Return to Vietnam

Between 1981 and 2016, thousands of American and Australian Vietnam War veterans returned to Việt Nam. This comparative, transnational oral history offers the first historical study of these return journeys. It shows how veterans returned in search of resolution, or peace, manifesting in shifting nostalgic visions of "Vietnam." Different national war narratives shaped their returns: Australians followed the "Anzac" pilgrimage tradition, whereas for Americans the return was an anti-war act. Veterans met former enemies, visited battlefields, mourned friends, found new relationships, and addressed enduring legacies of war. Many found their memories of war eased by witnessing Việt Nam at peace. Yet this peacetime reality also challenged veterans' wartime connection to Vietnamese spaces. The place they were nostalgic for was Vietnam, a space in war memory, not Việt Nam, the country. Veterans drew from wartime narratives to negotiate this displacement, performing nostalgic practices to reclaim their sense of belonging.

Dr. Mia Martin Hobbs is an Honorary Fellow in the School of Historical and Philosophical Studies, University of Melbourne. She has held fellowships and awards from the University of Melbourne, Australian Historical Association, Freilich Project, and Contemporary Histories Research Group Award, and has published prize-winning research on veterans and war memory.

Studies in the Social and Cultural History of Modern Warfare

General Editor
Robert Gerwarth, *University College Dublin*
Jay Winter, *Yale University*

Advisory Editors
Heather Jones, *University College London*
Rana Mitter, *University of Oxford*
Michelle Moyd, *Indiana University Bloomington*
Martin Thomas, *University of Exeter*

In recent years the field of modern history has been enriched by the exploration of two parallel histories. These are the social and cultural history of armed conflict, and the impact of military events on social and cultural history.

Studies in the Social and Cultural History of Modern Warfare presents the fruits of this growing area of research, reflecting both the colonization of military history by cultural historians and the reciprocal interest of military historians in social and cultural history, to the benefit of both. The series offers the latest scholarship in European and non-European events from the 1850s to the present day.

A full list of titles in the series can be found at:
www.cambridge.org/modernwarfare

Return to Vietnam
An Oral History of American and Australian Veterans' Journeys

Mia Martin Hobbs
University of Melbourne

Shaftesbury Road, Cambridge CB2 8EA, United Kingdom

One Liberty Plaza, 20th Floor, New York, NY 10006, USA

477 Williamstown Road, Port Melbourne, VIC 3207, Australia

314–321, 3rd Floor, Plot 3, Splendor Forum, Jasola District Centre, New Delhi – 110025, India

103 Penang Road, #05–06/07, Visioncrest Commercial, Singapore 238467

Cambridge University Press is part of Cambridge University Press & Assessment, a department of the University of Cambridge.

We share the University's mission to contribute to society through the pursuit of education, learning and research at the highest international levels of excellence.

www.cambridge.org
Information on this title: www.cambridge.org/9781108972666

DOI: 10.1017/9781108972987

© Mia Martin Hobbs 2021

This publication is in copyright. Subject to statutory exception and to the provisions of relevant collective licensing agreements, no reproduction of any part may take place without the written permission of Cambridge University Press & Assessment.

First published 2021
First paperback edition 2024

A catalogue record for this publication is available from the British Library

ISBN   978-1-108-83266-3   Hardback
ISBN   978-1-108-97266-6   Paperback

Cambridge University Press & Assessment has no responsibility for the persistence or accuracy of URLs for external or third-party internet websites referred to in this publication and does not guarantee that any content on such websites is, or will remain, accurate or appropriate.

For my parents

Contents

Acknowledgments		*page* viii
A Note on Spelling		xi
List of Abbreviations		xiv
	Introduction	1
Part I	**Return**	25
1	Reconciliation, 1981–1994	27
2	Normalization, 1995–2005	50
3	Commemoration, 2006–2016	73
Part II	**Việt Nam**	99
4	Relics and Remnants	101
5	Meeting the Enemy	127
6	Remembering the American War in Việt Nam	151
Part III	**Legacies**	175
7	Revisiting Vietnam	177
8	Veteran Legacies in Việt Nam	203
	Conclusion	229
	Appendix 1 Veteran Subjects	237
	Appendix 2 Interview Questions	245
	Bibliography	247
	Index	268

Acknowledgments

This book would not exist were it not for all the veterans who agreed to meet with me, shared their stories, and introduced me to others who, in turn, helped me. Thank you all for your generosity, your time, and your trust.

Seven years ago, this project began on a one-way ticket to Việt Nam. I had heard about veterans returning and was curious to find out more. That my curiosity evolved into a fully-fledged project is due to the guidance of my wonderful supervisor, Barbara (Ara) Keys. Ara helped me develop a PhD proposal from afar, encouraging me to think more broadly about my topic. Once back in Melbourne, she helped me find my feet in my PhD program and guided me toward becoming a more rigorous and thoughtful scholar. Ara's generous and constructive feedback helped me distill my ideas and find my voice. It was also through Ara that I discovered how much I love teaching history. I am indebted to Ara for her mentorship, and perhaps can only truly thank her by one day doing for others what she has done for me.

I am grateful to Julie Fedor, my PhD co-supervisor, for her invaluable feedback and for engaging me with new theories that sharpened my understanding of war memory.

I thank Stuart Macintyre, my Honors supervisor, for suggesting I undertake a PhD. I had never considered doctoral studies to be within my reach. Without Stuart's encouragement, I doubt I ever would.

I am grateful for the mentorship of Alistair Thomson, Noah Riseman, Kate McGregor, Carolyn Holbrook, and David Lowe, each of whom provided valuable guidance on research, writing, and working in academia. Thanks in particular to Al and Noah for their thoughtful feedback on drafts and for their advice on oral history problems. Scott Laderman advised me on recruiting veteran-participants and navigating fieldwork in Việt Nam, and supported numerous conference proposals from afar. Scott and Al were also my dissertation examiners, and their generous and encouraging reports helped me see my project in new ways and energized me in the shift from dissertation to book.

Acknowledgments

I have been fortunate to discuss my research with a broad community of scholars. Catherine Hall and Samia Khatun taught a brilliant class on "Race, Gender, Empire" early in my PhD, which led me to think about the Vietnam War in new ways. Conversations with participants at the 2017 "War and Memory" workshop at the University of Melbourne helped sharpen my early ideas. The panels, group discussions, and one-on-one conversations at the 2019 "Vietnam War in the Pacific World" conference at Macquarie University sparked new ideas about the war and its legacies. Emily Fitzgerald and Daniel Russo-Batterham at the Melbourne Data Analytics Platform helped me develop a digital map of my doctoral project, which allowed me to see new relationships between time and space in veterans' return journeys. Thanks also to the oral history group at Monash, whose thoughtful discussions often led to new ways of thinking about problems I had felt stuck on.

Many friends and colleagues contributed to the evolution of this book in more indirect ways. The postgraduate community at the University of Melbourne provided understanding, solidarity, and humor throughout my PhD. Amy Hodgson and Nayree Mardirian were a dream to teach with when I juggled new preps and my own research for the first time. In Việt Nam, thank you to Hà Giang, Hà Phước Hậu, Lê Hoàng Huy, and Lê Hạ Uyên for all your help, knowledge, advice, and most of all your friendship.

This work was made possible through the support of various funding bodies and organizations. A Melbourne Research Training Scheme scholarship gave me the luxury of focusing almost solely on my research for the duration of my degree. The Alma Hansen Scholarship, Norman Macgeorge Bequest, and Graduate Research Arts Travel Scheme supported my fieldwork in Việt Nam and the United States. The Gilbert Postdoctoral Career Development Fellowship, an honorary fellowship in the School of Historical and Philosophical Studies, and a residency in the Digital Studio at the University of Melbourne supported the development of dissertation into book proposal and then manuscript. I thank these organizations for their support.

At Cambridge University Press, I am grateful to my editor, Jay Winter, for seeing the potential in this project, and to Michael Watson, for shepherding the manuscript through the publishing process. My deepest thanks to Emily Sharp in the Cambridge Office for answering my many questions along the way, and to Angela Valente for her meticulous copyediting of the final manuscript. I thank the two anonymous reviewers who provided thoughtful and encouraging feedback on my manuscript.

An enormous thanks to the Baillieu Library and in particular to Richard Serle. Richard reached out to me when Melbourne first went into lockdown during the COVID-19 pandemic, letting me know he could order books I needed for teaching or research and mail them to me. Library mail was an absolute highlight of lockdown life, and I could not have completed this manuscript without the many, many books that arrived on my doorstep. Thank you.

The writing of this book was also helped by many wonderful artists, whose music energized me through writing blocks, and by my office companion, Miso, who tolerated my tendency to turn up the volume to get through a draft.

Finally, I am grateful for the close friends and family who supported me in so many ways. I thank Eleanor Lang, Bella Modlmayr, and Celie Martin Hobbs, each of whom possess a singular sense of humor (black, droll, and totally absurd, respectively) that kept me grounded. Tessa Cavanna is a lifeline from across the world, my biggest cheerleader and oldest friend. With enormous gratitude to Ben Martin Hobbs, for being badgered into reading everything I was too anxious to show anyone else. I thank my amazing partner, Tim Pierce, for his encouragement, his patience, for helping me muddle through so many ideas, for knowing when to tell me to stop and take a break. He lived this project with me, and this book would not have been completed without his love and support.

My parents, Jenny Martin and Jeremy Hobbs, are the reason this book exists. They instilled in me the values that underpin my research, always encouraged me to ask questions, and inspired me to try to understand more about the world. Thank you for everything you have done for me. This book is for you.

A Note on Spelling

This book explores the experiences of individuals from two English-speaking nations, in three countries, over three decades. These individuals, and the historians and journalists who discuss them, use a range of terms and spellings for groups, places, and ideas. In this book, American spelling is used for English-language words, except for quotations from Australian writers. Interviews that were transcribed by me are also in American spelling. Vietnamese words are ambiguous without diacritics, so I use Vietnamese spelling of Vietnamese words: "Việt Nam," "Hà Nội," "Long Tân," etcetera.[1] This spelling choice clarifies the difference between, for instance, Long Tân the place and Long Tan the battle, and indicates whether a place was named by Vietnamese inhabitants or its Western occupiers (such as Nui Dat, a base built and named by the Australian Task Force (ATF) – *núi đất* simply meaning "dirt hill").

This spelling distinguishes "Việt Nam" from "the Vietnam War." "Vietnam veterans" and "the Vietnam War" are used to describe the Australian and American experience in Việt Nam, while I use "the American War," as it is called in Việt Nam, to describe the Vietnamese experience. These spellings also reflect the intonations and implied connotations of returnees' speech in interviews. After returning to Việt Nam, many veterans tried to emulate the accent when using Vietnamese words. For example, "Việt Nam" was often pronounced with stress on the first word and deliberate separation between the words. This accent was not applied to "Vietnam," the war. One returnee explained that he found it useful to think of the war and the place as distinct through spelling, because "if you have a new spelling for a new word that is very emotional, or controversial for you, what if you were to respell it? Would that give you a new memory? . . . Spelling something in a new way, to have a new idea about an old problem, that made therapeutic sense to me."[2] Thus, in the

---

[1] Christina Schwenkel, *The American War in Contemporary Vietnam* (Bloomington, IN: Indiana University Press, 2009), xi.
[2] Interview with Ted, Skype, February 19, 2016.

quotations from returnees' interviews with me, I use the Westernized spelling of Vietnamese words for wartime references and Vietnamese spelling to refer to contemporary places and people.

Decisions about the use of Western and Vietnamese nomenclature for the Vietnam or American War have deep political implications. The common Western division of belligerents by territory misrepresents the nature of the conflict, inaccurately framing the war as divided between fixed geographical groups and implying, as historian Scott Laderman notes, an "invasion of a country called 'South Vietnam' by a country called 'North Vietnam.'"[3] Hence in this book the names of the governing authorities – the Democratic Republic of Việt Nam (DRV) and the Republic of Việt Nam (RVN) – are used instead. Because the civilian experience of war was determined by geography, civilians are described as northerners and southerners, as living in the DRV or RVN, or as living in northern, central, or southern provinces. I avoid politically charged names for events such as the "Fall of Saigon," "Black April," and "Liberation Day," referring to April 30, 1975 as "the end of the war."

Many returnees used the term "Viet Cong" (Vietnamese communist) to refer to the guerrilla forces of the National Liberation Front (NLF). The terms "North Vietnamese" and "NVA" refer to the conventional army of the DRV, the People's Army of Vietnam (PAVN). While official histories of the Socialist Republic of Việt Nam have retroactively grouped both the guerrilla and conventional forces as PAVN, in this book I maintain distinctions for the sake of specificity. Where both forces are referred to together, they are "revolutionary forces." Australian and US returnees used the acronym "ARVN" and the terms "South Vietnamese" or "local army" to describe the Republic of Việt Nam Armed Forces (RVNAF). Except when my sources use the terms "Viet Cong," "VC," "NVA," "ARVN," and "South Vietnamese," I use the terms NFL, PAVN, and RVNAF to describe Vietnamese fighting forces. It is worth noting that although many of these names originated as derogatory terms in colonial contexts (*Việt gian cộng sản* – communist traitor to Việt Nam) the terms "VC," "Viet Cong," and "ARVN" have been widely (and proudly) accepted by the Vietnamese and are not considered offensive in Việt Nam. Most returnees I interviewed had no idea that these are colloquial or incorrect terms and did not use them pejoratively.

Finally, there is ongoing debate regarding the proper descriptors for trauma-related mental health issues. Some veterans' groups oppose the inclusion of "disorder" in "post-traumatic stress disorder," arguing that it

---

[3] Scott Laderman, *Tours of Vietnam: War, Travel Guides, and Memory* (Durham, NC: Duke University Press, 2009), xi.

is stigmatizing or insulting. Some prefer "post-traumatic stress," others suggest changing "disorder" to "injury" could allow trauma to be included in the criteria for military awards. These arguments are entwined with debates around the social meanings and values of military service, as well as contemporary developments around mental health terminology. The US and Australian Departments of Veterans' Affairs (VA and DVA) and the American and Australian Psychological Associations use "PTSD," noting that "disorder" accurately describes the recovery period, healing methods, and variable susceptibility of individuals to long-term, maladaptive trauma issues. Except where returnees describe their own diagnosis differently, post-combat trauma stress is referred to as "PTSD."

Abbreviations

ANZAC/Anzac	Australia and New Zealand Army Corps
APC	Armoured personnel carrier
ARVN	Army of the Republic of Việt Nam (often used to refer to all RVNAF)
ATF	Australian Task Force
DMZ	Demilitarized zone
DRV	Democratic Republic of Việt Nam (often referred to as North Vietnam)
DVA	Department for Veterans' Affairs (Australia)
FUV	Fulbright University Việt Nam
MIA	Missing in Action
MONGO	My own nongovernmental organization
NGO	Nongovernmental organization
NLF	National Liberation Front (often referred to as Viet Cong)
NVA	North Vietnamese Army (People's Army of Việt Nam)
PAVN	People's Army Việt Nam (often referred to as North Vietnamese or NVA)
POW	Prisoner of War
PTSD	Post-traumatic stress disorder
R&R	Rest and Relaxation
RAR	Royal Australian Regiment
RSL	Royal Services League
RVN	Republic of Việt Nam (often referred to as South Vietnam)
RVNAF	Republic of Việt Nam Armed Forces (often referred to as South Vietnamese)
SASR	Special Air Service Regiment
SEAL	US Navy Sea, Air, and Land teams
SEATO	Southeast Asia Treaty Organization

SRV	Socialist Republic of Việt Nam (postwar government of Việt Nam)
UXO	Unexploded ordnance
VFP	Veterans for Peace
VFW	Veterans of Foreign Wars
VA	Veterans' Affairs (US)
VC	Viet Cong (National Liberation Front)
VVA	Vietnam Veterans of America
VVRP	Veterans Viet Nam Restoration Project

Introduction

"A lot of guys say, 'I almost feel like I'm coming home.'" So said Bill E., a former Marine from his home in Đà Nẵng. His personal experience of revisiting Việt Nam was so powerful that he began organizing tours for other veterans, bringing them back to sites of personal trauma and famous battlefields. He described how, after years of isolation, anxiety, and confusion, many veterans found healing and a sense of belonging when they finally returned to their former battlefields. Bill E. had originally deployed to Vietnam in 1969 with the Marines and served as a machine gunner along the demilitarized zone (DMZ). After a year in combat, he rotated out of Vietnam and was discharged, returning to the United States four days before the National Guard opened fire on an anti-war demonstration at Kent State University in 1970. Back in the United States, he wanted to talk about the war and his experiences, but found that people did not want to know or did not know how to ask. Bill E. joined the anti-war movement and was arrested for protesting on Veterans' Day. He tried college, but "didn't seem to fit in ... so I went to Mexico." Every day, he thought about the war. "I had this knot in my soul ... I just had to untie this knot." He began thinking about returning to Việt Nam, wanting to find out "why Vietnam is still the ghost that it is."[1]

Bill E. finally returned in 1994, a decision that transformed his life. For a decade, Bill E. shepherded groups of American veterans to Việt Nam. In 2006, his wife died, and two years later he decided to settle permanently to Việt Nam. He tried teaching English and became involved in Đà Nẵng's expatriate community. He reconnected with Anh, a tour guide he had met years before. They married in 2009, built a house together, and opened their own tour agency, Bamboo Moon. Bill E. visited the United States frequently to see family, but as soon as he was there he

---
[1] Interview with Bill E., Đà Nẵng, April 19, 2016.

would begin thinking about being back in Việt Nam. Being in Việt Nam, he said, just gave him "a little peace of mind."[2] In a letter to a fellow Marine, Bill E. explained: "Some say I changed in Vietnam. I say I was born here."[3]

This book examines why US and Australian veterans of the Vietnam War returned to Việt Nam and how they grappled with returning to the site of conflict. I conceptualize veterans as living legacies of war: they spend a formative part of their lives in the warzone, often with enormous personal consequences. They carry the memories of war with them, endure the physical and psychic costs of warfare, and often find their identity as individuals caught up with the meanings and debates around "their" war. For Vietnam veterans, these legacies are particularly fraught. The Vietnam War was deeply controversial in Australia and the United States, where substantial segments of the public questioned the justifications for the war. Veterans have struggled with ideas of patriotism, military honor, and the worldviews that led them to Vietnam in the first place. Furthermore, because the Western forces lost the war, Australian and US veterans who returned to Việt Nam did not do so as victors but instead were confronted with the reality that they had been defeated, with the country they fought in now governed by their former enemies.

Veterans returned to Việt Nam in search of resolution, or peace, in their individual relationships to the war. Their longing for peace manifested in nostalgia "for a home that no longer exists, or has never existed."[4] They described yearning to revisit their youth and the Vietnam they held in their memory, or to release the Vietnam that haunted their nightmares. Veterans who returned to Việt Nam were revisiting a site of violence that was deeply personal and often traumatic in their memories, demonstrating that nostalgic feelings can be more powerful than apprehension, and that trauma and fear can generate feelings of nostalgia. Many returnees expressed to me the idea that they were "born" in Vietnam: it is where their childhood ended, a "rite of passage" that "made them into men." This idea of being "born" in a warzone rests on the notion that violence is primordial and when experienced provides deep and authentic insight into the self. The shared experience of this "birth" compounds the sense of community that is created by modern military training: recruits are trained to depend on one another entirely for survival. Returnees described this to me as being a "link in a chain." Paradoxically, the warzone itself became "home": a place of emotional security and

---

[2] Ibid.
[3] Bill Ervin, "US Marine: This Is Why I Returned to Vietnam to Stay." *PRI.org*, May 6, 2015. www.pri.org/stories/2015-05-06/us-marine-why-i-returned-vietnam-stay
[4] Svetlana Boym, *The Future of Nostalgia* (New York: Basic Books, 2001), xiv.

profound understanding. This attachment to the place of the warzone was compounded by the experience of displacement upon repatriation from war: the inability to communicate traumatic experience, the lack of structure, the absence of a collectivized, entirely dependent unit. "Home" no longer feels like home after war. Returning to Việt Nam could then be experienced as a return to self and a return to truth: a return home.

Returning veterans thus acted as a diasporic community: one forged in war, sustained by ongoing debates about the war and its legacies in Australia and the United States, and linked by a shared, lost warzone home. Instead of ancestry, ethnicity, or familial ties, veterans' diasporic connection to Việt Nam flowed from their wartime experience. Where many diasporic communities imagine their homeland as it could be without or before war and catastrophe, for veteran-returnees, the imagined homeland *is* the war. Apocryphal stories of Vietnam veterans being mistreated in Australia and the United States fostered a sense of collective persecution, a central theme in diasporic consciousness.[5] Veterans came to think of Vietnam as the place where their identity was created, reflecting the "two core elements" of a diaspora: "the loss of 'home' and the ongoing link to some notion of it."[6] Their returns to Việt Nam were then a means to resolve the ongoing debates that swirled around the legacy of "their" war: attempts to find truth, heal trauma, honor friends, reclaim pride, or redeem their role in the war.

I identify three distinct strands of returnees, the first beginning in 1981, when veteran Bobby Muller returned with a delegation from the Vietnam Veterans for America Foundation – the first known return of a Vietnam veteran after the end of the war.[7] I follow their journeys and the journeys of a handful of other Americans and Australians who returned to Việt Nam in these early years to reconcile with their former enemies. These "reconciliation" returnees returned to address lingering questions about Việt Nam and the war, and their return journeys overwhelmingly took the form of political and humanitarian missions. Returning to Việt Nam had a profound impact on these veterans' emotional well-being and so became the precedent for "healing journeys." The numbers of returnees grew from 1995 to 2006, in what I categorize as the "normalization"

---

[5] William Safran, "Diasporas in Modern Societies: Myths of Homeland and Return." *Diaspora* 1:1 (Spring 1991): 83, 92.
[6] Nando Sigona et al. (eds.), "Introduction: The Self as Plural." In *Diasporas Reimagined: Spaces, Practices and Belonging.* (Oxford: Oxford University Press, 2015), 6.
[7] "25 Years from Vietnam: An Online Chat with Bobby Muller." *Revisiting Vietnam*, American RadioWorks. April 28, 2000. http://americanradioworks.publicradio.org/features/vietnam/muller_chat.html

period of return. I argue that "normalization" applies not only to the diplomatic status of Việt Nam to Western eyes but also to the very concept of returning. This period was characterized by "healing journeys," with most "normalization" returnees describing their return to Việt Nam as therapeutic. From 2006, returning for anniversaries and/or platoon reunions was increasingly common among Australian veterans, coinciding with major anniversaries of battles and significant war events. During this "commemoration" period, discourse on the war in Australia and the United States centered on remembering the service of veterans, rather than the war itself. "Commemoration" therefore refers to the context in which the war is discussed in Australia and the United States, as well as the rise in commemorative returns to Việt Nam. This last period of my study ends in 2016 when more than one thousand Australian veterans returned to commemorate the 50th anniversary of the Battle of Long Tan.

These changes in the nature of veterans' returns reflect broader trends in battlefield pilgrimage in Australia and the United States. American historians John Gatewood and Catherine Cameron find that early visits to Civil War battlefields were "rituals of reconciliation."[8] Over time, as battlefield tourism developed, historian Thomas Chambers argues they came to "serve as loci where societies and narrations invent and legitimize their histories, traditions, and myths."[9] In *What's Wrong with ANZAC?* (2010), Australian historians Joy Damousi and Mark McKenna concur, observing that Australian pilgrimages were increasingly ritual performances of national identity, "sentimentality and nostalgia," rather than mourning and reflections on individual experiences of total war, with numbers of pilgrims rising in tandem with political rhetoric that glorified war and soldiers.[10] These studies indicate that pilgrims who visited battlefields shortly after the conflict are likely seeking personal reconciliation, whereas those who do so much later tend to do so for broader commemorative purposes. Veterans' returns to Việt Nam echoed these existing patterns, demonstrating the different needs of veterans' life-stages and the consolidation of public war memories over time.

---

[8] John B. Gatewood and Catherine M. Cameron, "Battlefield Pilgrims at Gettysburg National Military Park." *Ethnology*, 43:3 (Summer 2004): 196.

[9] Thomas A. Chambers, *Memories of War: Visiting Battlegrounds and Bonefields in the Early American Republic* (Ithaca, NY: Cornell University Press, 2012), 15.

[10] Joy Damousi, "Why Do We Get So Emotional About Anzac?" In *What's Wrong with ANZAC? The Militarisation of Australian History*. Edited by Marilyn Lake, Henry Reynolds, and Mark McKenna (Sydney: University of New South Wales Press, 2010), 84–102; Mark McKenna, "Anzac Day: How Did It Become Australia's National Day?" *What's Wrong with ANZAC?*, 103–32.

Introduction   5

These shifts in the nature of veterans' returns, and the existing patterns in battlefield pilgrimage that they mirror, demonstrate different forms of nostalgia. In *The Future of Nostalgia* (2001), cultural theorist Svetlana Boym sets out two distinct forms of nostalgia: "reflective" nostalgia, which "lingers on ruins, the patina of time and history," and "restorative" nostalgia, which "manifests itself in total reconstructions of monuments of the past."[11] The trajectory from one form of nostalgia to another manifested in different visions of the diasporic warzone homeland: from the source of debates about "their" war, to the locus of trauma, to the origin place of veteran communities and war legacies. These visions of Vietnam corresponded to veterans' shifting goals for resolution, or peace, in the return to Việt Nam. Where reconciliation returnees focused on finding new understandings of the war, normalization returnees sought healing from war trauma, and commemoration returnees focused on marking "their" war in Việt Nam. In each return period, returnees demonstrated that their "fantasies of the past [were] determined by needs of the present," as cultural and political shifts prompted veterans to reflect on their war experiences and to reengage with Việt Nam.[12] Veterans' return narratives also illustrated that memories, as well as fantasies, were informed by the needs of the present, as each return cohort described their experiences through cultural discourses particular to their return period. The normalization returnees, for instance, used psychological theories and discourses of trauma, whereas commemoration veterans used language specific to the communities of veteran-expatriate enclaves in Việt Nam.

I use a comparative perspective to illuminate the effects of returning to the site of conflict. Perhaps surprisingly, given the prolific treatment of Vietnam veterans in oral history, there have been no comparative oral history studies.[13] Australian studies touch on how the Australian soldiers

---

[11] Boym, *Future of Nostalgia*, 41.   [12] Ibid., xvi.
[13] Comparative research on veterans in both countries has focused on veterans of different wars or on comparative health studies of veterans and their nonveteran peers. See for example: Effie Karageorgos, *Australian Soldiers in South Africa and Vietnam: Words from the Battlefield* (London: Bloomsbury Publishing, 2016); Valentine M. Villa, "Health and Functioning among Four War Eras of US Veterans: Examining the Impact of War Cohort Membership, Socioeconomic Status, Mental Health, and Disease Prevention." *Military Medicine*, 167:9 (2002): 783–89. Oral histories, quantitative histories, and psychological studies with Vietnam veterans provide a mass of information on trends and statistics on veteran adjustment as well as a literary footprint of veterans' postwar lives. See for example: John A. Wood, *Veterans Narratives and the Collective Memory of the Vietnam War* (Athens, OH: Ohio University Press, 2016); Stephen Garton, *The Cost of War: Australians Return* (Melbourne: Oxford University Press, 1996); Peter Siminski, "Employment Effects of Army Service and Veterans' Compensation: Evidence from the Australian Vietnam-Era Conscription Lotteries." *The Review of Economics and Statistics*

and veterans differed from their American counterparts in Việt Nam, but these comparisons focus on rejecting the application of perceived American stereotypes to Australian veterans rather than exploring the two experiences.[14] This book is the first comparative study of Australian and American Vietnam veterans. The justification for studying Australians and Americans and not, for instance, South Korean, Filipino, Thai, or even Vietnamese migrant veterans who have returned to Việt Nam, is partly logistical: there is a wealth of information about returning Americans and Australians, but little about other allies from the Southeast Asia Treaty Organization (SEATO) returning. While many Vietnamese veterans in the global diaspora long to return, many are afraid or unwilling to do so while Việt Nam is under socialist rule.[15] Although New Zealanders also fought in Vietnam, they did so in very small numbers and consequently I have not been able to track a national return movement – the only New Zealander I know of who returned fought in the Australian Army, lives in Australia, and is counted among the Australian returnees in this book.

Marked differences emerged between Australian and American veterans. Returnees tended to revisit places where they served, so while Australian returnees congregated in the province of Bà Rịa-Vũng Tàu, where the Australian Task Force (ATF) was based during the war, American veterans returned to provinces throughout central and south Việt Nam, and many were curious to see the north. These national geographies of return highlight the comparatively cohesive/disjointed nature of the Australian/American war experience, and mirror the different national imaginaries of Vietnam. Veterans' longing for resolution over the war was entwined with narratives about the Vietnam War in their

---

95:1 (2013): 87–97; Eric T. Dean Jr., "The Myth of the Troubled and Scorned Vietnam Veteran." *Journal of American Studies* 26:1 (1992): 59–74; Jerry Lembcke, *The Spitting Image: Myth, Memory and the Legacy of Vietnam* (New York: New York University Press, 1998); Carie Uyen Nguyen, "Whose War Was It Anyway?" *New York Times*, August 18, 2017.

[14] See for example: Peter Edwards, *Australia and the Vietnam War* (Kensington: NewSouth, 2014), 261–62.

[15] Nathalie Huynh Chau Nguyen observes that for overseas Vietnamese "the return to Vietnam is not a decision taken lightly." Nathalie Huynh Chau Nguyen, *Memory Is Another Country: Women of the Vietnamese Diaspora* (Santa Barbara, CA: Praeger, 2009), 141–60. Nguyen also finds that Vietnamese who return to provide aid to RVNAF veterans face scrutiny from Vietnamese authorities and fear repercussions for their activism. Nathalie Huynh Chau Nguyen, *South Vietnamese Soldiers: Memories of the Vietnam War and After* (Santa Barbara, CA: Praeger, 2016): 108, 150. Long T. Bui notes that while overseas Vietnamese are returning to Việt Nam, it is mostly younger refugees and second-generation Vietnamese who make the journey. Long T. Bui, *Returns of War: South Vietnam and the Price of Refugee Memory* (New York: New York University Press, 2018), 190–92.

Introduction 7

home countries. Their nostalgia hinged on how they conceptualized Vietnam as a site of conflict in their memories, which in turn reflected shifts in national war memory in Australia and the United States and changes in how the space of Việt Nam was understood. American veterans first returned when Việt Nam was a hostile nation to the United States: they returned as radicals, advocating for normalization and recognition of Vietnamese pain. Many were anti-war activists and situated themselves as atoning for their war participation and for America's war against the country at large. The first Australian returnees, on the other hand, had no diplomatic gap to bridge. Their returns coincided instead with Australia's "Anzac Revival," the creation of a national tradition of battlefield pilgrimage.

These early returns set the tone for future returnees from each nation: American returnees largely reflected anti-war and countercultural values, while Australian returnees were increasingly conservative, reflecting the domination of traditional veterans' organizations by Vietnam veterans through the late 1990s. These national differences created drastically different interpretations of peacetime Việt Nam. For instance, in Chapter 5 I unpack a near-uniform claim made by veterans that the Vietnamese bore no grudge for the war and welcomed veterans back to Việt Nam wholeheartedly. Because many American veterans positioned themselves as atoning for wartime participation and the crimes of their country, they viewed this reaction as forgiveness. Australian veterans, conversely, drew from Australia's national mythology to argue that the Vietnamese welcomed them back because they loved and respected Australian soldiers. The comparative approach in this book thus exposes similarities as well as differences, throwing national lenses and exceptionalist narratives into stark relief. While both groups of veterans interpreted Vietnamese welcomes as specific to their nations' historical relations with Việt Nam, commonalities across their experiences undermined these claims.

When they returned, many returnees found that new experiences in Việt Nam added to a "library of images" associated with the country, diluting their war memories with memories of peace. Returnees described this dilution as providing them enormous relief, with some even reporting decreases in specific trauma symptoms. As a result, veterans reported that returning to Việt Nam made it easier and less painful to remember war. Some conducted rituals at sites of personal significance to let go of their grief, or held memorial services to embed their war experience in collective traditions. Others found affirmation and solidarity through reconciling with old adversaries. Many found that simply seeing Việt Nam at peace lifted a weight and gave them some relief. Thus, the return to Việt

Nam was, for many veterans, a way of achieving resolution at a site of personal trauma. After returning, many veterans engaged with Việt Nam in new ways, reflecting their altered thinking about "Vietnam." Some returned again to explore the country as tourists, while others developed relationships in contemporary Việt Nam, with some even relocating permanently to reside with new partners and families. Many became dedicated to addressing the legacies of war in Việt Nam.

Yet peacetime Việt Nam offered its own challenges. Diasporic longing is defined by distance: we tend to feel that we belong to places most strongly when we are far from them; and upon return often feel estranged and out-of-place. The place that veterans were nostalgic for was Vietnam, a space of war in memory, not Việt Nam, the country. Veterans had returned to a place that was not theirs, but that continued to hold them. They were challenged by the physical erasure of their wartime presence; with the land they had fought in the hands of their former enemies. Many struggled with complex and conflicting emotions: both relief and sadness at the absence of war architecture. Returnees' emotional responses to the permanence or eradication of sites of personal significance showed powerful feelings of belonging and entitlement to Việt Nam as a space.

Returnees' responded to this sense of displacement by drawing on their wartime connections to Việt Nam; explaining challenges and contradictions through war memories and narratives. Their reactions to the physical space of Việt Nam revived the politics of memory about the war itself, as they contested Vietnamese authority over the past – and by extension the present – in those spaces. Geographer Karen Till defines the "politics of memory" in relation to place as "the spaces and processes of negotiation about whose conception of the past should prevail in the public realm. Because the meanings of these places are not stable in time or space, the politics of memory also refers to the ways and reasons groups attempt to 'fix' time and identity through the material and symbolic qualities of the place."[16] The extent to which returnees accepted Vietnamese sovereignty was directly related to their recognition of Vietnamese narratives of war. The extent of this recognition also shaped how returnees responded to the Vietnamese themselves: viewing them as active or passive, treating them as victims or perpetrators of violence, feeling solidarity with them or antagonism toward them. Geographer Tim Creswell argues that "the construction of places is more often than not achieved through the exclusion of some 'other' – a constitutive outside."[17] Returnees' selective inclusion and

---

[16] Karen E. Till, "Places of Memory." In *A Companion to Political Geography*. Edited by John Agnew, Katharyne Mitchell, and Gerard Toal (Oxford: Blackwell, 2003), 290.

[17] Tim Creswell, *Place: A Short Introduction* (Oxford: Blackwell Publishing, 2004), 290.

Introduction

exclusion of Vietnamese people, including Vietnamese veterans, by wartime allegiance, age, location, or status were influenced by their political beliefs, claims to place, and memory of the war. Furthermore, as the numbers of veterans returning to Việt Nam grew, the contestation over space extended to other Australian and American veterans, and their inclusion and exclusion of each other by nationality, service position, or even tourist "type" further illustrated the particular views of individual veterans toward place, memory, and the legacy of the war.

Returnees' responses to peacetime Việt Nam hinged on their relationship to war narratives in their home countries. Commemoration of the Vietnam War and its veterans followed an exceptionally contentious and highly political trajectory in Australia and the United States. When veterans reached Việt Nam they discovered that the Vietnamese narrative of the "American War" rendered them perpetrators of atrocities or, at best, passive victims of imperialist warmongering nations.[18] Vietnamese memories of victory were particularly jarring for those veterans who had absorbed narratives about winning "their" war. Returnees displayed a selective acceptance of Vietnamese commemoration and war memory. Across national and ideological lines, returnees tended to dismiss commemorative materials that contradicted their war memories and worldviews, while at the same time incorporating those elements of Vietnamese memory that supported their experiences. This confirmation bias is not exclusive to returnees, but was particularly notable given the war narratives through which they filtered Vietnamese memory.

Finally, many returnees negotiated the space of contemporary Việt Nam through a wartime lens. They performed social practices and political actions that echoed their military presence during the war. These practices – such as recreating a wartime "bar culture," or situating themselves acting as educators and liberators of the Vietnamese – both reiterated returnees' wartime connections to the country and tied them to the contemporary Việt Nam: collapsing time through space to find resolution and relocate their former warzone home.

Vietnam veterans' postwar experiences have been treated prolifically in historical research, popular culture, and journalism. However, the topic of veterans returning to Việt Nam is under-documented academically, with only a handful of scholars recognizing the phenomenon.[19] The

---

[18] See: Heonik Kwon, *After the Massacre: Commemoration and Consolation at Ha My and My Lai* (Berkeley, CA: University of California Press, 2006); Robert J. McMahon, "Contested Memory: The Vietnam War and American Society, 1975–2001." *Diplomatic History* 26:2 (2002): 159–84; Edwards, *Australia and the Vietnam War*.

[19] See: Isobelle Barrett-Meyering, "Pilgrimage to Vietnam: Australian Veterans as 'Ambassadors of Peace.'" *Venour V. Nathan Prize (Undergraduate)* (Sydney: University

earliest scholarship on returns came from returnees themselves, who reflected on their journeys in memoirs and articles.[20] Several scholars have analyzed the writing of American veteran-authors.[21] American scholars who consider early-return memoirs by veteran-writers tend to reach similar conclusions, partly because the sources they draw from are psychologically, socially, and politically similar. The returnees "acknowledge the personal and public desire of coming to terms with the past," seizing the return as "an opportunity for recovery or closure, a chance to replace difficult or painful memories with ones that are less so," and so the returns "are always written about as emotional as well as physical journeys."[22] Australian returnees also began to document their returns in memoirs; however, their reflections did not attract academic interest.[23]

The first veterans' returns coincided with increasing interest in the Vietnam veteran as a research subject. Academic interest in the Vietnam veteran began in the 1970s, and scholarship on the veterans quickly grew vast, focusing on the psychological impact of war and on its socially damaging effects.[24] This focus led veterans to return to Việt Nam

---

of Sydney, 2007). Veterans returning to Việt Nam are also briefly discussed in "Vietnam War Veterans." In *Encyclopedia of the Veteran in America*. Edited by William A. Pencak (Santa Barbara, CA: ABC-Clio, 2009), 438.

[20] W.D. Ehrhart, *Going Back: A Poet Who Was Once a Marine Returns to Vietnam* (Wallingford, CT: Pendle Hill Pamphlet, 1987); William Broyles Jr., *Brothers in Arms: A Journey from War to Peace* (New York: Alfred A. Knopf, 1986); Larry Rottmann, "A Hundred Happy Sparrows: An American Veteran Returns to Vietnam." *Vietnam Generation* 1:1 (January 1989): 113–40.

[21] Cultural scholar Julia Bleakney focused on returning to Việt Nam as one avenue for commemorating war service, historian Patrick Hagopian briefly considered returning veterans in his examination of healing in American discourse surrounding the Vietnam War, and Hai-Dang Doan Phan considered the politics of reconciliation in veteran literature in his 2013 doctoral dissertation. Julia Bleakney, *Revisiting Vietnam: Memoirs, Memorials, Museums* (New York: Routledge, 2006); Patrick Hagopian, *The Vietnam War in American Memory: Veterans, Memorials and the Politics of Healing* (Boston, MA: University of Massachusetts Press, 2009); Hai-Dang Doan Phan, "Rumor of Redress: Literature, the Vietnam War, and the Politics of Reconciliation." PhD Diss., University of Wisconsin-Madison, 2012.

[22] Doan Phan, "Rumor of Redress," 7; Bleakney, *Revisiting Vietnam*, 65; Hagopian, *Vietnam War in American Memory*, 415.

[23] Terry Burstall, *A Soldier Returns: A Long Tan Veteran Discovers the Other Side of Vietnam* (Brisbane: University of Queensland Press, 1990).

[24] See for example: Charles R. Figley and Seymour Leventman, "Introduction: Estrangement and Victimization." In *Strangers at Home: Vietnam Veterans Since the War*. Edited by Charles R. Figley and Seyour Leventman (New York: Praeger Publishers, 1980), xxi–xxxi; Paul Camacho, "From War Hero to Criminal." In *Strangers at Home*, 267–72; Robert J. Lifton, *Home from the War: Vietnam Veterans, Neither Victims nor Executioners* (New York: Simon & Schuster, 1973); Chaim Shatan, "The Grief of Soldiers: Vietnam Combat Veterans' Self-Help Movement." *American Journal of Orthopsychiatry* 43:4 (July 1973): 640–53.

to find healing through exposure therapy.[25] With the advent of Vietnam commemorations in Australia and the United States, and coinciding with rising popular culture interest in trauma and therapy, returnees' healing journeys became a fixture for human interest pieces in both countries throughout the 1990s, and veterans' pursuit of healing became a distinct focus in the scholarship on veterans returning to Việt Nam.[26] Because these healing journeys coincided with the normalization of US-Vietnam relations, and because many returnees found healing through activism and charitable works, American scholars began to consider the tensions between healing, humanitarianism, and paternalism in Việt Nam. Scholars such as Bich Ngoc Do and Christina Schwenkel suggested that veterans' healing journeys were efforts to redeem American "moral manhood" through "gendered rescue narratives."[27]

Scholarship on reconciliation and healing focused entirely on American veterans. Australia had established diplomatic relations with the Democratic Republic of Việt Nam (DRV) in 1973, so the notion of reconciliation held less cultural significance, and while there was certainly media interest in the healing journeys of veterans, these journeys were not considered radical as they were in the United States. This is because of Australia's traditions of battlefield pilgrimage, known as "Anzac."[28] In the early 1990s, to commemorate significant anniversaries of major World War I and II battles, Australian politicians made pilgrimage to overseas battlefields and performed public rituals that claimed these spaces as "in one sense, a part of Australia."[29] Over the following two

---

[25] See: Ray Scurfield, *Healing Journeys: Study Abroad with Vietnam Veterans*, Vol. 2 (New York: Algora Publishing, 2006).
[26] Barbara Crossette, "Vietnam Set for Tourists." *New York Times*, November 5, 1985; George C. Wilson, "Back to the Land of the Nightmares: Vietnam Vets Come Full Circle with Therapy." *San Francisco Chronicle*, March 18, 1990, 8; Andre Malan, "Return to Vietnam." *Canberra Times*, May 13, 1990; Lucy Hood, "Maine Native to Help Build Clinic in Vietnam." *Bangor Daily News*, September 3, 1990; "Vietnam as a Tourist Spot for Veterans." *Canberra Times*, September 30, 1992. In scholarship, see Jonathan Stevenson, *Hard Men Humble: Vietnam Veterans Who Wouldn't Come Home* (New York: The Free Press, 2002).
[27] Bich Ngoc Do, "Normalizing Vietnam: Vietnam Veterans and the Reconstruction of Postwar US-Vietnam Relations, 1985–2010." PhD Diss., University of Hawaii, 2011, 17; Schwenkel, *American War in Contemporary Vietnam*, 18.
[28] Australia's national military identity was forged in World War I in the Gallipoli Campaign, in which 8,000 Australian and New Zealand Army Corps (ANZAC) soldiers died. "Anzac Day" became Australia's national day of commemoration.
[29] Bob Hawke, "Speech by the Prime Minister: Dawn Service Gallipoli." April 25, 1990. http://pmtranscripts.pmc.gov.au/release/transcript-8013; Paul Keating, "Anzac Day: 25 April 1992." Ela Beach, Port Moresby, April 25, 1992. www.keating.org.au/shop/item/anzac-day-25-april-1992. Australia's tradition of reimagining overseas battlefields as a spiritual extension of the nation speaks to the lack of publicly acknowledged wars on Australian soil. The Frontier Wars, armed conflict between colonial settlers and

decades this association between pilgrimage to overseas battlefields, national commemoration, and national identity strengthened in the cultural imagination and became a distinct field of inquiry in Australian scholarship.[30] The very first Australian returns to Việt Nam coincided exactly with this Anzac Revival. Consequently, returns to Việt Nam were easily incorporated into scholarship on Australian battlefield pilgrimage.[31]

Throughout the 2000s, veterans' journeys continued to receive media coverage, and as the return became normalized their journeys were treated increasingly as traditional pilgrimages.[32] This treatment clouded the overlap of veteran pilgrimages – and healing journeys, and reconciliation missions – with tourist ventures. Tourists visit war sites to learn about the cultural and political heritage of a country; pilgrims visit war sites to pay respects, mourn, and take part in ritual. These are artificial distinctions to

---

Indigenous tribes between 1788 and the mid-1800s, are still not officially commemorated on Anzac Day.

[30] See: Bruce Scates, *Return to Gallipoli: Walking the Battlefields of the Great War* (Cambridge: Cambridge University Press, 2006); Ken Inglis and Jan Brazier, *Sacred Places: War Memorials in the Australian Landscape* (Melbourne: The Miegunyah Press, 2008); Antonio Sagona et al., *Anzac Battlefield: A Gallipoli Landscape of War and Memory* (Melbourne: Cambridge University Press, 2016); Gary McKay, *Going Back: Australian Veterans Return to Vietnam* (Crows Nest: Allen & Unwin, 2007).

[31] Journalist Mark Dapin situates the expatriate-veteran community in Vung Tau – what he calls the "Vung Tau RSL" – in the context of the Australian tradition of "diggers return[ing] to the battlefields," while Garrie Hutchinson's survey situates Việt Nam as a space for military pilgrimage alongside Gallipoli, the Western Front, Kokoda, Korea, and Timor-Leste. Mark Dapin, "At the Vung Tau RSL." *The Monthly*, April 2013; Garrie Hutchinson, *Pilgrimage: A Traveller's Guide to Australia's Battlefields* (Melbourne: Black Inc., 2006).

While the United States has a history of battlefield pilgrimage, Việt Nam does not fit neatly in this category. American tourist-pilgrims are more likely to visit battle sites in the United States than they are to travel overseas for battlefield tourism, and while some American veterans make pilgrimages to the battlefields of World War II and Korea, they tend not to visit sites of recent and more controversial wars. There are many American battlefield tours to France, Japan, and South Korea, but not to Panama, Kuwait, Bosnia-Herzegovina, and Somalia. The former are sites where the United States can claim (partial) victory, while the latter are morally fraught and, in some cases, still recovering from war and US military presence. Pilgrimages to World War II and Korean War sites may also reflect war memory stabilizing over time; increasing numbers of US tour agencies offering military tours to Việt Nam suggests that this stabilizing has begun to occur with the Vietnam War as well. In the case of Việt Nam, Pauline Gueno Curtis argues that it is difficult for American veterans to glorify their wartime experience on the battlefield because the United States lost and because American atrocities are so well documented in Việt Nam. Paulette Gueno Curtis, "Locating History: Vietnam Veterans and Their Returns to the Battlefield, 1998–1999." PhD Diss., Harvard University, 2003, 140, 183, 196.

[32] Didier Lauras, "A Pilgrimage to the Battlefields." *Sydney Morning Herald*, January 2, 2005.

lay on traditional battlefield visitors, but in Việt Nam, these distinctions fall away entirely. The nature of guerrilla warfare changed the spatial relationship of combat and so of battlefield pilgrimage. All southern provinces were a battlefield in the Vietnam War, so the war tourist cannot realistically cross a threshold and become a pilgrim. The return to Việt Nam thus blurs battlefield pilgrimage, war tourism, nostalgia tourism, and "dark" tourism, that is, tourism to places associated with death and suffering.[33] Reflecting these overlapping heritage niches, the most recent scholarship on returning veterans considers the tourism potential of veteran pilgrimages, showing how pilgrimage has been commodified by the tourism industry.[34] American tourists and veterans who visit Việt Nam intending to bear witness to American suffering find themselves challenged by the unambiguous presentation of the West as the perpetrator of Vietnamese suffering. Returning veterans thus faced conflicting messages about their place in contemporary Việt Nam.

Perhaps because of the dominance of healing journeys, many scholars have focused on the effect of returning on veterans.[35] Scholars have reached different conclusions about what the effects are: Hai-Dang Doan Phan and Patrick Hagopian find that veteran authors who return to Việt Nam for reconciliation generally find some kind of closure, while Julia Bleakney finds that Vietnamese commemorative practices can be challenging for veterans.[36] I explore these contradictory experiences in detail Chapters 5 and 6, and find evidence that supports both contentions. The returnees discussed in this book unanimously reported that returning offered them a measure of peace; however, because I study a broader range of returnees than veteran-authors, my findings develop Doan Phan and Hagopian's conclusions. Because early anti-war returnees found closure through reconciliation, later anti-war veterans returned to heal through reconciliation activities. Their return journeys

---

[33] Anthropologist Victor Alneng observes that the Vietnamese tourism industry has responded to growing demand from Western tourists by promoting a kitsch phantasm of "Nam" in which memory is drawn from nostalgia for "the cinematic wartime Saigon." Victor Alneng, "'What the Fuck Is a Vietnam?' Tourist Phantasms and the Popcolonization of (the) Vietnam (War)." *Critique of Anthropology* 22 (2002): 462. See also: Laderman, *Tours of Vietnam*.

[34] Joseph Lema and Jerome Agrusa, "Revisiting the War Landscape of Vietnam and Tourism." In *Tourism and War*. Edited by Richard Butler (New York: Taylor and Francis, 2013), 250.

[35] Even studies assessing the potential of Vietnam veterans as tourists note that those who return do so "for consolation." Jerome Agrusa et al., "Determining the Potential of American Vietnam Veterans Returning to Vietnam as Tourists." *International Journal for Tourism Research* 3 (2006): 228.

[36] Doan Phan, "Rumor of Redress," 31–32; Hagopian, *Vietnam War in American Memory*, 416; Bleakney, *Revisiting Vietnam*, 178.

were predicated on the potentially healing experience of reconciling with their former enemy. In addition, the Australian veterans I spoke to did find closure or healing, but generally they did so through visiting battlefields and attending memorial services rather than through reconciliation activities. Furthermore, many interviewees confirmed Bleakney's findings, expressing discomfort and even anger at Vietnamese memorial sites because they found the narratives there challenging. I find that returnees navigated these challenges by drawing on Western war narratives to interpret Vietnamese memory. In doing so, they found a way to coexist more comfortably with Vietnamese commemorative practices.

Veterans' return journeys flowed in parallel to a mass migration away from Việt Nam: the Vietnamese diaspora. From 1975, millions of Vietnamese left Việt Nam: to escape the end of the war, flee persecution, find their families, work, or study.[37] Their journeys, relationships to their homeland, and imaginings by their host countries became the focus of many scholars in critical refugee studies: Yến Lê Espiritu untangles the ways in which the Vietnamese diaspora were militarized by the US government and society to resuscitate American national identity as liberator, while Long T. Bui considers how "South Vietnam" lingers in the memories of the Vietnamese diaspora as a "ghost nation" – both as a warzone and a lost home.[38] Veteran-returnees might be conceptualized as a parallel to the Vietnamese diaspora, many of whom "see themselves as sojourners, hopeful they can return to their country someday."[39] Yet as critical refugee studies scholars note, US veteran narratives have dominated Western war discourse, eliding Vietnamese (both from within Việt Nam and from the diaspora) voices.[40] Because of this dominance, and because the Vietnamese, Cambodian, and Laotian diasporas unfolded in parallel to veterans returns, simply claiming veteran-returnees as a diaspora risks what Nguyễn-Võ Thu-Hương describes as "an act of cannibalism," appropriating a key site of Vietnamese resistance to that dominating historical discourse.[41] Instead, this book draws on Rogers

---

[37] Phuong Tran Nguyen, *Becoming Refugee American: The Politics of Rescue in Little Saigon* (Chicago, IL: University of Illinois Press, 2017), 5–6; Christina Schwenkel, "Socialist Mobilities: Crossing New Terrains in Vietnamese Migration Histories." *Central and Eastern European Migration Review* 4:1 (2015): 13–25.

[38] Yến Lê Espiritu, *Body Counts: The Vietnam War and Militarized Refugees* (Berkeley, CA: University of California Press, 2014), 2; Bui, *Returns of War*.

[39] Ronald Takaki, *Strangers from a Different Shore: A History of Asian Americans* (New York: Penguin, 1989).

[40] Yến Lê Espiritu, "About Ghost Stories: the Vietnam War and 'Rememoration.'" *PLMA* 123:5 (2008), 1702.

[41] Nguyễn-Võ Thu-Hương, "Forking Paths: How Shall We Mourn the Dead?" *Amerasia Journal* 31:2 (2005): 172.

Brubaker's call to speak more precisely of "diasporic stances, projects, claims, idioms, practices" to examine the ways in which veterans attempted to relocate a lost home in Việt Nam.[42]

The field of diaspora studies emerged in the late 1980s in response to the plethora of transnational links and flows fostered by war and globalization through the twentieth century. As the field proliferated, scholars established certain patterns to define diasporas. Veteran-returnees echo many of these patterns: they are dispersed from their imagined homeland, which they retain a collective memory of, and they share a "diasporic consciousness" with others in their community.[43] Like other groups who act like diasporas, veteran-returnees put particular emphasis on a perceived alienation or persecution.[44] As this book will show, veteran-returnees attempted to maintain the homeland upon return through nostalgic practices that worked to bring "Vietnam" back to Việt Nam.[45] Returning veterans were also migrants and travelers *to* Việt Nam, with generational tides among them. In the same way that the "first wave of migrants can be seen as a generational cohort that laid a foundation for the diasporic group," veterans' journeys were molded around the patterns established by earlier returns.[46] There are, however, key differences between veteran-returnees and diasporas. Veterans are not a dispersed ethnic group. They do not face the challenges of the refugee: they experience no forcible displacement or resettlement; they do not deal at all with statelessness. Despite feelings of alienation, veterans are not actually persecuted: unlike the Vietnamese diaspora, for instance, veterans do not have their citizenship rights contested by virtue of their connection to Việt Nam. Where many diaspora communities relate to their community through family and shared cultural heritage, such as food, art, and language, veteran-returnees found belonging in community through shared war experiences.[47] Finally, many members of diasporas embark on pilgrimages to homeland to learn about their heritage, such as in *taglit* pilgrimages to Israel.[48] While early returnees travelled to learn about

---

[42] Rogers Brubaker, "The 'Diaspora' Diaspora." *Ethnic and Racial Studies* 28:1 (2005): 13.
[43] Safran, "Diasporas in Modern Societies," 83–99.
[44] Elizabeth McAlister, "Listening for Geographies: Music as Sonic Compass Pointing Towards African and Christian Diasporic Horizons in the Caribbean." In *Geographies of the Haitian Diaspora*. Edited by Regine O. Jackson (New York: Routledge, 2011): 225.
[45] Safran, "Diasporas in Modern Societies," 84.
[46] Danny Ben-Moshe et al., "The Vietnamese Diaspora in Australia: Identity and Transnational Behaviour." *Diaspora Studies* 9:2 (2016): 112–27.
[47] Nathalie Huynh Chau Nguyen found that for four Vietnamese women who returned after the war, emotional attachments were the central motivation: "Vietnam means above all, family." Nguyen, *Memory Is Another Country*, 141–60.
[48] Paulla A. Ebron, "Tourists as Pilgrims: Commercial Fashioning of Transatlantic Politics." *American Ethnologist* 26:4 (November 1999): 911.

Vietnamese perspectives of war, over time veterans adopted the role of educator in Việt Nam, inverting diasporic community patterns by privileging their war knowledge over local memory.

In recent years, historians have increasingly examined the ways in which war lingers beyond the battlefield. Edwin A. Martini traces a "new phase of the American war" through a punitive, heavy-handed policy of "bleeding" Việt Nam coupled with a cultural recuperation of American honor in new war narratives of "mutual destruction."[49] Christian Appy considers how the traumas of Vietnam continue to reverberate in US culture, while Peter Yule argues that Australian veterans live in the "long shadow" of war.[50] Ellen Wu calls for a centering of war in migration history, to consider the ways in which "war-making seeded and nurtured new human connections across borders."[51] Mary Dudziak unpacks the concept of "war time" itself, noting that "built into the idea of war time is a conception of the future ... a place beyond war."[52] This book draws on these conceptions of war, trauma, time, space, and memory by exploring how Western veterans sought to find that "place beyond war" – namely, peace – by returning to Việt Nam.

This book reveals the history of Australian and American return journeys through the testimony of veterans who returned. I draw primarily from oral history interviews I conducted with returnees, supplemented with memoirs, media interviews, and blogs.[53] Through my interviews with over fifty veterans, I reached a very broad range of returnees, tracing their individual stories against the unfolding transnational histories of Việt Nam, Australia, and the United States. An oral history approach also provided me with insight into not only individuals' memories, but "the formation and narration of memory stories" in the interview itself; revealing how veterans locate their journeys in broader "web[s] of meaning" about the return journey, about Việt Nam, and about the war itself.[54]

---

[49] Edwin A. Martini, *Invisible Enemies: The American War on Vietnam, 1975–2000* (Amherst, MA: University of Massachusetts Press, 2007), 2–10.

[50] Christian Appy, *American Reckoning: The Vietnam War and Our National Identity* (New York: Penguin, 2015); Peter Yule, *The Long Shadow: Australia's Vietnam Veterans Since the War* (Sydney: NewSouth, 2020).

[51] Ellen D. Wu, "It's Time to Center War in US Immigration History." *Modern American History* 2:2 (2019): 221.

[52] Mary Dudziak, *War Time: An Idea, Its History, Its Consequences* (Cary, NC: Oxford University Press, 2012), 22.

[53] Because the focus of this project is veterans' returns to Việt Nam, many well-known veteran-authored works are not included (for example, *The Things They Carried* by Tim O'Brien and *A Rumor of War* by Phillip Caputo) because the authors either did not return to Việt Nam or did not write about their return journey.

[54] Lynn Abrams, "Memory as Both Source and Subject of Study: The Transformations of Oral History." In *Writing the History of Memory*. Edited by Stefan Berger and Bill Niven (London: Bloomsbury, 2014), 90.

Introduction

My interviews were structured around key questions regarding why veterans returned to Việt Nam and their wartime, postwar and post-return experiences and views. The interviews were free-flowing or "semi-structured" to provide more power and control to the participant. Psychologists argue that in less structured interviews, "the interviewee is reconceptualized as an active participant in the production of knowledge in the research process."[55] Semi-structured interviews have the dual benefits of encouraging trust and reciprocity between the researcher and participant and providing the interviewer with more context about specific experiences.[56] This flexible model is also beneficial to participants who may be suffering from trauma. Oral historian Sean Field, for instance, suggests using "empathic imagination" which "requires patient listening to what interviewees want to talk about and helps in eliciting responses."[57]

The source material in this book is as much shaped by the dynamics of my interviews and my position as an interviewer as by the veterans' personal histories. Feminist oral historians such as Brigid Limerick, Tracey Burgess-Limerick, and Margaret Grace argue that a conscious exploration of the "politics of interviewing" can enhance our understanding of the narrator's story.[58] Interviews are palpably contrived events. Both interviewer and interviewee work consciously and unconsciously to find a comfortable rapport, often falling into normative roles shaped by social hierarchies of race, gender, class, age, and status. Such power dynamics were apparent in my interviews. Not only was I a civilian speaking to veterans, and a woman speaking to men, I was twenty-four years old – younger than many of my interviewees' children. I am certain that my social positioning inhibited discussion of topics that veterans perhaps considered impolite or unsavory to discuss with a young woman, and I explore some of these limitations in Chapter 8. Social dynamics also affected how I behaved as an interviewer. There were many times when I considered redirecting the interview focus, or asking a candid question, but it was clear that doing so would have been received

---

[55] Brigid Limerick et al., "The Politics of Interviewing: Power Relations and Accepting the Gift." *International Journal of Qualitative Studies in Education* 9:4 (2006): 458.

[56] Juliet Corbin and Janice M. Morse, "The Unstructured Interactive Interview: Issues of Reciprocity and Risks When Dealing with Sensitive Topics." *Qualitative Inquiry* 9:3 (2003): 337.

[57] Sean Field, "Beyond 'Healing': Trauma, Oral History and Regeneration." *Oral History* 34:1 (Spring 2006): 38. For further discussion on navigating trauma in oral history research, see: Robert Reynolds, "Trauma and the Relational Dynamics of Life-History Interviewing." *Australian Historical Studies* 43:1 (2012): 78–88.

[58] Limerick et al., "The Politics of Interviewing," 450. See also: Valerie Yow, "'Do I Like Them Too Much?': Effects of the Oral History Interview on the Interviewer and Vice-Versa." *The Oral History Review* 24:1 (Summer 1997): 55–79.

by veterans as improperly directive on my part, and would have subdued the interview rapport. However, my social positioning also provided some advantages. Most veterans responded to me with an avuncular and sometimes protective manner, in contrast to a prickliness I witnessed in response to other researchers (mostly older, male journalists) who were present in Đà Nẵng, Vũng Tàu, and Washington, DC. My youth, gender, and lack of experience with the military appeared to neutralize the threat posed by an outsider asking questions, and combined with my interest and concern in their stories, seemed to allow interviewees to become vulnerable during their interviews. I was often surprised at their openness with me, and many said that they had not anticipated discussing (unasked) some very personal and sensitive aspects of their biography. The emotional depth of the interviews explored in this book demonstrates this vulnerability.

I conducted interviews between December 2015 and June 2017. The interviews took place in person in Việt Nam and Australia, and over Skype, Facetime, and telephone. Returnees were recruited for interviews through organizations such as the Vietnam Veterans Association and Veterans for Peace (VFP), as well as through personal contacts and referral from existing participants. Emails were sent to organizations with recruitment information so that returnees could opt in. Prior to the interview, while going over the consent form, participant interviewees were offered a copy of their interview transcript, as well as the final report on the findings of the project. Because of the number of participants I interviewed, and because I travelled very briefly through cities while conducting fieldwork and often recruited potential participants through local contacts in those cities, narrator-review was not possible for this project. I transcribed interviews with the goal of retaining participants' natural colloquial styles in order to capture their individual voices. Although most veterans gave permission for their names to be used, to err on the side of caution, in this book only first names or pseudonyms are used to identify interviewees. This naming choice also serves to differentiate interview sources from sources found only in published materials, conveying my relationship to the source through the first name/last name distinction. For example, I draw from articles and a memoir written by US politician and Vietnam prisoner of war (POW) John McCain, and refer to him by his surname, but because his fellow POW and politician Douglas "Pete" Peterson was among my interviewees, I refer to him as "Pete" to indicate our interview relationship. In the case of a few veterans whose public work is linked to

Introduction

Table 1 *Enlisted and volunteer veterans*

	Australian	US	Total
Drafted/Conscripted	10	6	16
Enlisted	16	37	53
• Volunteer	• 14	• 33	• 47
• Draft Volunteer	• 2	• 4	• 6

their returns, such as Pete's, identifying information is included where relevant to the context.[59]

Of the sixty-nine returnee accounts discussed in this book, forty-three are US veterans and twenty-six are Australian veterans. These demographics are not proportionate to demographics in the war – 2.7 million American soldiers served "in country", compared to 60,000 Australians – but are robust sample sizes for a comparative study.[60] Of the sixty-nine veterans, sixteen were drafted: six American and ten Australian (see Table 1).[61] However, four of the US returnees were "draft volunteers" who enlisted to avoid the draft, because drafted men were more likely to serve in the infantry which had significantly higher casualties. One Australian described himself as a "draft volunteer" who volunteered for National Service to guarantee that he would see service, not to avoid the infantry. One other Australian enlisted "on advice from a magistrate," indicating his choice was jail or enlistment; I have included him as a "draft volunteer."[62] Draftees or conscripts constitute around 25 percent of both US and Australian fighting forces in Việt Nam: therefore, in my interviews draftees are slightly overrepresented in the Australian accounts and slightly underrepresented in the American accounts. The difference in draft or conscript numbers among my return sample might result from the different social welfare systems in Australia and the United States, which minimized postwar income inequality among Australian veterans.

---

[59] For this reason, interviewee and author W.D. Ehrhart is referred to as W.D. in text to link him to his pen name, because I draw extensively from his books as supplementary sources.

[60] Only about 1 percent (30,000) of US soldiers and 5 percent (3,000) of Australian soldiers have returned to Việt Nam. These estimates are gathered from personal communication with veterans and tour guides.

[61] The breakdown of drafted veterans by nationality and return group are as follows: three US "reconciliation" veterans; two "normalization" veterans – one Australian, one American; and ten "commemoration" veterans – nine Australian, one American.

[62] Interview with Ken, Melbourne, May 25, 2016.

Sixty-eight of the sixty-nine returnees are white, reflecting what I believe to be the vastly disproportionate rate of return of white veterans relative to black, Hispanic, Asian, Native American, and Indigenous Australian veterans. The homogeneity of my book subjects reflects a broader problem in historical research on Vietnam veterans.[63] The same institutional discrimination that has inhibited lower socioeconomic and nonwhite narratives from being produced and published also impacts the ability to afford or even consider international travel.[64] In this book, I attend to how the comparative affluence and racial privilege of the overwhelming majority of veterans who returned to Việt Nam shaped their experiences and attitudes upon return.

In order to track patterns and trends in the return to Việt Nam, the veterans discussed in this book are divided into three groups (see Table 2). As patterns emerged among returnees' stories, I considered how cultural influences, social processes, and politics of remembering shaped their individual memories. I show, for example, that veterans identified "stepping-stones" on a healing journey back to Việt Nam (Chapter 2), and that returnees embraced Vietnamese mythology into understandings of warfare (Chapter 6), demonstrating how "remembering always entails

Table 2 *Veterans grouped by periods of return*

Type	Australian (26)	American (43)	Total (69)
Reconciliation (1981–1994)	4	23	27
Interviews	2	12	14
Other Source	2	11	13
Drafted/Conscripted	0	4	4
Enlisted	4	19	23
Normalization (1995–2005)	6	10	16
Interviews	5	9	14
Other Source	1	1	2
Drafted/Conscripted	1	1	2
Enlisted	5	9	14
Commemoration (2006–2016)	16	10	26
Interviews	16	10	26
Other Source	0	0	0
Drafted/Conscripted	10	1	11
Enlisted	6	9	15

---

[63] Wood, *Veteran Narratives and the Collective Memory of the Vietnam War*, 22.
[64] Curtis, "Locating History," 23–24.

the working of past experiences into available cultural scripts."[65] My approach draws on memory research on how we "compose" memories in ways that are psychologically comfortable: striving "for a version of the self that can be lived with in relative psychic comfort."[66] Returnees' memories – both of the war and of returning to Việt Nam – were "composed" in this sense, as veterans sought "recognition and affirmation for [their] life stories."[67]

My research is also informed by the concept of "particular publics," developed by historians Graham Dawson and Alistair Thomson.[68] Where "public memory" refers to the collective recollections of the general public and so is broad and impersonal, particular publics are the social groups that have the most significance to our lives and so play the largest role in affirming our memories and identities. Within these groups certain memories are reiterated and become privileged over others, because they represent and resonate with the values of the group.[69] The effect of particular publics – of ongoing composure of memories over time through the process of re-remembering within a specific group – was particularly apparent among Australian veterans. This is because Australian veterans constitute a smaller group than US veterans generally – producing a more cohesive group identity – and because returning Australians were densely concentrated in one area of Việt Nam.

Finally, I draw from work on emotion and masculinity to explore a contradiction in my interview data. Every single veteran described returning as a very positive experience. However, the content of their interviews was largely negative in tone. My interview questions (see Appendix 1) do not explain this contradiction. I draw from historian Michael Roper's work with letters of soldiers in the Great War to explore this problem. Roper finds within these letters a "secret battle" for emotional survival in total war.[70] He argues that beneath every memory there is an "underlay," the individual, emotional experience that is fundamental to the meaning of the memory as the cultural references that shape the memory over time.[71] Roper's theory of underlay was useful in helping me

---

[65] Alistair Thomson, "Anzac Stories: Using Personal Testimony in War History." *War & Society* 26:2 (2006): 183.
[66] Graham Dawson, *Soldier Heroes: British Adventure, Empire and the Imagining of Masculinities* (New York: Routledge, 1994), 23.
[67] Thomson, "Anzac Stories," 5. [68] Dawson, *Soldier Heroes*, 24.
[69] Alistair Thomson, "Anzac Memories Revisited: Trauma, Memory and Oral History." *Oral History Review* 42:1 (2015): 26.
[70] Michael Roper, *Secret Battle: Emotional Survival in the Great War* (Manchester: Manchester University Press, 2009).
[71] Michael Roper, "Re-Remembering the Soldier Hero: The Psychic and Social Construction of Memory in Personal Narratives of the Great War." *History Workshop Journal* 50 (Autumn 2000): 184.

consider how returnees' memories and emotions, particularly those connected to war, were mediated through a prism of masculinity. The negative tone in interviews generally conveyed a hostility which, in Western culture, is perhaps the only socially acceptable expression of emotion by men. Using Roper's concept of underlay, I read the subtext of veteran criticism of, for instance, the development of infrastructure in contemporary Việt Nam, finding that beneath this hostility lay an expression of loss over "their" Việt Nam.

This book is made up of three parts. In the first part, "Return," I chart the chronology of veterans' returns, addressing the reasons why they returned, discussing how they were affected by their returns, and situating their returns in the political and cultural context of the time. Chapter 1 examines the experiences of the earliest returns by veterans to Việt Nam, from 1981 to 1994. Chapter 2 follows the journeys of veterans who returned between 1995 and 2005, as the concept of returning "normalized." Chapter 3 tracks patterns of return from 2006 to 2016, focusing on a rising trend of reunion and anniversary orientated returns.

The second part of the book examines how returnees have responded to Việt Nam since the end of the war. Part II is divided into three chapters, addressing how returnees respond to war remnants (or lack thereof), Vietnamese people, and Vietnamese memories of the war. Chapter 4 explores the reactions of returnees to the presence and absence of war in peacetime Việt Nam. In Chapter 5, I show that the majority of returnees viewed the Vietnamese through an Orientalist lens, reflecting both the wartime views of Việt Nam and the broader legacies of colonial thought in Australia and the United States. Chapter 6 explores how returnees reacted to Vietnamese memories of "their" war.

Part III considers the broader story of veterans' returns. Vietnam veteran identity is entwined with war legacies. In Chapter 7, I explore returnees' views on key legacies of the war, mapping their views against the various schools of thought in the historiography of the war to unpack why certain groups of returnees were drawn to specific historical narratives. My final chapter considers the impact of returning veterans for Việt Nam, as well as veterans' own perceptions of their role in peacetime Việt Nam, arguing that both their return activities and their perceptions of those activities were mediated through the Western war narratives. Finally, I conclude by considering how veterans reflect on their return journeys as living legacies of war.

By speaking of veterans as living legacies, this book aims to make a broader point. The experiences of survivors reveal how war continues to manifest in peacetime: through their journeys, relationships, practices, traumas, memories, identities, bodies, and loss. Though returnees found new ways of thinking about Vietnam that brought them a measure of peace, their return journeys were defined by nostalgic longings, diasporic claims, and lingering wartime biases. In so doing, they brought fragments of their war back to peacetime Việt Nam, and to the Vietnamese – who are also living legacies – working to overcome war's enduring consequences. The return journey thus reveals the inevitable permanence of war: creating ripples beyond the battlefield and perpetually reemerging in myriad ways.

Part I

Return

1 Reconciliation, 1981–1994

"The memories would not go away. That is why we had to go back," wrote US Marine and Vietnam veteran Mike P. in his private journal in 1989.[1] Between 1980 and 1994, a trickle of Australian and American Vietnam veterans made the first journeys back to Việt Nam. I call this group "reconciliation" because their journeys were attempts to make contact, discover their enemy, engage in diplomacy – even find friendship. For some, the rise in Vietnam War commemoration provided an opening to explore their wartime pasts. For others, contemporary political issues set them on the path of a personal mission. Major economic changes within Việt Nam acted as a cue for many veterans, which indicated a longing to return. These changes, known as Đổi Mới, also lessened restrictions on foreign travel to Việt Nam, and from 1986 veterans returned to Việt Nam in increasing numbers. By the early 1990s, American and Australian travel agencies were organizing tours to Việt Nam. Some veterans described their return as a turning point that challenged them to atone for the war. Others found Việt Nam offered new opportunities and relationships. In their interviews, reconciliation returnees broadly agreed that returning to Việt Nam transformed their lives by releasing them from wartime memories and bringing them a measure of peace. Their focus on the challenge they had overcome and the relief they experienced by returning nearly obscured the historical reality that reconciliation was not initiated by the veterans themselves. It was Việt Nam that reached out and asked them to come back.

Following the end of the war in 1975, Prime Minister Phạm Văn Đồng invited the United States to normalize relations under the conditions of the 1973 Paris Peace Accords, including Nixon's secret promise of

---

[1] Mike P., "1989 VVRP Journal w Intro." Private journal shared with the author, May 14, 2016.

$3.2 billion in reconstruction aid.[2] The Ford administration refused, arguing that Việt Nam had violated the Accords' terms by failing to account for missing American servicemen.[3] These alleged Prisoners of War (POWs) and Missing in Action (MIA) became the basis of decades-long hostility between the US and the Socialist Republic of Việt Nam (SRV), with successive US administrations insisting on transparency and the SRV maintaining that they withheld no prisoners or soldiers' remains.[4] In 1981, the SRV invited representatives of Vietnam Veterans of America (VVA) to Hà Nội in order "to stir public opinion" in favor of reconciliation.[5] Four veteran members agreed to return, including the founder and director Bobby Muller.[6] News of the VVA tour rippled through veteran communities, attracting condemnation from the Veterans of Foreign Wars, the American Legion, and the National League of POW-MIA families.[7] Publicly, the Reagan administration maintained their focus on POWs/MIAs, with a public statement from the State Department supporting "efforts by private citizens to join Government efforts in achieving a full accounting for those missing in action." Privately, however, the returning veterans were warned that they would be "used for propaganda purposes."[8] Undeterred, Muller pushed forward with negotiations for the trip, which he described as a "soldier-to-soldier" discussion.[9] The VVA team focused on veteran advocacy issues, including accounting for POWs/MIAs and sharing research on the

---

[2] Steven Hunt, *The Carter Administration and Vietnam* (London: Macmillan, 1996), 19.
[3] Ibid.
[4] Historian H. Bruce Franklin documents how the Nixon administration "lumped together" the categories of POW and MIA into the acronym "POW/MIA" under the grouping "Unaccounted For" to galvanize support for the war and buy time and power in the peace negotiations. After the Peace Accords, the separate category of Killed in Action/Body Not Recovered was added to the grouping, leaving the United States with over 2,500 "Unaccounted For" Vietnam soldiers framed by the administration as potential prisoners of war. Bruce Franklin, *MIA, or, Mythmaking in America* (New Brunswick, NJ: Rutgers University Press, 1993), 13. See also: Joseph Siracusa and Hang Nguyen, "Vietnam-US Relations: An Unparalleled History." *Orbis* 61:3 (2017): 404–22; Michael J. Allen, *Until the Last Man Comes Home: POWs, MIAs, and the Unending Vietnam War* (Chapel Hill, NC: University of North Carolina Press, 2009).
[5] Bernard Weinraub, "Hanoi, In Economic Straits, Seeks to Move Toward Ties with US." *New York Times*, December 28, 1981.
[6] Michael Kranish, "No Retreat, No Surrender." *Boston Globe*, March 9, 2003. www.boston.com/ae/music/articles/2003/09/03/no_retreat_no_surrender/
[7] Mary McGrory, "For a Moment at Christmas, Vietnam Evokes the Old Emotions." *Washington Post*, December 29, 1981.
[8] Bernard Weinrub, "Vietnam Invites 4 US Veterans to Visit Hanoi." *New York Times*, December 13, 1981. Despite accusations from the VFW of treachery, the VVA trip was entirely legal: the US embargo was established under the Trading with the Enemy Act (1917), so there was nothing to stop private citizens undertaking humanitarian and fact-finding missions in Việt Nam.
[9] Bobby Muller, quoted in Weinrub, "Vietnam Invites 4 US Veterans to Visit Hanoi."

consequences of Agent Orange. By returning to Việt Nam, Muller and the VVA showed faith in Việt Nam's declarations regarding POWs and demonstrated to Vietnamese and Americans alike that reconciliation was possible. Muller said he hoped that the trip would "start a process of healing" and "initiate a dialogue between our people, Americans and Vietnamese, after years of bloodshed and strain."[10]

Veterans in government were also engaged in the POW/MIA debate. In 1985, former POW and US Senator John McCain returned to Hà Nội with a CBS documentary team to "bring visibility to Americans still listed as missing in action."[11] McCain returned several times in the 1980s and 1990s in an official capacity, accounting for POWs/MIAs and promoting normalization efforts between the two countries.[12] Air Force colonel and former POW Douglas "Pete" Peterson returned in 1992 as a congressman, to "make sure that what we were saying about looking for MIA/POWs was an honest assessment." Pete remembered that the Bush administration claimed to be prioritizing the POW/MIA issue and blaming delays on the Vietnamese. He told me, "some of us in Congress took some angst about that, thinking that it might not be true."[13] While these veterans' personal experiences as POWs undoubtedly affected their determination to resolve the POW/MIA issue, Pete and McCain made it clear that they returned primarily in their capacity as politicians.

These first political returns to Việt Nam coincided with a shift in cultural representations about the Vietnam War and its veterans in American and Australia. During the war, Vietnam veterans had increasingly been depicted in popular culture as dangerous and unstable, with symptoms of their trauma represented as indicators of moral decay.[14] The United States, and to a lesser degree Australia, collectively diagnosed the Vietnam veteran in an effort to shrug off the responsibility and blame for the damage done to society, and consequently, "the 'Vietnam veteran' was taken to symbolize someone who was both physically and mentally

---

[10] Bobby Muller, quoted in Weinrub, "Vietnam Invites 4 US Veterans to Visit Hanoi."
[11] Michael Kilian, "The War Hero Is a Senator Now." *Chicago Tribune*, July 19, 1987.
[12] John McCain, "A Former POW on Vietnam, Four Decades Later." *Wall Street Journal*, March 13, 2013.
[13] Interview with Pete, Melbourne, May 12, 2016.
[14] For example, *Deathdream* (1974, also released as *The Veteran*, 1972 and *Dead of Night*, 1972), was a supernatural horror film in which a soldier dies in combat only to return to his hometown in zombie form, killing and syphoning the blood of his victims with a syringe. *Deathdream* invoked the fears emerging around Vietnam veterans abusing heroin: returning to the United States contaminated and threatening to spread the epidemic among Middle America. *Deathdream*, directed by Bob Clarke (Toronto: Quadrant Films, 1974). See also: *Motorpsycho!*, directed by Russ Meyer (Hollywood, CA: Eve Productions, 1965); *Nam's Angels*, directed by Jack Starrett (Hollywood, CA: Fanfare Films, 1970).

damaged."[15] Toward the late 1970s Vietnam veterans began to be represented as antiheroes rather than villains, reflecting a new social willingness to discuss the war.[16] Francis Ford Coppola's *Apocalypse Now* (1979), for instance, points to the betrayal of soldiers by the military, complicating the hero-villain narrative by giving Marlon Brando's Colonel Kurtz logical reasons for his insanity: "there's nothing I detest more than the stench of lies."[17] By the 1980s, Vietnam veterans were "remasculinized" and cast as protagonists, with their trauma and isolation portrayed sympathetically "to represent the United States as the primary victim of the war."[18] The defining image of the 1980's Vietnam veteran was John Rambo, who, in *First Blood: Part II* (1985), rescues POWs abandoned in Vietnam and insists that all veterans want is "for our country to love us as much as we love it."[19] Such sympathetic cultural representations opened up a new space for veterans to reflect on their personal war legacies.

For example, US Army infantry veteran Fredy Champagne recalled from a line in Oliver Stone's 1986 film *Platoon*: "those of us who did make it have an obligation to build again, to teach to others what we know and to try with what's left of our lives to find a goodness and meaning to this life."[20] Champagne was motivated by this: "we veterans had to return and rebuild in order to make some sense of it all. That line stuck with me subconsciously."[21] Champagne became one of many reconciliation veterans who returned to Việt Nam on humanitarian volunteering missions, inspired by Veterans Peace Actions Teams in Central America. Peace Action Teams were the brainchild of anti-war Vietnam veterans who saw US-sponsored wars in Central America as evidence that the United States

---

[15] Peter Edwards, "Fifty Years On: Half-Century Reflections on the Australian Commitment to the Vietnam War." In *New Perceptions of the Vietnam War: Essays on the War, the South Vietnamese, the Diaspora and the Continuing Impact*. Edited by Nathalie Huynh Chau Nguyen (Jefferson, NC: McFarland, 2015), 73.

[16] In the late 1970s, see: *Taxi Driver*, directed by Martin Scorsese (Los Angeles, CA: Columbia Pictures, 1976); *The Deer Hunter*, directed by Michael Cimino (Los Angeles, CA: Universal Pictures, 1978).

[17] *Apocalypse Now*, directed by Francis Ford Coppola (Beverly Hills, CA: United Artists, 1979).

[18] Susan Jeffords, *The Remasculinization of America* (Indianapolis, IN: Indiana University Press, 1989); Martini, *Invisible Enemies*, 8. In the 1980s, see: *First Blood*, directed by Ted Kotcheff (Los Angeles, CA: Orion Pictures, 1982); *Missing in Action*, directed by Joseph Zito (Beverly Hills, CA: The Cannon Group, 1984); *Vietnam*, directed by Chris Noonan and John Duigan (Sydney: Roadshow, February 23–April 27, 1987).

[19] *First Blood: Part II*, directed by George P. Cosmatos (Los Angeles, CA: Anabasis Investments and Estudios Churubusco, 1985).

[20] *Platoon*, directed by Oliver Stone (Los Angeles, CA: Orion Pictures, 1986).

[21] Fredy Champagne, "The Founding of the VVRP." Veterans Viet Nam Restoration Project. www.vvrp.org/?page_id=133

1 Reconciliation, 1981–1994

had failed to learn from the mistakes of Vietnam.[22] Champagne recalled hearing that a "team of vets, many of them Vietnam vets, had just rebuilt a medical clinic [in Nicaragua] ... I thought that was a really cool idea."[23] In 1988, he initiated Veterans Viet Nam Restoration Project (VVRP), a nongovernmental organization (NGO) that took teams of veterans back to Việt Nam to help with postwar reconstruction.[24]

Reconciliation veterans on volunteering missions described a deep preoccupation with Vietnam that preceded their returns. Many had struggled to reintegrate in the United States, dwelling on their warzone home and wondering what had happened to Việt Nam. After the war, US Army infantry veteran Mike Boehm lived in solitude, filled with "blackness" and a "hatred for what I had been a part of."[25] In 1991, he volunteered to help rebuild hurricane-damaged houses in Puerto Rico, which led him to wonder "if we can do this in Vietnam."[26] This preoccupation echoes Boym's "reflective" nostalgia: these veterans "see everywhere the imperfect mirror images of home, and try to cohabit with doubles and ghosts."[27] Boym was describing here the nostalgia of "diasporic intimacy" among migrant communities, a connection to a lost home defined by "uprootedness and defamiliarization."[28] Veterans acted as another kind of diaspora, one linking those who shared a lost home at war. Among these reconciliation volunteers, diasporic longing was particularly apparent: after learning "to live with alienation" and reconciling with the "uncanniness of the world," "there comes a surprise, a pang of recognition."[29] They explained their returns as a gradual path from disillusionment to action. Mike P. remembered: "I was, as they say, in deep denial. But in the early 80s, I ... saw the eloquent Bobby Muller as he was trying to start up the Vietnam Veterans of America." Mike P. began studying international relations and development practices at the University of California under Pentagon Papers coauthor Mel Gurtov, which "re-awakened [him], Big Time, back to Việt Nam." He read about a Vietnamese village where Combined Action Platoon Marines had served, which "triggered memories and feelings I had so studiously put down."[30] As a member of the VVA in the late 1980s, Mike P. spent time reviewing literature for "any number of causes," eventually coming across mail from the VVRP "and, I thought, 'oh wow, that's kinda

---

[22] S. Brian Wilson, "History of the Idea of the Veterans Peace Action Teams." February 1, 1987, republished on *brianwilson.com* in 2017. www.brianwillson.com/history-of-the-idea-of-the-veterans-peace-action-teams-vpat/
[23] Champagne, "The Founding of the VVRP."   [24] Ibid.
[25] Dan Kaufman, "Reconciliation at My Lai." *New Yorker*, March 24, 2013.   [26] Ibid.
[27] Boym, *Future of Nostalgia*, 251.   [28] Ibid., 252.   [29] Boym, *Future of Nostalgia*, 254.
[30] Mike P., "1989 VVRP Journal w Intro."

cool.'"³¹ Champagne and Mike P. returned to Việt Nam with the VVRP on its first mission in 1989, and Boehm returned on a VVRP mission in 1992.

These veteran volunteers felt a moral obligation toward Việt Nam. VVRP members, for instance, were mostly anti-war veterans who felt they had a duty to right the wrong in which they had participated. Mike P. described VVRP members (including himself) as a "group of potheads ... [who] thought it would be groovy to wage peace."³² Most were antiestablishment and critical of organized religion and its influences on US politics. However, there were political outliers. Maurice, a US Army draftee, first returned to Việt Nam in 1973 after his tour had ended to work as a medic in Sài Gòn, staying after the war "to encourage the Christian church and particularly pastors to stay and minister to their flock." Maurice felt he had a personal responsibility to shoulder the burden of protecting Christians and upholding Christianity in the newly communist state: "I can't ask somebody else to do it if I'm unwilling to stick around and have the consequences myself."³³ He continued working for the International Red Cross, and even applied for Vietnamese citizenship, but was turned down and returned to the United States on one of the last flights out organized by the United Nations in 1976.³⁴

Throughout the 1980s, commemorative events, veteran memoirs, popular culture, and political dialogues reintroduced Vietnam into American society, indicating growing public interest in the war and its veterans. In 1980, President Ronald Reagan declared Vietnam "a noble cause" and equated Vietnam veterans with veterans of historic wars.³⁵ In his inaugural address, Reagan told the American people that the United States was not "doomed to an inevitable decline."³⁶ The fear of this decline had been termed "Vietnam Syndrome," and the promise that the syndrome could be cured through patriotism helped some veterans to feel proud of their service and engage in public commemoration.³⁷ The Vietnam Veterans Memorial in Washington DC, known as "The Wall," was dedicated in 1982, and the "Three Soldiers" statue was added to the

[31] Interview with Mike P., Skype, May 11, 2016.   [32] Ibid.
[33] Interview with Maurice, Skype Interview, July 26, 2016.
[34] David A. Andelman, "49 US Citizens and Dependents Fly from Saigon." *New York Times*, August 2, 1976, 1.
[35] Ronald Reagan, "Peace: Restoring the Margin of Safety." *Veterans of Foreign Wars Convention*, Chicago, Illinois, August 18, 1980. www.reagan.utexas.edu/archives/reference/8.18.80.html
[36] Ronald Reagan, "Inaugural Address." *The American Presidency Project*, online by Gerhard Peters and John T. Woolley, January 20, 1981. www.presidency.ucsb.edu/ws/?pid=43130
[37] Andrew Bacevich, *The New American Militarism: How Americans Are Seduced by War* (New York: Oxford University Press, 2013), 107–08.

site of The Wall with another dedication in 1984. In the early 1980s, small, locally organized Welcome Home parades were held all over the United States.[38] The absence of parades after the war had ended disappointed many veterans who felt they were being stigmatized and neglected.[39] The small parades in the 1980s thus operated both as a belated recognition for war service and an apology for wartime non-recognition, culminating in a 200,000-veteran strong parade in Chicago in 1986 attended by about 300,000 civilians.[40] These cultural signals legitimized their war service and encouraged them to reflect on their experience, memories, and nostalgia. With public debates about Vietnam settling in their home countries, veterans began to consider the return as a way of addressing internal conflict over the war. US Marine veteran Bill E. attributed changing culture as a factor in his return in 1994: "probably for maybe four or five years before I came back, I was really starting to think about, 'it would be good to come back'.... It was a progression of things that would come up that would just kinda start to focus more and more on the past, and on the war."[41]

The role of commemorations in sparking thoughts of return reveal the interconnections between war memory, debates around the war, veteran identity, and nostalgia for Vietnam. Many veterans first contemplated returning when they visited war memorials. US Army veteran and writer Kevin Bowen wrote that at The Wall, "against the reflecting surface of black granite etched with the names of the 58,000 dead, we began a dialogue with Vietnam ... for many veterans it seems the time has come for reengagement, for a new campaign of hearts and minds, a campaign that involves returning to the land where they fought."[42] The Wall is made of black, shining stone. Over seventy-five meters in

---

[38] Scholars agree that these parades were largely a response to the end of the Iranian hostage crisis in 1981. The "emotional welcoming" of released American hostages engendered a swell of support toward Vietnam veterans. John Hellman, *American Myth and the Legacy of Vietnam* (New York: Columbia University Press, 1986), 101. See also: David Fitzgerald, "Support the Troops: Gulf War Homecomings and a New Politics of Military Celebration." *Modern American History* 2 (2019): 6; Appy, *American Reckoning*.

[39] Historian Eric T. Dean Jr. found that "the lavish parades of which veterans of past wars supposedly received are often more a myth than reality," so the veterans' memories of "lavish parades" likely come from films and television that celebrated World War II veterans with montages of ticker-tape parades, as well as iconic photos from "V-Day." Dean Jr., "The Myth of the Troubled and Scorned Vietnam Veteran," 67.

[40] William Mullen, "At Peace, At Last: After 11 Years and an Emotional Parade, Vietnam Vets Finally Feel Welcome." *Chicago Tribune*, August 17, 1986. www.chicagotribune.com/news/tribnation/chi-1986-chicago-tribune-magazine-vietnam-parade-article-20110610-story.html

[41] Interview with Bill E.

[42] Kevin Bowen, "Seeking Reconciliation in Vietnam." *Christian Science Monitor*, November 10, 1988.

length, it lists the names of more than 58,000 US soldiers killed in action in Vietnam. The surface of The Wall acts as a mirror, so as visitors approach they are faced with their own image behind the names of the dead. Former US Marine and writer William Broyles Jr. described how visiting the memorial forced him to think of the Vietnamese. "As I stood mesmerized by all those names at The Wall, I saw something else. I saw my own reflection. It fell across the names like a ghost. 'Why me?'. . . 'Why them' . . . . And then I realized that other names weren't there – the names of the men and women we fought, our enemies. . . . Who knows their names?"[43] Thus the visual experience of The Wall could provoke self-reflection and contemplation about how many Vietnamese died, and how long a wall with their names might be. Debate surrounding The Wall and its construction emphasized national reconciliation and healing, but Broyles indicated that his experience reopened old wounds and made them raw, igniting new questions about the legacies of the war. In 1984, Broyles returned to Việt Nam "to find the pieces of myself I had left there, and to try and put the war behind me."[44]

Commemoration is a public acknowledgment of war that grants permission for grief to become visible and be felt collectively through shared mourning: a social act that supports and validates the emotions of the bereaved. Historian Daphne Berdahl describes The Wall as "healing a nation through breaking a silence," validating Vietnam veterans by refusing to accept "the American public's desire to forget the controversial war."[45] Early Australian veterans also cited public remembrance as a catalyst for their returns. Australian Army veteran Graham E. explained that commemorations allowed him to reflect on his service and consider returning to Việt Nam. Graham E. had lost both of his legs to a landmine, and he half-joked that he returned because "I left a fair portion of myself, both physically and mentally in the country, perhaps I wanted to go back and reclaim that." Like Broyles, Graham E. told me that he thought if he returned to Việt Nam, he would be able "to move on."[46]

Graham E.'s memory of commemorations sparking his return illustrates the malleability of memory and shows how, over time, different events can link together and become imbued with new significance in our memories. He recalled that "I think it was probably 1990, [or] 1989, we had the unveiling of the Vietnam Veterans War Memorial, in Canberra. And that's when I really determined that I'd just go back and chase down

---

[43] Broyles Jr., *Brothers in Arms*, 13.   [44] Ibid., 226.
[45] Daphne Berdahl, "Voices at the Wall: Discourse of History and National Identity at the Vietnam Veterans Memorial." *History and Memory* 6:2 (1994): 91.
[46] Interview with Graham E., Perth, December 18, 2015.

a few ghosts, I guess."⁴⁷ In fact, however, the Australian Vietnam Forces National Memorial was unveiled in Canberra in 1992, two years after Graham E. returned.⁴⁸ His memory of this public, official recognition for Australian Vietnam veterans as the cue for his return suggests a deeper importance of the broader commemorative period.

Australian memory of Vietnam was saturated with and informed by American experiences, both with television coverage during the war and with cultural representations afterwards. As a result, Australian veterans themselves internalized and promoted American narratives about the war.⁴⁹ The American Welcome Home parades had inspired Australian veterans to organize their own Welcome Home parade in Sydney in 1987, despite the fact that each Australian battalion had received a Welcome Home parade during the war and that Australian Vietnam veterans already marched in national parades each year.⁵⁰ Yet this Americanized identity also led Australian Vietnam veterans to complain "that they were being written out of Anzac history – the poor cousin, even the black sheep, of the legend."⁵¹ The Anzac legend originated in World War I when soldiers at Gallipoli were eulogized for their "fighting spirit," with the battle declared "the birth of the nation," producing a martial nationalism where Australian masculine identity was defined by the qualities of Anzac: "mateship, sacrifice, and noble manly endeavour."⁵² Because the Anzac mythology hinges on martyrdom of the "diggers," claiming Anzac status requires "an ongoing creation of victimhood."⁵³ In the case of Vietnam, this resulted in the incorporation of American myths of public antipathy and anti-war hostility toward veterans into Australian memories.⁵⁴ Thus Vietnam War commemoration in Australia was not only about recognizing Vietnam veterans and their service; it was also

---

⁴⁷ Interview with Graham.
⁴⁸ *The Australian Vietnam Forces National Memorial*. Vietnam Veterans of Australia Association. www.vvaa.org.au/memorial.htm
⁴⁹ See: Jeffrey Grey, "In Every War but One? Myth, History and Vietnam." In *Zombie Myths of Australian Military History*. Edited by Craig Stockings (Sydney: NewSouth, 2010), 211.
⁵⁰ Historian Elizabeth Stewart points out that "veterans themselves have either forgotten or dismiss the fact that every returning battalion except one had a welcome home march." My interviews mirrored this finding. Elizabeth Stewart, "Vietnam: The Long Journey Home." In *New Perceptions of the Vietnam War: Essays on the War, the South Vietnamese Experience, the Diaspora and the Continuing Impact*. Edited by Nathalie Huynh Chau Nguyen (Jefferson, NC: McFarland, 2015), 110.
⁵¹ Garton, *Cost of War*, 235.
⁵² Stephen Garton, "War and Masculinity in Twentieth Century Australia." *Journal of Australian Studies* 22:56 (1998): 86.
⁵³ Mia Martin Hobbs, "'We Went and Did an Anzac Job': Memory, Myth, and the Anzac Digger in Vietnam." *Australian Journal of Politics and History* 64:3 (2018): 482.
⁵⁴ Ibid., 489–94.

about acknowledging a distinctly Australian Vietnam veteran identity and incorporating Vietnam veterans into the Anzac legacy.

The 1987 Sydney March provided veterans with this recognition. The march was followed by a concert at which members of the Australian folk band *Redgum* performed their iconic song "I Was Only Nineteen (A Walk in the Light Green)."[55] The song uses colloquial Australian vernacular and references Australian place names and army slang. Based on the stories of a veteran close to the songwriter, it was widely considered by Australian veterans to be an authentic representation of their Vietnam experience. The song's performance at the 1987 march was a public display of acceptance of Australian Vietnam veteran identity. Following the success of the 1987 parade, Prime Minister Bob Hawke announced an annual Vietnam Veterans Day to be commemorated on the anniversary of the Battle of Long Tan, and in 1988 the Hawke government gave its support to building a national Vietnam memorial, upon which *Redgum's* lyrics were inscribed.[56] Graham E.'s memory of the memorial dedication being the spark for his return to Việt Nam thus reflects the intense burst of commemoration from the broader Australian community in the late 1980s and early 1990s that centered on a distinctive idea of the Aussie digger in Vietnam.

Veterans also returned in reaction to Việt Nam's economic reforms in 1986, known as Đổi Mới ("renovation"). As soon as Greg, a former Marine read about Đổi Mới, he began organizing his 1988 trip back: "in 1987 I read a little blurb ... that said Vietnam is changing its policy and it's going to issue visas to Westerners. So, I knew right then I had to get a visa and go." Greg "was always going to go back and see the country, I was always gonna return someday I just knew it ... I knew all along. I didn't know why, exactly, I just knew that I was gonna go back."[57] Logistically, the Đổi Mới reforms did not make it much easier for US veterans to return to Việt Nam. The US embargo, effectively a "continuation of war by other means," isolated Việt Nam diplomatically and economically by denying them access to aid, capital, and membership in the United Nations, and prevented US citizens from engaging directly with Việt Nam through the US Trading with the Enemy Act.[58] Americans had to go through another country to get visas, could not access American bank accounts from within Việt Nam, and American travel agents were

---

[55] Redgum, "I Was Only Nineteen (A Walk in the Light Green)." *Caught in the Act* (Sydney: Epic Records, 1983).
[56] Long Tan saw the highest Australian casualties in a single battle in Vietnam and was consequently commemorated by veterans.
[57] Interview with Greg, Hồ Chí Minh City, March 25, 2016.
[58] Martini, *Invisible Enemies*, 14.

1 Reconciliation, 1981–1994

prohibited from providing economic assistance to a hostile nation by organizing tours, so the veterans had to organize trips themselves or find a travel agent willing to take the legal risk.[59] US Army veteran John Z. explained to me that he "had thought about it but I didn't really know that it was possible, you know we didn't have diplomatic relations and it was – it was kinda scary."[60] However, many veterans had been waiting for an opportunity to return, and for them, Đổi Mới was a signal. John C., a US Army draft volunteer, told me that returning "was always in my mind," and once he heard of Đổi Mới, he and his brothers immediately began shopping around for ways to return, finally locating a travel agency that could organize visas through Thailand in 1989.[61]

Several veterans identified Đổi Mới as one link in a chain of events that led them back to Việt Nam. Chuck, a US Army intelligence specialist, started thinking about returning when he flew out of the war in 1967. "I remember thinking, actually with some bitterness I think, that one day I'll have determined to come back here, and I hope it'll be in a time of peace." There was no question about whether to return or why, only when: "I just sort of assumed in the recesses of my mind that one day I'd come back." In the early 1990s, Chuck ran into "an old army buddy ... [we] realized that both of us had thought over the years about one day returning to Vietnam." Chuck linked this chance meeting to Đổi Mới, which had taken hold in the early 1990s and made it "somewhat easier to come back to Việt Nam than even three years or five years earlier," along with fortuitous timing with his work.[62] Bill E. described a similar pattern: thinking about Việt Nam more and more over a few years, in 1994 he decided to go back. "I'd just sold my business. Had a little bit of time, little bit of money. And decided if I was gonna do it, it'd be a good time to do it."[63] The inevitability in returnees' narratives reflects the tendency for diasporas to see their homeland as "a destiny to which ... [they] are now 'awakening.'"[64] Some veterans explicitly attributed their returns to destiny, or "fate – or as it's called in Vietnam, *đinh-mệnh*."[65]

While some veterans were waiting for the right opportunity or following their fate, others presented their returns as prompted by simple curiosity. Ralph, a US Army draftee and the brother of John C., returned in 1989

---

[59] In 1990, the Connecticut-based Lindblad travel agency was fined $500,000 in fines and legal fees for organizing tours for US veterans and Vietnamese Americans to Việt Nam. They subsequently declared bankruptcy. James Fallows, "Shut Out." *The Atlantic Monthly* 267:3 (March 1991), 42–43.
[60] Interview with John Z., Skype, November 15, 2016.
[61] Interview with John C., Skype, June 23, 2016.
[62] Interview with Chuck, Hà Nội, April 21, 2016.   [63] Interview with Bill E.
[64] Brubaker, "The 'Diaspora' Diaspora," 13.
[65] Rottmann, "A Hundred Happy Sparrows," 113.

with his brothers "just to see more of the country. It was always just a curiosity."⁶⁶ Bill E. "was curious about what happened over here. About what happened to me, what happened to the country."⁶⁷ The 1980's rhetoric around Vietnam, particularly in films, was often melodramatic and exploited veterans' trauma with distorted caricatures. In their interviews, Ralph and Bill E. indicated a weariness with cultural histrionics around Vietnam and veterans and showed a determination not to be caricatured themselves. Renewed media interest in Việt Nam as a country had also revived moral debates about the war, provoking veterans to return as a means to decide the truth for themselves. For example, McCain's 1985 return to Việt Nam was the focus of a heavily promoted CBS documentary, *Honor, Duty and a War Called Vietnam*, which opened with Walter Cronkite describing Vietnam as "the war America did not win."⁶⁸ Former Marine Joe Bangert said that he "was so sick and tired of these fucking dickhead fucking anchor-men. These media mogul guys going back and trying to – And I said, I'm going back. I'm not gonna listen to the networks anymore."⁶⁹ Bangert made his way back in 1985 through connections with Vietnamese staffers at the United Nations.

Yet far more common were stories of veterans who felt a deep, internal, psychological need to return. Former Marine W.D. wrote that "for years I have wanted to go back ... I felt certain that if I could only see the Vietnamese getting on with their lives, the war gone and the awful wreckage of the war grown over and forgotten, I too would be able to let go."⁷⁰ His longing to "let go" of the war by seeing Việt Nam at peace demonstrates reflective nostalgia, which, Boym writes, "dwells in *algia*, in longing and loss, the imperfect process of remembrance."⁷¹ W.D., a 1984 returnee, explained that his purpose in returning was to replace his memories of Vietnam, all of which "were in black-and-white."⁷² He "wanted to see the country" in full color, not shaded by the war. He thought that if he could see experience Việt Nam "without fear," he would achieve "emotional catharsis."⁷³ Similarly, Australian Army veteran Terry Burstall found himself weighed down by his war experience. Determined to "take an academic stance" as he studied the war at university, he discovered that "the more I looked, the murkier it

---

⁶⁶ Interview with Ralph, Skype, June 27, 2016.
⁶⁷ Interview with Bill E.
⁶⁸ *Honor, Duty and a War Called Vietnam*, produced by Burton Benjamin (New York: CBS, 1985).
⁶⁹ Joe Bangert, interview in *Going Back: Echoes of War* [US version], directed by Kaley Clements, 2016. Unreleased documentary shared with me by the filmmaker on Vimeo.
⁷⁰ Ehrhart, *Going Back*, 5.   ⁷¹ Boym, *Future of Nostalgia*, 41.
⁷² Interview with W.D., Email, January 12, 2016.   ⁷³ Ibid.

1 Reconciliation, 1981–1994

became ... the monkey on my back was becoming a baboon."[74] Burstall returned in 1986. As Boym writes, reflective nostalgics are "aware of the gap between identity and resemblance."[75] Burstall and W.D. knew that their memories did not define Việt Nam. They returned to release their wartime memories, experiences, understanding or emotions by reframing, reexperiencing, and rediscovering Việt Nam in a different context.

Other veterans returned out of nostalgia for their past selves. US Army veteran Ted Heselton returned in 1990 "to mourn for myself, to mourn the death of the person I was before," invoking the idea of death and rebirth on the battlefield.[76] Australian and American gender norms linked masculinity with military service and combat, and for the Vietnam generation – whose fathers and uncles had served in World War II and Korea – the idea of baptism by fire as the rite of passage to manhood was powerful. Some veterans interpreted the displacement and isolation they experienced as a result of the forced maturing required by the war: turning teenagers into soldiers, cutting short their adolescence, returning from war not simply as veterans but as "men." These returnees felt the need to grieve the boys they were before they went to war, before their childhood was subsumed by violence, by returning to the site of that rite of passage. Bowen, for example, was drafted into the US Army and served in the First Air Cavalry Division. He returned to Việt Nam in 1987 and wrote in an article the following year that "Vietnam was where we spent our youth; some would say where we lost it .... Where we lost our innocence. At the very least, it was a place, real and symbolic, that still held us."[77]

Returnees' nostalgia for their warzone home, the place of their rebirth, demonstrated again the concept of diasporic intimacy. They were "haunted by the images of home and homeland," unable either to explore or forget their war memories.[78] Many drew on metaphors of walls, doors, glass, and gates to explain how returning to Việt Nam was a return to memories they had sealed away. Bowen drew on The Wall in Washington, DC to describe his memories: "to touch down again in Vietnam is to take the first wary step into the silent worlds locked in the reflecting granite of the memorial. To return again is to attempt to crack the wall of silence."[79] US Army veteran Rottmann described his memories as subterranean, threatening to emerge as he returned: "my apprehension is so powerful .... So terrible are these memories and truths that I've

---

[74] Burstall, *A Soldier Returns*, 14.   [75] Boym, *Future of Nostalgia*, 50.
[76] Ted Heselton, "Ted Heselton's Yen Vien Journal: Team III." *VVRP.org.* http://033a4c3.netsolhost.com/?page_id=1123
[77] Bowen, "Seeking Reconciliation in Vietnam."   [78] Boym, *Future of Nostalgia*, 253.
[79] Bowen, "Seeking Reconciliation in Vietnam."

never allowed them to come fully to the surface. These memories far darker than the worst nightmares."[80]

Veterans described how both nostalgia and apprehension built as their return approached, culminating in an emotionally fraught entry into Việt Nam. Many experienced a flood of visceral memories as their flights descended. Ted, a US Air Force veterans, described looking out the window at the landscape of Việt Nam during his "entrance to the evil city [Hà Nội]," experiencing "some sort of white noise situation … it seemed like all the years, from the time I was in Vietnam until that moment, all the stuff that's been going on in between in my life, it was just kinda rushing through like a film that is going real fast."[81] Heselton, likewise, found himself overwhelmed, "I can't stop the flood of strange thoughts."[82] Some struggled with the adrenaline rush and the distressing contrast between past and present. Broyles reflected that "it was peaceful, bucolic. But it brought back less peaceful memories …. I could smell all those odors of war – gunpowder, excrement, fear … I had to struggle with the impulse to flee. For a brief moment I wanted a weapon."[83] Many veterans described wanting to turn around and get back on the plane. US veteran Tom Bird, part of Muller's VVA team, actually did get back on the plane when he saw the Vietnamese soldiers "waiting to greet him. Mr. Bird swiftly returned to the plan, trembling. 'My first instinct was to call the whole thing off …. It's just too strange. I feel a little out of control.'"[84]

Surviving the airport memory flood was just the first step. Most veterans returned with a specific place or personal agenda in mind in their search for resolution: somewhere or something (sometimes themselves) to find or release. On these missions, war memories were profoundly challenged. On Burstall's second trip back in 1987, he sat down with Vietnamese veterans of the Battle of Long Tan to understand their perspective. Their memories of the battle confused and distressed him. Colonel Khánh presented Burstall with evidence that two of the Australians who had died in the battle were not killed by the National Liberation Front (NLF) but had been captured and killed alongside their captors by Australian artillery. "My head was spinning and there was bile in my throat as I sat looking at him and wanting to lash out all around me. I wanted to cry out bullshit … bullshit … bullshit. But I couldn't."[85]

---

[80] Rottmann, "A Hundred Happy Sparrows," 118.   [81] Interview with Ted.
[82] Heselton, "Ted Heselton's Yen Vien Journal."
[83] Broyles Jr., "The Road to Hill 10: A Veteran's Return to Vietnam." *The Atlantic*, 225. April 1, 1985.
[84] Weinraub, "Vietnam Veterans Take Emotional Journey to Hanoi." *New York Times*, December 19, 1981.
[85] Burstall, *A Soldier Returns*, 72.

1 Reconciliation, 1981–1994

This loss was exacerbated by a disagreement between Burstall and his Vietnamese hosts over the NLF body count at the Battle of Long Tan. According to the Australian narrative, 250 NLF died. The Vietnamese insisted the body count was much lower. Colonel Bào asked Burstall, "How did you count them?" Burstall wrote that this question "really put me back on my heels. The count was done in a slipshod fashion .... Would a shell-shocked digger count an arm, a trunk and a leg scattered over several meters as one body or three bodies?" Burstall was forced to reflect on the capacity and limits of his own memory: "One hundred and fifty dead bodies in a 2 square kilometer area is a mind-numbing sight. It is a great deal of death: and 250 dead bodies is the same. The mind cannot cope with the sight of destruction of that magnitude. The difference between 150 and 250 is not something that those who were there could even look back on with anything like an objective view."[86] This realization tempered Burstall's belief in the Australian narrative of the battle as a David and Goliath feat, which brought into question the value of commemorating battles as feats at all.

Not all return journeys were fraught with memory confrontations. Pete and McCain visited one of their "old lodgings," Hòa Lò Prison, together in 1992 on an official US delegation.[87] At the time, Hòa Lò – commonly known in the United States as the Hanoi Hilton – was still operating as a prison. McCain reflected: "no tidal wave of remembrance washed over me as I stared into the faces of the Vietnamese who were occupying my old cell. In fact, curiously, I felt little emotion at all beyond sympathy for the poor bastards who were living there now. It had been a long time. What's past is past."[88] It is possible that because these veterans experienced such graphic and prolonged wartime experiences, they were unable to avoid their memories and were forced to reckon with their trauma long before returning to Việt Nam.

For some returnees, memory confrontation was a cleansing experience, allowing a release of their grief. Ted, for example, still had many of his war photographs, including one of his old base camps in the village of Lai Khê. When he returned to Việt Nam he decided to rephotograph the "exact same place" and gave the old photograph to his Vietnamese guide. Returning to the vehicles, he felt something missing:

The only way I can explain this, it's like, having a pipe, like under your sink, your pipe that goes down for your garbage, your water drain. It's like having one of

---

[86] Burstall, *A Soldier Returns*, 78.
[87] John McCain and Mark Salter, *Worth the Fighting For: A Memoir* (New York: Random House, 2002), 262.
[88] Ibid., 261–62.

those inside, and over the years, it's filled up. And it just was filled with shit. It was the fear, the anger, all of the things, the memories, everything that was associated with the war. And after, even. And it wasn't there anymore. It felt like a physical object was not either on, or in my body.... Something was literally gone. And it's like that tube was clean. It was whistle clean... I gave away the old emotions. And by doing that I cleaned myself out."[89]

Others explained that simply by mourning at a personal site, they found peace. Rottmann returned to Việt Nam in 1987 and experienced a single, defining moment of catharsis at a place of great significance to him. He returned to My Khe beach in Đà Nẵng, a Rest and Relaxation (R&R) location for Americans in the war and allowed himself to mourn. "The waves on China Beach advance and retreat the way wartime memories ebb and eddy around the edges of my daily routine at home, repeating over and over the gentle whisper of Ho Chi Minh, 'The wheel of life turns without pause.... Men and animals rise up reborn.' The waves on China Beach advance and retreat, and I kneel on the sand and weep the grief I've hoarded for twenty years."[90]

These veterans indicate that their nostalgia for Vietnam had been resolved by returning to Việt Nam – not ended, but accepted. Ted described it as "an opening... there was not closure at all, not for a long time."[91] Boehm found peace after demonstrating grief and mourning for soldiers on all sides of the war at My Lai: "I finally realized that I would never understand it, but I had to mark it somehow. So, I went to the My Lai memorial.... And I played Taps on my fiddle, for all the pain and suffering of both the Americans and Vietnamese. And now having made that gesture, I think I can move on."[92] Coming to terms with the war in Việt Nam was a powerful and expressive experience. US Army draftee James likened it to "a twenty-four hour a day open heart massage."[93] Rottmann described a twenty-year, "repressed, constipated pain" becoming a "cathartic pain, a pain of release – almost as if I were giving birth to a new awareness. I haven't exorcised all my demons... but I know this trip is helping me reach an accommodation with them."[94] Despite this pain, many returnees found that revisiting their memories brought a degree of peace. Bowen described it as "an affirmation – reopens the heart to hope. It cannot change the past, but it can reconnect with the present, so allowing the silence to be broken."[95]

[89] Interview with Ted.   [90] Rottmann, "A Hundred Happy Sparrows," 130.
[91] Interview with Ted.
[92] Mike Boehm, "A Union of Like Hearts – A Unique Collaboration." *Project Leaders, MQI Vietnam*. www.mqivietnam.org/project-leaders
[93] James, "Hoi An Epiphany." Private journal entry shared with the author, 1993.
[94] Rottmann, "A Hundred Happy Sparrows," 125.
[95] Bowen, "Seeking Reconciliation in Vietnam."

1 Reconciliation, 1981–1994

Some veterans explained that while returning in peacetime did not erase their wartime memories or emotions, it made it easier to deal with darker thoughts by adding new, positive ones. Bill E. remembered that before he returned, "I'd hear the word 'Vietnam' spoken in the background, and I'd start thinking of the war in Vietnam." However, after he had returned, "I'd hear somebody mention Vietnam and I'd try and think about the food, the kids, the neat experience of coming back. So, it just kinda changed the library of images that accompanied my mind."[96] Greg, who said the return experience "changed my life completely," explained:

> All of my memories from Vietnam were negative. Anything that came up in my mind was just horrible. Just the war part, all of the guys that I saw shot up, the Vietnamese that I saw shot up, my friends, all of that. It wasn't till I came back in '88 that I could replace those memories, those old bad memories, with now memories of smiling children, about people happy to see us, about people trying to pick up their lives and move on and go forward and stuff. So, I replaced all those bad memories with good memories.[97]

This changing of the "library of images" reflected an increasing focus on "image replacement" for the treatment of post-traumatic stress disorder (PTSD).[98] Small numbers of veterans began returning specifically to confront their trauma in Việt Nam. Veteran and psychologist Raymond Scurfield led a team of veterans, all diagnosed with PTSD, to Việt Nam in 1989. In his analysis of the efficacy of returning as treatment, he observed: "where once there were memories only of war-time Vietnam, now I have essentially an equivalent number of *both* wartime *and* peacetime Vietnam."[99] As Chapter 2 explores, the psychological benefit of returning to Việt Nam reported by reconciliation veterans became a motivating factor in later veterans' returns.

Adding to the library of images sometimes had broader consequences. Most veterans were aware that the views they held of their former enemy were caricatures but were less conscious of how the war environment had shaped their attitudes toward Vietnamese civilians. Once they were physically back, some veterans recognized how they had dehumanized all Vietnamese. James explained that shortly after returning, he encountered some Vietnamese women: "and they saw me, and big smiles and laughter, and in a flash of a moment, I thought, 'prostitutes.' I assumed it. *M: Because they were smiling at you?* Yeah. I assumed that. And just that quickly again, I went, 'no.'" As a soldier living on a military base in

---

[96] Interview with Bill E.   [97] Greg, interview in *Echoes of War*.
[98] Dr. Matthew J. Friedman, quoted in Alan C. Miller, "Veterans Find Peace in Vietnam." *Los Angeles Times*, July 5, 1990. http://articles.latimes.com/1990-07-05/news/mn-136_1_vietnam-veterans
[99] Scurfield, *Healing Journeys*, 206.

Cam Ranh Bay, James had frequented a local brothel and befriended the sex workers and owners. Because his wartime experiences with Vietnamese women were isolated to that bar and its context, James realized that for him, Vietnamese women smiling had always been associated with solicitation. "I thought, 'my God. The way our minds can change, to think.' And it's like our minds get stuck in time until we replace – well not replace, until we add some new information. So, I added a little bit of information, and that moment was an important one. And I never did that again."[100]

This challenge incited some to redress their wartime perceptions, which were imbued with orientalism and misogyny. Rottmann focused on meeting as many people as possible on his return trip: "I need more data ... I need names and faces. I never got to learn who these people were the last time .... And these are real people. Not slant-eyed rifle range caricatures."[101] Returning to Việt Nam therefore had the effect of forcing veterans to actively confront their own biases proactively, often with profound and positive effects. John Z. said that "it's gone on to make me a fuller person. To make me realize that you know these, the people in Việt Nam, are real people. They're not cardboard cutouts that are trying to kill me. I've met them in their houses, I met them on the streets and there and everywhere, and ... I think it's made me a more rounded person."[102]

Thus, returning to Việt Nam often resulted in reclaiming or reassessing what Vietnam meant in a peacetime context. For Bowen, "going back ... is an attempt to reassert through our own action the probity of our purposes."[103] Flying into Việt Nam for the first time since the war, Mike P. felt "fulfilment; twenty years having come full circle. Contentment. Rightness.... Tears, then a quiet fullness." For Mike P., spending time in Việt Nam not only brought "contentment," he also reframed how he felt about the former enemy territory. Over time, as he worked on a VVRP project alongside Vietnamese people, "the little alleys and side streets lost their terrors."[104] Burstall considered how after his return, "Hanoi now meant people, laughing, crying, loving. It no longer symbolized alien ideologies or ideals that we in our arrogance thought we could not live beside in Asia."[105] The recognition of Vietnamese as people and not as the face of an enemy ideology had a lasting impact on many returnees' lives. John Z. noticed changes in his outlook. "The return visits have changed my attitudes. They've made me more friendly. I mean hey,

---

[100] Interview with James, Hà Nội, April 23, 2016.
[101] Rottmann, "A Hundred Happy Sparrows," 132. [102] Interview with John Z.
[103] Bowen, "Seeking Reconciliation in Vietnam."
[104] Mike P., "1989 VVRP Journal w Intro." [105] Burstall, *A Soldier Returns*, 32–33.

1 Reconciliation, 1981–1994

when I was there at war ... I was at war! I wasn't making friends with anybody! And by going back, that's changed that attitude."[106]

Some returnees found that this change in perspective drew them back to Việt Nam time and again. Graham E. told me that returning "changed my life. It's given me a greater appreciation of life. It's given me a motivation to be involved in things. And while there's never a day that I don't lament the fact that I don't have legs, there's never a day that I don't appreciate the fact that I'm still alive when so many lost their lives." Graham E. returned to Việt Nam almost every year since 1990, becoming involved in the campaign to ban landmines. His return instilled in him "a strong sense of responsibility for the innocent kids particularly, who would come across landmines ... it just made me appreciate how lucky I was."[107] Some veterans made the decision to relocate permanently. Greg moved to Hồ Chí Minh City in 1992 and became an English teacher. He explained: "coming back was probably the best thing I could have done, in my life. Because the direction I was headed in America was a dead end. And I don't think I coulda kept all that stuff inside of me much longer. So, I think coming back gave me that spin that I needed to go forward again. I was going backwards, for sure. Drinking, and other problems. So, coming back turned me around."[108]

Many returnees found personal worth in "healing-through-helping." Heselton explained this in his VVRP journal: "I've come because I'm an experience junkie .... An important part of the 'high' is experiencing the feeling of struggling for a cause you know to be right on both political and humanitarian grounds."[109] These veterans acknowledged the self-interest of their work. Greg described teaching in Hồ Chí Minh City: "the feeling of actually contributing and helping somebody to get a little bit farther along in their career or get into a program that's gonna help them out. ... It's a good feeling! Much better than it was as a soldier. So, carrying a briefcase to class was much better than carrying a rifle." Greg especially enjoyed the relationships he built with his students: "they're all very grateful, they highly respect teachers."[110] Almost all of the veterans involved in healing-through-helping work labored to impress upon me how generous the Vietnamese were with their gratitude and respect for veterans' work. Chuck told me, "the Vietnamese give us all much more appreciation than we deserve for what we're actually doing here, it's very, very disproportionate. And I know that. And I also understand that part of what I'm doing here, I'm doing for myself. Cause I have to live with myself."[111]

---

[106] Interview with John Z.   [107] Interview with Graham E.   [108] Interview with Greg.
[109] Heselton, "Ted Heselton's Yen Vien Journal."   [110] Interview with Greg.
[111] Interview with Chuck.

As Chuck suggests, atonement played an important role in veterans' return activities. Chuck returned to Việt Nam repeatedly in the early 1990s before relocating to Hà Nội in 1995 to work on a rehabilitation project. From there, he learned of the ongoing effects of unexploded ordnance and Agent Orange on the Vietnamese and became dedicated to those causes. Chuck's work gave him "some level of hope that I've been able to correct, in small ways, some of the damage that we did here, during the war. I know that ... what we do is a drop in the ocean. But, you know, enough drops will eventually fill up the ocean." His actions in Việt Nam were redemptive. Chuck reflected that "in a small way, I'm trying to meet the expectations of my parents and my extended family and the country that I grew up in and the values that I was raised to believe. So it's, so that's why I have been here and it's not entirely satisfactory, it never will be, it's never enough. But it's the best that I can do, and it's something that I have to do."[112]

Other returnees atoned simply by bearing witness to the Vietnamese experience of war. Burstall had asked his Vietnamese guide, Dy, to show him some photographs of Hà Nội in the late stages of the war. Burstall's intention was to understand academically the scale of the "Christmas bombing" campaign, but viewing the images forced him to bear witness to the "horror, the terror, the futility of the exercise hit me from the first page. By the time I had been through one book I was sickened and emotionally distraught." Burstall tried to hand the books back to his guide Dy, who refused and told him, "Perhaps this is your penance, my friend, the way of loosening the monkey you told me you thought was on your back," Burstall reflected on this: "as I looked at him standing there like a schoolmaster gently chastising a student, I thought he just may have been right."[113] Others bore witness to survival, rather than devastation. Rottmann explained:

> I need to be reassured that we didn't kill or poison them all. Or destroy their individuality or their collective spirit .... I don't give a damn at this point in time (and perhaps I never did) about who won the war. But I need to know that the country is alive and viable. It feels very good to know that Vietnam lives.[114]

Heselton reflected that "my real goal was not a physical location but to be forgiven by the Vietnamese people. That has happened. I can go home now."[115]

---

[112] Ibid.   [113] Burstall, *A Soldier Returns*, 32.
[114] Rottmann, "A Hundred Happy Sparrows," 132–33.
[115] Heselton, "Ted Heselton's Yen Vien Journal."

1 Reconciliation, 1981–1994

For anti-war veterans, returning in search of forgiveness was relatively straightforward in terms of internal logic. Veterans who maintained a sense of pride in their military service faced a more complex relationship between their war memories, their personal grief, and their return to Việt Nam. These returnees focused on reconciliation with the enemy. US Army veteran Harold Moore returned to Việt Nam three times in the 1990s to research the Vietnamese experience of the Battle of Ia Drang. In 1993, Moore returned to his battlefield site with his former enemy. He described a prayer at the Ia Đrăng valley among American and Vietnamese veterans:

> General An stood directly across from me in the circle, and when we broke he walked straight to me, his right hand extended. As we shook hands my old enemy pulled me to him and kissed me on both cheeks. Old enemies can become friends .... We had much in common as military men who had fought our country's wars, even though duty and orders pitted us against each other during one of those wars .... Each of us had a reservoir of respect for the man who commanded on the other side.[116]

Moore's experience parallels the pilgrimages of other veterans of US wars, notably the commemorative Civil War reconciliation events held at Gettysburg, where the 25th, 50th and 75th anniversaries of the battles were celebrated with reunions and "'rituals of reconciliation' in which Union veterans extended offers of friendship and forgiveness to the Southern veterans."[117] Like those Civil War reunions, which excluded black veterans and papered over the war's legacies with "unifying myths" and "values of manliness, valor, sacrifice, and a mutual sense of honor," Moore's reunion narrative excluded "the causes, transformations, and results of the war."[118] By framing his reconciliation as a traditional – and, importantly, a traditionally *masculine* – ritual of pilgrimage, Moore distanced the notion of anti-war atonement from his return.

In parallel to traditional reconciliations between former soldiers were veterans conducting diplomacy through political and volunteer missions. Muller and the VVA visited Việt Nam regularly in the early 1980s on invitation from the Vietnamese. "Our government will not talk to them. So, we do represent the only channel with which to exchange information."[119] Muller and the VVA's primary concern was proving

---

[116] Harold G. Moore and Joseph L. Galloway, *We Are Soldiers Still: A Journey Back to the Battlefields of Vietnam* (New York: HarperCollins, 2008), 1, 98.
[117] Gatewood and Cameron, "Battlefield Pilgrims at Gettysburg National Military Park," 196.
[118] David W. Blight, *Race and Reunion: The Civil War in American Memory* (Cambridge: Harvard University Press, 2001), 9, 199.
[119] Bobby Muller, quoted in Bernard Weinraub, "Hanoi Asks US Veterans for Talks." *New York Times*, April 22, 1984.

Việt Nam trustworthy to Americans, putting their safety in Vietnamese hands and lobbying for the recognition of Việt Nam upon their return. They saw themselves as "providing a bridge to Vietnam, a conduit to dialogue."[120] Other veterans' groups promoted similar goals: the VVRP wanted to "break down the embargo ... to do people-to-people diplomacy."[121] Pete and McCain were quickly convinced that there were no POWs in Việt Nam and that the Vietnamese were doing their best to assist the US government in finding US remains. They became the most prominent government advocates for normalization of relations, with Pete appointed the first US Ambassador to the SRV in 1997. Both veterans were very proud of the fruits of their efforts. Pete told me: "there's always a personal feeling of accomplishment if you do something you think has advanced a good cause. And I think that was a good cause."[122]

Finally, one universal component in veterans' returns was enjoying Việt Nam as a tourist or expatriate, and not focusing on the war. This was particularly true of veterans who returned to Việt Nam frequently or who had relocated there. Maurice said he "found that fascinating, to go to the north with my wife," after years of stopping through Hồ Chí Minh City en route to Cambodia, where he worked throughout the 1980s.[123] Cultural immersion was important for Bill E., who told me that a big part of his happiness is "Việt Nam itself, being married to a Vietnamese woman, I get involved in the family and the culture. And I enjoy seeing that side of it, I find it interesting and touching a lot of times. I don't get involved, you know, with both feet at all times, but you know, yeah I enjoy seeing that there's more than one way to do something, and how different belief systems can still be compatible."[124] Some veterans who had struggled with postwar readjustment in their home countries realized that Việt Nam offered them a more harmonious life. Greg found enjoyment and satisfaction in Việt Nam because of the contrast between Việt Nam and the United States. "I was able to come over here and fulfil the American dream. In America I couldn't. ... It was hollow. It was so meaningless. There was no substance to it at all. ... Over here, I got to do what I wanted to do. I got to make my life like I wanted it to be."[125]

Reconciliation veterans portrayed their return experiences as positive and profound. As Australian and American debates swirled and settled around "their" war, returnees were drawn back to Việt Nam to address lingering questions and satisfy nostalgic longing. While they found some answers and some peace, none reported that their return terminated their

---

[120] Ibid. [121] Champagne, "The Founding of the VVRP." [122] Interview with Pete. [123] Interview with Maurice. [124] Interview with Bill E. [125] Interview with Greg.

1 Reconciliation, 1981–1994

connection to Việt Nam. On the contrary, they demonstrated that by returning, they built emotional ties to and memories of Việt Nam that became as important to them as their wartime experiences. Differences between Australian and US veterans were not pronounced in this group because the numbers of Australian returnees were so few. The US veterans offer a clue for these demographics: most reconciliation veterans returned for political or humanitarian reasons, partly in response to the hostility of the United States toward Việt Nam surrounding the POW/MIA issue. Australia's diplomatic ties with the Democratic Republic of Việt Nam (DRV) were established in 1973, and the six Australian soldiers classified as MIA at the end of the war were all presumed Killed in Action.[126] Australian veterans did not experience a prolonged debate around the possibility of POWs/MIAs, or by proxy the debate around establishing relations with Việt Nam. US veterans had an imperative in returning to establish these truths and demonstrate their allegiances: Australian veterans had no such urgency. The following chapter includes a more balanced number of Australian and US veterans' accounts, as more veterans from both countries began to return to Việt Nam in the new political climate of "normalization."

---

[126] Ashley Ekins, "Australian MIAs of the Vietnam War – 'Missing in Action' or 'No Known Grave'?" *Wartime* 23 (2003). www.awm.gov.au/wartime/23/no-known-grave/

2 Normalization, 1995–2005

"Before 2000 it wasn't that easy to get here. Before '95, very few people came here. Before 1990, nobody came here, because it was under the Iron Fist."[1] So said David W., an Australian Army veteran who returned to Việt Nam for the first time in 2004. The establishment of diplomatic relations between the United States and Việt Nam in 1995 opened the door to veteran returns, offering symbolic security to tentative veterans who had watched the reconciliation process from afar. I call this group "normalization" because their returns coincided with the normalization of political relationships as well as the normalization of the idea of Việt Nam as a friendly nation in the Western imagination. The lifting of travel restrictions offered opportunities to veterans who had long thought of returning, as well as allowing others to consider it for the first time. The effects of Việt Nam's economic reforms took hold, leading to a growing tourism industry that gave veterans more latitude in how they returned and with whom, resulting in a more diverse return group. Yet despite the increasingly diverse reasons for and methods of return, one narrative came to dominate the story of veteran returns: healing in Việt Nam. "Normalization" thus also describes the normalization of post-traumatic stress disorder (PTSD) in Australian and American culture and society. A dominating discourse of trauma and healing influenced how veterans described the Vietnam they held in memory, the effects of their return, and the actions they took when they returned. Underneath this discourse, however, normalization veterans echoed earlier returns, focusing on releasing their past and finding new meaning in Việt Nam.

The normalization of diplomatic relations between the United States and Việt Nam offered symbolic security to veterans. In 1997 the US Congress confirmed Pete Peterson as the first US Ambassador to Việt Nam. Pete's status as a Vietnam veteran, former prisoner of war (POW),

---

[1] Interview with David W. Vũng Tàu, August 17, 2016.

2 Normalization, 1995–2005

and congressman who had lobbied for normalized relations may have emboldened veterans who were interested in returning. A similar comforting effect may have been produced by coverage of President Bill Clinton's visit to Việt Nam in 2000, when "thousands of Vietnamese gathered on the road from the airport and thousands more convened in front of his hotel to get a glimpse of their American guest ... [the crowds] waved and applauded."[2] Footage from this first ever visit by a US president to Hà Nội presented a warm image of the Vietnamese that countered Cold War notions of a cold, oppressive, communist state. Australia tapped into the zeitgeist of reconciliation by emphasizing their wartime bonds and regional relationship. In 1996, Vietnam veteran and Deputy Prime Minister of Australia Tim Fischer visited Việt Nam to profile bilateral cooperation, friendship, and trade opportunities, "reaffirming that Australia, like Vietnam, looks to the future in the relationship."[3] Fischer drew attention to burgeoning Vietnam veterans' nongovernmental organizations (NGOs) in Vũng Tàu and attended a commemoration with a veterans' delegation for the 30th Anniversary of the Battle of Long Tan. Like the Đổi Mới reforms for reconciliation veterans, these political reconciliations had a symbolic effect on normalization veterans' returns: signaling that Việt Nam itself was "normalizing," that is, mirroring and converging with the West. For Australians and Americans alike, Việt Nam seemed safer.

One example of this "normalcy" and safety was a gesture of reconciliation from the Socialist Republic of Việt Nam (SRV) toward Vietnamese in exile. In the aftermath of war, millions who supported the Republic of Việt Nam (RVN) were imprisoned in reeducation camps or forcibly displaced under the New Economic Zones program, leading hundreds of thousands to flee Việt Nam between 1975 and 1995.[4] Communist Party reformer Nguyễn Văn Linh considered this diaspora a potential source for capital and from 1986 to 1991, under his tenure as Party Secretary, Việt Nam altered its stance toward overseas Vietnamese in an effort to draw back educated and wealthy migrants.[5] Anthropologist Ashley Carruthers argues that this was a watershed moment: "a

---

[2] "Vietnam: Bill and Hillary Clinton Visit Hanoi." *AP Archive.* www.aparchive.com/metadata/youtube/92023f9b409a456f39e610084b653a23

[3] Tim Fischer, "Visit to Brunei Darussalam and Vietnam by Deputy Prime Minister and Trade Minister, The Hon. Tim Fischer MP." *The Department of Foreign Affairs and Trade, Australia*, August 9, 1996. http://trademinister.gov.au/releases/1996/tr53.html

[4] For experiences of RVNAF living in the SRV, see: Nhgia M. Vo, *The Bamboo Gulag: Political Imprisonment in Communist Vietnam* (Jefferson, NC: McFarland, 2003).

[5] Lynellyn D. Long, "Viet Kieu on a Fast Track Back?" In *Coming Home? Refugees, Migrants, and Those Who Stayed Behind.* Edited by Lynellyn D. Long and Ellen Oxford (Philadelphia, PA: University of Pennsylvania Press, 2004), 67–68.

fundamental shift in conceptualizing the role of Viet khieu [overseas Vietnamese]," from imperialist "puppets" to Vietnamese visiting their homeland.⁶ Việt Nam's outreach to the Vietnamese diaspora caught the attention of veterans who were observant of political and cultural change in the region. If Việt Nam was welcoming back refugees, then perhaps it was safe for American and Australian veterans not only to return, but to try and locate their colleagues, friends, and girlfriends. US Army veterans Francis and Robert J. Reilly both returned in 1998 with the intention of finding people they knew, as did Derrill, an Australian Army veteran, in 2003.⁷ Derrill and Reilly wanted to locate people they had worked with, whereas Francis remembered the children who lived in the village where he operated and "wanted to go back and see if there were any of them who returned, grown up, thirty-five, forty years old."⁸

These changes in the political status of Việt Nam led to a greater political diversity among returnees. Some veteran communities had condemned reconciliation veterans as "commie sympathizers" and "traitors" for engaging with a hostile nation, but as the shadow of the Cold War receded, officially friendly relations between the United States and Việt Nam allowed more conservative veterans to return.⁹ In 1995, a former Marine called Paul S. returned on invitation from the Vietnam Veterans of America (VVA) to liaise with Vietnamese scientists and Agent Orange advocacy groups. Paul S. was not eager to return to Việt Nam. However, one of his sons had died in early childhood and his surviving boys had severe health conditions. He suspected that his wartime exposure to Agent Orange was the cause. Paul S.' interest in the effects of Agent Orange on Vietnamese survivors and their children outweighed his apprehension about returning: "I swore I'd never do it again, but there I was, on the airplane."¹⁰

Normalization also made the logistics of returning to Việt Nam less complicated. Official diplomatic relations lifted travel restrictions on Americans, which opened a broad range of return pathways. Where previously veterans' groups had to organize small tours themselves,

---

[6] Ashley Carruthers, "Vietnamese Language and Media Policy in the Service of Deterritorialized Nation-Building." *Language, Nation and Development in Southeast Asia* (Singapore: Institute of Southeast Asian Studies, 2007), 198.

[7] Interview with Derrill, Skype, June 27, 2016; Interview with Francis, Skype, May 11, 2016; Robert J. Reilly, *Return of the Warriors: Vietnam War Veterans Face the Ghosts of Their Past on Their Personal Battlefields* (Victoria, BC: Trafford Publishing, 2010), 17.

[8] Interview with Francis.

[9] Interview with Greg. Muller and his delegation were called a "total disgrace," accused of "kowtowing to the North Vietnamese" and "urinating on the American flag" for participating in commemorative and reconciliation activities in Việt Nam; McGrory, "For a Moment at Christmas, Vietnam Evokes the Old Emotions."

[10] Interview with Paul S., Skype, January 19, 2016.

large American organizations and companies could now organize and conduct tours. Francis returned on the 1998 World T.E.A.M. Sports Vietnam Challenge, a sponsored bicycle ride with able-bodied and disabled veterans from Hà Nội to Hồ Chí Minh City. Francis had "always been interested in returning. . . . I didn't have any rational reason to do it, or at least one that I could explain to the rest of my family."[11] The Vietnam Challenge provided Francis with the reason he needed: "it just all seemed to come together. It was the right time, the right place. If that had happened ten years earlier I probably would have done it then, or if it happened ten years later I probably would have done it then."[12] Within Việt Nam, a burgeoning tourism industry sprang up in the 1990s.[13] This shift allowed some veterans to return on a whim. David W. was visiting China in 2004 and found it far too cold, so he bought a flight to Hồ Chí Minh City.[14] Richard, a former Marine, insisted it was nothing more than "idle curiosity" that brought him back in 2002: "I hadn't been thinking of returning at all."[15] US Army veteran Don returned in 2005 when some friends "kinda drug [sic] me along."[16] The nonchalance of David W., Richard, and Don illustrates how returning to Việt Nam had been popularized and "normalized."

Yet like reconciliation returnees, many normalization veterans described long-held dreams of returning. Reilly knew, even during the war, that he "needed to return someday – someday when no one is shooting at me."[17] Echoing early returnees, they described Vietnam as a foundational rite of passage, and were both nostalgic for the place as it had been and wistful about what it could be. US veteran Mike C. told me:

I came back because I always loved this place. And I wanted to see it when it was peaceful. . . . There was something about this place that was always with us. It was the biggest experience, the most traumatic and powerful experience of our life. . . . I always believed that this country really is beautiful and that it had the chance to really become a wonderful place to live, without colonialism and the American War, French War, all of that stuff.[18]

Despite their nostalgic longing, normalization returnees also recognized that what they experienced in the war was "Vietnam," not Việt Nam. A common theme, perhaps surprisingly so among combat veterans with

---

[11] Interview with Francis. [12] Ibid.
[13] Prema-chandra Athukorala and Tran Quang Tien, "Foreign Direct Investment in Industrial Transition: The Experience of Vietnam." *Journal of the Asia Pacific Economy* 17:3 (2012): 446.
[14] Interview with David W. [15] Interview with Richard, Đà Nẵng, April 16, 2016.
[16] Interview with Don, Nha Trang, March 31, 2016.
[17] Reilly, *Return of the Warriors*, 11, 17.
[18] Interview with Mike C., Nha Trang, March 31, 2016.

memories of a war-torn environment, was sentimentality for the Vietnamese landscape. Australian Army veteran Brian contemplated returning for a long time to "actually see what Việt Nam was like," because in the midst of war, "there were glimpses of sort of beautiful sights and things."[19] Even US veteran Ron, who as an army photographer had captured images of the massacres at My Lai in 1968, remembered beauty in Việt Nam: "it's a beautiful country and I wanted to see what it was like, you know, from prior years."[20]

Underlying many normalization returns was the objective of healing in Việt Nam. The 1990s saw increasing awareness and interest in trauma and psychology in the West, an interest itself linked to the Vietnam War. As a consequence of veteran activism and the 1970's psychology boom, "post-Vietnam syndrome" emerged as a Vietnam-specific incarnation of "battle fatigue" or "shell shock," eventually designated in 1980 as PTSD in the third edition of the *Diagnostic and Statistical Manual of Mental Disorders* (DSM-III).[21] Inclusion of PTSD in the DSM legitimized veterans' psychological problems when the Veterans' Affairs (VA) and Department of Veterans' Affairs (DVA) – and by extension the US and Australian militaries and governments – had avoided responsibility for them. In response, both the VA and the DVA increased the scope of their services and the veterans' entitlements.[22] Consequently, and in conjunction with the healing discourse that now came to surround memorials in Australia and the United States, more and more veterans began to seek out compensation and care for mental health issues. Brian explained that returning "was something that was playing on my mind since I was diagnosed," because "I felt that I needed to go back to the place where it all started." Brian's desire to return to "the place where it all started" demonstrates the shifting vision of a warzone homeland in returnees' memories through a trauma narrative. Trauma is often theorized as repetitive, involuntary returns in memory, and so treatments tend to focus on remembering and reintegrating traumatic experiences by revisiting them in therapy.[23] As travel to Việt Nam normalized, increasing numbers of veterans in treatment began to consider literally revisiting the physical site of their trauma. Brian was diagnosed in 1996, and "after

---

[19] Interview with Brian, Skype, June 23, 2016.
[20] Interview with Ron, Skype, April 5, 2016.
[21] Chaim Shatan, "Post-Vietnam Syndrome." *New York Times*, May 6, 1972, 35.
[22] Kenneth W. Kizer, "The 'New VA': A National Laboratory for Health Care Quality Management." *American Journal of Medical Quality* 14:1 (Jan/Feb 1999): 3; "Veterans' and Veterans' Family Counselling Service – Summary of Background and Current Events." Vietnam Veterans Association of Australia. www.vvaa.org.au/vvcs2.htm
[23] Ruth Leys, *Trauma: A Genealogy* (Chicago, IL: University of Chicago Press, 2000), 242–52.

2 Normalization, 1995–2005

going through the PTSD programs and learning more about post-traumatic stress," he returned in 2002.[24]

The notion of Việt Nam as the locus of trauma mirrored a broader medicalization of Vietnam.[25] The war and its veterans had long been pathologized in psycho-medical terms: "Vietnam Syndrome" encompassed "trauma," "malaise," "shame," and "guilt."[26] From the late 1980s, political and social discourse about Vietnam in the United States and Australia centered on healing: healing within, healing through recognition, healing the national political and social divides caused by the war. "The Wall" came to be known as "a national healing shrine," while the dedication of the Australian Vietnam Forces National Memorial in 1992 was described by memorial chairman and Vietnam veteran Peter Poulton as "the final healing process."[27] The notion of healing was further promoted in political discourse. Clinton framed reconciliation with Việt Nam as an imperative for locating possible remaining POW/MIA (missing in action) soldiers and healing the effects of "Vietnam Syndrome": "another crucial step which will carry us forward to help our nation and redeem the sacrifices for freedom that brave Americans made in Vietnam."[28] In a statement to the Australian Senate, the Minister for Veterans Affairs Bruce Scott described Fischer's 1996 veteran delegation to Long Tân as a "profoundly healing" experience which he linked repeatedly to reconciliation and to the positive relationship between Australia and Việt Nam.[29] Political leaders in Australia and the United States therefore framed normalization as a continuation of the "healing process" initiated by the memorials, expanding the terms of reconciliation over the war to a global scale.[30]

At the same time, memories of a hostile homecoming dominated discourse about the war, veterans, and trauma. The US-led coalition entered the Gulf War in 1990 with widespread public support generated by a "Support the Troops" campaign.[31] Historians Thomas D. Beamish et al. argue that the campaign "made the ongoing problems of Vietnam

---

[24] Interview with Brian.
[25] Kali Tal, *Worlds of Hurt: Reading the Literatures of Trauma* (Cambridge, MA: Cambridge University Press, 1996), 6, 60–61.
[26] Hagopian, *Vietnam War in American Memory*, 73–74, 162.
[27] Peter Poulton, quoted in Inglis and Brazier, *Sacred Places*, 387.
[28] William Clinton, "Announcement of Normalization of Relations with Vietnam." *The White House*, July 11, 1995. Online by Gerhard Peters and John T. Woolley, *The American Presidency Project*. www.presidency.ucsb.edu/ws/?pid=51605
[29] Bruce Scott, "Vietnam Veterans' Delegation to Vietnam." Ministerial Statements, Australian Senate, 38th Parliament, 1st Session, 1st Period, Canberra. September 11, 1996, 3283–85.
[30] Hagopian, *Vietnam War in American Memory*, 93.
[31] Fitzgerald, "Support the Troops," 1–22.

veterans a result of protesters' activity rather than resulting from the war experience and the failures of government policy toward veterans."[32] Similarly Australia's "Anzac Revival" in the 1990s "disarm[ed] the critique of Australian participation in war by casting it as an attack on Anzac and the nation itself."[33] Despite ample evidence that stories of anti-war hostility and nonrecognition of Vietnam veterans were apocryphal, the mistreatment of Vietnam soldiers continued to dominate war memory.[34] Framing anti-war protesters as traitors and veterans as betrayed heroes allowed the distrust, anger, and shame between veterans and civilians to scar over. The myth of hostile homecomings worked to deepen links between veterans, fostering a diasporic consciousness through collective memories of marginalization.[35]

The narrative of the betrayed hero informed theories of trauma promoted through the early 2000s by prominent writers who historicized the traumatized soldier. Psychologist Jonathan Shay, veteran Ray Scurfield, and therapist Edward Tick drew parallels between Vietnam veterans and Homeric and Shakespearean representations of trauma, creating an archetypal trauma narrative in which the "warrior" (veteran) undergoes a "rite of passage" (combat) in "the Underworld" (warzone) and returns to an unrecognizable home where he (always he) is subjected to "demeaning and dishonoring" treatment.[36] The betrayed hero narrative displaced gendered notions of victimhood by establishing combat as an esoteric masculine experience and casting the civilian (feminine) body – the anti-war protester – as the "traitor" to the transformed "warrior." As Boym notes, "modern nostalgia is a mourning for the impossibility for the

---

[32] Thomas D. Beamish et al., "Who Supports the Troops? Vietnam, the Gulf War, and the Making of Collective Memory." *Social Problems* 42:3 (1995), 355.

[33] Marilyn Lake, "How Do Schoolchildren Learn About the Spirit of Anzac?" In *What's Wrong With ANZAC? The Militarisation of Australian History*. Edited by Marilyn Lake and Henry Reynolds (Sydney: University of New South Wales, 2010), 156.

[34] See: Beamish et al., "Who Supports the Troops?"; Ann Curthoys, "'Vietnam': Public Memory of an Anti-War Movement." In *Memory in Twentieth Century Australia*. Edited by Kate Darian-Smith and Paula Hamilton (Melbourne: Oxford University Press, 1994); Lembcke, *Spitting Image*; Stewart, "Vietnam: The Long Journey Home"; Dean Jr., "The Myth of the Troubled and Scorned Vietnam Veteran"; Chris Dixon, "Redeeming the Warriors: Myth-Making and Australia's Vietnam Veterans." *Australian Journal of Politics & History* 60:2 (2014): 214–28; Mark Dapin, "'We Too Were Anzacs': Were Vietnam Veterans Ever Truly Excluded from the Anzac Tradition?" In *The Honest History Book*. Edited by David Stephens and Alison Broinowski (Sydney: NewSouth, 2017), 77–91; Martin Hobbs, "We Went and Did an Anzac Job."

[35] Safran, "Diasporas in Modern Societies," 83.

[36] Jonathan Shay, *Odysseus in America: Combat Trauma and the Trials of Homecoming* (New York: Scriber, 2002), 137; Ray Scurfield, *A Vietnam Trilogy: Veterans and Posttraumatic Stress, 1968, 1989, 2000* (New York: Algora Publishing, 2004), 106; Edward Tick, *War and the Soul: Healing Our Nation's Veterans from Post-traumatic Stress Disorder* (Wheaton, IL: Quest Books, 2005), 195.

mythical return," a longing for "clear borders and values" where there are none.[37] This narrative appealed to veterans like Brian, who were proud of their service and who felt that the veterans had been "criticized, verbalized, humiliated" by the anti-war movement, and to Reilly, who wrote in his memoir *Return of the Warriors* (2010): "I ask no more of you than you not vilify these sons."[38]

Reilly's return to Việt Nam illustrates how veterans who did not seek out psychological support were influenced by a new "discourse of trauma" in which the traumatized subject was the hero and nostalgia for the war was the norm.[39] When Reilly returned from service, he had nightmares so severe he would attack his wife in his sleep, believing her to be "my Viet Cong attacker. The more she thrashed about, the harder I tried to kill her/him." Reilly did not recognize his experiences as trauma symptoms until the 1990s, when PTSD was widely represented in a way that was sympathetic to the traumatized subject. When he accepted that his nightmares, violence, and hypervigilance were symptoms of PTSD, Reilly wrote: "I reasoned that I could see a psychiatrist and be medicated.... I could see a psychologist and undertake a year or two of talk therapy... or I could return to the land of my fears."[40] His decision to "return to the land of my fears" in 1998 reflected popular PTSD treatments treatment at the time, including "flooding," immersion, and exposure or desensitization therapies. At the same time, his decision to return instead of seeking psychological help in the United States suggests a reaction against the therapy craze of the 1990s: a valuing of stoicism and self-reliance in mental health that reflected the remasculinization of victimhood.

"Healing journeys" were particularly appealing to anti-war veterans. Reconciliation returnees had made use of media exposure and veteran-activist networks to spread their stories, which appealed to an anti-war demographic. Reconciliation returnee and psychologist Ray Scurfield's 1989 "PTSD tour" was filmed by PBS for a documentary, *Vietnam: Two Decades and a Wake-Up* (1990), which emphasized recovering "inner peace" by letting go of "twenty years of hate" toward the Vietnamese.[41] Some reconciliation returnees, such as Greg, became dedicated to telling "the truth" about Việt Nam: "this time I'm not gonna make the same mistake and stay quiet. I'm going to tell people what I saw. Because

---

[37] Boym, *Future of Nostalgia*, 8.
[38] Interview with Brian; Reilly, *Return of the Warriors*, 14.
[39] Claire Sisco King, *Washed in Blood: Male Sacrifice, Trauma and the Cinema* (New Brunswick, NJ: Rutgers University Press, 2011), 79.
[40] Reilly, *Return of the Warriors*, 12.
[41] *Vietnam: Two Decades and a Wake-Up*, produced by Steven Smith (Arlington, VA: PBS, 1990).

I think what I saw, they need to know."[42] The idea of healing journeys rippled through veteran and anti-war communities. Mike C., for instance, returned in part because after working as a counselor for the VA and "listening to so many vets in so many different places, and participating in the healing process, I just wanted to do my own recoveries." Mike C. had become anti-war during his 1966–67 tour of duty, evaluating psychiatric cases. "Like Kafka ... we certainly did our job, didn't we?" The assassinations of Martin Luther King Jr. and Bobby Kennedy in 1968 turned Mike C. into an activist: it "woke me up to the violence inherent in the country at that time." In the 1990s, Mike C. had been working as a VA vet counselor in Alaska when he heard about Friendship Village in Hà Nội, an organization started by a close friend from the anti-war movement, George Mizo. Mike C. thought Mizo had died. When he visited Friendship Village "under the wing" of reconciliation returnee Chuck, he discovered his old friend was alive. Mike C. described his healing as "a story from one vet to another, from the beginning."[43]

Anti-war veterans' familiarity with the language and methods of psychotherapy appeared to shape the format of their memories of return. Many described a pattern of "stepping-stones," mirroring common understandings of classical psychoanalysis and "talk therapy" in which the subject works through their past to pinpoint defining events that affected their psychological state. Although individual steps varied, common steps included prewar patriotism, wartime disorientation, postwar isolation, gratification, and reflection during the commemorative era of the 1980s, and increased political awareness. Most experienced a major traumatic event after the war that led them to seek psychological help: hitting "rock bottom" with substance abuse, acts of violence, arrests, divorce, or the death of a child or spouse. Diagnosis of PTSD and counseling were commonly the final steps before returning to Việt Nam. This stepping-stone pattern demonstrates Alistair Thomson's theory of "composure" in individual recollections in which we "construct or compose memory narrative drawing upon the language and meaning available in our culture, from the time of the event through to the time of telling ... we also seek to create a past we can live with."[44] Veterans who remembered their return journeys through a series of stepping-stones were composing a narrative that incorporated and accommodated the most traumatic and desperate moments of their lives: building stories that made sense of how they struggled, progressed, and, by returning to Việt Nam, became whole.

---

[42] Interview with Greg.   [43] Interview with Mike C.
[44] Thomson, "Anzac Memories Revisited," 22–23.

2 Normalization, 1995–2005

Former Marine Suel was "a conservative young Texas boy" who volunteered for the Marines out of feelings of patriotism and duty. He was raised with the "mythology" of America "always wearing the white hat, always doing the right thing, we won World War II." Suel served in Vietnam from 1968 to 1969, and when he returned "nothing seemed real anymore ... everything looked dangerous." He described walking into his family home as "almost like walking into a jail. I felt so uncomfortable."[45] He spent years living alone in Alaska abusing alcohol and drugs. In 1987 he went to Poona, India, to attend a psychological group in an ashram, where he finally asked himself "the question I feared the most. Was there a depth of evil in my soul? Was I truly the Nazi killer or a kid who had been misled by his elders and government?"[46] Suel struggled with his guilt and responsibility for the war, coming to the realization that "I'm a good guy. And I had good intentions. The Nazis were in Washington DC." After his trip to India, Suel began connecting with anti-war groups, realizing that they were people that he liked and respected. "It was the best thing I did ... I want to be part of this." Eventually, he sought help from a PTSD program in Seattle. It took a full decade from that first confrontation of guilt in the ashram to work up to returning to Việt Nam. Suel finally returned in 1998 with Mike C. to "meet the enemy.... 'Cause I never met any of them, I never talked to any of them. Cause I really just realized I've been over here fighting and killing people and I have no idea." He described returning as "really stepping off an abyss in a sort of Buddhist way, you're just gonna go over there and find out what in the hell is going on."[47]

Central to these anti-war returns was an emerging discourse of trauma that incorporated morality, politics, and spirituality. Judith Herman's *Trauma and Recovery* (1992) and Jonathan Shay's *Achilles in Vietnam* (1994) both made explicit links between anti-war activism, recognition of trauma, and the morality of the war.[48] Herman argued that "the moral legitimacy of the antiwar movement and the national experience of defeat in a discredited war had made it possible to reorganize psychological trauma as a lasting and inevitable legacy of war."[49] Shay coined the term "moral injury" to describe the emotional violation experienced by Vietnam veterans: "we begin in the moral world of the soldier – what his

---

[45] Interview with Suel, Đà Nẵng, April 14, 2016.
[46] Suel D. Jones, *Meeting the Enemy: A Marine Goes Home* (N.p.: Booksurge.com, 2008), 146.
[47] Interview with Suel.
[48] Judith Herman, *Trauma and Recovery* (New York: Basic Books, 1992); Jonathan Shay, *Achilles in Vietnam: Combat Trauma and the Undoing of Character* (New York: Atheneum, 1994).
[49] Herman, *Trauma and Recovery*, 27.

culture understands to be right – and betrayal of that moral order by a commander."[50] These emerging theories framed moral injury through the broader cultural trauma of Vietnam in the United States, reflecting the shift in American conceptualizations of the war: "'Vietnam' had gone from something 'we' did to the Vietnamese, to something Vietnam did to 'us,' and finally to something 'we' did to ourselves."[51] Because moral injury theory situated the veteran as a victim of the war as well as a participant, and recognized the war experience as psychospiritual trauma, it permitted veterans to grieve their Vietnam experience – an experience that, since the Reagan era, they had increasingly been told to feel proud of. John A., a former Marine, said that "I wished I hadn't made it back. Because of what I'd been doing, what I knew about the futility, the worthlessness of the whole endeavor.... I felt a lot of shame and guilt for being a part of it ... I thought I would have been better off getting killed over there." That prominent psychologists were communicating that this shame and guilt was not only understandable, but legitimate, allowed veterans like John A. to reflect on their legacy in Vietnam in a way that they felt was more honest than the "noble cause" commemorations of the 1980s. John A. began attending group therapy sessions in the late 1990s, where he met politically similar veterans who had returned to Việt Nam. He himself returned in 2000.[52]

Veterans returning for healing purposes attracted a great deal of media attention, and press coverage of veterans' returns frequently flattened the entire experience into "healing," erasing the political nuances and multiplicity of reasons why veterans return. For example, a 2001 article in *Good Weekend* briefly discussed the variety of factors involved in returning to Việt Nam, including retirement, empty nests, business opportunities, curiosity, and "a nostalgic interlude."[53] Yet most of the article focused on trauma and catharsis, promoting the idea that healing was always the underlying purpose of returning to Việt Nam. The promotion of healing journeys by veteran psychologists, who wanted to promote the positive outcomes of their therapy models, contributed to the prominence of this story. Scurfield organized a second "PTSD tour" in 2000 and published a book based on his experiences, while Tick took up the cause of healing journeys in the early 2000s.[54] Tick characterized PTSD as a "moral and spiritual wound as much as a psychological wound" and, crucially, he argued that veterans could be cured from PTSD by returning to Việt Nam.[55]

---

[50] Shay, *Achilles in Vietnam*, 3. [51] Martini, *Invisible Enemies*, 157.
[52] Interview with John A., Facetime, August 12, 2016.
[53] Mark Baker, "Going Back." *Good Weekend*, November 10, 2001, 21.
[54] Scurfield, *A Vietnam Trilogy*, 67.
[55] Edward Tick, quoted in Ann Piccininni, "Author Details How He Helps Veterans Heal." *Daily Herald (Arlington Heights)*, November 10, 2005.

2 Normalization, 1995–2005

As a consequence of this dominant healing narrative, veterans began to be coerced into returning by friends and family. Australian Army veteran John W. had decided that he "just wasn't going to go back. Ever. Ever going back ... I never thought I was gonna leave Vietnam alive ... just to get out of Tân Sơn Nhất Airport and be free of that country, it was like being reborn. It was just like: I've got a chance at life again." It was reconciliation returnee Graham E., a close wartime friend of John W.'s, who pushed him to return to Việt Nam. Their regiment reunion had been cancelled, and Graham E. seized the opportunity. "He rang me every day, every day for a week, and he kept saying 'the reunion is not going to happen, come to Việt Nam.' Until in the end, out of sheer frustration, I went, 'Right then, bugger you, I will.'"[56] Graham E., John W. and another veteran returned together for Anzac Day, 2000. Other veterans were persuaded (or instructed) to return by their partners. Derek, an Australian Army veteran, returned to Việt Nam in 1999. "My wife said, 'we should go and visit Việt Nam,' I hadn't been particularly interested, as a lot of veterans aren't, but she convinced me and off we went."[57] Emboldened by the media coverage of returns and the new discourse on trauma, spouses began to encourage their partners to return to Việt Nam. With the advent of commemorations, memorials, and increasing turnout at Anzac Days and reunions in the 1990s, some veterans' wives – particularly those whose partners were integrated in veteran communities – wanted to visit Việt Nam themselves in order to build a frame of reference for the anecdotes and memories that dominated their social lives. Derek told me that his wife wanted to go "so that when I had other conversations with people, she knew those places."[58] Others were determined to go in search of a cure.

Increasing numbers of civilians engaged with the idea of a healing return to Việt Nam. US infantry veteran Deryle described being "tricked" into returning to Việt Nam in 1995 by a younger friend who taught at an international school in Singapore. His friend flew him to Singapore to run a course – Deryle worked with low-income high school students – but when he arrived, school was on a break. "I said, 'Man, what's this about?' ... He said, 'you're supposed to go to Việt Nam, these weeks. Don't you have 5,500 dollars in your pocket?' I said, 'well I do.' He said, 'go to Việt Nam.' So, I did!" Deryle's friend effectively organized and paid for his trip to Việt Nam by contracting him for three weeks in Singapore with only one week's work when he arrived. Deryle explained his friend's interest in getting him to Việt Nam: "there are some younger men, American guys, who were impacted by the Vietnam War, and didn't

---

[56] Interview with John W., Skype, May 23, 2016.
[57] Interview with Derek, Skype, May 16, 2016. [58] Ibid.

go. . ... They were our little brothers."[59] Civilian psychotherapist Tick was one such "little brother," who described the "Vietnam guilt" of his generation: "[we] suffer because we chose not to perform a primary and expected rite of passage."[60] Deryle indicated that his friend orchestrated his return out of the same feelings of "Vietnam guilt."

Like reconciliation returnees, many normalization returnees described visceral memories at the descent into Việt Nam and upon revisiting sites of personal significance. John W., for instance, remembered how the descent into Việt Nam "put the heebie-jeebies in me, because it was like revisiting a nightmare. And that was my concern, and as I said, getting out, and getting out alive, I never thought would happen. Achieving it, I never wanted to put myself back in that situation again. Of fear, and death, and all of that . . .. It's not something you want to revisit."[61] However, where reconciliation veterans relied largely on metaphor and emotional language to describe memories, normalization veterans used trauma-specific language and ideas. Deryle described a flashback on his second trip back to Việt Nam in 1996:

A truck comes by, and it backfires, and I knew in my head it was a backfire from an American 2-in-1 half-tonne truck 'cause I was responsible for one of them when I was over there. I knew what thing sounded like. Boom! It backfires, and it's the middle of the day and I just try to melt myself into the side of this building. And I'm stuck upside this building, realizing, "holy shit, what the fuck do I look like."

Deryle explained that although his friend had sent him to Việt Nam in 1995 on a "wounded veterans" tour, "I didn't really address the core of it."[62] When he returned again in 1996, intending to visit the country as a tourist, not a veteran, he was less prepared for his psychological wounds to come to the surface and was caught off guard by his memories.

In some cases, the new discourse of trauma led veterans to dwell on memories of war. For example, John A.'s return led him to reconnect with a close war buddy, Barr. Barr described an event that John A. had no memory of. His platoon was "walking point" and came across a deserted village and checking the hooches: "[I] step inside, I hear movement, and I just opened up. Because it's a reflex." John A. remembered this far in the story. Then Barr asked him, "'don't you remember what happened?' And there were civilians hiding behind the hooch. And I hear a movement and I opened up. And it's civilians." Barr told him that as John A. "opened up" fire, he (Barr) had "snapped," dragging one of the civilians out and firing rounds into her corpse. John A. had no recollection of this: "I don't

---

[59] Interview with Deryle, Skype, 29 August 2016.
[60] Edward Tick, "Apocalypse Continued." *New York Times*, January 13, 1985, 60.
[61] Interview with John W.   [62] Interview with Deryle.

2 Normalization, 1995–2005

have those pictures, I don't have those sounds, smells, feels, nothing. But I have everything leading up to it, and afterwards."[63]

John A. was understandably distressed by the idea that, first, he killed civilians and that his friend mutilated a body, and second, that he could not remember it. "For decades I'm sure only bombs and artillery and psychopaths killed innocents, that I'd remained pure . . . Barr's revelation blows away my belief that I'd never knowingly caught Vietnamese civilians in the middle of a fight."[64] He became convinced that he had repressed this memory, likely influenced by the popularity of repressed memory theory in the early 1990s: "my brain blocked it for my own good. That might have been the straw that broke me."[65] However, repressed memory theory has been largely discredited. Psychologist Elizabeth Loftus emphasizes that emotion and environment can heavily distort memory and argues that "memory is malleable even for life's most traumatic experiences."[66] It is possible that Barr recounted a distorted or "amplified" traumatic memory to John A., and that John's memory of Barr's story became further distorted as John A. tried repeatedly to remember his missing memory.[67] "I kinda started getting more pieces to that incident . . . . The story's just coming into my head, you know, I'd be somewhere, and then I'd be lost, because this incident was starting to write in my brain." John A., an author and poet, used narrative to "write out" his trauma. He decided to revisit his memoir to account for this repressed memory, because "that's a big part of the story: how your brain protects you from trauma."[68] The repressed memory of trauma became entwined with returning to Việt Nam where he was, still, "searching for the remnants of his soul."[69]

Many normalization returnees responded to questions about war memories by engaging in debates about the nature and function of memory and how memory relates to PTSD. Veterans' positions can be broadly mapped against Boym's categories of "reflective" and "restorative" nostalgia. Some explicitly rejected the concept of memory malleability, demonstrating restorative nostalgia. John A. said:

---

[63] Interview with John A.
[64] John A. "More High Weirdness." Personal essay shared with the author, April 24, 2020.
[65] Interview with John A.
[66] Elizabeth Loftus, "The Reality of Repressed Memory." *American Psychologist* 48:5 (May 1993): 530.
[67] Jacinta M. Oulton et al., "Memory Amplification for Trauma: Investigating the Role of Analogue PTSD Symptoms in the Laboratory." *Journal of Anxiety Disorders* 42 (August 2016): 60–70; Deryn Strange and Melanie K.T. Takarangi, "False Memories for Missing Aspects of Traumatic Events." *Acta Psychologica* 141:3 (November 2012): 322–26.
[68] Interview with John A.
[69] John Akins, "Vietnam War Books & Writing." www.johnakins.com

… they say your memory changes and stuff like that, but I don't think the people that say, you know, when they test people on memory, cognitive testing, I don't think that they've tested a whole lot of people where their life was on the line for over a year, and they had to keep themselves and the guys they were with alive and stuff. 'Cause those images, those days are burned into my brain.[70]

This belief in perfect memory recall was part of the reason John A. was so troubled by his lack of recollection of the incident Barr described. Other returnees pointed to evidence that their memories were stable and accurate. Derek told me: "I kept diaries. So, I didn't need to have something to trigger a memory."[71] These veterans did not accept that their memories were susceptible to change and thought of them not as "nostalgia, but rather as truth."[72] John W. told me: "those sorts of memories indelibly imprinted on your mind forever. They don't change."[73] Because the concept of trauma was closely linked to Vietnam veterans, and because Vietnam was, for some veterans, the defining experience of their life, the suggestion that they did not remember it accurately was understandably a threat to their very identity.

Yet most normalization returnees exhibited reflective nostalgia, contemplating the subjectivity of memory, debating memory recall and "call-[ing] it into doubt."[74] I asked Don about a flashback he had written about in his 2008 memoir, *Into the Heart*. He had visited the Sơn Mỹ Memorial and Museum in 2005, which portrays the My Lai massacre in graphic detail. The exhibition triggered a memory of a search-and-destroy patrol, a "terrible day of fire, swirling smoke, screaming and death so long ago."[75] Don explained that it was the feeling, more than the facts, that mattered in memory: "what you remember is the visceral. It can viscerally come back at you." He advised me: "memory is a very faulty thing…. Anybody who will tell you the truth, will tell you that there's really nothing too sure about some of the things, how they're remembering them."[76]

With the increasing numbers of veterans returning to Việt Nam, veterans were not only challenged by Vietnamese war memories but the memories of other Australians and Americans. Suel met Bill E., a reconciliation veteran, when he returned to Việt Nam. They had served in the same company and fought in a battle together. "He and I were on the same hill, that we got ran off of. We had a big ass battle. All day long. We fought all day long. I did not think I was going to get out alive. When

---

[70] Interview with John A. [71] Interview with Derek.
[72] Boym, *Future of Nostalgia*, xviii. [73] Interview with John W.
[74] Boym, *The Future of Nostalgia*, xviii.
[75] Don Blackburn, *Into the Heart* (N.p.: CreateSpace, 2013), 148–49.
[76] Interview with Don.

we talk about that battle, it doesn't – there is not one common thing about it." Talking with Bill helped Suel recognize the fluidity of his memory. This realization was at first threatening, destabilizing the identity that was built on the memories that Suel thought were true. "I don't know what's real. I have no concept of what's real anymore. I mean, from what actually happened, to what you think happened, to what you've heard happened, to the movies, and the stories, and dreams, you don't have a clue what really happened."[77] This totalizing doubt seemed traumatic in itself, but Suel explained that it helped him to detach from the memories that were troubling him the most.

The growing number of returnees who had become counselors after the war were acutely aware of the unstable nature of memory. They reveled in change, demonstrating reflective nostalgia that "cherishes shattered fragments of memory and temporalizes space."[78] When I asked Mike C. about his memories, he said "I've got more of them. That's a natural process. You have more, and when you're back here and you relax and you start smelling and seeing and you start talking to other people, and you say, 'Oh, I remember that' .... And then you reach a point where '[shrugs] I don't need to remember anything else.'" Mike C. encouraged other veterans to return to Việt Nam to counter negative memories implanted from Western media.

If you were here, you have your own memories that are stuck in the past. So, when you come back, well I tell people, all of your pictures change. All of the pictures and scripts in your mind are destroyed, all at once, when you come back .... You know, they have a picture of Rambo and Viet Cong and NVAs with black pajamas, VC, things that only came from the media but in reality it all looked different.[79]

This theory mirrored the "library of images" described by reconciliation returnees. Deryle remembered: "you think that because the war's so powerful in your life, it's etched in your memory, that if you go back 'cause you were there in that event, it's gonna be like it was. And it ain't. It ain't, 'cause the war ended and things changed and life went on. Nothing's etched, nothing's permanent except change. So, it changed."[80]

Thus, normalization returns echoed the patterns established by reconciliation returnees, describing processes of reframing or reclaiming what Vietnam meant but filtering them through discourses of trauma and healing. Suel often visited a place called Razorback Ridge, a personal battlefield of his: "It's where I go to hear the ghosts .... There's something about coming back here coming back to the place where you fought. There's no bodies, there's no screaming, there's you, standing here in

[77] Interview with Suel. [78] Boym, *Future of Nostalgia*, 50. [79] Interview with Mike C.
[80] Interview with Deryle.

the silence, and understanding that it's truly, truly over. Not here [pointing to his heart], but truly, truly over."[81] Suel's acceptance of the past reflected the changing and reclaiming of meaning described by reconciliation returnees. John W., similarly, reminisced:

> ... going back, and just seeing it in peacetime, and seeing the people that weren't living in fear, and living underground ... to see them in peacetime, in real peace, that was, I think what hit me within the first twenty-four hours .... Everywhere you looked when I was up there [in the war], there were Americans, there was military. And when I went back in 2000, there was none of that. There was no sign of military at all.[82]

Where reconciliation returnees described feelings of peace or closure, normalization returnees linked their "life-affirming" experiences to significant decreases in specific PTSD symptoms.[83] John W. explained: "when I first came home, I had a lot of horrendous memories, a lot of horrendous memories. One or two in particular. And it put to rest, if you like, nightmares that had gone on for forty years."[84] Similarly, Reilly wrote: "since returning from this trip my nightmares have stopped and my soul is at peace."[85] Derrill even advised another veteran, "this [visiting Việt Nam] will cure you. Let me tell you, this will cure you."[86]

Many veterans reported that, as a consequence of healing in Việt Nam, their lives completely changed. Brian reported that "one guy just recently said to me, 'your attitude has changed, you're not as angry .... You seem to be much happier and freer.'"[87] A common symptom of PTSD is "numbing," or suppression of emotion. Numbing allows the sufferer to avoid traumatic thoughts and feelings and maintains emotional safety by limiting interpersonal vulnerability.[88] Anger, being harder to control, is sometimes the only emotion that shows through, and is a very common symptom of combat-related PTSD.[89] Some veterans reflected that they were raised to view emotion as weakness among men, a lesson that was later ingrained in the military. Francis described it as "the macho façade, you know, tough and nothing upsets me ... that's a natural male thing." He remembered "wandering through the streets of Huế, early in the morning, seeing the people coming out and sweeping the streets and setting up their little stands, it struck me: what a wonderful, beautiful place this was. And it also struck me that, that was the point I recognized,

---

[81] Interview with Suel.   [82] Interview with John W.   [83] Interview with Mike C.
[84] Interview with John W.   [85] Reilly, *Return of the Warriors*, 183.
[86] Interview with Derrill.   [87] Interview with Brian.
[88] Lizabeth Roemer et al., "A Preliminary Investigation of the Role of Strategic Withholding of Emotions in PTSD." *Journal of Traumatic Stress* 14:1 (2001): 150.
[89] Raymond W. Novaco and Claude M. Chemtob, "Anger and Combat-Related Posttraumatic Stress Disorder." *Journal of Traumatic Stress* 15:2 (2002): 129–30.

2 Normalization, 1995–2005

that I realized, that I had never, ever dealt with the emotions that I had in Vietnam. And so that particular moment was a big revelation for me." During the Vietnam Challenge, Francis and the rest of the bicycle team visited a memorial to the Unknown Soldier in Hà Nội: "[we] were overcome with emotions ... we were hugging each other, and crying .... [And] it occurred to me that in my entire tour of Vietnam ... I never once cried." Because returning helped him realize that emotions are part of the human experience, Francis became more in touch with and accepting of his emotions. He explained that now if he cried in front of me, a near stranger, he would no longer feel "mortified": "now I would say, that's just part of your feelings leaking out, and you're human."[90]

At the end of the Vietnam Challenge, Francis visited Nhơn Đức, a village where he had been stationed during the war. He set up a program donating money to the school there and visited every few years. This kind of post-return philanthropy was a common feature among normalization veterans. Derek first returned to Việt Nam in 1998 but became involved with an orphanage in 2007. A friend who had been working at the orphanage left, and Derek thought: "it's time to step up to the plate, cause I think we left the country in a bit of a mess ... the ethnic minority people in particular, who fought alongside Australian and Americans, and the orphanages were ethnic minority kids. So, I decided I'd take over where she'd left off. So, we've been going back ever since."[91] Veterans' projects often led to deep and lasting connections with Việt Nam. After his 1998 return, Suel became involved with Friendship Village. "I thought, I'm gonna go home and raise money and bring it back one time. Well, I went home, raised money, brought it back, went home, raised money, brought it back, went home, raised the money [he laughed] and I thought, this is getting expensive ... I just came over."[92] Suel's work with Friendship Village encouraged him to become more active in Veterans for Peace (VFP). Eventually he started his own chapter, *Hòa Bình* ("peace"), raising money for Vietnamese NGOs that assist victims of Agent Orange, unexploded ordnance, and poverty.[93]

Increasing numbers of returnees became involved in bringing some resolution to the families of an estimated 300,000 revolutionary soldiers still MIA.[94] When Brian returned in 2002, he visited a personal battlefield near Lai Khê. He was accompanied by a representative of the Local

---

[90] Interview with Francis.   [91] Interview with Derek.   [92] Interview with Suel.
[93] "About VFP Chapter 160." Veterans for Peace Chapter 160: Hòa Bình Việt Nam. https://vfp160.org/about-vfp-chapter-160/
[94] Estimates from The Information Center for Martyrs (MARIN). RVNAF soldiers are not included in this estimate as they are not remembered as martyrs by Việt Nam. www.nhantimdongdoi.org/?mod=gioithieu

People's Committee, who informed Brian that forty-two soldiers from the Battle of Coral-Balmoral were still listed as MIA. Brian remembered that in the aftermath of that battle, a number of bodies were buried together in a bomb crater. Finding the mass grave became a personal mission for him, and he returned to the battle site six times. "I did everything I possibly could to try and find that location.... It was important to me, and it was my goal to locate these men and have their remains returned."[95] With an increased understanding of their own trauma and their experiences of closure upon return to Việt Nam, veterans became more aware of how the war continued to affect the Vietnamese. After Derrill's first trip back in 2003, he developed the idea of "Operation Wandering Souls," a project that collects personal items taken by Australian soldiers from the bodies of killed Vietnamese soldiers and returns them to their families. The program was named after a psychological warfare (psy-ops) campaign: during the war, Operation Wandering Soul broadcast "ghost tapes" over revolutionary troops, recordings of voices claiming to be the despairing souls of Vietnamese who could not rest. Derrill, who worked in psy-ops, told me: "we'd play on beliefs. And the belief is, if they die violently, or die where they are not known, their spirit will wander.... We played on people's fears." The idea of Derrill's Operation Wandering Souls was to reverse the effects of this psy-ops campaign. "[Australian soldiers] took those letters, took the diaries, took watches, took things, kept them. And we started collecting these. And then we thought, we'll have this program and bring them home."[96]

Like reconciliation returnees, normalization returnees were open about the emotional benefits that volunteer work afforded them. Don moved to Nha Trang and became a VFP Hòa Bình Chapter liaison, explaining that volunteer work "makes me feel so good. It doesn't get rid of the guilt, but it's built something new in me, new things, gives me something to look forward to, wake up to every day."[97] Derek also focused on "healing-through-helping": "the satisfaction ... we've got a long way to go, but that's my reward. We're trying to mend what we broke."[98] Francis ruminated on his work:

I guess maybe there's some self, trying to deal with some issues that I have ... anything I can do to pay back the families of those kids, by helping them in some little way, makes me feel good. So, I guess that's a selfish motivation that may be a little bit of help to somebody. I do it primarily for myself, rather than anybody else, I guess.[99]

---

[95] Interview with Brian. [96] Interview with Derrill. [97] Interview with Don.
[98] Interview with Derek. [99] Interview with Francis.

2 Normalization, 1995–2005

Normalization returnees centered the injustice of children, who "had nothing to do with it," being affected by war legacies.[100] This focus reflected the increasing numbers of people living with unexploded ordnances (UXOs), poverty, and the ecological and biological effects of Agent Orange who were born after the war. It also indicated a gradual depoliticization of veteran volunteer work as relationships between the United States and Việt Nam normalized. Where reconciliation returnees framed their efforts as supporting "the people" (who, they implied, supported the revolutionaries), normalization returnees eschewed wartime binaries by focusing on children.

There were other differences between reconciliation and normalization veterans who engaged in healing-through-helping activities. Where most reconciliation returnees conceptualized this healing practice as a form of atonement, normalization returnees were divided by nationality. None of the Australian normalization returnees described either seeking out or being granted forgiveness. Even Derek, who was healing-through-helping by "mend[ing] what we broke" did not consider his work atonement. Americans, in contrast, centered atonement and forgiveness. I asked Deryle what his work in Việt Nam accomplished: "shit, made me feel like a human being! [We] ran these people out, went over and committed what I would consider the ultimate insult to, and they take me back like... I still don't get it. And I study Buddhism, I know it's about compassion and forgiveness, but phew!"[101]

Among the redeemers, there were further differences. Reconciliation veterans had focused on their atonement, remembering raw, emotionally fraught experiences. Normalization veterans, in contrast, focused on Vietnamese forgiveness and remembered positive, invigorating experiences. Mike C. described a meeting with generals from the PAVN,

> ... sitting down as if we were just old friends. And that changes you, when you have that kind of experience, it transforms you, your whole view of a country and a war. And I was so overwhelmed. I mean, it's a beautiful place. It's a beautiful people. And we did our damndest to kill them. And that has never left [me].... [So] my return really taught me forgiveness.[102]

Perhaps because most normalization veterans had returned after receiving counseling, they were more prepared for the profound and often painful experience of atoning and being forgiven.

Normalization accounts indicated that the Vietnamese were increasingly accustomed to contrite foreigners. Suel wrote about meeting a man on his first day in Hà Nội: "'Oh!' he exclaimed, pointing at me with a long,

---

[100] Interview with Francis. [101] Interview with Deryle. [102] Interview with Mike C.

thin finger. 'You the enemy!' My heart almost fell into my stomach and I wanted to run, run as fast from the confrontation as I could. Then he reached out to me, threw both arms around my shoulders, and gave me a big hug while laughing, 'Welcome Vietnam.'"[103] The man's jesting and embrace suggests that he was familiar with the phenomenon of returning veterans and comfortable welcoming them to his city. Yet Suel remained incredulous of this easy acceptance. Suel remembered meeting a group of Vietnamese veterans at Friendship Village and someone saying to him, "the war is over, we forgive you." Suel told me he decided to give them "the American test":

I said, "now wait a minute. We bombed your country. We killed millions of your people. We raped your daughters, we made whores out of them. We poured poison all over it, and you tell me you're not angry? You're full of shit, too." And, of course, you never say that. And it got very quiet. And this beautiful old man stood up, no teeth, a farmer, you'd think he's probably as ignorant as you could get. And he told me, he says: "I choose to live in the future. I can live in the past, and I can live in the pain, but I choose to live in the future. If you want to live in the pain, and you want to live in the past, don't bring it to me." I went: "Oh shit. Holy shit."[104]

Despite the many stories about Vietnamese encouraging returning veterans to "look to the future," some normalization returnees tended to indulge in restorative nostalgia, submerging themselves in the past. Paul S. reminisced: "you're back in this place where you had nothing but death and mayhem surrounding you twenty-four hours a day, and here you are, a married man, back in the place where you spent the best days of your youth as it were, and it's ... wow. It's an adventure. It's an adventure. And you gotta have some adventures."[105] As the distance of time between war and the present extended, increasing numbers of veterans returned with a longing to collapse time through space. For example, after John A. returned in 2000, he began dreaming about building a house in a specific area between Đà Nẵng and Tam Kỳ. I realized after our interview that this place was the base of his "bunch of misfits" three-man Combined Action Platoon during the war: "our Shangri-La."[106] From his memoirs and interviews, it was clear that this place, with these men, was the time John A. felt most alive and the only time he ever felt free. He fantasized about the freedom from taboo, sexualizing the adrenaline rush of combat: "in a nutshell ... pure pussy."[107] He romanticized

---

[103] Jones, *Meeting the Enemy*, 166.   [104] Interview with Suel.
[105] Interview with Paul S.
[106] John Akins, *Nam Au Go Go: Falling for the Vietnamese Goddess of War* (Port Jefferson, NY: Vineyard Press, 2005), 217, 183.
[107] John Akins, *Drowning Out the Drums: A Marine Comes Home* (Hà Nội: Thế Giới Publishing, 2014), 166.

2 Normalization, 1995–2005

"walking point" in the bush with the "band of lost boys," his renegade platoon with whom he felt unconditional trust and friendship, "a bond tighter than any marriage."[108] This nostalgia for war was complicated by his profound guilt and shame over his participation in the war, shame that intensified the taboo memory of "the goddess of war luring me on" and sublime tranquility in combat.[109] John A. thought he could harmlessly relocate that tranquility by reclaiming the only place he had ever felt it, revisiting time through space and "rebuild[ing] the lost home."[110] However, his "old area" – the high ground off the beach, between Trường Giang river and the East Sea – had become prime real estate. When he visited Nha Trang he realized he could recreate it, living with "the river on one side and the ocean on the other."[111] John A. came to see his home in Nha Trang as "my getaway, my Shangri-La."[112]

Despite their searches into the past, none of my interviewees found their wartime friends. However, they and many other returnees found satisfaction in new friendships and in seeing new places. Francis told me: "it's important for me to get to know the people."[113] Don and Richard married Vietnamese women and moved to Nha Trang and Đà Nẵng, respectively. Don told me, "I've had a lotta good days at the beach! I met my wife and my family here."[114] John A. had a child with a Vietnamese woman; he and his daughter live half the year in Seattle, half in Nha Trang. He prefers Nha Trang: "It's beautiful... I like the weather. I love the South China Sea. I like swimming. I love riding my bike up and over the mountain and back, and taking my daughter to school, and meeting people." He also admitted he likes it there because "it's not America. So, it feels good."[115]

Like reconciliation veterans, normalization veterans had overwhelmingly positive experiences when they returned to Việt Nam. Richard described it as "miraculous. The whole trip was miraculous. It was full of profound experiences; I think every day I was brought to tears about something.... It changed my life."[116] Where reconciliation veterans used literary language to describe such experiences, however, normalization veterans drew from a psychological lexicon. Reilly wrote that his trip was "highly therapeutic... it seemed so palpable that I could almost hear and feel the healing take place."[117] Mike C. described it as "closure. Of all

---

[108] Akins, *Nam Au Go Go*, 164, 161. [109] Ibid., 131.
[110] Boym, *Future of Nostalgia*, 41. [111] Interview with John A. [112] Ibid.
[113] Interview with Francis. [114] Interview with Don. [115] Interview with John A.
[116] Interview with Richard. [117] Reilly, *Return of the Warriors*, 87, 88.

these dangling thoughts and feelings and distortions."[118] Paul agreed that "there's been a sense of closure."[119] For John W.,

> ... it was the best thing I've done in my last forty years, it was just wonderful. It was very cleansing .... To go back there and leave, I left at peace. Whereas I had brought back a lot of guilt, I carried a lot of guilt with me for forty years after Vietnam. And going back and being there – I was amazed ... Graham said to me, "it'll put a lot of ghosts to bed," and it did. For me it certainly did.[120]

---

[118] Interview with Mike C.   [119] Interview with Paul.   [120] Interview with John W.

3   Commemoration, 2006–2016

The last period of Vietnam veteran returns was defined by the commemoration of war, and so I call this group "commemoration." Official Vietnam War commemorations surged in Australia and the United States in the mid-2000s for a string of major anniversaries linked to key milestones in the war. These commemorations corresponded with changes within Việt Nam. The earlier "normalization" of Việt Nam had coincided with the globalization boom at the turn of the millennium, allowing Việt Nam's growing tourism industry to tap a new international market of Western travelers. Responding to this new market, and specifically to the increasing numbers of veteran-tourists, Việt Nam's tourism industry turned toward kitsch reproductions of war, creating souvenirs and tour experiences that hinged on American memories of the war. Organized tours became more popular as travel experiences were increasingly tailored and packaged to niche markets. Australian veterans preferred commercial battlefield tourism and private troop reunion tours, while Americans favored peace- or healing-orientated tours. All of these tours shared a common fixation on commemoration, with memorial services and truth-telling as central goals and effects. Commemoration tours were refined over the decade, entrenching narrative pathways that coagulated into rigid individual war memories. The commemoration decade was characterized by a diasporic vision of Vietnam as the origin place of veterans' communities and war legacies, and their returns were defined by a desire to mark "their" war in Việt Nam.

In 1990, Australian Army veteran Graham E. negotiated a small commemorative service at Long Tân with the Đất Đỏ District People's Committee, or local government.[1] Graham E. and "former enemy"

---

[1] The Battle of Long Tan took place on August 18, 1966, between the Australian Task Force's (ATF's) D Company, 6RAR, and the NLF battalion D445. Eighteen ATF

attended the service together before sharing morning tea.[2] Over the next two decades, increasing numbers of veterans returned to the site to mourn the eighteen soldiers killed in the Battle of Long Tan, linking the space of Việt Nam to Australia's Vietnam veteran identity.[3] For the 40th anniversary of the battle in 2006, Australian current affairs television program *60 Minutes* accompanied several veterans on their battlefield pilgrimages, while in the nearby town of Vũng Tàu, John Schumann of the band *Redgum* performed "I was Only Nineteen (A Walk in the Light Green)," the "unofficial anthem for veterans" of Australia's Vietnam War.[4] Between 2006 and 2016, increasing numbers of veterans returned, and for the 50th anniversary in 2016 over 3,000 Australians, with roughly 1,000 veterans among them, descended on Vũng Tàu.[5]

With this ritual of pilgrimage, the space of Long Tân became linked to Australian national military identity through the modern phenomenon of Anzac commemoration. In 1915, 8,000 Australian soldiers died in the ten-month Allied Gallipoli campaign in Turkey. Wartime eulogies and official histories of the campaign glorified the courage and character of the Anzac troops, disseminating the idea that at Gallipoli, "on the 25th of April 1915 . . . the consciousness of Australian nationhood was born."[6] In 1927, "Anzac Day" became a national public holiday, and small, infrequent services were held on the beaches of Gallipoli by Australian soldiers and veterans' families. These pilgrimages petered out, were briefly revived in the 1960s, and diminished again. In 1990, Prime Minister Bob Hawke attended a service at Anzac Cove and proclaimed that because "these hills rang with their voices and ran with their blood," the Turkish territory was "in one sense, a part of Australia."[7] This marked the beginning of the "Anzac Revival," in which thousands of Australians participated in Anzac pilgrimages to lands bestowed with "some form of

---

soldiers died, which was the highest casualty for Australia in a single battle during the Vietnam War. Three years later, 6RAR erected a cross to mourn the ATF soldiers killed and among veterans the day became associated with remembering those who died in Vietnam. When the Prime Minister declared the anniversary "Vietnam Veterans Day" in 1987, the day took on a broader national significance.

[2] Interview with Graham E.
[3] See for example: "A Place Called Long Tan with Meaning for All." *The Age*, August 18, 2002. www.theage.com.au/articles/2002/08/17/1029114030988.html
[4] Rowan Callick, "Battles Put to Rest." *The Australian*, August 18, 2006.
[5] Lindsay Murdoch, "Why Vietnam Objected to the Long Tan Commemoration." *Sydney Morning Herald*, August 18, 2016. www.smh.com.au/world/why-vietnam-objected-to-the-long-tan-commemoration-20160817-gqv9aw.html. Estimates of veterans based on the author's discussions with tour guides in Việt Nam.
[6] Charles Bean, *The Official History of Australia in the War of 1914–1918, Vol. II, The Story of ANZAC from 4 May, 1915, to the Evacuation of the Gallipoli Peninsula*, 11th ed. (Canberra: Australian War Memorial, 1941), 910.
[7] Hawke, "Speech by the Prime Minister: Dawn Service Gallipoli."

sovereignty" through their relationship to Australian military history, and established the practice of Australian leaders sanctifying foreign land as "Australian."[8] In 1996, Deputy Prime Minister Tim Fischer cemented this tradition of political commemoration in Việt Nam. The formalization of Anzac pilgrimage – itself a nostalgic creation – in Việt Nam is a demonstration of "restorative" nostalgia: it "characterizes national and nationalist revivals all over the world" by "engag[ing in the antimodern myth-making of history by means of a return to national symbols and myths."[9] For many Australian returnees, returning to Việt Nam became about locating a home for "their" war in national remembrance practices.

From the mid-2000s, commemorative battlefield tours and troops reunions rose in popularity as modes of return, with memorial services the "focal point" of the tour.[10] Where reconciliation returnees had been inspired by commemorations in their own countries, this last group of returnees returned to commemorate the war in Việt Nam itself. Australian veteran Wal explained that his platoon held reunions every year in different parts of Australia, and that in 2014 they decided to hold their reunion in Việt Nam.[11] Special Air Service Regiment (SASR) veteran Robin had thought about returning since 2007, when the SASR celebrated the 50th anniversary of formation. The SASR celebration revived old friendships and established regular troop reunions, leading to his troop returning in 2016 for a reunion service on Anzac Day. "We focused it on Anzac Day to give us a reason, rather than just visiting."[12] Australian Army veteran Rodney returned on a battlefield tour in 2016 for the 50th anniversary of Long Tan. He had a holiday planned in Thailand and thought, "it's not very far to come down, so we'll come down for the service ... it's fifty years." Rodney told me he had not thought much about returning before he decided to come to the anniversary, but that celebrating with other veterans – "meet[ing] up with other people and go[ing] to bars and beer drinking" – was a big part of why he wanted to come back.[13]

American interviewees did not demonstrate the same instinct to gather together for reunions and official commemorative services. While the United States has a strong tradition of overseas battlefield pilgrimage,

---

[8] Bart Ziino, "Who Owns Gallipoli? Australia's Gallipoli Anxieties 1915–2005." *Journal of Australian Studies* 88 (2006): 1–12; Martin Ball, "What the Anzac Revival means." *The Age*, April 24, 2004.
[9] Boym, *Future of Nostalgia*, 41.   [10] "A Place Called Long Tan with Meaning for All."
[11] Interview with Wal, Skype Interview, May 18, 2016.
[12] Interview with Robin, Melbourne, July 26, 2016.
[13] Interview with Rodney, Vũng Tàu, August 17, 2016.

the "sacred patriotic spaces" – the graveyards and battlegrounds that echo America's founding myths – reside on American soil.[14] The demographics of veterans recruited for this project also factor into this difference. The Australian returnees I interviewed were proud of their service in Vietnam, and the majority felt they were helping the local people. Their memories of warfare and sense of identity reflected the Anzac legend. In contrast, the Americans I interviewed felt that their actions in Vietnam hurt the local people, and most aligned with countercultural narratives in the United States. Among US returnees, the commemorative era had a different significance. Vietnam commemorations coincided with a cultural shift toward remilitarization, generated by the shifting political landscape post-9/11. Because many US returnees felt they had been recruited into Vietnam by national memories that glorified World War II, these veterans opposed war commemoration on principle and viewed the Vietnam commemorative resurgence as a recruiting tool for the US military. Rather than being drawn back through nostalgic remembrance practices, US veterans returned to Việt Nam in reaction to the so-called War on Terror.

When David E. left the Marines, he joined the Veterans of Foreign Wars (VFW), and by the early 1990s he was employed by the veterans' group. He became an alcoholic and the VFW facilitated his heavy drinking, insulating him socially and politically. At the time, he "could give a shit less about Việt Nam. We had two thousand [prisoners of war] POWs here, that they were keeping us from." He believed that "we should *never, ever* get normal relations with Việt Nam. Truly, that was my hardcore ... [he began to beat his fist against his chest]." David E. indicated that his political views were a manifestation of trauma and survivor's guilt. He could not bear the post-Cold War culture in which a "draft-dodger" was president and former enemies were suddenly friends. He remembered: "I wanted to die in the battlefield, that was an honorable death. I was getting ready to sell the farm, go to Chechnya, buy an AK47, fight the Russians." David E's politics softened as he stopped drinking, which removed him to some degree from the social world of the VFW. It was the Iraq War, however, that triggered his political revolution. "When Bushie boy went into Iraq, I had this terrible, terrible gut feeling. I was sick, I was physically sick the day we invaded Iraq. It affected me that much ... I just prayed .... It was the Bush presidency [that] definitely changed my political views. That's when I started doing a little research." David E. completely reversed his political views during the Bush

---

[14] See: Edward Tabor Linenthal, *Sacred Ground: Americans and Their Battlefields* (Chicago, IL: University of Illinois Press, 1993), 3.

presidency and began spending time with different kinds of veterans. "I heard about guys coming back, and it was always a positive, and I said, 'man, I'd really like to do that.'"[15] David E. returned in 2007.

US veterans linked their political triggers to the form of their return, which were largely peace- or healing-oriented. Many returned on organized, expatriate-chaperoned Veterans for Peace (VFP) tours. Anti-war expatriate veterans developed an "insiders 2-week tour" to "address the legacies of the American War" in 2012, and the linking of past war experience with political engagement and contemporary activism appealed to veterans who were retraumatized by America's newest wars.[16] Former Marine John K. first began to think about returning in the early 2000s, after a close friend died of an illness associated with Agent Orange. Then the United States invaded Iraq.

> [That] was very devastating for me ... the Vietnam War was only, it only seemed like it was fairly recent, and I was surprised that you know, we were gonna go and step in the same bucket again, and that there would be a lot of people that would die for no cause ... my thoughts were that if we should have learned one thing about Vietnam, it's that we don't go back and do something stupid again, and we did.

John K. began a personal crusade against the war. He became so immersed in his resistance that he almost lost his job, and his friendships began to break down. "I really didn't understand what I was going through ... I was denying that it was anything related to Vietnam, anything like that." John K. sought help from Veterans' Affairs (VA) and was diagnosed with post-traumatic stress disorder (PTSD). He retired from the corporate world and became heavily involved in the veteran community, joining conservative groups including the Vietnam Veterans of America (VVA) and Disabled American Veterans as well as the leftist VFP, which he found helpful because "it's a lot of likeminded individuals."[17] Increasing awareness of how Agent Orange was affecting veterans and associating with groups who had been involved in Việt Nam gradually encouraged him to return. John K. returned on a VFP tour in 2016.

Building on trends from the normalization era, increasing numbers of veterans were pressured into returning by other veterans, spouses, and friends. US Navy veteran Michael said that although he had worked with

---

[15] Interview with David E., Đà Nẵng, April 8, 2016.
[16] "Veterans for Peace Annual Spring Tour to Việt Nam 2017." *Veterans for Peace*, October 21, 2016. www.veteransforpeace.org/who-we-are/member-highlights/2016/10/21/veterans-peace-annual-spring-tour-viet-nam-2017
[17] Interview with John K., Skype Interview, August 2, 2016.

veterans, "I didn't realize how that worked. How this going back to the scene of the crime, so to speak, helped you to heal from it."[18] Michael was an alcoholic for many years until his children put him in a rehabilitation program at the age of sixty. His son was diagnosed with leukemia just as Michael was released from the program, and he attributed his son's diagnosis as the force behind his permanent sobriety. Two years later his son died, and Michael began attending a "healing circle" for veterans at his church. The healing circle had already returned to Việt Nam and members began encouraging Michael to join them on another trip. He was very reluctant to return. "I just don't want to go face it, because I'm pretty sure that they probably don't like Americans over there. I know if somebody had invaded my country, and killed a bunch of my neighbors and everything, I would not be welcoming them back for any reason. So, I know they're going to resent me and I don't want to face it." It took pressure from the healing circle, his wife, and a close wartime friend before he agreed to go back. Even then, he had to find a clear motivation within himself. Michael's trauma centered on one specific incident, so he made the decision to go back to the site of that event "to see if anything happens, because in a way that's where I lost my childhood. So, they asked me 'why are you going,' and I said, 'Well I just wanna see where I left my childhood behind, because when that was done, I was no longer a child.'"[19]

Stories of pressure by the veteran community show both the process and the effect of "particular publics," a term coined by Graham Dawson to describe the "shared, communal forms" of memory within small social groups.[20] The more significant the group to our personal identity, the more the values of the group influence our memories through recognition and rejection in retellings. Michael's healing circle had immense significance for him: it was a spiritual retreat, it was where he worked through the grief of his son's death, and it was full of people who were like him – veterans or their partners searching for healing. Michael's memory of coercion was filtered through cultural frameworks that he learned at the healing circle: identifying "stepping-stones," naming fears and anxieties, echoing earlier ideas about Vietnam as the locus of trauma by returning to "the scene of the crime."[21] His decision to bow to coercion and return to Việt Nam flowed from this frame, re-remembering war in such a way that made sense of returning. Thus, Michael's return story shows how memories that are composed among and validated by significant social groups can create new pathways and direct future actions.

---

[18] Interview with Michael, Đà Nẵng, April 15, 2016. [19] Interview with Michael.
[20] Dawson, *Soldier Heroes*, 24. [21] Interview with Michael.

3 Commemoration, 2006–2016

Among my interviewees, far fewer Americans than Australians expressed reluctance about returning. There are a number of possible factors for this difference, each indicating that it was simply easier for the friends and family of Australian veterans to persuade them to return that it was for the concerned loved-ones of American veterans. Many US returnees said that they tried to convince veteran friends to return and but were met with resistance. The long delay in establishing diplomatic relations between the United States and Việt Nam sustained a broader cultural hostility toward a political enemy within the United States. A trip to Việt Nam might be considered unusual and even dangerous in the United States, whereas holidaying in Southeast Asia is common among Australians. The Anzac Revival also embedded the concept of overseas battlefield pilgrimage in broader Australian culture. Finally, the affordability of travel between Australia and Việt Nam is a likely factor in the numbers of reluctant Australian returnees. Australian Army veteran John B. described planning to return several times at the behest of others and "pull[ing] the pin" at the last minute. Each time men from his platoon asked him to return, John B. would agree and then back out before the final arrangements were made, because "there was nothing happy for me in Vietnam when I was there." One friend who tried to convince him to return in the early 2000s was Brian, of the normalization group. Brian and John B. both served in the Battle of Balmoral, and Brian hoped that John B. would help him find the crater they had used for a mass grave to bury the Vietnamese missing in action (MIA). John's response was, "Brian, I couldn't give two fucks about it. We killed the bastards, and I really don't care." Finally, when his friend Paul organized another trip in 2007, John B. called Paul to cancel and was told that his son had already paid for the trip. "'So, you have to go' ... I got railroaded."[22] His son's trick, of forcing his hand by prepaying for his trip, would be a much costlier gamble in the United States.

Most Australians downplayed their reluctance. Army veteran Ray, for instance, was "sort of talked into going for the first time" by his daughter. "We were gonna do it together ... I wouldn't do it. And that upset me."[23] He implied that his shame over letting down his daughter motivated him to join his bowling club on their team holiday in Việt Nam. He returned for the first time in 2008, a year after he backed out of the trip with his daughter. Australian Army veteran Rod was similarly offhand: "a couple of my mates convinced me that it was very worthwhile coming back. I think we all left here originally saying we'd never come back to that

---

[22] Interview with John B., Skype, May 16, 2016.
[23] Interview with Ray, Melbourne, May 19, 2016.

shithouse, but we're all back."²⁴ This nonchalance reflected the broader machismo in Australian culture where stoicism is rewarded, and emotion and fear is considered weak. In contrast, US veterans were much more expressive: Michael's explanation for how he returned to Việt Nam covered his addiction, denial, personal tragedy, anxiety, and personal resolution. Most Americans I interviewed described their process for returning in similar detail. Only one Australian veteran expressed in similar emotional depth his reluctance to return. Andy told me that he had "no incentive or motivation to go back.... I would have probably just said no, except on this occasion I was pushed." He explained that growing up, he was very aware of the hatred his family felt toward the Japanese after the bombing of Darwin in 1942. He assumed that the Vietnamese would feel toward him the way his family felt toward the Japanese: "I imagined that they would have no reason to feel goodwill towards the people that invaded their country and interfered with their politics." When he shared his apprehension with his friend, she told him, "it's alright to go back," and "it just stuck with me."²⁵ Andy returned in 2008.

At the same time as these reluctant veterans were persuaded and pushed into returning, increasing numbers of veterans became curious about Việt Nam, encouraged by changes in technology and tourism. Images of Việt Nam from tourist agencies featured on travel websites, on television, in magazines, with images and videos of pristine beaches, national parks, traditional markets, lantern festivals – showing another side to Việt Nam. These marketing campaigns piqued a diasporic curiosity, leading veterans to wonder how "their" areas had changed. Australian SASR veteran Ken "wanted to see how much the place had changed, either for better or worse."²⁶ Fellow Australian Peter returned in 2013 "to have a look at what the area that I'd been to ... when the country had settled down, just to see, you know, how it had all turned out."²⁷ Australian Army veteran Bill A. returned in 2006 to "compare in my mind what Vũng Tàu was then and what Vũng Tàu is now, you know, just compare from then to now."²⁸ Bill A. and Peter explained that their wives were also curious about Việt Nam and wanted "a little bit of insight" into their wartime experiences.²⁹ Bill A. even indicated that it was his wife's idea to return: "she just wanted to have a look at the areas that we talked about. Nui Dat and Vũng Tàu and the Horseshoe, all these things that in conversation with other Vietnam veterans she had

---

[24] Interview with Rod, Vũng Tàu, August 19, 2016.
[25] Interview with Andy, Melbourne, June 13, 2016. [26] Interview with Ken.
[27] Interview with Peter, Melbourne, February 8, 2016.
[28] Interview with Bill A., Vũng Tàu, August 18, 2016. [29] Interview with Peter.

overheard. So, she said it would be nice to go back and to actually have a look."³⁰

The nonchalant curiosity of these Australian returnees contrasted sharply with the emotional expressions by Americans, mirroring the national differences between reluctant returnees. David A. was a US Army veteran who was drafted into the war. His wartime experiences "sickened" him: "I just hated the war." At the same time, he fell in love with Việt Nam. He told me: "I couldn't wait after the war was over to get back here and see the beautiful country, the beautiful people, the beautiful food, and as far as I'm concerned ... the most beautiful women in the world. I couldn't wait to get back." He read about the country, the war, the political climate, and concluded that the United States had committed "a genocide worse than Hitler" just because "they wanted to sell bullets." He became a "functional alcoholic": highly successful, but with a "dysfunctional life ... for thirty years, drinking and drugging." David A. had tried repeatedly to get clean but continued to struggle. He faced racial discriminated from employers and was denied treatment and shuttled around by the VA. Finally, he found a counselor who helped, diagnosing him with PTSD and attention deficit issues. "My questions are answered, why? I always wondered why I was a fuck up!"³¹ David A. finally began receiving medical care and compensation and gradually began to work with the veteran community, joining the VFP and returning on the 2016 tour.

Heiko, a US Air Force veteran, explained "it's always on my mind ... it was very significant in terms of my development as a human being. So, I always had that desire to go back." He also "had this longing to see what happened to some people over there," and decided to try to find his wartime girlfriend and translator.³² Commemorations between Australians, Americans, and revolutionary forces received international publicity, motivating veterans such as Heiko and Australian Army veteran Les to return to settle the "unfinished business" of seeing how his Republic of Việt Nam Armed Forces (RVNAF) friends were being treated by the Vietnamese government.³³ Given the radical changes Việt Nam had experienced over the decades – with millions uprooted by war, forced displacement, environmental desertification, and economic pressure and development – the odds of commemoration returnees finding their wartime friends seemed slim. However, the Internet provided new opportunities. US Air Force veteran Jim returned in 2012 to find his

---

³⁰ Interview with Bill A.
³¹ Interview with David A., Hồ Chí Minh City, March 29, 2016.
³² Interview with Heiko, Skype, May 10, 2016.
³³ Interview with Les, Skype, July 1, 2016.

wartime girlfriend, crediting his timing partly to his second divorce, and partly to technological changes.[34] Internet access and increased digital literacy helped veterans connect with each other, share anecdotes about returning, and research their options. Jim discovered "Father Founded," the website of Brian Hjort, a Danish man who took on the plight of Amerasian (Vietnamese fathered by American soldiers) children in the early 1990s with several success stories.[35]

A handful of commemoration veterans returned as Agent Orange advocates. SASR veteran Ric was invited to Hà Nội by the Socialist Republic of Việt Nam (SRV) to speak at a conference. Ric told me that Việt Nam wanted "'non-compliant veterans' ... non-compliant – they wanted veterans who'd tell the truth, and not follow the party line if you like, as far as the government goes."[36] Herbicidal warfare was controversial in the United States and Australia. Many veterans believed that their governments conspired to avoid recognizing the poisoning of soldiers and paying them compensation.[37] The SRV, however, recognized the effects of dioxin poisoning in the 1970s and sought to build networks and exchange information with veterans in Australia and the United States. American advocacy increasingly came in the form of VFP tours, which had broad themes of solidarity, and because these tours offered established networks to veterans interested in Agent Orange (such as John K.), targeted advocacy returns like those of Bobby Muller and Paul S. diminished. Among Australians, however, there were no tour groups focusing on Agent Orange, and as Australian veterans noticed diseases among their community rise, the issue of Agent Orange gained traction.[38] Ric, who described himself as "an opposition to the [Department for Veterans' Affairs] DVA," began researching for his presentation and realized that the chemical companies "knew that that stuff was deadly, even before they started ... all they were interested in was selling this crap to the government and making a heap of money." He became determined to "get the message out that yes, [Vietnamese] people deserved reparations" for the ongoing effects of Agent Orange.[39] Ric returned to Việt Nam in 2006. Other veterans were driven by personal experiences with

---

[34] Interview with Jim, Hồ Chí Minh City, March 23, 2016.
[35] Father Founded. http://fatherfounded.org/
[36] Interview with Ric, Telephone, August 5, 2016.
[37] For an exploration of transnational Agent Orange politics, see: Edwin A. Martini, *Agent Orange: History, Science, and the Politics of Uncertainty* (Amherst, MA: University of Massachusetts Press, 2012).
[38] See: Graham Walker, "The Official History's Agent Orange Account: The Veterans' Perspective." In *War Wounds: Medicine and the Trauma of Conflict*. Edited by Elizabeth Stewart (Wollombi: Exisle Publishing, 2011), 148–61.
[39] Interview with Ric.

3 Commemoration, 2006–2016

Agent Orange. Australian Army veteran Robert was motivated by his wife's multiple miscarriages and the deaths of his children. One of his daughters died shortly after being born. His adult son died in 2009. "They couldn't tell me what he died from. I'd had a lot of health problems. I knew a lot of other veterans that had a lot of health problems, their children had problems .... I was pretty angry, and I started asking questions ... I thought, now this is getting to me, I've got to go back."[40]

Like earlier returnees, those in the commemoration period explained that their returns hinged largely on opportune moments. However, where earlier returnees had seized opportunities offered by global shifts, these veterans focused on opportunities offered by their private lives. This period saw a dramatic rise in the number of veteran officers or "career soldiers" returning after retiring from the military. Other returnees finally began receiving compensation from the VA and DVA for health issues. Jim, for example, had heart issues in 2010 and was told by a doctor that his health problems were possibly caused by indirect exposure to dioxin and that he should claim for compensation. Jim had never considered being affected by Agent Orange and was gratified to be paid in arrears. "That's when I decided, I'm gonna go back, and this basically pays for my trip."[41]

As the average age of veterans rose, more and more chose to return on organized tours, indicating the convenience and variety offered by Việt Nam's growing tourism industry. Americans tended to return on nonprofit or "voluntourism" tours. Because these tours were often run by Vietnam veterans who either returned regularly or were expatriates in Việt Nam, they offered a sense of security to nervous returnees, mirroring the safety in numbers of the volunteer tours organized by the reconciliation group. Fredy Champagne's Veterans Viet Nam Restoration Project (VVRP) continued to "wage peace" until 2014, and a flyer for the 2009 tour caught the eye of US Army veteran Mark: "I thought it might be a pretty good way of me giving back to Việt Nam."[42] Veteran volunteering tours offered authenticity: US Army veteran Paul R. explained that the 2016 VFP tour was appealing because "it was totally not a trip to Waikiki."[43] Australian veterans, in contrast, favored commercial and battlefield tours, although again they tended to choose tours run by or tailored to Australian Vietnam veterans. Peter and Bill A. both returned on tours organized for and by Vietnam veterans. Peter liked that "we were roughly all on the same wavelength," and Bill A. told me that "it was just

---

[40] Interview with Robert, Melbourne, July 1, 2016. [41] Interview with Jim.
[42] Interview with Mark, Đà Nẵng, April 14, 2016.
[43] Interview with Paul R., Hồ Chí Minh City, March 28, 2016. Waikiki is a resort beach in Hawaii.

that the opportunity came up ... the people that was in the [tour] group were the people we know, in the Vietnam veterans' group."[44]

The prominence of organized veteran tours both reflected and reinforced the commemorative trend in this period. Veterans increasingly returned with an awareness of previous returnees' journeys. Early return itineraries became templates that shaped later returnees' journeys, and groups of veterans created rituals to commemorate their return which were then recreated and reinvented by subsequent groups. Commemorative returns were shaped by the dominance of the "healing journeys" in the normalization era. The healing narrative had popularized the idea of revisiting a personal combat space specifically for the purpose of traumatic release (rather than for remembrance, as in traditional battlefield pilgrimages). Because the SRV had increasingly relaxed its restrictions on tourists, more veterans were able to access their personal combat territories. John B. returned to his former combat zone at Long Điền and was pleased that "we could actually retrace our footsteps, 'cause there were landmarks, and we had a guide. So, we retraced our footsteps." Because the healing narrative emphasized that combat memories would be revisited upon return, commemoration veterans were prepared to some extent for their trauma symptoms to heighten. John B. described how at Long Điền "we could reflect, and we were, like, back there .... I said to Paul, 'how'd you sleep?' He said, 'I slept shithouse.' I said, 'me too, were you thinking about [the battle at] Long Điền?' He goes, 'yeah.'" The discourse of trauma that had emerged in the "normalization" period made it easier for veterans to discuss their PTSD symptoms with each other, as well as describing them to me. John B. explained that revisiting Long Điền was like when "you hear a song, and you're back there ... or you have a smell and you're back there again. We all have that."[45] However, the promise of catharsis could not insulate veterans entirely. Ray described how "they couldn't get me off the plane the first time I went there. Seriously, I wanted to stay on the plane and go back ... I got flashbacks. And I just sat in the seat, grabbed the seat, wouldn't get off."[46]

When I asked commemoration returnees about how returning affected their memories, they focused more on recovering or verifying memory than calling traumatic memory into doubt. Michael told me that he was tormented by the confused memory of one experience. Michael was a gunner in the Navy, based off Vũng Tàu in 1967. A spotter plane ordered a fire mission on two women working in the river. Michael thought they were digging clams, but the spotter plane thought they

[44] Interview with Peter; Interview with Bill A. [45] Interview with John B.
[46] Interview with Ray.

were planting mines: "So the gunnery officer gave the command to fire, and we blew them away. It happened this fast: 'commence fire,' I give the guys the signal and boom, boom. Maybe fifteen second and it was done with." These fifteen seconds haunted Michael ever since the war.

I suppressed those memories for a long time. Suppressed them to the point that thirty years after the fact, I couldn't even remember if I had been there. All my thoughts and dreams and daydreams of that time, I would have picture dreams as I was daydreaming, and I would remember that day, but I didn't know if it was, if I was making it up in my head or if it had actually happened. And I had those for many, many years. But I go through that, this horrible scene, you know, I thought, "I don't know if that happened, or if I'm making it up, or if I dreamed it or what," you know, I just couldn't work it out.

Michael could not literally retrace his footsteps by returning to his Navy posting, so he chose an alternative view. "In my imagination I was going to be able to get up on this mountain and look down on the river where we were when this horrible thing happened." This bird's eye view clarified his memory. "I killed a couple of innocent women," he told me.[47]

Michael's story demonstrates how veterans sometimes became fixated on traumatic memories. Where earlier anti-war returnees used the return to embrace the fluidity of memory and forgive themselves for the past, for commemoration returnees, lingering questions of responsibility in their memories of violence led some veterans to dwell instead in regret. Larry was a patrol leader of a Marine Recon platoon. He returned to Việt Nam in 2008 because he was haunted by memories of a woman who had died in labor on My Khe beach: "You don't escape, I couldn't escape the eyes of Việt Nam, or that woman. And, so, my wife told me I needed to go back here." Larry implied that he returned to let go of his traumatic memories. Yet after returning to Việt Nam, he became more aware of his wartime responsibilities, dwelling on how captured enemy were treated as POWs under his care. "One of my Marines that I'd sent down there guarding these guys said, 'Sir, they're torturing prisoners down there.' And, you know, you're in the middle of everything, you think, I can't let them go, they'll turn around and kill some of my people. I can't shoot them. I kept sending them back." Larry thought he would have lost his job had he confronted his superior. Still, "I wish I had done that."[48]

The increasing numbers of veterans returning to Việt Nam, growing expatriate communities, and the commercialization of the return led to

---

[47] Interview with Michael. Michael spoke about this event on the record to the *Plain Dealer*. Brian Albrecht, "Vietnam Surprises Vets Returning to Battleground." *Plain Dealer*, November 11, 2016. www.cleveland.com/metro/index.ssf/2016/11/vietnam_vets_return_to_old_bat.html
[48] Interview with Larry, Đà Nẵng, April 18, 2016.

concentrations of veterans in certain areas. David E. met another veteran visiting Đà Nẵng who "was talking about how the Da Nang [Air Base] ammo dump got mortared, got overran, blew up." The visitor's memory of the ammo dump explosion told a story of Vietnamese aggression, suggesting the United States was defeated by underhand, unfair methods of warfare. David E. was stationed at Da Nang Air Base in May 1969, and remembered the ammo dump explosion vividly: "it was the biggest mushroom cloud I've ever seen. The first thing I thought: 'oh shit, the mother fuckers dropped an atom bomb!' I swear to God, it looked like an atom bomb." However, David E. recalled the story in a different way to the visiting veteran: "some Marines were burning some trash, they caught some grass on fire, and *that's* what blew up the Da Nang ammo dump." David E.'s memory told a story where the Americans were responsible for their own defeat, illustrating how memories of minor incidents often tell a much broader story about the war. The visiting veteran's memory was his interpretation of the war, which contested David E.'s memory and interpretation. David E. told me that he checked in with Bill E. and Larry, both of whom live in Đà Nẵng, and they verified his version of events. "So, I just gained a little validity, 'cause I thought maybe I forgot some of this stuff, maybe this thinking isn't right."[49]

Growing numbers of veterans returning to Việt Nam changed how returnees were challenged by memories of the war. The reconciliation group found their memories contested by Vietnamese memory. The normalization group found their memories contested by Vietnamese and American or Australian memory. Because commemoration veterans mostly returned on tours and stayed in veteran-expatriate enclaves, many were so isolated from Vietnamese memory and so immersed in American or Australian war narratives that their memories were not contested at all. Instead, they performed restorative nostalgia by reconstructing their memories of the war. This reconstruction was particularly common among reunion tour returns. When I asked Robin if his memories had been affected by returning to Việt Nam, he told me: "it started about two months before we went to Việt Nam." A phone call from a platoon member reminded him to look through the patrol notes he had kept from the war. "A lot of things came out then. I sat down that night and wrote down a whole heap of things, and so far I've enjoyed doing it... it's inspired memories." This remembering continued upon return to Việt Nam, but the stories and memories were inspired by former platoon members, not by revisiting the landscape itself. The shift in returnees' memory focus mimics trends in diasporic migrant communities, where

---

[49] Interview with David E.

the diasporic consciousness in younger generations is not "oriented toward the homeland. Rather, it is a consciousness that takes the diaspora, not the homeland, as the point of reference."[50] Robin described how he and seven men from his platoon sat in a hotel room in Việt Nam discussing a patrol that had gone wrong, trying to combine their memories to understand why. When compared with the memory exploration of reconciliation veteran Terry Burstall, who sought out Vietnamese veterans from enemy battalions to understand their view of battles and strategies against the Australians, Robin's memory reconstruction illustrates how the space of Việt Nam was sometimes ignored by returning veterans. Robin told me that for him, and for his platoon, "being in Việt Nam was a bonus, as a backdrop. But what's important, it being a reunion, is the people."[51]

Perhaps the defining feature of commemoration veterans' memories was their rejection of the concept that memory changes over time. Memory recovery or verification was accepted, but memory change – the fluidity that had caused so much debate among the PTSD-aware normalization veterans – tended to be dismissed. Wal told me, "one thing I do have is a pretty good bloody memory."[52] Consider how Michael and David E. considered their verified memories of war as the correct version of events, or "the absolute truth."[53] Commemoration veterans also tended to provide evidence for the veracity of their memories. Australian Army veteran Dave, for example, explained: "I had a very clear idea of what I was doing, and what I done, partly because I was an officer ... I had the map, and the radio, I was pretty certain where we were going. I had a bigger overall picture than the average digger .... Việt Nam, the present day, simply confirmed my own convictions of what had happened."[54] This use of proof mirrored how normalization veteran Derek pointed to his diaries to prove that his memories had not changed. Because I asked the veterans open-ended questions about memory, the tendency to use evidence in their answers indicated that the returnees were responding to broader cultural contestation of memory. Bill A. told me, "Long Tan never goes away. Long Tan will be with me until the day that I die. There's always something that will trigger a memory .... Imagine if you were in a plane, and it crashed, and a third of the passengers were killed and you survived, you walked away from that plane crash.

---

[50] Ji-Yeon Yuh, "Moved by War: Migration, Diaspora, and the Korean War." *Journal of Asian American Studies* 8:3 (October 2005), 287.
[51] Interview with Robin.   [52] Interview with Wal.   [53] Boym, *Future of Nostalgia*, xviii.
[54] Interview with Dave, Melbourne, June 27, 2016.

I mean you would never forget that, that's with you until the day that you die. Well, so is Long Tan."[55]

Because most commemoration veterans believed strongly in the accuracy of their memories, witnessing change in Việt Nam and acquiring new memories was not described in the same "library of images" way as earlier returnees. The few returnees who did describe changes to memory offered specific anecdotes, rather than discussing a broader phenomenon of memory. For example, Bill A. showed me some photographs of an orphanage he had visited in Vũng Tàu. "That little fellow there, he's the spitting image of my five-year-old great grandson back in Australia. I mean look at the kids! That was absolutely beautiful. These are the memories that I'll now be taking back to Australia, not any awful memories about the war or anything like that."[56] Similarly, David A. said that the only memory change was "just how I remember it. The craters, the cities, destroyed. Now looking at it – Look out that window!" He gestured at the cityscape view of Hồ Chí Minh City from inside his skyscraper hotel: "This is what I was hoping for. You know, this is what I been dreaming about."[57]

Despite the influence of the healing narrative, commemoration veterans did not widely report reductions in trauma symptoms. In fact, only one veteran cited a reduction in specific traumatic symptoms. Rod had suffered from recurring nightmares about vulnerability and helplessness since the end of the war and reported that his nightmares had stopped since he returned to Việt Nam.[58] Yet most commemoration returnees emphasized that trauma was chronic, possibly in reaction to the promises of normalization veterans that returning to Việt Nam would "cure" them. David E. recalled how, one day walking with his family in the Vietnamese countryside, "all of a sudden I see this one bamboo in a way that was just there, I just couldn't go on no more. It was that spot. It was that scene." David E. gave me several other examples of how his trauma continues to manifest.[59] His interest in this subject reflects the culture of veteran groups in Việt Nam and the heated debates they often had about the war, about trauma and its causes, and whether it was curable or chronic. David E. was hosting Mark at the time of our interview, and Mark told me he cured himself from PTSD.[60] David E.'s emphasis on flashbacks may have been a response to Mark's insistence that PTSD was curable.

In place of the focus of curing trauma, commemoration returnees – particularly Australians – used metaphors to imply release, catharsis, and

---

[55] Interview with Bill A. [56] Ibid. [57] Interview with David A.
[58] Interview with Rod. [59] Interview with David E.
[60] Interview with Mark. His story about curing trauma was not related to returning to Việt Nam.

resolution. Rod said, for instance, that returning had "taken away all the demons of the past."[61] In Australian narratives, metaphors of "ghosts" and "demons" were repeated with unusual frequency. This feature was established by reconciliation returnees: Graham E. decided to "go back and chase down a few ghosts" and Kevin, a New Zealander who served in the Australian Army, returned to "lay the ghosts, you might say."[62] Normalization returnees picked up on this language – John W. frequently used the "ghost" metaphor – and media coverage of returns during the normalization period used the same language.[63] Mark Baker's 2001 *Good Weekend* article noted: "now thousands of Australian ex-servicemen are being drawn back to Vietnam – to revisit their youth, do a little business, exorcise their demons" and described Việt Nam as "a place to exorcise the ghosts of a war."[64] By the time of the commemoration returns, "ghosts" and "demons" had become the standard form of expression for trauma among Australian veterans. Robin used the term "demons" to explain patterns of postwar alienation that he had seen in generations of returned servicemen.[65] Ray and Ken both used variations on theme to explain why they returned: "the prime reason was to lay some demons to rest"; "I guess I had a ghost to kill."[66]

Traumatized people often use metaphors to build coherent narratives of their experiences. Because trauma can be "unspeakable," metaphors offer "psychological scaffolding" that provide meaning to the survivor and allow them to make sense of their experience.[67] Given the uniformity of the specific terms "ghosts" and "demons" among Australian narratives, it is possible that these were recommended or offered metaphors by veterans' counseling services in Australia, reflecting the 1990's popularity of trauma theory in which combat was conceptualized as hell and/or the Underworld. Spectral metaphor suggests a blurring of past and present and implies perpetual preoccupation and unresolved issues: "battling inner demons" meaning grappling with conscience; "haunting" evoking the arrested state of traumatic memory. The abstraction of emotional pain into supernatural metaphor also facilitates discussions among veterans who feel vulnerable, mythologizing trauma without feminizing it. This masculine function of ghostly metaphor was particularly apparent when contrasted with the psychologically specific and emotionally deliberate language used by many US veterans to describe trauma. Other common themes in Australian narratives were the forceful defenses of

---

[61] Interview with Rod. [62] Interview with Rod. [63] Interview with John A.
[64] Baker, "Going Back," 20. [65] Interview with Robin.
[66] Interview with Ray; Interview with Ken.
[67] John P. Wilson and Jacob D. Lindy, *Trauma, Culture, and Metaphor: Pathways of Transformation and Integration* (New York: Routledge, 2013), 35.

Australia's conduct in Vietnam, pride in their service, and the unfair vilification of veterans by the anti-war movement. Working from the basis that civilians do not – cannot – understand the depths of violence in warfare, it is logical that Australian veterans would not want to discuss explicitly the experiences that they found traumatizing. To do so would call into question the honor of the ATF and undermine their service. The use of "ghosts" and "demons" by the small handful of US veterans who also feel proud of and unfairly vilified for their service supports this.

Australian veterans' use of "ghost" and "demon" metaphors suggested that they, like the Americans, found some resolution or internal peace by returning to Việt Nam. Les told me that it "is was good for me to go back, and I guess kinda faced my demons."[68] John B. described putting "demons, I suppose, to rest."[69] Ken said that "lay[ing] some demons to rest" was a goal for his return: when I asked if he had succeeded, he answered "yes. Well, I put them to sleep. They wake up every now and again, yeah."[70] Where Australians draw on supernatural metaphors, commemoration Americans employed Vietnamese philosophies, memories, and maxims. However, because very few veterans actually spoke Vietnamese, this often resulted in mangled appropriation. Mark told me: "I'm at peace. What they call boa dinh, peace."[71] What "they" call peace is in fact "*hòa bình*" not "boa dinh" and "boa dinh" has no meaning in Vietnamese. Nonetheless, Vietnamese philosophy and memory helped veterans find closure. David E. explained that "the Vietnam War haunted me every day and every night in America. And today, when I'm in Việt Nam, the American War was over forty years ago. So, I just feel very peaceful."[72]

Once they returned, commemoration veterans formed intense attachments to place in Việt Nam. David E. remembered how, when he first saw the land of his former base in Đà Nẵng and climbed Marble Mountain, he almost said to his friend, "I can't leave. I'm gonna have to stay here, you're gonna have to go on without [me]."[73] Perhaps because they had returned so recently, these veterans were hyperaware of how different they felt in Việt Nam. John B. told me, "I just find a bit of solace in going back there. It's just really strange, I feel comfortable."[74] Ray found that this comfort was established on his second trip back in 2010, when he visited places that were relevant to his war experience. "That was a bit of healing. Yes, it took a long time, but the healing process is there ... [a] bit of closure. For a start, I now know that I can [return]."[75]

---

[68] Interview with Les.   [69] Interview with John B.   [70] Interview with Ken.
[71] Interview with Mark.   [72] Interview with David E.   [73] Ibid.
[74] Interview with John B.   [75] Interview with Ray.

Australian veterans focused in particular on communing in Vietnamese spaces with other Australians, indicating that civilian recognition of their connection to Vietnamese spaces was important to them. When Peter returned to his base at Nui Dat, he encountered an Australian man and his daughter there. "He said, 'my father got killed on this hill.'" Peter showed them where his father would have been, helping them imagine the base camp and describing his father's experience there. Building an emotional connection with someone who was not a veteran, but who shared an attachment to the land, was cathartic for him. "That got a lot of emotion out from me.... That kind of opened [me] up a little bit and let a little bit out."[76] Returnees' interactions with other Australians suggests that civilian recognition in Việt Nam validated the integration of Vietnam into the Anzac pilgrimage tradition. Andy explained that he "used to blot it out and ignore it. Just not think about it. I might even have got away with that when I came back," he added, except for a surprise organized for him by a civilian on his tour. She "had organized for the Long Tân memorial to be opened to us, so we were in this van driving around, she said, 'let's get out and walk' ... we stood around, and she gave me a little card to read. And boy. That was cathartic. So that just poured out the emotion for me. That was a relief. The relief of forty years."[77] This veteran had not fought in the battle, but nonetheless felt a deep attachment to Long Tân, illustrating the growing significance of the memorial not only to all Vietnam veterans, but to civilian Australians, as it came to represent the Anzac identity.

For Australian and American commemoration returnees the meaning of "Việt Nam" changed, corresponding with a shift in attitude. Ken told me that the whole experience was "brilliant, absolutely. It's very difficult to describe the feelings ... I came back happy. Happier."[78] These changes were particularly apparent among expatriate veterans. Rod, who moved to Vũng Tàu, told me, "I'm a more relaxed person now. I'm happy with the way I'm living here, and I just have more respect and love for the Vietnamese people ... we never really got too many chances to really communicate with the Vietnamese in those days."[79] David E. reflected that "my attitude has changed greatly since I've been here.... When we're here it's the American War, it looks a lot different. It feels a lot different."[80] American commemoration veterans focused in particular on the relationship between returning, atonement, and healing. David A. explained that he felt "real bad, participating in the genocide ... I feel a lot better now." He described the return as "therapeutic as hell. I'm in

---

[76] Interview with Peter.   [77] Interview with Andy.   [78] Interview with Ken.
[79] Interview with Rod.   [80] Interview with David E.

heaven.... It's provided the therapy for me that I needed."[81] Similarly, Paul R. explained that "I always felt like it was just stuck... and of course I was devastated that I had participated in that just be being there. And there were things, you know, having to do with the way I behaved as a man." US veterans put a strong emphasis on returning as more self-aware people. Paul R. had earlier alluded to engaging with sex workers during his wartime tour, as "a young guy, who wasn't even aware of the notion of a moral compass, just sort of doing the things that young guys do in those situations." He explained "It was nice to come back as a feminist," Paul R. told me; "it's a way of completing the circle."[82]

Like earlier returnees, many commemoration veterans volunteered in or supported Vietnamese communities after returning. They donated to fundraising agencies, joined other veterans' projects, volunteered with nongovernmental organizations (NGOs) based in Việt Nam, and initiated their own projects. In a new trend, returnees acted as envoys between overseas Vietnamese and their families in Việt Nam. Some, such as Ray, focused on those exiled from the war. He worked closely with the local Vietnamese community in Frankston, most of whom were refugees. "So, we sort of take messages from these people, 'cause they obviously can't or don't want to go back."[83] Others worked with younger Vietnamese. Ric took gifts from Vietnamese students to their parents in Việt Nam and liked to think of himself as a connection between them. He explained that if he could help a Vietnamese family, "it makes them feel better, it just makes me feel better ... it makes you feel good."[84] Both Australians and Americans focused on how it helped them to help Việt Nam – a continuation of the "healing-through-helping" story. John K., who fundraised for the VFP, valued "the feeling that I'd made, or I have made and will make more of a difference for them."[85] Several explained that, like earlier returnees, they needed to forgive themselves. Robert told me, "it was not who I was. The person inside of me didn't want to go and shoot anybody. The person inside of me didn't want to be abusive to my wife and to my children. I didn't want these feelings of guilt, for my infractions when I was away." By returning, he recognized that the war did not define him: "it's what you say to yourself, and you've gotta be happy with who you are."[86]

However, for the commemoration returnees, the process of forgiveness was more complicated than for the reconciliation or normalization returnees. The healing narrative had established forgiveness as a common theme in veterans' return stories, but some veterans were not

[81] Interview with David A. [82] Interview with Paul R. [83] Interview with Ray.
[84] Interview with Ric. [85] Interview with John K. [86] Interview with Robert.

ready to be forgiven – or to forgive. Ken told me that he does not "believe in atoning for the sins of the past, because things are done at a particular time according to society's beliefs at the time."[87] Even more forthright was Dave, who told me, "I didn't have a monkey on my back, I wasn't under any apprehension as to whether we were helping the locals or not helping the locals, there's no question, I was quite happy with what had been done [in the war]."[88] Other returnees had lived so long with their grief and sorrow that accepting the forgiveness offered to them was impossible. Three veterans told me three different stories, demonstrating the various ways that returnees reacted to forgiveness in Việt Nam.

When Michael first returned to Việt Nam, he stayed in a homestay on the Mekong Delta run by a Vietnamese couple, both of whom had fought in the National Liberation Front (NLF). The husband had been shot by American soldiers, the wife captured and beaten. They showed Michael their scars and told him their war stories. Michael asked the husband if he was still angry. The wife translated for him: "'he turned that page of that chapter of his life a long time ago. And he doesn't see any need to go back and read it again … we let the wounds heal, and you Americans seem to keep picking your scabs' …. I thought, wow. That's good thinking." Although the couple suggested Michael forgive himself, he continued to be tormented by Vietnam, still picking at his scabs and trying to pay his "moral rent." He viewed volunteer work and NGO support as a "civic obligation" because the United States never gave reparations for the war, but also described his work as "penance." Michael told me that he carried a lot of guilt, and he did not know that God could forgive him. He seemed caught in a loop of cyclic atonement, and it was evident that for him, no amount of work would ever pay his "moral debt."[89]

The second story followed in the tradition of reconciliation and normalization veterans, of forgiveness and mutual recognition between soldiers. David E. described his experience of forgiveness in Việt Nam as a reciprocal act. "What's humbling is, you know, when these people find out that you were here in the war, you come back? … They really treat you like a comrade-in-arms." David E. described an incident where he returned to Marble Mountain, and a woman his age approached him. "She looked me right in the eye, she said: 'you Marine?' I said, 'Yes, I was a Marine.' She said, 'Well, I'm [Viet Cong] VC, I'm sorry for killing Marines.' And I said, 'Well, I'm sorry for killing VC.'" David E. went to dinner with her, and "the whole village showed up. And I was the guest of

[87] Interview with Ken. [88] Interview with Dave. [89] Interview with Michael.

honor. Because I was stationed there at Marble Mountain. It was like some lost comrade had come home."[90]

Lastly, some veterans focused on forgiving the Vietnamese. Ric told me "what stung a little bit" when he returned was the attitude of the revolutionary forces. "They said, 'when we won,' and when we this, and when we that." Ric, like most Australian returnees, believed that "we didn't lose, the pollies [politicians] lost it for us." He was irritated by what he felt was boasting. He decided to "get over it" by laying poppies on the graves of the People's Army Việt Nam (PAVN) uncle of a friend. His friend was astonished, "'you were fighting, and now you're doing this, for them.' And I said, 'Well that's it, he was a soldier, I was a soldier. And that's what it's about, you know'?"[91] The final forgiveness story shows how veterans who contest Vietnamese notions of victory – and the numbers of those veterans were increasing, particularly among the Australians – were able to "forgive" the Vietnamese for disrespecting their memory of the war.

Despite almost every commemoration returnee knowing other veterans who had returned before them, they were still surprised at the warmth of the Vietnamese toward them. Ric was nervous about talking to revolutionary veterans at the Agent Orange conference he was attending. "I didn't know what to say, I mean, the whole security thing, and you're thinking, 'oh shit, you know, loose lips sink ships.'" Only once they begun talking together did Ric realize, "they're not your enemy anymore … these guys are the same as our guys … it was quite an eye-opener for me."[92] Robin had a similar reaction on his second visit in 2016. He and another veteran met with NLF veterans together and had tea together. They initially felt "a little bit as though we were walking on eggshells," worried that they would say the wrong thing, but "we spent about four hours together, talking about experiences in the war …. It was very relaxed."[93]

Stories about Vietnamese forgiveness from the normalization period indicate that the Vietnamese had become accustomed to returning and repentant veterans and had developed scripts for reconciliation meetings. Commemoration stories reinforce this theme. John K. said that "one of the most enlightening things that I found was the fact that the Vietnamese didn't hold any grudges." John K. returned on a VFP tour, and the in-country VFP veterans who acted as the tour hosts (among them: Suel, Mike C., Don, and Chuck) had established friendships with Vietnamese veterans. When John K. entered a room of Vietnamese soldiers on the VFP tour, it is

---

[90] Interview with David E. [91] Interview with Ric. [92] Ibid. [93] Interview with Robin.

3 Commemoration, 2006–2016

very likely that those Vietnamese soldiers had participated in many similar reconciliation meetings. John K. told me that one man approached him after their meeting:

he says, "you, Marine. You, I remember your face. I'll never forget your face." And I kinda looked at him, he had his buddy standing behind him, and I kinda smiled at him, and I said, "well, I never forgot yours either." And so then he came over, he had one of his arms shot off, and he put one of his arms around me and I put my arms around him, and he said, "we're comrades, we're friends, we need to get along, the war is over." And for me that was very, very powerful.[94]

The frequency of this kind of story in the narratives of returning veterans – where the Vietnamese veteran initiates aggressively but then goes on to embrace the returning veteran – suggests that the Vietnamese soldiers involved in reconciliation meetings had developed repertoires to carry the emotional labor through these events, perhaps also indicating that these meetings were somewhat routine.

Unlike the normalization veterans, all three commemoration veterans who returned in search of wartime friends were at least partially successful. Les tracked down some of the people he had worked with in the war. Heiko could not find his wartime girlfriend, but when he tried to find his translator Hùng, "I found somebody that thought they knew where Mr. Hùng was." He set off on a hunt through the outskirts of Nha Trang: directed to a church, where the priest wrote him a note and summoned a man on a bicycle. Heiko sat on the back of the bicycle as the man rode through the jungle for a few miles. "And we came to this most beautiful setting in the jungle, something out of a movie, it was that gorgeous … and there were all these young nuns." Heiko's cyclist took the note, went into the nunnery, and brought out a woman, who told Heiko that Hùng was in California. Heiko connected with him when he returned from Việt Nam.[95] Last of all, Jim found his wartime girlfriend, Hạnh, in September 2015, three years after his search began. "[I] actually never really thought I'd find her. How could …. And what happened in '75, how could I even think that she might be around?" Hạnh had joined the RVNAF after Jim left her and was sent to a reeducation camp for two years after the war. She had remarried and had children, after giving her first daughter to an orphanage. Jim had not believed nineteen-year-old Hạnh when she said she was pregnant. She did not know where their child was. After their reunion, Hạnh and Jim began searching together for their daughter.[96]

---

[94] Interview with John K.   [95] Interview with Heiko.   [96] Interview with Jim.

For some veterans, their return to Việt Nam was the first of many. They built friendships, explored more of the country, and developed new travel interests. Many veterans continue to return because of close friendships they have built, and to explore more of the country. Robert made a friend in Hội An he liked to visit regularly. Andy returned again because he particularly liked Hội An and wanted to go back.[97] Ric returned as often as he could, to see somewhere new and catch up with people he met before. "I just go for, I dunno, I just go," he said, "I sort of fell in love with the place again. I wasn't in love with it at first ... you know, the first time."[98] John B. concurred, "I really can't explain it, I just fell in love with the place."[99] They emphasized how beautiful and interesting they found Việt Nam. John K. told me that returning "gave me a more of an appreciation for their culture, their way of life."[100] Les said that because he could not "smell the roses when we were there before, so it was nice to actually do a bit of touring around, see some of the beautiful country."[101] Wal summarized that visiting Việt Nam was "just a bloody good holiday."[102]

For a growing number of returnees, Việt Nam became home. Rod, Larry, and David E. built lives in Việt Nam. Rod told me, "people say to me, 'I seen you walking up the street, what were you smiling about?' And it's just the kids, the old ladies that say hello, they give you a greeting a smile, a little high five for the kids and that. Yeah, I love all that. That's the good part of it."[103] These veterans became part of larger expatriate groups with strong community ties. Larry explained that he had a relationship "not just with the Vietnamese but the Americans and the others who are here that is unique. Because you are a relatively small group, and in a different culture, different language, so it's a little bit tighter group."[104] They built relationships and families. David E. described seeing his wife, Ushi, for the first time: "she's got this humungous smile. And she's eating watermelon seeds .... We started dancing in the street there, and I don't know, we just kinda been dancing in the street ever since." Expatriate veterans emphasized that Việt Nam offered them much more than just resolution from the war. As David E. said:

Let's face it, let's really face it, please don't paint no grim picture. When I'm riding down this road, looking at this palm tree and the Lady Buddha, I'm on my motorbike, I gotta pinch myself! .... I'm very grateful that I have ended up here.

---

[97] Interview with Andy.   [98] Interview with Ric.   [99] Interview with Robert.
[100] Interview with John K.   [101] Interview with Les.   [102] Interview with Wal.
[103] Interview with Rod.   [104] Interview with Larry.

Cause if I hadn't stopped drinking, I'm sure right now I'd be in the VFW, drinking, telling some damn sob story about Vietnam. But instead, I'm here in paradise, I've got a very beautiful wife. She's got four beautiful children, we've got six beautiful grandchildren, and I just . . . I feel very fortunate. In 1968 I came here to die for my country. In 2013 I just come here to die.[105]

---

[105] Interview with David E. A giant statue of Lady Buddha on Sơn Trà mountain overlooks the bay of My Khe beach in Đà Nẵng.

Part II

Việt Nam

4   Relics and Remnants

Returning veterans often engaged in battlefield pilgrimage as a way to reflect on the past, encountering or visiting war remnants in the form of battle locations or military bases. Their descriptions of these encounters reveal how survivors of war conceptualize space and invest it with emotion and memory. However, for the Vietnamese, the remnants of war were not limited to battlefields and military architecture. I take a broad view of "relics and remnants," considering alongside military battlefields and bases the ecological, social, and individual effects of war on those who lived through it and those born in its aftermath. These more subtle remnants were obvious to some returnees, but to others, they were invisible. Exploring veterans' reactions to the presence or absence of war remnants in these forms illuminates further remnants of war: the biases and other lingering effects of wartime ideologies of the Australians and Americans who returned.

This chapter is based around several questions that I asked in interviews and applied to memoirs and articles. Because many veterans returned to revisit specific places, I asked veterans what it was like to see their old bases or battlefields again. I also asked two more general questions: "what did the war do to Việt Nam?" and "how has Việt Nam changed since the war?" These questions were intentionally ambiguous so as not to lead the interviewee. Despite their open-endedness, it was striking how often specific focuses emerged, while other issues were notably absent from veterans' discussions. For example, most returnees described how infrastructure had changed in Việt Nam over the years, remarking on roads and buildings, but very few responded to these questions by discussing the effects of war on people. To raise the human dimension of war legacies, I began to add follow-up questions: "how do you think the war affected the Vietnamese?" or "how do you think the war impacted their way of life?" When returnees spoke at length about post-traumatic stress disorder (PTSD) among Western veterans but did not mention trauma in Việt Nam, I asked them whether they thought the war had affected the Vietnamese psychologically as well. The interview data that this chapter draws on are therefore subjective: all the interviews followed a semi-structured method, and later interviewees were asked more questions than those I interviewed earlier in the fieldwork process. The specific content of this chapter also reflects a subjective perspective on war remnants in Việt Nam: discussing war remnants that the veterans themselves described as significant (such as bases and battlefields) alongside the issues that continue to be a major concern to the Vietnamese people and government: psychological impact, social effects, and war-related sickness, injury, and death.

When reconciliation veterans returned to Việt Nam, the country was littered with physical war remnants. Some battle areas were still strewn with shell casings, bullets, and armor. US veterans David Roberts and Edward Marcin returned on psychologist Ray Scurfield's 1989 PTSD tour and visited Hải Vân Pass, a mountain range road connecting Huế and Đà Nẵng. At the top of the pass lie the ruins of a French-built fort later used by the US military and Republic of Việt Nam Armed Forces (RVNAF). Roberts and Marcin wandered the ruins, picking up dead ammunition, and wept and laughed together. They held an old helmet and traded healing aphorisms: "we need to put the war and the memories of it in the same place as this helmet is . . . gone," "that's not reality today." As they examined M16 shells, Marcin mused they were "all used up, like the war is," and Roberts clutched him, laughed, and said "and it can't do any harm, it can't do any harm any longer . . . it's gone!"[1] Recognizing the powerlessness of weaponry and armor offered the men a profound moment of catharsis. Other reconciliation veterans noted how war remnants had been turned into scrap metal or repurposed in their existing form by the Vietnamese. US Army veteran Larry Rottmann wrote that when he looked carefully, he could see "US military hardware which has been turned to peacetime usage: defused bombs made into flower pots, GI steel helmets used as buckets, jet wing tanks turned into bathtubs and boats, and aircraft aluminum cut into roofing material, cooking utensils, and even a merry-go-round."[2] The ingenuity and resourcefulness of these adaptations and the symbolic peace of the neutralized weaponry brought these veterans hope for Việt Nam's future.

As military hardware became scarcer and more veterans returned, repurposed remnants and relics became tourist souvenirs. Particularly

---

[1] David Roberts and Ed Marcin, quoted in *Vietnam: Two Decades and a Wake Up*.
[2] Rottmann, "A Hundred Happy Sparrows," 137.

popular were bullet shell pendants, Zippo lighters, combat jackets, military patches, and dog tags. Because a steady market for war memorabilia was only established in the late 1990s, by which time most war remnants had been recycled or repurposed, the overwhelming majority of these items were replicas. Anthropologist Christina Schwenkel describes these relics and replicas as "souvenirs of death," "embodying memory and sacredness" through "alleged connection[s] to a tragic past" that becomes "an object of fetishized tourist desire."[3] The replica dog tags caused outrage among tourists and among veteran communities in the United States due to the emotional resonance of the prisoner of war/missing in action (POW/MIA) issue.[4] However, no returning veterans seemed troubled by this commodification of their wartime presence. They either realized the items were replicas or were aware of how often tags were lost and replaced in the war.

Returnees were generally far more interested in collecting kitsch memorabilia of Vietnamese war experiences. Particularly popular were "Viet Cong" helmets, propaganda posters, and commemorative Hồ Chí Minh plates. These kitsch artifacts reflect a broader, deliberately ambiguous nostalgic war memory promoted by the Vietnamese tourism industry to attract foreign tourists.[5] They are marketed as mementos of Vietnamese culture, rather than as markers of wartime hostility, sold alongside conical hats, bamboo instruments, and Hội An silks. Tourism scholars Richard Sharpley and Philip R. Stone argue that kitsch reproductions are a way of comfortably interpreting tragedy and the macabre by sanitizing violent memory.[6] Flimsy, mass-produced "Viet Cong" helmets are sold in stacks outside shops, while depictions of the revolutionary leader are flattened and almost saintlike: Uncle Ho plates are lined up alongside miniatures of Lady Buddha. Propaganda posters show "long-haired warriors" in idyllic Vietnamese landscapes, but the context of the original posters – created

---

[3] Christina Schwenkel, "Recombinant History: Transnational Practices of Memory and Knowledge Production in Contemporary Vietnam." *Cultural Anthropology* 21:1 (February 2006): 10.
[4] "Vietnam-Era Unaccounted for Statistical Report." Vietnam-Era Prisoner of War/Missing-in-Action Database, POW/MIA Databases & Documents, Library of Congress. http://lcweb2.loc.gov/frd/pow/Nov0701.html, 2; Colleen Mastony and Tet Gregory, "Real or Fake, Vietnam Dog Tags Stir Up Emotions." *Chicago Tribune*, October 30, 2002.
[5] Laurel B. Kennedy and Mary Rose Williams, "The Past Without Pain: The Manufacture of Nostalgia in Vietnam's Tourism Industry." In *Country of Memory: Remaking the Past in Late Socialist Vietnam*. Edited by Hue-Tam Ho Tai (Berkeley, CA: University of California, 2001), 151.
[6] Richard Sharpley and Philip R. Stone, "(Re)presenting the Macabre: Interpretation, Kitschification and Authenticity." In *The Darker Side of Travel: The Theory and Practice of Dark Tourism*. Edited by Richard Sharpley and Philip R. Stone (Bristol: Channel View, 2009), 109–28.

among guerrilla units in the midst of war – is lost in the souvenir reproductions.[7] Their messages of hope, glorious victory, peace, and independence, roughly translated on the back of the posters in Biro, appear quaint. Many returnees were consumers of this communist nostalgia. Some purchased kitsch souvenirs ironically, wearing their "Viet Cong" helmet to a local bar or sewing a red star patch onto their bags next to the Australian or American flag. Others, including many anti-war returnees, purchased kitsch memorabilia to signal their allegiance, proudly displaying propaganda posters in their residences alongside other cultural artifacts.

While returnees responded to small arms, hardware, and kitsch reproductions with optimism and positivity, large-scale remnants such as military bases were more controversial. Veterans' responses reflected their individual views on the war, on reconciliation with the Vietnamese, and their attitude toward the Socialist Republic of Việt Nam (SRV). For instance, reconciliation returnees John Z., Graham E., and Paul Murphy all returned within two years of each other and visited southern provinces. John Z. said that in 1988, "there were very few signs of the war." He visited Long Bình military base in Đồng Nai, once one of the largest military bases in the world, and found "there was nothing there ... you could see the asphalt of the perimeter ring, but the only other thing was the eucalyptus trees. Nothing else."[8] Graham E. described how at Hồ Chí Minh City's Tân Sơn Nhất Airport in 1990, "we could still see the remnants of the war, the old buildings, the bays that were built for protection of planes and helicopters, bunkers, things like that."[9] Murphy returned to Suối Nghệ in Bà Rịa-Vũng Tàu, a refugee camp for forcibly resettled civilians where he had engaged in an operation that "to this day shames me to sleeplessness." He was "totally mentally shattered to find that Sui Nghi [sic] remains a blot on the landscape": isolated, dilapidated, and poor. "I could not come to terms with the fact that nothing had changed for the better in the intervening years," he wrote.[10] While these veterans all observed the disrepair of wartime structures – bases, airstrips, camps – in neighboring areas (the provinces of Hồ Chí Minh City, Bà Rịa-Vũng Tàu, and Đồng Nai border one another), their interpretations of disrepair indicated differing perspectives on the Vietnamese recovery from the war. John Z. saw the overgrowth at Long Bình as a symbol of progress and reconciliation: "for them, the war was over. It was past, and

---

[7] Sandra C. Taylor, "Long-Haired Women, Short-Haired Spies: Gender, Espionage, and America's War in Vietnam." *Intelligence and National Security* 13:2 (1998): 61–70.
[8] Interview with John Z.   [9] Interview with Graham E.
[10] Paul Murphy, *The Quiet Australians: Saints and Sinners* (Self-Published: Book Pal, 2011), 195, 198.

they were trying to get on, and they moved on."[11] Graham E. disagreed, interpreting the remains as evidence of Việt Nam's struggle to recover: "nothing much had changed except that they weren't fighting."[12] Murphy viewed the military structures as evidence of the SRV's poor governance, writing that "with the fall of the south in 1975, Vietnam closed her doors to the west and the west in turn placed a total trade embargo on Vietnam. Hence she sat isolated, slowly decaying from within."[13]

Among later returnees, perceptions of military structures were even more varied, as different places were maintained, modified, or demolished. For the most part, there was less war architecture to see as Việt Nam increasingly built over old battlefields and bases. As many veterans returned to visit "their" areas, it was difficult to find them unfamiliar or even unrecognizable. Veterans reacted with the "oscillating sense of belonging" that characterizes diasporic returns, a pattern "that returnees adopt to (re)assess and/or (re)define their identities and sense of belonging."[14] Many remembered a mingling of nostalgia, melancholy, and relief in these spaces. When commemoration returnee Wal returned in 2015: "there was nothing there of the war, for me. We went back to Nui Dat, and tried to locate our position . . .. But time's moved on and yeah, it's very hard to find anything that resembles anything from the war days."[15] "You wouldn't know it happened," Andy agreed, "I hardly recognized anything."[16] Coming to terms with the erasure of "their" places allowed some returnees to feel more at peace. Australian Special Air Service Regiment (SASR) veteran Ken explained: "the whole place has changed, so it wasn't like I was there. So, all those memories are gone now. I remember what it was like, just, but it's all gone now. And, so it should be, you know, we don't need to keep all those places."[17]

A handful of returnees were less accepting of change in Việt Nam. These veterans had strong feelings of belonging to and possession over Vietnamese spaces. They were unprepared for the modern-day Việt Nam that displaced the diasporic homeland they clung to in memory. When Richard, a former Marine, returned in 2002, he was "expecting this place to be populated with American military, just the way we left it . . . you're not really prepared to go back to your old neighborhood and find that all the houses are gone."[18] Les, an Australian Army veteran, complained that

---

[11] Interview with John Z. [12] Interview with Graham E.
[13] Murphy, *Quiet Australians*, 198.
[14] Nanor Karageozian, "Diasporic 'Return' Migrations." In *Diasporas Reimagined: Spaces, Practices and Belonging*. Edited by Nando Sigona et al. (Oxford: Oxford University Press, 2015), 69.
[15] Interview with Wal. [16] Interview with Andy. [17] Interview with Ken.
[18] Interview with Richard.

"the 'new management' over there went out of their way to replace anything that resembles something to do with significance to our allies. There's no trace of our units, it's been bulldozed, they've built pagodas in places that were of significance to us ... they've actually obliterated all that stuff." Les, more so than any other veteran, found this upsetting, and was especially angry about the demolition of a "place called the Horseshoe .... They're just a bit fanatical to change things. It's just childish, but they've done it."[19] The Horseshoe was a fire support base on a raised hill near Đất Đỏ. Les' expectation that the Horseshoe be preserved, and particularly his perception that the Vietnamese mined the hill to spite their former enemies – rather than to quarry their natural resources – suggests lingering feelings of entitlement to Vietnamese spaces. Geographer Tim Creswell argues that place is entwined with memory: "places have many memories ... [so] places become sites of contestation over which memories to evoke."[20] The Horseshoe was the physical space for Les' memories: he experienced its absence as an attempt to reduce the significance of experiences that were formative for him, and so interpreted the quarrying as malicious.

This attachment of memory to place was also evident among returnees who found their former bases repurposed by the Vietnamese Army, revealing a core conflict between the diasporic claim and contemporary Việt Nam. Many veterans tried to return to these sites, only to be turned away.[21] Air Force veteran Heiko, for instance, decided to visit his old base in Nha Trang: "we took the cyclo .... I said, 'go ahead.' He says, 'no no,' he shook his head, he got all nervous, and it reminded me, I looked at the floor of the ground and sure enough, there was the old white line. The old white line that no Vietnamese could cross. There were always two machine guns pointing out at the Vietnamese in case one of them did cross." Heiko suddenly found himself in the same position as his cyclo driver – whom he implied was an RVNAF veteran – of being prohibited from entering a space where he once felt he belonged. "And so that just blew my mind away ... everything we had ever put in Việt Nam, all decaying. All sitting there."[22] Because they still thought of these bases as "theirs," this sudden restriction and reversal of power was jarring for veterans, and sometimes elicited resentment. Scurfield described a veteran called Jake on the 1989 "PTSD tour" who tried to return to his old airbase near Nha Trang. "Even though this is where he 'belongs,'

---

[19] Interview with Les.   [20] Creswell, *Place*, 89–90.
[21] This experience, of turning up at old bases and being turned away, was more common among veterans who had served in support positions, because veterans who had served in combat tended to focus on visiting personal battlefields.
[22] Interview with Heiko.

Jake will get no closer … it's very frustrating to travel 7,000 miles and be stopped 200 yards short …. All that the Americans did and built here, all of that is disappearing and gradually but relentlessly being reclaimed by vegetation and by Vietnamese people."[23]

Because this reminder of Vietnamese sovereignty disrupted returnees' "healing journeys" to "their" areas, a small number reacted in ways that undermined their missions of peace and reconciliation. One veteran on Scurfield's tour claimed he "snuck in" to his old base, buried a marker, and "said his goodbyes."[24] He felt this was the only way he could achieve peace when the Vietnamese would not allow him in to commemorate his war. However, by breaking into the base, he violated Vietnamese law. War remnants, and veterans' attempts to revisit them, thus brought to light an ongoing conflict in the story of veterans' returns. The pilgrimages, rituals, and memorial practices that individual veterans planned for their journeys often clashed with Vietnamese laws and etiquette. Although most returnees maintained that they respected Vietnamese rules and accepted Vietnamese sovereignty as part of their commitment to reconciliation, some tried to circumvent these rules and prioritized their individual healing over the broader reconciliation agenda.[25] When veterans described restrictions on revisiting certain sites, few seemed to have considered how their own country would respond if a former enemy turned up to a military site expecting access, or broke into an army barracks to "say goodbye."

The SRV gradually responded to the increasing numbers of returnees and war tourists by developing war sites in significant locations, mostly marking US actions in Vietnam. Anthropologist Victor Alneng notes that "while the war left most heritage sites otherwise destined for great tourism in ruins, it 'blessed' Vietnam with other sites – the Cu Chi tunnels, My Lai, the [demilitarized zone] DMZ, China Beach, Hamburger Hill, Khe Sanh, the Rex."[26] Some veterans felt a deep sense of loss when they saw how war tourism had appropriated and commodified "their" wartime places. Former Marine John A., for example, returned several times to Khe Sanh, one of his personal battlefields. The first time, in 2000, "it just rooted me to the ground, and my skin was crawling and everything. It was an overcast day, and I got up there and I looked at those mountains in front of me, and it gave me a serious case of the heebie-jeebies. I was just froze [sic] there, with the hair standing up." John A. held his arms out and

---

[23] Scurfield, *A Vietnam Trilogy*, 160–61.
[24] Scurfield, quoted in *Vietnam: Two Decades and a Wake Up*.
[25] Apart from Scurfield's veteran, this was most apparent in the Australian challenges of Vietnamese terms of visitation at the site of Long Tan, discussed in Chapter 6.
[26] Alneng, "What the Fuck Is a Vietnam?" 462.

closed his eyes, indicating that the atmosphere in 2000 was authentic to his wartime memory. However, rising tourism from the United States led the Vietnamese to develop the site. The next time John A. visited, he was disappointed to find that "they've phonied up the strip area ... they've set up a kind of phony airstrip, a phony ditch. They've made it a tourist attraction."[27] Such perceptions of "phoniness" are not exclusive to veterans. Perceptions of authenticity are intrinsic to every traveler, as Alneng notes, because "daydreaming of potential destinations precedes every act of voluntary travelling," and the fidelity of the location to the daydream informs the tourist's perception of authenticity.[28] For veterans, however, the daydream of Việt Nam was based in the wartime memory of Vietnam: war itself was the locus for authenticity. Any departure from the war memory was perceived as deviation from historical truth: as "phoniness."

Other returnees felt that Vietnamese preservation and modification of war remnants provided them with healing opportunities. During the war, the extensive National Liberation Front (NLF) tunnel network frustrated the RVNAF and their Western allies. Soldiers trained as "tunnel rats" to conduct underground search-and-destroy missions. Most tunnel rats who returned to Việt Nam were not able to return to the specific tunnels they fought in: the tunnel labyrinth covered most of the country, and even if returnees found the right place, many tunnels were bombed, collapsed, or have since been built over. However, the Củ Chi tunnels were preserved, developed into a tourism site, and expanded to allow visitors to pass through the small passages more easily. Jake, the veteran from Scurfield's PTSD tour, suffered severe trauma as a result of fighting in tunnels. Jake held himself responsible for the death of one of his friends in the tunnel. He himself was buried alive in a collapsed tunnel and for years had nightmares about suffocating. In 1989, Jake successfully made his way through one of the tunnels at Củ Chi. Although they were not "his" tunnels, Jake's journey through the tunnel provided him with profound catharsis: "twenty years ... yeah, maybe things'll change .... I'm gonna leave Việt Nam in good shape I think .... Very good shape."[29] The Vietnamese decision to preserve and capitalize on the tunnels provided Jake with the opportunity for "flooding" or immersion therapy, and the inauthenticity of these war remnants ceased to matter.

Because many of the staff at sites like Củ Chi are Vietnamese veterans, these places repeatedly emerged as stages for reconciliation among veterans. Veteran and author Wayne Karlin described how at Củ Chi, another US veteran and a Vietnamese guide "show[ed] each other the

---

[27] Interview with John A.   [28] Alneng, "What the Fuck Is a Vietnam?" 464.
[29] Smith, quoted in *Vietnam: Two Decades and a Wake Up*.

4 Relics and Remnants 109

puckered flesh of their wounds, raising trouser cuffs and shirts."[30] Australian Army veteran John B. remembered returning to the site of the Battle of Balmoral in 2014 and meeting a Vietnamese general with a scar on his leg.

And I decided to show my wounds, I said, "look at this one." And then he showed me another one. And I said, "have a look at this one here!" All our scars. And he showed me another one, I lifted me shirt up, said, "have a look at this one, got one like that?" And it was really funny, we ran out of scars, but we gave each other a big hug, and it was a funny moment.[31]

Physical war remnants and the politics of Vietnamese preservation, eradication, or modification faded into the background as bodies – Australian, American, and Vietnamese – became points of connection.

Vietnamese bodies were themselves another kind of war remnant. Generations of Vietnamese lives were changed, shaped, and created by war. Yet apart from occasional moments of connection at military sites – when veterans could bond over wounds and scars – Vietnamese bodies, and Vietnamese lives more broadly, were remarkably absent from veterans' discussions about the effects of war. Literature scholar Việt Thanh Nguyễn argues that "every war has these human consequences that are not easy to frame in ways that would make them more acceptable, these amputees, these blind, these depressed, these suicidal, these insane, these jobless, these homeless, these side effects and delayed effects whose existence keeps memories of the war alive when most citizens would rather forget, or, at best, remember in circumscribed fashion."[32] But returning veterans were themselves legacies or "human consequences" of the war. Their lack of recognition of the effects of war on Vietnamese lives and bodies suggests, as Schwenkel notes, "that [veterans'] own processes of healing are frequently in tension with the conferment of the status of suffering on Vietnamese bodies."[33]

This was particularly the case when veteran recognition of Vietnamese suffering might require accepting responsibility for that suffering. For example, the war created tens of thousands of "Amerasians," the children of Vietnamese women and foreign soldiers.[34] After the war, Amerasians

---

[30] Wayne Karlin, *Wandering Souls: Journeys with the Dead and the Living in Viet Nam* (New York: Nation Books, 2009), 211.
[31] Interview with John B.
[32] Việt Thanh Nguyễn, *Nothing Ever Dies: Vietnam and the Memory of the War* (Cambridge: Harvard University Press, 2016), 25.
[33] Schwenkel, *American War in Contemporary Vietnam*, 33.
[34] "Amerasian" usually refers to American-Vietnamese people, but there does not seem to be an equivalent term for Australian-Vietnamese people. Sabrina Thomas estimates that

were treated by the Vietnamese as physical symbols of betrayal and fraternization with the occupying soldiers. Some grew up in "reeducation camps." Many were abandoned by their mothers and became street children, described in Việt Nam as *bụi đời*, "dust of life." Hundreds camped together in a Hồ Chí Minh City park opposite their gateway to America: the Foreign Affairs Office that processed their emigration claims.[35] The sight of hundreds of teenagers and young adults sleeping in a park in the former Republic of Việt Nam (RVN) capital attracted the attention of the handful of American journalists in Việt Nam in the late 1980s, creating media pressure for action on this "national embarrassment."[36] Scholars agree that the American "rediscovery" of Amerasians reflected anxieties about race, the Vietnamese refugee diaspora, and American desires to reclaim "benevolent supremacy" after the war.[37] Media coverage fostered popular support for legislation that affirmed Amerasians' American citizenship, with the Amerasian Homecoming Act (1987) providing preferential immigration to the Vietnamese children of US soldiers. The Act saw Amerasians turn "from dust to gold": bought, bribed, or conned into posing as the family members of rich Vietnamese who tried to use them as "a ticket out" of Việt Nam.[38]

US soldiers alone left behind 30,000–50,000 Amerasian children. Sabrina Thomas, "Blood Politics: Reproducing the Children of 'Others' in the 1982 Amerasian Immigration Act." *Journal of American-East Asian Relations* 26 (2019): 51–84.

[35] Thomas A. Bass, *Vietnamerica: The War Comes Home* (New York: Soho, 1996), 19.

[36] Jana K. Lipman, "'The Face is the Roadmap': Vietnamese Amerasians in the US Political and Popular Culture, 1980–1988." *Journal of Asian American Studies* 14:1 (2011): 54. For example of media coverage, see: Laura Palmer, "A City of Forgotten Children." *Deseret News*, September 1, 1989.

[37] Heather Stur, "'Hiding Behind the Humanitarian Label': Refugees, Repatriates, and the Rebuilding of America's Benevolent Image after the Vietnam War." *Diplomatic History* 39:2 (April 2015): 223–44; Thomas, "Blood Politics"; Allison Varzally, *Children of Reunion: Vietnamese Adoptions and the Politics of Family Migrations* (Chapel Hill, NC: University of North Carolina Press, 2017); Lipman, "The Face Is the Roadmap,"55–59.

[38] Trin Yarborough, *Surviving Twice: Amerasian Children of the Vietnam War* (Washington, DC: Potomac Books, 2005), 103, 118. Amerasians lived in poverty and were uneducated, so they often needed assistance in reading and filling out the forms for the Orderly Departure Program. Rich Vietnamese helped them to fill out these forms or bought them fake papers connecting them to US soldiers, but insisted that they were listed as family on the Amerasians' applications. This meant that legitimate Amerasians often handed in fraudulent applications to the Orderly Departure Program. Some Amerasians were denied approval when their families turned out to be fake. Others were abandoned by their "family" as soon as they had left Việt Nam. See also: Marykim DeMonaco, "Disorderly Departure: An Analysis of the United States Policy Toward Amerasian Immigration." In *Asian Indians, Filipinos, and other Asian Communities, and the Law*. Edited by Charles McClain (New York: Garland Publishing, 1994): 217–86; Caroline Kieu-Linh Valverde, "From Dust to Gold: The Vietnamese Amerasian Experience." In

Despite the focus on Amerasians in the United States, few reconciliation returnees spoke of the hundreds of teenagers living on the streets of Hồ Chí Minh City. US Army veteran Ralph remembered that in 1989 "all at once, within minutes we were surrounded by thirty or so kids, all with pictures, saying 'do you know my father?'"[39] American reconciliation veterans who met Amerasians described feeling drawn to them. Ralph "ended up spending a lot of time in the park with those kids."[40] One girl, Hương, told former Marine W.D. that she had her papers and was going to visit America to see her father soon. W.D. quickly realized "that there are no papers and there is no father waiting eagerly to receive her ... she asks me why I am crying. 'I'll miss you,' I tell her."[41] After meeting an Amerasian girl in Đà Nẵng, former Marine William Broyles Jr. wrote, "we had left behind a new generation neither American nor Vietnamese ... victims, trapped in an eternal no-man's-land of a war they never knew."[42] Despite, or perhaps because of these feelings of connection, Americans who mentioned Amerasians often indicated an impulse to keep some emotional distance. Mike P. wrote in his 1989 journal: "Friendship in Việt Nam means a special commitment. I didn't want to get close to any of the kids, only to further disappoint and hurt them once it was time for me to go."[43] W.D.'s visit to the Amerasian Transit Center on his second trip demonstrated that Amerasians, for him, were too close for comfort. "It was positively eerie: several hundred teenagers and young adults ... stared at us as if we were their fathers .... What could we say to these children, who gazed at us with penetrating eyes, as if trying to see their own futures?"[44] For these veterans, the potential responsibility of surrogate fatherhood overwhelmed them.

The Amerasian Homecoming Act led roughly 23,000 Amerasians to migrate to the United States throughout the early 1990s, diminishing public concern in the United States, while in Việt Nam the Orderly Departure Program established increasingly strict burdens of proof for Amerasian applicants. The group of teenagers sleeping in the park disappeared as Amerasians became adults and gave up hope of emigration. Among later returnees, only one raised the subject. After reconnecting with his wartime girlfriend Hạnh in 2015, US veteran Jim began looking for his daughter, but stories of traffickers and frauds intimidated him. One woman approached him who "thought she was our daughter. But she

---

Racially Mixed People in America. Edited by Maria P. Root (London: Sage, 1992): 144–61.
[39] Interview with Ralph.   [40] Interview with Ralph.   [41] Ehrhart, *Going Back*, 28.
[42] Broyles Jr., *Brothers in Arms*, 128.   [43] Mike P., "1989 VVRP Journal w Intro."
[44] W.D. Ehrhart, *In the Shadow of Vietnam: Essays, 1977–1991* (Jefferson, NC: McFarland, 1991), 185.

turned out to be, I don't know. I had her on Facebook for a while, and it seemed OK, but then she started demanding things, and it's like ... she basically wanted me to accept her as my daughter. And I said, well I'm gonna wait for DNA." Jim wasn't hopeful. "I don't think she liked that, and eventually she just ... we don't talk, at all."[45]

Because Amerasians were flesh and blood legacies of soldiers' personal presence in wartime Việt Nam, I had expected veterans to bring up the subject: perhaps their fear that they may have fathered and abandoned a child, or their anger at the mistreatment of Australian and American children by the Vietnamese state and society, or skepticism toward those who claimed to be Amerasian. Despite high rates of unprotected sexual intercourse between foreign soldiers and Vietnamese women during the war, no other veterans raised Amerasians as a lingering concern or in connection with wartime and postwar responsibilities.[46] Wartime racism and sexism, particularly the ingrained suspicion of Vietnamese women, likely limited soldiers' concern about pregnancies. Jim acknowledged, for instance, that he had not believed Hạnh when she said she was pregnant. Yet most veterans returned with a more reflective perspective on war, and ongoing media coverage of the plight of Amerasians into the 2010s sustained the link between wartime soldiering, potential children, and modern-day Việt Nam.[47] Perhaps later returnees did not think of Amerasians because they did not see them. Nonetheless, it appeared that both Australian and US veterans chose to overlook their potential, and very personal, legacies of war.

---

[45] Interview with Jim.
[46] Medical researcher Gavin Hart found that nearly two-thirds of all Australian soldiers had heterosexual intercourse while they were in Vietnam, while historian Amanda Bozcar argues that given the higher ratio of US soldiers in support roles (between 75–90 percent), US soldiers would have similar or higher participation in the wartime sex industry. Hart's findings, along with the research from the US Army Office of Medicine, indicate very low and inconsistent use of prophylaxis. Gavin Hart, "Sexual Behavior in a War Environment." *Journal of Sex Research* 11:3 (August 1975): 220; Amanda Bozcar, "Economics, Empathy and Expectation: History and Representation of Rape and Prostitution in Late 1980s Vietnam War Films." In *Selling Sex on Screen: From Weimar Cinema to Zombie Porn*. Edited by Karne Ritzenhoff and Catriona McAvoy (Lanham, MA: Rowman & Littlefield Publishers, 2015), 71; Brig. Gen. Andre J. Ognibene et al., *Internal Medicine in Vietnam, Vol. II: General Medicine and Infectious Diseases* (Washington, DC: Surgeon General and Center of Military History United States Army, 1982), 233–36.
[47] See: James Dao, "Vietnam Legacy: Finding GI Fathers, and Children Left Behind." *New York Times*, September 15, 2013; Sue Lloyd-Roberts, "A US soldier Searches for His Vietnamese Son." *BBC News*, April 27, 2014; Linda Davidson, "Legacies of War: Forty Years After the Fall of Saigon, Soldiers' Children are Still Left Behind." *Washington Post*, April 17, 2015; Samantha Hawley, "US Veterans Who Fathered Children in Vietnam Gather on 50th Anniversary." *AM: The Full Story. ABC News*, May 15, 2015.

4 Relics and Remnants

The ongoing effects of Agent Orange and unexploded ordnances (UXOs) on Vietnamese bodies were similarly absent from most veterans' observations, particularly early returnees. American reconciliation veteran Chuck remembered that initially, "I was not aware of [it]. It's kind of embarrassing to say, but at the time I didn't really imagine there was a problem of unexploded ordnance, old bombs and mines." It was only after a long visit that he became aware of these war remnants: "it was in the news here ... because every few days, at least once a week, there was an accident here somewhere and some kid was killed or had his arms blown off."[48] Reconciliation veterans who did focus on these issues were those who were personally affected by them. Graham E. said that seeing the effects of UXOs on the Vietnamese "just made me appreciate how lucky I was, in that when I trod on my landmine, I was with people who knew exactly what they were doing." Graham E. became involved in the campaign to ban landmines because he knew that "lots of these kids just died, horrifically, agonizingly, lonely, slow deaths. Or, they survived, without any help of prosthetics."[49] Paul S., a former Marine who returned to investigate the effects of Agent Orange after suspecting it had poisoned his family, said: "these people are living in an environment, today, forty years after the end of the war, where people are constantly being exposed to the war, the soil, and all of the other conditions that exist, and children are being born in this environment. And suffering birth defects that are just incredible."[50]

The development of Vietnamese towns into modern cities provided a stark backdrop for the thousands of disabled people who were still affected by war, and because later returnees saw Việt Nam as a rapidly developing country, this visible vulnerability was shocking. Les observed that "they're still digging up mines, they're still losing their legs ... it's still really in their face. Agent Orange is still a very, very big problem."[51] Several later returnees were fixated on the bodily destruction, redirecting almost every interview subject to the bodily harm caused by war. Robert, an Australian veteran, returned "to see for myself the effects of Agent Orange on the children, and the population, on the country, the food chain." Describing some women "doing needlework, and they're making these beautiful patterns and craft and everything," he recalled, "this is where I see again the deformities ... there's a lot of deformities, there's a lot of illness, there's a lot of crippled."[52]

Robert demonstrated an underlying wartime bias when observing people with Agent Orange-related disabilities working.[53] "I might be

---

[48] Interview with Chuck.   [49] Interview with Graham E.   [50] Interview with Paul S.
[51] Interview with Les.   [52] Interview with Robert.
[53] The Vietnam Association for Victims of Agent Orange has centers around the country that train and employ disabled victims in handcrafting jewelry and souvenirs.

wrong, but I think it is the sense that maybe the north is saying 'well OK, we've got these victims, we've got these people who are crook [sick]. The ones that supported the south, we will make them work. The ones that supported the north, we'll look after as best we can.'"[54] The disproportionate number of disabled people working in southern provinces is a consequence of US strategy during the war. Only provinces south of the 17th parallel were sprayed with the Agent Rainbow herbicide group. Vietnamese in northern provinces with Agent Orange-related disabilities were mostly People's Army Việt Nam (PAVN) who fought in or below the DMZ before returning north. They are far outnumbered by the millions of Vietnamese, RVNAF, NLF, and civilian, who not only fought but lived in the central and southern provinces and thus were exposed to ongoing dioxin contamination.[55] Robert's perception of biased welfare by the Vietnamese government elides the central factor affecting Agent Orange disability in the Vietnamese population: where the herbicides were sprayed.

More than forty-five million liters of Agent Orange were sprayed on the RVN during the war.[56] Although deforestation was the purpose of herbicidal warfare, few soldiers were stationed in one place long enough to observe the landscape and foliage over time. For Burstall, returning in 1986 to see the barren land was distressing.

> The once majestic ranges, covered in forest when I last saw them, were bare of growth.... Where were all the great trees? Now there were only rocks. The whole range on the southern side was just a vast expanse of bare mountain and boulders – bare, eroded slopes with great scars down the sides where the erosion had started to tear the mountain apart.[57]

As veterans learned more about Agent Orange upon their return, the role of the landscape took on greater significance. Dioxin, the contaminant in

---

[54] Interview with Robert.

[55] Agent Orange Record identifies three population groups who have been impacted by Agent Orange. The first is the population who were directly exposed during the war: up to 4.5 million Vietnamese who lived in areas that were sprayed, and an additional 1 million RVNAF and North Vietnamese Army (NVA) (soldiers from southern and northern provinces) who traveled through areas that were sprayed. The second population group are those who lived in areas sprayed with dioxin during and since the war, as the ecological systems they live off were contaminated by the spray. This population group are all in provinces below the 17th parallel. The third group are those who are still being exposed to dioxin in "hotspots" or high concentration areas. They are also all in provinces below the 17th parallel. The offspring of all three groups are at risk of dioxin poisoning. "Impact on Vietnam," Agent Orange Record. www.agentorangerecord.com/impact_on_vietnam/health/

[56] Jeanne Mager Stellman et al., "The Extent and Patterns of Usage of Agent Orange and Other Herbicides in Vietnam." *Nature* 422 (April 2003).

[57] Burstall, *A Soldier Returns*, 45.

4   Relics and Remnants   115

Agent Orange, settles in rivers and poisons ecological systems. Anything that grows or lives off the contaminated land and water is potentially dangerous. The scale of damage was such that some returnees pointed to the poison as the root cause of all of Việt Nam's problems, disregarding postwar factors that have affected the environment: climate change, infrastructural development, agricultural disruptions to ecosystems, pollution.

For example, in 2016, masses of dead fish washed up on Việt Nam's beaches. Several returnees assumed that Agent Orange contaminants in the seabed were responsible. Australian Army veteran Ric said "all these fish got washed ashore, poisoned, and they couldn't figure out why they were dying, and that was the first thing I thought of. Something shifted under the sea and the dioxin's been there, started floating around, killing the fish."[58] Edwin A. Martini argues that the politics of uncertainty in establishing causal links between Agent Orange exposure and illness, coupled with refusal by chemical companies and the US government to take responsibility toward potential victims, has led victim-advocates to overstate the possible ramifications of dioxin.[59] Veterans who drew connections between the fish kill and Agent Orange were deeply invested in combatting the ongoing effects of dioxin. It is likely that they connected the fish kill to recent research and activism in the United States and Australia on the exposure of "Blue Navy" (open water) servicemen to Agent Orange.[60] Yet few mentioned the scientific findings that the fish were poisoned by toxic chemical waste flushed into the ocean by a foreign-owned steel plant. These findings caused outrage in Việt Nam, leading to mass demonstrations by fishermen, environmental activists, and political protesters which were widely covered in Vietnamese and international media.[61] However, only one veteran, Pete, the former US ambassador to Việt Nam, described the fish kill protests in context: as an environmental issue that also involves civil rights, political representation, and the economic future of Việt Nam.[62]

---

[58] Interview with Ric.   [59] Martini, *Agent Orange*.
[60] Charles Ornstein and Terry Parris Jr., "40 Years After Vietnam, Blue Water Navy Vets Still Fighting for Agent Orange Compensation." *ProPublica*, September 11, 2015. www.propublica.org/article/after-vietnam-blue-water-navy-vets-fighting-agent-orange-compensation
[61] Liam Cochrane, "Mass Fish Kill in Vietnam Solved as Taiwan Steelmaker Accepts Responsibility for Pollution." *ABC News*, July 1, 2016. www.abc.net.au/news/2016-07-01/mass-fish-kill-in-vietnam-solved-as-steelmaker-admits-pollution/7559906
[62] Interview with Pete.

At the same time, returnees failed to connect contemporary problems to their wartime origins. Despite their broad focus on the legacy of Agent Orange in Việt Nam, few veterans mentioned the herbicide when they expressed concern about Vietnamese urbanization. The herbicides used in Operation Ranch Hand were so effective that many people in southern and central provinces became ecological refugees. Geographer Jim Glassman explains how a decade of herbicidal warfare led directly to the rapid urbanization of Việt Nam, with ongoing effects: deforested areas flood more easily, food security continues to be threatened, and increasing numbers of Vietnamese continue to move to cities.[63] Many veterans had negative perceptions of Việt Nam's urbanization, holding nostalgic views of the agrarian lifestyle they remembered from the war and criticizing the scale of Việt Nam's development, social problems in urban areas, and a perceived loss of culture. These issues were direct consequences of denatured land.

Sex work and sex tourism were one such impact. I did not ask veterans about the sex trade in Việt Nam, and was not anticipating that interviewees would raise this issue. Most did not. However, a handful of veterans complained about the growth of the sex industry in their interviews, but did not see the correlation between this phenomenon and the war's consequences for mass urbanization of Vietnamese cities that created so much poverty and desperation. Australian Army veteran Ray said, "it's getting a bit sleazy now, it was never really that – I mean, like, we had the girls and all that stuff, in wartime situation, but now it's getting sleazy and underhanded."[64] John A. agreed that "it's getting bad with all the boomtown thing [sex work] in Nha Trang."[65] Việt Nam's contemporary sex tourism industry originated from a wartime industry that sprang up around the foreign soldiers, where many of the sex workers were war refugees, with the support of the National Tourism Office of the RVN.[66] Historian Scott Laderman notes that "having originally sprouted in response to the foreign military presence, mass prostitution was, by 1973, being enthusiastically touted [by the tourism office] as one of the waves of Vietnam's touristic future."[67] Once created, this tourism niche soon overflowed: sociologist T.S. Taylor observes that the combined effects of the embargo and the economic vacuum created after 1975 left generations in desperate poverty and more vulnerable to traffickers.[68] Yet

---

[63] Jim Glassman, "Counter-Insurgency, Ecocide and the Production of Refugees: Warfare as a Tool of Modernization." *Refuge* 12:1 (June 1992): 27–28.
[64] Interview with Ray.   [65] Interview with John A.
[66] Heather Stur, *Beyond Combat: Women and Gender in the Vietnam War Era* (Cambridge: Cambridge University Press, 2011), 163
[67] Laderman, *Tours of Vietnam*, 35.
[68] T.S. Taylor, "Sex Tourism and Inequalities." In *Tourism and Inequality: Problems and Prospects*. Edited by S. Cole and N. Morgan (Cambridge: CABI, 2010), 49.

neither Ray nor John A. acknowledged sex commerce as a legacy of the war.

This oversight was particularly notable given that the "boomtown thing," or culture of sex tourism, tapped into wartime nostalgia. As John B. pointed out, within the "bar culture" (bars operating as brothels), "everything else is the same, the only thing different is the girls are the great granddaughters of whomever they were before."[69] Taylor notes that places with wartime reputations for sex availability, such as former Rest and Relaxation (R&R) centers like Vũng Tàu and Nha Trang, "became models for tourist 'playgrounds' and the development of the tourist prostitution industry in Asia."[70] Sex workers use wartime slang terms to solicit clients, popularized in the Vietnam film genre, and perform Western stereotypes of Asian women: dragon lady, china doll, village girl. This presentation taps into the fetishization of Asian women which, as historian Amanda Bozcar notes, was established before the war and influenced soldiers' perceptions of Vietnamese women as "available, innocent, but highly sexualized," becoming deeply ingrained in Western perceptions in the aftermath of the war.[71] Workers in the sex tourism industry tap into these orientalist tropes: sociologist Kimberly Kay Hoang observed how Vietnamese sex workers capitalized on the specific desires of Western clientele, notably fantasies of the white savior and white sexual superiority.[72]

The marketing of war nostalgia in the sex trade reveals an inverse blind spot to that of Ray and John A. Several veterans spoke of an absence of sex work in Việt Nam. US Army veteran Paul R., for example, said of Hà Nội in 2016, "I didn't see very many prostitutes actively working, I didn't see any pimps doing their thing."[73] His observations directly contradicted the reality of contemporary Việt Nam. Historian Thu-Hương Nguyễn-Võ notes that "commercial sex became integral to the Vietnamese economy in the first decade of marketization," that is, the 1990s.[74] Although illegal, the sex industry grew rapidly. Historian Gabriel Kolko argues that by 1996 there were more sex workers in Hồ Chí Minh City than there were in Sài Gòn "at the peak of the war."[75] Nguyễn-Võ wrote in 2008 that, based

---

[69] Interview with John B.   [70] Taylor, "Sex Tourism and Inequalities," 50.
[71] Bozcar, "Economics, Empathy and Expectation," 73.
[72] Kimberly Kay Hoang, "Flirting with Capital: Negotiating Perceptions of Pan-Asian Ascendency and Western Decline in Global Sex Work." *Social Problems* 61:4 (2014): 515–17; Kimberly Kay Hoang, *Dealing in Desire: Asian Ascendency, Western Decline, and the Hidden Currencies of Global Sex Work* (Berkeley, CA: University of California Press, 2015), 129–53.
[73] Interview with Paul R.
[74] Thu-Hương Nguyễn-Võ, *The Ironies of Freedom: Sex, Culture and Neoliberal Governance in Vietnam* (Seattle, DC: University of Washington Press, 2008), 3.
[75] Gabriel Kolko, *Vietnam: Anatomy of a Peace* (London: Routledge, 1997), 108.

on the rate of increase in the sex work industry, there would be "roughly half a million women involved in the sex trade" in Việt Nam.[76] Việt Nam's domestic sex industry is far larger than the sex tourism industry, but while both sex industries disguise themselves behind other businesses, the sex tourism "disguise" replicates wartime bar culture.[77] Consequently, it is the sex tourism industry that is most visible to foreigners – and as John B., Ray, and John A. pointed out, it is highly visible.

Paul R.'s perceptions were all the more surprising given his awareness of the relationships between the war, the sex industry, returning veterans, and sex tourism. Paul R. identified as a feminist, and explained how he and his wife had ethical questions about returning on a veteran tour because of "this thing, these vets, coming back to Việt Nam, marrying these Vietnamese women, and seeing it as a real sort of easy way to maintain this imbalance, you know, this privilege. This male privilege. Over here they can get away with it."[78] Paul R. returned on the 2016 Veterans for Peace (VFP) tour, which focused on community development and war recovery in Việt Nam. The itinerary of the tour curated an experience that was sentimental and reverent of Vietnamese tradition and authenticity, largely avoiding backpacker areas that emphasize Việt Nam's "party" tourism scene. Paul R.'s observations show how returnees increasingly isolated their travel within the country by tailoring their experience to their preferences.

There were also returnees who described an absence of sex work and tourism in areas where they almost certainly would have seen these practices. Australian Army veteran John W. compared wartime Vũng Tàu to his perceptions of the town in 2000. During the war "probably six out of every ten buildings were brothels … whereas now they're reputable houses and business and industry."[79] As Taylor notes, Vũng Tàu quickly developed as a sex tourism destination after the war, building off its reputation established during the war as a place for R&R.[80] Yet John W., like Paul R., did not "see" these signs. Possibly because Vũng Tàu was so renowned for sex work during the war, the visibility of the trade was diluted for the returning veteran who noticed instead the signs of "reputable" civilian life. However, the hospitality and tourism industry in Vũng Tàu still trades on nostalgia for wartime sexuality and economy. This was a further impact of sex work and sex tourism on veterans' returns

---

[76] Nguyễn-Võ, *Ironies of Freedom*, 5.
[77] Kimberly Kay Hoang, "Economies of Emotion, Familiarity, Fantasy, and Desire: Emotional Labor in Ho Chi Minh City's Sex Industry." *Sexualities* 13:2 (2010): 260, 263, 266.
[78] Interview with Paul R.   [79] Interview with John W.
[80] Taylor, "Sex Tourism and Inequalities," 50.

that went largely undiscussed in interviews: the overlapping categories of sex tourism, war tourism, nostalgia, and expatriate culture. Bars in tourist spaces, particularly those that catered to older clientele, almost always hired young women as waitstaff. The women were usually university students, taking on jobs in hospitality and tourism to develop their conversational English. They were not sex workers, but because of the combined influence of nostalgia, war tourism, the sex trade, and power imbalances in these spaces, these women were frequently conceptualized – and treated – by tourists and expatriates as the contemporary embodiment of wartime "bar girls," or sex workers.

For example, Tommy's Bar in Vũng Tàu is a popular bar among veteran expatriates and visitors. It has no reputation for sex work, focusing instead on philanthropy and the ties of friendship between Vietnamese and Australians past and present. The Australian owner taught his staff to sing "Cheap Charlie," sung by sex workers about Australian servicemen, *úc đã lợi*, who refuse to pay for their services. A rendition of "Cheap Charlie" is performed each Anzac Day at Tommy's by staff, after which a hat is passed around for veterans and visitors to donate to a local charity. This performance is both nostalgic and ironic. The young women mimic chorus dancers and end the performance shaking their fists at the audience of "cheap Charlies," who "cop to it" and donate as penance for their wartime stinginess. The event is self-reflexive and good humored, but because the staff are still called "bar girls" by the clientele and are performing to solicit money, their performance embodies the blurred lines between socializing and sexual economy during the war. Furthermore, although the intention of the performance is a jocular rebuke of the veterans, the lyrics and performance instead make the sex worker the subject of the humor. The singer is forced by a "cheap Charlie" to "give him one for free," punished by her *"mamasan"* (brothel madam), made pregnant, and abandoned – all of which is parodied through camp choreography.[81] The Anzac performance of "Cheap Charlie" illustrates nostalgia for wartime sexuality that was prominent throughout veteran-expatriate spaces in Việt Nam.

Returnees' attitudes toward the sex tourism industry echoed their broader views of postwar Việt Nam. John A.'s belief that "it's getting bad" mirrored his nostalgia for the pre-industrialized Việt Nam, lamenting the corruption of spaces he once felt were his "Shangri-La."[82] Ray believed that the war was a righteous cause and that by the end the

---

[81] A video of the rendition is available on YouTube: "Cheap Charlie (ANZAC Day 2013 Tommy's Sports Bar Vung Tau Viet Nam)." www.youtube.com/watch?v=3CjH2dMpl0M
[82] Interview with John A.

Australians had "achieved our goals." He had very negative views of the SRV, suggesting that the Vietnamese had "lost their innocence" and were "trying to get the money."[83] Paul R., on the other hand, expressed support for the SRV as a continuation of his anti-war opposition to wartime imperialism. He saw the best in Việt Nam, focusing on the positive to the extent that he overlooked very real problems – stemming both from the war and postwar governance.[84] Finally, John W. focused heavily on the virtues of Australian soldiers and veterans in his interview. He suggested that the development of Vũng Tàu from a "shanty town" to "suburbia" was a credit to Australian contractors.[85] His perception of Vũng Tàu as "reputable" therefore conformed to his worldview where the Vietnamese and Australians developed a positive relationship because of the war, and supported his feelings of pride and belonging in Vietnamese spaces that were controlled by Australians during the war.

The last "war remnant" was the psychological impact of war on the Vietnamese. Veterans described social impacts in their own countries – homelessness, employment difficulties, alcohol and drug dependency, family breakdown, and domestic violence – but did not recognized similar effects in Việt Nam as a mirror to their own experiences.[86] Instead, signs of PTSD were attributed to the failures of communism, cultural degeneracy, or, from the racial essentialist perspective, primitiveness. Rather than observing what makes them similar, many returnees abstracted trauma out of the Vietnamese experience, concentrating on ideological differences.

In Australia and the United States, the war and its veterans are closely linked to the idea of trauma and to the diagnosis of PTSD. Diagnosis of "post-Vietnam syndrome" emphasized experiences perceived as particular to the Vietnam War – combat brutalization, survivor's guilt, postwar alienation – before being linked to shell shock, soldier's heart, battle fatigue, and other historical war "syndromes" under the rubric of PTSD.[87] As a result, Australian and American Vietnam veterans tend to see PTSD as part of the legacy of "their" war. Many were surprised to see little evidence of PTSD among their former enemies and allies. Broyles, for example, wrote that he "tried to explain post-traumatic stress syndrome – the flashbacks, the blackouts, the bitterness, the paralysis of will, that seem to afflict many Americans. It was incomprehensible to

---

[83] Interview with Ray. [84] Interview with Paul R. [85] Interview with John W.
[86] Le Minh Giang et al., "Substance Use Disorder and HIV in Vietnam since Doi Moi (Renovation): An Overview." *Journal of Food and Drug Analysis* 21:4 (2013): S42–S45.
[87] Shatan, "Post-Vietnam Syndrome"; Marc-Antoine Crocq and Louis Crocq, "From Shell Shock and War Neurosis to Posttraumatic Stress Disorder: A History of Psychotraumatology." *Dialogues in Clinical Neuroscience* 2:1 (2000): 47–55.

4 Relics and Remnants

them."[88] A paradoxical logic emerged: returnees acknowledged the greater stakes and suffering of the Vietnamese but then went on to dismiss the impact of this very same suffering. Jim said that "other than a lot of family dying, and stuff, in the war, they seem to be pretty resilient... they seem to forget pretty easily."[89] This Western perception of an absence of Vietnamese trauma has been attributed by academics to racist attitudes cultivated during the war. Journalist Arnold R. Isaacs interpreted Broyles' belief that the Vietnamese lacked self-reflection and "were sustained then, and are now, by simple ideas" as echoing myths about Vietnamese in particular and Asians in general:

> The condescension was unconscious, no doubt, but to believe that the Vietnamese had so easily buried their own experiences – or that they were satisfied by "simple ideas," or that a foreigner could truly fathom the war's impact in a few hours – came disturbingly close to believing that they didn't quite fully share human feelings. It recalled old clichés about the cheapness of life in Asia, reflected in Gen. William Westmoreland's notorious wartime comment that the Vietnamese didn't value human life in the same way Americans did.[90]

Other veterans produced nuanced explanations about the presence and manifestation of trauma and reasons for trauma's presence or absence. These veterans based their opinions on conversations with Vietnamese survivors. Choosing to believe the Vietnamese whom they spoke to, veterans drew on a variety of theories to explain the apparent absence of trauma. The theory held by any one veteran reflected his view of trauma, why and how it manifests, and the dominant narratives about war and trauma within their country.

One idea reflected psychiatrist Jonathan Shay's theory of "moral injury", raised in Part I of this book. Shay argues that "veterans can usually recover from horror, fear, and grief once they return to civilian life, so long as 'what's right' has not also been violated."[91] Veterans who subscribed to this view argued that the Vietnamese did not suffer moral injury because they were fighting to defend themselves, their land, and their people. Under this logic of moral injury, the Vietnamese were less traumatized than US or Australian soldiers because (revolutionary) Vietnamese soldiers were fighting for "what's right" – and because they won. This view of moral injury was popular among anti-war veterans who sympathized with the revolutionary cause. "I don't think the Vietnamese hardly even have given it a thought," said Chuck, "I don't think they see it

---

[88] William Broyles Jr., "The Road to Hill 10."   [89] Interview with Jim.
[90] Broyles Jr., "The Road to Hill 10"; Arnold R. Isaacs, *Vietnam Shadows: The War, Its Ghosts, and Its Legacy* (Baltimore, MA: JHU Press, 2000), 190.
[91] Shay, *Achilles in Vietnam*, 20.

as something terrible, other than, you know, our country was screwed up and now it's not so bad."[92] Chuck's characterization of the Vietnamese being psychologically unaffected by the war focused entirely on the political and pragmatic, skipping over the fear, violence, and death that people all over the country experienced for over a decade.

The moral injury argument mirrors the narrative put forward by the SRV, which focuses on historic victories against invaders and situates the American War as one further victory for Việt Nam. Official historians, such as Phan Huy Lê, Hà Văn Tấn, and Trần Quốc Vượng, produced for the regime what historian Patricia Pelley describes as "marxish" histories: informed by Marxist–Leninist theories but promoting a "history of broad social unity and … the 'tradition of resistance against foreign aggression.'"[93] All three historians were contributors and editors of a core text in Việt Nam's national history curriculum, *Lịch Sử Việt Nam Tập 1* (1983), which details Vietnamese history from *thời nguyên thủy* (the "primitive era") to 1838 and emphasizes continuity in the territory, culture, and national characteristics of Việt Nam.[94] It is logical that veterans were given variations on this perspective from the Vietnamese they asked about the war. Because they were embedded in Vietnamese culture, expatriate veterans were particularly influenced by these ideas of moral injury and ingrained resilience. Former Marine David E. explained:

the French were here giving them shit for a hundred and fifty years, and then the Japanese were here really terrorizing them for a few years. And then the French come back in for a few more years. We're just here bombing the shit out of them for ten years. You know it was all part of their – they just take it in their stride, they just keep on chugging.[95]

Other veterans argued that Vietnamese veterans were less susceptible to trauma because they were properly recognized by their society. Anthropologist Sebastian Junger suggests that long-term trauma is created during the adjustment period by societies who do not accept – or do not know how to accept – their soldiers back into the community.[96] This theory of reintegration and social recognition can, when divorced from context, implicitly shift blame to wider society for the trauma of combat

---

[92] Interview with Chuck.
[93] Patricia Pelley, *Postcolonial Vietnam: New Histories of the National Past* (Durham, NC: Duke University Press, 2002), 61, 45.
[94] Phan Huy Lê et al., *Lịch Su Viet Nam Tập 1*. Hà Nội: Ministry of Education and Training, 1983.
[95] Interview with David E.
[96] Sebastian Junger, "The Bonds of War." *Psychotherapy Networker Magazine* 42:46 (1 September 2016): 42–48.

veterans. Such blame was effectively deployed in the United States with the first Gulf War and in Australia with the 2003 invasion of Iraq, with Vietnam as the referent, so veterans were generally aware of this narrative and compared an apparently cohesive and supportive Việt Nam with the divisions in Australia and the United States. This interpretation of absent trauma was most common among veterans who returned on healing journeys. They described how they could not be recognized and heal in their home nation and instead framed the return to Việt Nam as their true homecoming. These veterans suggested that because the Vietnamese had a shared and generational experience of war, they accepted each other and could move on as a community. Reconciliation returnee Greg explained that "the Vietnamese had had literally six or seven generations of people who have lived under constant war, no break at all ... you gotta quickly deal with it and then get on with life. You can't sit around and cry and mope about it."[97]

Sociologists Bussarawan Teerawichitchainan and Kim Korinek studied the health of civilians and veterans in the Red River Delta, a northern province east of Hà Nội, and found some evidence to support these theories of absent trauma. They found "a near absence of military service effects on later-life health" among their entire study group, including effects on mental health, and suggested that "the violence and trauma of war, when viewed through a lens of moral certainty (that the war was justified), common purpose (fighting for independence), and victorious outcome, can lend resilience that heals and buffers from physical and psychological ills in the long run."[98] They also offered support for the social recognition theory, hypothesizing that the "valorization" of revolutionary veterans and "the extensive institutional support extended to them might have buffered against the psychological anguish felt by American veterans who experienced PTSD."[99] However, these sociologists cautioned against taking these possibilities as absolute. Psychologists and anthropologists disagree about the extent to which Western conceptions of traumatic stress can be applied cross-culturally.[100] Korinek and Teerawichitchainan argued that two additional factors be considered: the

---

[97] Interview with Greg.
[98] Bussarawan Teerawichitchainan and Kim Korinek, "The Long-Term Impact of War on Health and Wellbeing in Northern Vietnam: Some Glimpses from a Recent Survey." *Social Science & Medicine* 74 (2012): 2002–03.
[99] Kim Korinek and Bussarawan Teerawichitchainan, "Military Service, Exposure to Trauma, and Older Adulthood: An Analysis of Northern Vietnamese Survivors of the Vietnam War." *American Journal of Public Health* 104:8 (2014): 1482.
[100] See for example: Peter Yeomans and Evan M. Forman, "Cultural Factors in Traumatic Stress." In *Culture and Mental Health: Sociocultural Influences in Theory and Practice.* Edited by Sussie Eshun and Regan A.R. Gurung (Oxford: Blackwell, 2009).

cultural "constraint in expressing emotion" in Việt Nam and the "tendency toward somatic complaints about depression" within their study group.[101] Furthermore, all of these theories for the absence of trauma – moral injury, homecoming, or recognition, and a social narrative of resilience – erase the experiences of RVNAF soldiers and supporters, and their descendants.

Some veterans recognized that the Vietnamese went through a brutal and protracted war and were likely profoundly traumatized. However, these veterans tended to focus on civilian trauma. Australian Army veteran Derek imagined how "while [war] was all going on, the old normal farmer had to curry favor with the [Viet Cong] VC or there'd be consequences, he had to curry favor with the south, because there'd be consequences. I mean both sides were fairly ruthless ... how can that not have affected the people?"[102] His separation of "the old normal farmer" as distinct from "both sides" renders the "old normal farmer" as passive. This characterization was common among Australian veterans, who empathized with the civilians who were caught up in the war but rarely acknowledged that civilians might have chosen, rather than be coerced, to side with the revolutionaries.

Other returnees spoke about familial grief. As anthropologist Mai Lan Gustafsson notes, "with more than 5 million or 13 percent of the population killed," the scale of loss was so great in Việt Nam that "it was statistically probable that every family *would* lose somebody."[103] Many veterans knew that familial grief has a particular spiritual resonance in Việt Nam because of the US and Australian "Wandering Souls" psy-ops campaign. However, few realized that this idiom for distress represents a culturally distinct phenomenon, *con ma*, that cannot be understood solely as mourning, PTSD, or even as psychosomatic trauma.[104] Instead, returnees described familial grief as they could comprehend it, communicating what had been stressed to them in conversation with Vietnamese survivors. US veteran Mark said that "there are families that have been broken apart, a lot. Especially in north Việt Nam, there's a lot of people that died in that war. Like, a million, or two ... everything

---

[101] Korinek and Teerawichitchainan, "Military Service, Exposure to Trauma, and Health in Older Adulthood," 1486.
[102] Interview with Derek.
[103] Mai Lan Gustafsson, *War and Shadows: The Haunting of Vietnam* (Ithaca, NY: Cornell University Press, 2009), xi.
[104] *Con ma* are the spirits of those who died violent or unnatural deaths and for whom the traditional death rites could not be performed. They become angry ghosts, "wandering souls" who are unable to rest in the afterlife. Surviving family members believe they are haunted by these angry ghosts, who cause chronic illness, misfortune, and even possess and act through their surviving kin. Gustafsson, *War and Shadows*.

like that is a huge psychological thing for these people."[105] Similarly, Australian Army veteran Derrill thought about "older people who were there during the war whose relatives are missing, it's a deep psychological scar."[106] While this emphasis on familial grief reflects veterans' experiences in postwar Việt Nam, once again the traumatized subject was framed as a witness to war, not a participant or survivor. There was no acknowledgement that many Vietnamese were also veterans of the war, or that they, like the returning veterans, likely suffered from *combat* trauma. While these veterans empathized with families grieving for those lost on the war, none proposed that Vietnamese veterans might experience the same feelings of guilt, fear, and flashbacks that tormented the returning veterans.

Some returnees believed that the Vietnamese had been traumatized, but thought that Vietnamese culture had provided them with helpful philosophies for coping with pain. These veterans were anti-war activists who used Buddhist teachings as a method to cope with their own PTSD. Suel, a former Marine who described his spirituality as confused between "a southern Buddhist or a Zen Baptist," explained, "they live in terrible, wretched pain. They just choose to always keep a positive look ahead, not live in the past." However, Suel also acknowledged the impact of this determination to "look ahead" on social understandings of trauma. "The young people here have no concept of the war," he said, "none whatsoever. And old people don't want them to have it. They want everybody to look to the future." Suel worried about the impact of this silence on the Vietnamese: "you don't go through that – you simply do not do it. The whole country has PTSD. All the women, all the children, everyone who went through that bombing, in those times. Everybody. But they have no way of dealing with it."[107] Fellow American veteran Deryle appreciated the capacity for forgiveness of the Vietnamese, but was skeptical:

> These people being Buddhist, it's a whole different – their mindset is entirely different, right? But you know what? I honestly think that what's going on in Việt Nam about the war is an extreme denial. I think they really are forgiving and kind people, and they're Buddhist and Buddhists say, "don't worry about the past, and there is no future, there's only today." And the Vietnamese will say to me, "Deryle, war's over. War's over." And they mean it. But ... no one who's impacted by that event at any stage in their lives is ever gonna get over it. Little children, old women, soldiers, politicians, whether they admit it or not, you know?[108]

They tried to accept Vietnamese philosophies on war and forgiveness, but could not let go of their belief that war always leaves an imprint. As traumatized veterans who, for a period, repressed their own trauma to

---

[105] Interview with Mark. [106] Interview with Derrill. [107] Interview with Suel.
[108] Interview with Deryle.

conform to their nation's ideology, Suel and Deryle concluded that anyone who claimed to be unaffected by war was equally repressed.

The most plausible theory for this perceived absence of trauma in Việt Nam is that it is not absent but that it is hidden. Many symptoms of trauma are hard to recognize unless the observer knows the traumatized person well – signs such as hypervigilance, quick changes in temperament, or self-isolation. A handful of returnees acknowledged this, stating that regardless of "evidence": "war affects everybody, and they still suffer. They suffer from PTSD."[109] US Army veteran Mike C., for instance, recognized that Việt Nam had its own ways of managing and making sense of the war experience. Reflecting on his experience as a Veterans' Affairs (VA) counselor, he said: "If I engage with them and found out this, and found out that, they probably show up in the same profile of a PTSD combat veteran in the US. But because they won, they hide . . . it wasn't as profound. But it was there."[110] These veterans emphasized that combat trauma is a personal and individual experience, and could only begin to be understood in close relationships or through shared experiences. These shared experiences, and the friendships and understanding that returnees found in them, are discussed in Chapter 5, "Meeting the Enemy."

[109] Interview with John B.   [110] Interview with Mike C.

5   Meeting the Enemy

The phrase "meeting the enemy" was used broadly by returning veterans: in interviews, in memoirs and articles, and as titles of speeches about their return.[1] Not all Vietnamese had been "the enemy," of course: veterans of the Republic of Việt Nam Armed Forces (RVNAF), their families, and civilians who supported the Republic of Việt Nam (RVN) were allies. However, because the space of Việt Nam was conceptualized as the battlefield by returnees, its inhabitants became former adversaries by default. Many returning veterans thus constructed all Vietnamese as potential enemies, regardless of their wartime allegiance, and feared animosity and rejection. In their interviews and memoirs, veterans focused on meetings with People's Army Việt Nam (PAVN) and National Liberation Front (NLF) veterans, which became rituals of the "healing journey." Meanwhile, RVNAF veterans, scapegoated as "puppets" in Western and Socialist Republic of Việt Nam (SRV) narratives alike, are unrecognized by the SRV and cannot freely organize as a community, making it nearly impossible for returning veterans to organize meetings with them.[2] These factors – apprehension about returning, returning to "the battleground," erasure of wartime allies, and the emphasis on meetings with former revolutionaries – led veterans to frame the Vietnamese broadly as "the enemy," both before and during the return.

I did not ask veterans directly about how they were received in Việt Nam, but many responded to questions about the return journey – "what was it like going back?" or "was it a good experience for you?" – with comments about how they were received and their interactions with

---

[1] Interview with Dave; Jones, *Meeting the Enemy*; Brendan Nicholson, "Vietnam's Long Tan Reunion Ban Fuels Outrage." *The Australian*, August 18, 2016. www.theaustralian.com.au/national-affairs/defence/vietnams-long-tan-reunion-ban-fuels-outrage/news-story/602e1dd87f7e1701f4ddd9ee860335e1

[2] Espiritu, *Body Counts*, 109.

Vietnamese. In Chapter 4 I discussed how my interview methodology evolved as certain topics proved to be noticeably absent from interviews. One of the questions I introduced to address an absence – "how did the war affect the people of Việt Nam?" – yielded many responses about how the veterans were received by the local population upon return. Additionally, anti-war Americans and conservative Australian veterans were especially likely to focus on Vietnamese attitudes toward returning veterans throughout their interviews – albeit for very different reasons.

Returnees repeatedly stated that the Vietnamese welcomed them back to Việt Nam, accepted them, and bore no animosity toward them. Veterans made sense of this welcoming attitude in a variety of ways. Some interpretations reflected the same ideas about the causes and manifestations of trauma discussed in Chapter 4. US Air Force veteran Mike M. remembered that "most of the Vietnamese that I met who were my age thanked me for going back. I don't think they have the hostility, of course, they won the war .... The victors always look at it a little differently."[3] Another interpretation was that the Vietnamese had higher priorities than holding grudges. Reconciliation American returnee John C. remembered "an odd thing: I never heard a huge amount of negativity towards the United States, or at least towards the United States people, from the Vietnamese. I would have been inclined to be a lot more difficult .... They had bigger problems. They couldn't really dwell on it; they didn't have the luxury of dwelling on it."[4] Another American veteran, Michael, observed the youth of the Vietnamese population and recognized that most people he met in 2014 "were not old enough to even remember the Vietnam War. So, if I were home in America and some Germans came over or something, some French or Russians, I wouldn't think a thing about it .... They had heard about it like I had heard of World War II. But it was just a concept, you know, it wasn't reality."[5]

The most common interpretation, however, was that the Vietnamese collectively had an exceptional capacity for acceptance and kindness. This interpretation relied on orientalist tropes about Asian people: as spiritual, peaceful, timeless. Ralph, for example, remembered a bus driver he spoke to in 1989, who "expressed to me what I think was the general attitude of the Vietnamese that we came across, and that was: 'the war is behind us. And we can't live in the past, we have to live in the future.' And they have the uncanny ability to really move forward, and not be left out, anchored, holding back."[6] Ralph's interpretation of the bus driver's

---

[3] Interview with Mike M., Skype, May 20, 2017.   [4] Interview with John C.
[5] Interview with Michael.   [6] Interview with Ralph.

statement – which could also be interpreted as "let bygones be bygones" – as "uncanny" reflects notions of Asian people as the Other, experiencing time differently, with an "imaginative, quasi-fictional quality."[7] US Army veteran Robert J. Reilly wrote that "the Vietnamese ... strike me as an essentially happy people," while Australian Special Air Service Regiment (SASR) veteran Ken said, "I believe that the Vietnamese are one of the most beautiful races ... so friendly, hospitable, outgoing."[8] The emphasis on friendliness, happiness, and gentleness in these comments highlights an important absence: none of these veterans brought up the political tensions of "meeting the enemy" – the tensions of being the winner or loser, invader or defender, perpetrator or victim. Instead, these veterans provided simple explanations: they noted Vietnamese acceptance, praised it, identified it as a racial quality, and moved on.

In contrast, one group of veterans focused intently on these political tensions. Most anti-war returnees had a heightened awareness of the scale of violence wrought upon the Vietnamese, and consequently could scarcely believe that the Vietnamese accepted them. US Army veteran Mike C., for example, believed that war crimes against the Vietnamese were pervasive and a product of a "dysfunctional" US military, remembering that "there was something fucking wrong" in Vietnam; "everyone knew, this was not right."[9] Although he was not in combat – he evaluated psychiatric cases at a hospital in Nha Trang during the war – he felt profound guilt for his participation in the war, and returned to Việt Nam feeling as though he represented the perpetrators of atrocities against the Vietnamese. Veterans like Mike C. strongly suggested that they not only anticipated but also felt they deserved reproach, anger, and rejection. US Army veteran Chuck, for example, flew out of Vietnam in 1967 "in a context of much anger and pain and confusion ... questioning, you know, what I'd done here and what we'd done, as Americans." When he returned in 1992, he was amazed by the "incredible welcome that we experienced from the Vietnamese people. And the complete absence of any blame towards us, or any anger, or hostility, or bitterness."[10] Consequently, the acceptance they received often confounded them: "I was overwhelmed. It's a beautiful place. It's a beautiful people."[11]

Anti-war veterans framed the Vietnamese as more spiritually evolved than Westerners, demonstrating what historian Judy Tzu-Chun Wu terms "radical orientalism." In her study of American activists who travelled to Vietnam during the war, Wu argues that they "ironically followed

---

[7] Edward Said, *Orientalism* (London: Penguin, 1978), 55.
[8] Reilly, *Return of the Warriors*, 45; Interview with Ken.   [9] Interview with Mike C.
[10] Interview with Chuck.   [11] Interview with Mike C.

an orientalist tradition of perceiving a dichotomy between the East and the West ... they inverted and subverted previous hierarchies: American travelers idealized the East and denigrated the West."[12] This inversion was reflected in anti-war returnees' idealizing of the Vietnamese. They found acts of kindness or decency unfathomable. David A. remembered that a hotel staff member offered him a Band-Aid. "'Here! Here!' He can't speak English. What the fuck? I don't need no Band-Aids, what the hell? And he points to my hand. And there's blood running down my hand, I didn't even know I cut myself! This guy don't know me! Went and got some Band-Aids and comes running!" David A. held out his hands and shook his head, indicating that he was lost for words. "So, there's been so many experiences here, the beauty of the Vietnamese people." He later returned to the same example: "[they] have certain qualities that [Americans] couldn't even come close to having. The spirit, the love that I've experienced over here. As if there's somebody running up to me in America with a Band-Aid!"[13] Like Wu's activists, the anti-war veterans "questioned the United States' global policies [and] wanted to name American imperialism" and desired to "distanc[e] themselves from what they perceived as the militaristic, materialistic, and racist values of mainstream [American] society." Both groups constructed Việt Nam as a more spiritual and peaceful space where they could be "enlightened."[14]

It is understandable that many veterans returned to Việt Nam anticipating hostility or hatred, particularly those veterans who came to see the war as wrong and themselves as aggressors, and that they would respond positively when their expectations were confounded. Returnees' praise also suggests that some were responding to and seeking to correct widespread representations of the Vietnamese that were circulated during the war and in prominent war memoirs. Historian John A. Wood notes in his study of veterans' narratives of the war that the Vietnamese were often portrayed as "pitiless exploiters" who performed an "exaggerated kindness" in order to manipulate or steal from soldiers.[15] Returning veterans highlighted the authenticity of their experiences, emphasizing that "the friendliness that they show towards you is sincere. It's not false, 'I've got to be your friend here because of tourism,' and all that, there's none of that. They are a very friendly and outgoing and loving sort of people."[16]

---

[12] Judy Tzu-Chun Wu, *Radicals on the Road: Internationalism, Orientalism, and Feminism During the Vietnam Era* (Ithaca, NY: Cornell University Press, 2013), 4, 5. See for example: Susan Sontag, *Trip to Hanoi* (New York: Farrar, Straus and Giroux, 1968).
[13] Interview with David A. [14] Wu, *Radicals on the Road*, 5.
[15] Wood, *Veteran Narratives and the Collective Memory of the Vietnam War*, 37.
[16] Interview with Bill A.

5 Meeting the Enemy 131

Vietnamese do not all think alike, of course, and their feelings toward and opinions of returning veterans are as varied and individual as veterans' experiences. Yet returnees' stories described the Vietnamese as universally welcoming, accepting, and forgiving. Mike M. and Ralph suggested that because they won the war, Việt Nam emerged with a more cohesive national identity than the United States or Australia, both of which were deeply divided in the aftermath of war.[17] There is some truth in this, in the sense that Việt Nam was unified into one state and subsequent generations were educated with a national curriculum that focused on common heritage, victory, and reunification.[18] However, given that the war was also a civil war, the scale of loss on both sides, and the punitive treatment of the "losers" by the SRV after the war, there are undoubtedly lingering resentments. John C. suggested that the Vietnamese faced such a difficult and protracted recovery from the war that they "did not have the luxury of dwelling" on the war.[19] This is a partial truth: destruction and rebuilding may have received immediate and public attention, but this does not mean that trauma, mourning, and pain were not felt privately.

Returnees' perceptions of Vietnamese acceptance neglected several factors that affect interactions between strangers of any culture and in any country: social and cultural norms, context, politeness, and language barriers. These contextual factors were often implicit in veterans' memories but overlooked by the narrator himself. For example, many returnees remarked on the hospitality they received. Describing his first reaction to Việt Nam in 1989, former Marine Mike P. was "astounded by the hospitality of the Vietnamese," while Australian Army veteran Graham E. remembered that the Vietnamese people he met in 1990 were "quite friendly, they were quite warm, and they were quite hospitable ... very accommodating."[20] Both appeared to overlook the fact that almost all Vietnamese they interacted with were working in the hospitality industry. As anthropologist Julian Pitt-Rivers argues, hospitality works to protect the host as much as it honors the foreigner, as it works to neutralize the "always potentially hostile" stranger by transforming them through socialization into a guest.[21] Additionally, most returnees described the

---

[17] Interview with Mike M.; Interview with Ralph. For scholarship on the effects of Vietnam on Australian and American society and national identity, see: Marilyn Lake and Carina Donaldson, "Whatever Happened to the Anti-War Movement?" In *What's Wrong with ANZAC? The Militarisation of Australian History*. Edited by Marilyn Lake et al. (Sydney: NewSouth, 2010), 57–83; Barbara Keys, *Reclaiming American Virtue: The Human Rights Revolution of the 1970s* (Cambridge: Harvard University Press, 2014), 48–74.
[18] Pelley, *Postcolonial Vietnam*, 41.   [19] Interview with John C.
[20] Interview with Mike P.; Interview with Graham E.
[21] Julian Pitt-Rivers, "The Law of Hospitality." *HAU: Journal of Ethnographic Theory* 2:1 (2012): 506–09.

Vietnamese as "just friendly people," remarking on how happy they seemed, but in Việt Nam, smiling is a socially appropriate response to a variety of situations, and "may show emotion, politeness, or hide true feelings."[22]

Veterans' observations of Vietnamese behavior correspond to the image of Việt Nam presented by the Ministry of Culture, Sports and Tourism, as well as Việt Nam's international image reported by travelers, so veterans are not alone in their perceptions.[23] However, some veterans interpreted hospitality, friendliness, and respect as specific to returning veterans, linking the reception they received with their sense of belonging in Việt Nam. Former Marine Larry remembered sitting with a group of Vietnamese men at a formal dinner celebrating Tet. After the toasts the group began playing music together. Larry remembered, "I stood up and sang the United States Marine Corps hymn. And they all stood up, with their beers, they knew it was patriotic for me. And at the end, I did a toast, *một, hai, ba, vô!* [One, two, three, cheers!] ... I knew these people only by sight, and [they were] sitting down basically with strangers and drinking beer and toasting together." Larry interpreted this gesture as evidence that Vietnamese recognize US veterans as, in his words, "long lost brothers."[24] It is equally likely that because Larry was a guest and had signaled that this song was meaningful to him, the men at the table responded with a gesture of respect.

Larry's interpretation of this meeting introduces an important aspect of the return to Việt Nam: solidarity among soldiers. Although most Vietnamese men who were around the same age as the returning veterans were almost certainly veterans of the American War, returnees also met formerly with former NLF or PAVN. These meetings became an important ritual in the return to Việt Nam. US Army veteran Harold Moore remembered meeting with "a large table of Vietnamese war veterans .... Any apprehension at such a chance meeting of old enemies were quickly laid to rest as the Vietnamese veterans smiled and held up a hand-lettered sign that read, in English: Welcome American Veterans. Some of us blinked back tears."[25] Returnees' memories of these soldier-to-soldier moments emphasized the importance of physical contact and emotional bonds. At another meeting, Moore remembered how General Võ Nguyên

---

[22] Interview with James; Vu Mai Yen Tran, "Vietnamese Expressions of Politeness." *Griffith Working Papers in Pragmatics and Intercultural Communication* 3:1 (2010): 18.

[23] See for example the "Charming Viet Nam" campaigns by the Ministry of Culture, Sports and Tourism which tout the Vietnamese as "simple, amiable and hospitable." "Welcome to Viet Nam." *Tuổi Trẻ News*, September 23, 2015. http://tuoitrenews.vn/news/national/20150923/watch-viral-tourism-promotion-clip-welcome-to-vietnam/38531.html

[24] Interview with Larry. [25] Moore and Galloway, *We Are Soldiers Still*, 48.

5 Meeting the Enemy

Giáp "held me like a son in his arms" after they exchanged gifts.[26] Their memories parallel narratives of the war, which as Wood notes "portray Vietnam as a very masculine experience: groups of men mostly fighting other men, proving their manhood, and forming deep bonds with each other."[27]

These meetings were almost always orchestrated events – the "chance meeting" at this Hà Nội restaurant was arranged by the Vietnamese veterans for the returning Americans.[28] Veterans' interviews indicate that two groups of revolutionary veterans were responsible for meeting the majority of returnees in official capacity. One was D445, the NLF battalion who fought Australians at Long Tân. Many Australians reported meeting veterans of this battalion at veteran-expatriate bars in Vũng Tàu. The other was a group of senior military in Hà Nội, including General Giáp before his death in 2013. These senior officers met with Bobby Muller on his 1981 tour, with Moore in 1993, and with the Veterans for Peace (VFP) annual tours. The political status of these groups of veterans as celebrated war heroes indicates that the perception of solidarity between soldiers was based in part upon heavily curated experiences with willing Vietnamese veterans.

The curated nature of these experiences draws out a political underlay in the narrative of solidarity between soldiers. From the earliest veteran returns, the official Vietnamese stance toward returnees has been to offer reconciliation and solidarity. This position originated with the invitation from the SRV to Muller's Vietnam Veterans of America (VVA) group in 1981.[29] The four veterans were overwhelmed by the "reaction of the Vietnamese [which was] ... 'incredibly warm and sensitive and friendly.'" Vietnamese officials proffered messages of reconciliation and "inevitably point out that they have 'never had any animosity toward the American people.'"[30] The VVA was later asked by the SRV to continue returning every few months in lieu of diplomatic ties with the United States, indicating that the SRV hoped to negotiate a formal relationship and end the embargo.[31] To maintain political legitimacy while seeking reconciliation with the United States – an imperial invader – the idea of reconciliation was constructed in a way that validated the SRV and their

---

[26] Moore and Galloway, *We Are Soldiers Still*, 32–33.
[27] Wood, *Veteran Narratives and the Collective Memory of the Vietnam War*, 73.
[28] See also: the Vietnamese Veterans Association of ex-Communist combatants facilitating tour visits for returning Americans. Keith Richburg, "Returning to Vietnam for Comfort – or Cash." *Washington Post*, April 27, 1995.
[29] Weinraub, "Vietnam Invites 4 US Veterans to Visit Hanoi."
[30] Bernard Weinraub, "American Veterans Treated Warmly in a Threadbare Hanoi." *New York Times*, December 22, 1981.
[31] Weinraub, "Hanoi Asks US Veterans for Talks." *New York Times*, April 22, 1984.

ideology.[32] Christina Schwenkel argues that the official SRV approach to returning veterans "underscore[s] a classic socialist construct of 'war between governments' and 'solidarity between people' ... [which] recollects the US soldier as enemy *and* fellow victim of US imperial ambitions."[33] This narrative aligns the returning veterans with the "revolutionary struggle of the Vietnamese people over the past half century" and frames them as part of "the forces of national independence, democracy and peace throughout the world which have actively supported the just cause of the Vietnamese people."[34]

Veterans rarely observed this political motivation. Instead, they frequently compared their experiences of "meeting the enemy" with their repatriation experiences after deploying. John W. remembered how he felt when he first returned: "I can't believe this. These people treat us better and respect us better than our own countrymen."[35] Returnees' juxtaposing of Vietnamese welcomes with the "betrayed hero" narrative reflects the central theme of persecution in a diasporic claim, "cultivat-[ing] a rhetoric of feeling marginalized (and sometimes even martyred)" which justifies the longing for (and belonging to) homeland.[36] Former Marine Richard described meeting a man in Đà Nẵng in 2002, who shook his hand and said, "'I want to thank you, and your country, for coming to help my poor country try to stay free. I'm so sorry for all the young boys that had to come here and die.' And then he just kept saying thank you, and dropped my hand. Turned around and left me quietly weeping. Because nobody had ever thanked me for anything."[37]

These comparisons hinged on concepts of identity politics and victimhood that emerged in the decades after the war. All the veterans I interviewed considered themselves victims – of the war, but also of the anti-war movement, of an apathetic or ignorant public, of their government, or (among anti-war veterans) of the "US military-industrial complex."[38] Complex tensions between victimhood, masculinity, and martial identity were drawn out in the Vietnam era, and veterans who became scholars drew on the language of civil rights, women's liberation, sexual liberation, and the expanding field of psychology to explain the Vietnam experience. Vietnam veteran and sociologist Paul Camacho argued in 1980 that the Vietnam veteran "suffers from status inequality

---

[32] The exclusion of RVNAF veterans and their descendants from SRV gestures of reconciliation and solidarity until the 1990s highlights the political dynamic at work here.
[33] Schwenkel, *American War in Contemporary Vietnam*, 26.
[34] Preamble to the 1980 Constitution of the Socialist Republic of Vietnam, cited in Mark Sidel, *The Constitution of Vietnam: A Contextual Analysis* (London: Hart Publishing, 2009), 68.
[35] Interview with John W.   [36] McAlister, "Listening for Geographies," 225.
[37] Interview with Richard.   [38] Interview with David A.; Interview with Chuck.

in much the same way as do racial/ethnic (black/Hispanic) groups and other minorities such as the elderly."[39] A transnational identity of the victimized Vietnam veteran worked to reintegrate veterans into broader remilitarizations of national myths: in Australia, a "cultural script" of neglect and exclusion restages the Anzac narrative of mateship, sacrifice, and martyrdom in Vietnam, while in the United States, the "troubled and scorned" Vietnam veteran became the vehicle for a "new American militarism" which coalesced around the "survivor-as-hero."[40] For veterans themselves, comparisons to historically disenfranchised groups were a common method for describing feelings of isolation: Australian Army veteran Dave told me that being a Vietnam veteran was like "walk[ing] into a room full of people and say[ing] 'I've got AIDs.'"[41] My interviews strongly suggest that many veteran counselors and mental health workers drew analogies to oppressed groups in order to help veterans understand and accept their trauma and pain without challenging masculine values of stoicism and strength.[42]

Most veterans thus returned to Việt Nam with a flattened understanding of structural oppression. Consequently, they demonstrated narrow conceptions of solidarity among soldiers of the war. The Leninist narrative promoted by the Vietnamese state – that all people are the victims of wars between governments – was accepted by returning veterans as reality rather than ideology. Their sense of victimhood within their own countries coupled with the Vietnamese solidarity narrative erased the power relations between themselves and their former enemies. Despite their keen observations of differences in power and status among various Vietnamese groups – such as former PAVN, former NLF, former RVNAF, the Degar and Hmong, and the descendants of veterans and allies of these groups – returnees smoothed over these differences in relation to themselves. American veteran Deryle enjoyed the fact that when he was in Việt Nam, "I carry the status a bit, I do only love it, you know. I do walk among it, like, 'yeah, hell yeah I got a right to be here. I spilt blood on this ground.' So whomever I encounter I have something to talk about."[43] Schwenkel notes that because "of their traumatic and experiential relationship to the war, US veterans were thought at times to have more in common with non-tourists, such as Vietnamese nationals, than they did with other travelers

---

[39] Camacho, "From War Hero to Criminal," 276.
[40] Martin Hobbs, "We Went and Did an Anzac Job"; Dean Jr., "The Myth of the Troubled and Scorned Vietnam Veteran"; Bacevich, *New American Militarism*, 2.
[41] Interview with Dave.
[42] For discussion on the relationship between military identity, masculinity, and trauma, see: Christina Twomey, "Trauma and the Reinvigoration of Anzac: An Argument." *History Australia* 10:3 (2013): 85–103.
[43] Interview with Deryle.

who were not veterans."⁴⁴ The notion of collective victimhood and solidarity between foreign veterans and Vietnamese thus became grounds for returnees' diasporic claims to Việt Nam.

Returnees' claims to status as soldiers in solidarity were not immune to threat. There was a perceptible resentment – usually masked as wistfulness for a less "touristy" Việt Nam – among more recent returnees who felt they were received with occasional indifference. This resentment highlighted a significant feature of returning veterans: almost all of them were white. Over the return period, increasing numbers of Việt Nam's tourists arrived from majority-white countries (the United States and Australia, along with Germany, Russia, England, and France).⁴⁵ While early returnees were treated with curiosity and interest, rising tourism (and veteran returns) also corresponded with rapid urbanization, so Vietnamese became accustomed to white tourists in their cities. Put simply, by the commemoration period, being white was no longer a novelty in many areas of Việt Nam, nor was being a veteran. However, as David A. explained, "now, I'm Black ... quite a bit of attention is directed at me cause I'm Black. How many Black folk you see in Việt Nam?" David A. observed that other members on his VFP tour were irritated by the attention he received: "I notice, the people in the group are checking it out, how, you know, [the Vietnamese] are checking out the Black guy ... the rest of the people, they're actually getting upset because of the popularity – I'm like a celebrity!"⁴⁶

The attention David A. received – and the resentment he felt from other veterans – reflected a specific link of solidarity between Black Americans and Vietnamese veterans: the shared experience of being oppressed by and fighting against American white supremacy. David A. felt this solidarity deeply, as he had questioned the war on these grounds when he was drafted. "I was like Muhammed Ali. 'No [Viet Cong] VC ever called me a n*****.' So why you gonna send me over there to kill VC?"⁴⁷ Vietnamese veterans he met with recognized this connection. As part of the VFP itinerary,

---

⁴⁴ Schwenkel, *American War in Contemporary Vietnam*, 29.
⁴⁵ Viet Nam National Administration of Tourism, Ministry of Culture, Sports and Tourism, "International Visitors to Vietnam from 1995 to 2003." December 1, 2003. http://vietnamtourism.gov.vn/english/index.php/items/489; Viet Nam National Administration of Tourism, Ministry of Culture, Sports and Tourism, "International Visitors to Viet Nam in December and 12 Months of 2016." December 27, 2016. http://vietnamtourism.gov.vn/english/index.php/items/11311
⁴⁶ Interview with David A.
⁴⁷ This phrase was used by civil rights leaders and Black protesters in anti-war marches and demonstrations. It later became associated with Muhammed Ali, linked with his actual quote: "I ain't got no quarrel with them Viet Cong."

5 Meeting the Enemy

... we went to a meeting with the VC up there [in Hà Nội], and I told them how I felt about my experience in Vietnam and my love for Việt Nam, and I told them that when I went home [after the war] and I talked to my father, I told him, I said, "Daddy, if I was a Vietnamese, I'd be a VC." When I said that, the VC, they got the biggest smiles on their face.

David A. was proud to have "made two newspapers up there [in Hà Nội]" for stating his solidarity with the NLF, but he also felt that it was this media attention that the white veterans particularly resented. The experience of oppression that David A. and revolutionary veterans shared challenged a central theme of dominant American war narratives: that the war was an equalizing or "raceless experience" for soldiers, with white veterans and commentators suggesting "that, against all odds, they understand the black grunt."[48] The solidarity David A. found disrupted the notion of all soldiers being equal victims in the war, undermining white returnees' sense of belonging in Việt Nam. He chose to ignore this resentment, focusing on his experiences of connection and solidarity with the Vietnamese: "I have to appreciate it, I have to stay humble, and it's a blessing. All these years I've been wanting to get back, and I've come back, and look at this. Look at the way they're treating me."[49]

There was one group of Vietnamese who were excluded from returnees' memories of soldier solidarity: women. Hundreds of thousands Vietnamese women served in combat as well as in support positions in the PAVN and NLF.[50] Propaganda from the Democratic Republic of

---

[48] Herman Beavers, "Contemporary Afro-American Studies and the Study of the Vietnam War." *Vietnam Generation* 4: A White Man's War: Race Issues and Vietnam (1989): 13, 10.

[49] Interview with David A.

[50] Because of the nature of the war, the duties of combat and support positions were blurred for Vietnamese fighters. In total, 1.5 million women joined the PAVN. Almost one million of them served in local guerrilla and militia forces. These women carried supplies, cared for the wounded, maintained agricultural and industrial production, and also protected their villages by shooting at American planes. Another 60,000 served in the PAVN regular forces, along with thousands in support positions. In addition, between 70 and 80 percent of the volunteer youth (170,000 young people) were women, protecting hot zones along the Ho Chi Minh trail. Karen Gottschang Turner with Phan Than Hao, *Even the Women Must Fight: Memories of War from North Vietnam* (New York: Wiley, 1998), 20–21. In the NLF, women's service in guerrilla and militia units ranged from 2.59 percent in some districts to 51.3 percent in others. Sandra C. Taylor, *Vietnamese Women at War: Fighting for Ho Chi Minh and the Revolution* (Lawrence, KS: University Press of Kansas, 1999), 61. Women also fought for the RVN: one million women were "actively involved in the defense of their nation" in the RVNAF through the war. Over 4,000 served in the Women's Armed Forces Corps in support roles, "to provide 'woman power' to release men from assignment in combat areas." In the RVN's People's Self-Defense Force (local militias), 130,000 women served in defensive combat forces, and over 1,000 volunteered in Saigon for combat roles. Phung Thi Hanh, *South Vietnam's Women in Uniform* (Sài Gòn: Vietnam Council on Foreign Relations, est. 1970), 3–17.

Việt Nam (DRV) during the war relied heavily on imagery of vengeful mothers and the woman-as-soldier, and SRV commemoration promotes the same imagery.[51] Women guerrilla fighters appear frequently in veteran narratives of the war, both in the interviews I conducted and in the broader Vietnam memoir genre, where they feature in numbers disproportionate to the population of women in combat in the war, likely reflecting the confronting experience of seeing "a woman in the bush."[52] The prominence of women in veterans' memories of combat contrasted with women's absence from soldier solidarity upon return. Most veterans described seeing men their age when they returned and wondering if they were veterans, where they might have served, whom they might have fought against. None described wondering the same about women. Some returnees referred to Vietnamese veterans from both sides as "brothers" because of their shared war experience, implicitly excluding Vietnamese women.[53] Women who survived the war were mothers, sisters, daughters, victims – but never veterans.

Combat memories provide some clues for this absence. Some returnees suggested that the Vietnamese only put women in combat to psychologically confront US and Australian soldiers, arguing that when "the VC used the woman [sic], it was so that we wouldn't shoot them."[54] This implies that Vietnamese women did not fight voluntarily, for a variety of reasons, and on both sides.[55] Others remembered women fighters as beautiful and innocent, underscoring the cruelty of war. John A. remembered

> ... standing over a young, barefoot girl, about 16 years old.... She lay on her back, eyes closed. Beautiful, with delicate features, perfect skin and one layer of silky clothing. Rounds had tore [sic] through her chest, but she looked like a sleeping beauty.... I couldn't even imagine that she wanted to kill us. We carried her to

---

[51] These aspects of Vietnamese remembrance are discussed in Chapter 6: Remembering the American War in Việt Nam.
[52] Interview with Dave.
[53] Broyles, *Brothers in Arms*; Interview with Suel; Interview with Ralph; Interview with Larry.
[54] Ibid.
[55] Stories from Vietnamese women veterans show that many volunteered and fought for the same reasons as Vietnamese men: "to protect our country, to protect our people," to prevent outsiders from "trying to control and take my country." Additionally, some Vietnamese women fought to emancipate themselves from patriarchal oppression. Nguyễn Thị Hoa described how she joined the NLF to escape the confines of traditional Vietnamese culture which forces women to be dependent on their fathers, husbands, and sons: "when I was young, I knew we had to figure out how to escape from this oppression. And the only way to do it was to follow the revolution." Ngô Thị Thương, Hoàng Thị Nở, and Nguyễn Thị Hoa in Elizabeth D. Herman, "The Women Who Fought for Hanoi." *New York Times*, June 6, 2017.

5 Meeting the Enemy 139

a good ambush spot, pinned a cruel note on her bloody shirt, and hid in the tree line .... We opened up on the sobbing Viet Cong comrades who found her.[56]

Both memories ignore the agency of women fighters, casting them as puppets or victims and not as soldiers in their own right. Consequently, when veterans returned, they did not conceptualize women as veterans. Instead, Vietnamese women who were generational peers of veterans played a specific role that is central to veterans' memories of "meeting the enemy": the role of the forgiver.

Vietnamese forgiveness of returning veterans establishes a crucial dynamic of moral accountability. As Schwenkel notes: "the image of the remorseful US veteran on his knees asking for – and ultimately being granted – forgiveness from the Vietnamese nation has emerged from the post-war embers of US-Vietnamese relations to symbolize a moral victory for Vietnam and the beginning of the end to ideological warfare and US historical unaccountability."[57] The actions of reconciliation veterans – such as Muller's laying of a memorial wreath at the tomb of Hồ Chí Minh in 1981, or the commitment of the Veterans Viet Nam Restoration Project (VVRP) to "wage peace" – fed this narrative, symbolizing solidarity with the Vietnamese through penance.[58] Because the redemption-forgiveness narrative received widespread media coverage in Việt Nam, most returnees who discussed their war service would have been understood by the Vietnamese people they spoke to as redeemers.[59] Redemption and forgiveness thus became central to Vietnamese understandings of returning veterans.

Many veterans accepted Vietnamese forgiveness and solidarity unconditionally. Anti-war veterans explicitly acknowledged Việt Nam's moral victory, while moderate veterans avoided political overtones and simply accepted the forgiveness extended to them. However, a very small number of Australian veterans included the caveat that they did not seek out forgiveness, likely in reaction to the widespread notion of returning to Việt Nam as an act of redemption. While these veterans addressed the misconception that they returned seeking forgiveness, they did not reject the forgiveness that was offered to them. Ken, for example, said: "I don't

---

[56] Akins, *Nam Au Go Go*, 73.
[57] Schwenkel, *American War in Contemporary Vietnam*, 27.   [58] Interview with Mike P.
[59] See for example: Larry, "I did not know I was fighting against freedom," in a dubbed-over interview for *VTV4*, a state-owned television channel; and Suel, "I was a murderer here," in an article printed in Vietnamese and English in *Thanh Niên*, a major newspaper. "Câu Chuyện Của Cựu Chiến Binh Mỹ, Larry Vetter Tại Việt Nam (The Story of Veteran American Larry Vetter in Vietnam)." *VTV4*, July 24, 2015; "Cựu Binh Mỹ Và Hành Trình Trở Lại Việt Nam Giúp Đỡ Nạn Nhân Chiến Tranh (American Veterans and their Journey Back to Vietnam to Help Victims of War)." *Thanh Niên*, April 30, 2016.

believe in atoning for the sins of the past, because things are done at a particular time according to society's beliefs at that time ... it was the yellow peril coming down from the North and we were in it." Yet he also remembered that "the acceptance of the Vietnamese people was something that really blew me away. The fact that, here we were forty years earlier invading their country and now they welcomed us with open arms, and loved to talk to us, that really was quite something."[60]

A very small number of veterans felt animosity from the Vietnamese. Some of these veterans clearly returned with some suspicion of the Vietnamese and appeared to project their animosity onto those they met. Moore, for example, interpreted the bureaucratic difficulties he experienced when trying to return to his personal battleground as deliberate, politically motivated, and malicious:

> ... the Vietnamese government officials in Hanoi had flatly refused permission for such a journey [to Ia Đrăng], uncertain whether we had some hidden agenda among the restive Montagnard tribal people ... it was becoming clear that the Vietnamese were going to have things their way ... knowing what we had hoped to achieve by this visit, the Vietnamese were wasting our time and doubtless enjoying our visible impatience.[61]

Moore's interpretation had some element of truth – these central highlands were Degar (Montagnard) territory. State-sponsored colonization of the highlands by Việt Kinh (ethnic Vietnamese) from first the RVN and then the SRV led to an armed resistance by the United Front for the Liberation of Oppressed Races, supported by Cambodia and China. Outright hostilities ended in 1992 when the guerrillas surrendered to the United Nations, coinciding with Moore's return journeys.[62] It is very likely that the SRV refused foreign access to a contested territory, but there is no evidence to support Moore's suspicion that the Vietnamese were prohibiting him from embarking on a personal pilgrimage out of spite.

Other accounts, however, suggested that some Vietnamese did harbor animosity. Australian Army veteran Terry Burstall met a woman, Mrs. Xiu, in 1987, who burst out "why did you come here? What right did you have to destroy my sons? I had never heard of your country before your soldiers came here."[63] Paul Murphy, another Australian Army veteran from the reconciliation era, wrote about his experience meeting the deputy chairman of Long Điền People's Committee in 1990. The

---

[60] Interview with Ken. [61] Moore and Galloway, *We Are Soldiers Still*, 2, 26, 27.
[62] Sidney Jones et al., *Repression of the Montagnards: Conflicts Over Land and Religion in Vietnam's Central Highlands* (New York: Human Rights Watch, 2002), 42.
[63] Burstall, *A Soldier Returns*, 85.

deputy chairman's father had died in the war. He asked Murphy through the interpreter: "why did Australian soldiers shoot unarmed women?"[64] These kinds of memories were sparse in veterans' accounts and mostly occurred among reconciliation veterans. Only one recent returnee, Larry, described anything similar. Interviewing survivors from Côn Đảo prison in the early 2010s, a woman asked him how many Vietnamese he had killed.[65]

Larry, Burstall, and Murphy responded to these questions in different ways. Larry answered the question directly: "they were trying to kill me, I was trying to kill them, and I can't say how many people were killed. I can better count how many people around me were killed." He believed that the Côn Đảo women accepted this: "they just moved on. Like, let it go at that."[66] Burstall was overcome with grief and sorrow, and the authenticity of his reaction touched the Vietnamese he met. Bảo, his guide, "said quietly, 'I think you have made some friends here, Terry.'"[67] Murphy, however, responded with anger: "well fuck me, who was this asshole and why present him to us? ..... I sat him down and said that I would answer him." Murphy provided a defensive explanation about collateral damage, implied that killed civilians were at fault for wandering into "clearly marked 'free fire zones' where everything is a target," and stated that "Australian soldiers were well trained, and their fire control was as good as it gets .... Shit happens in war!"[68] From his account, this explanation was (understandably) unsatisfactory to the deputy chairman.

Each of these reports of animosity show someone who was personally affected by the war demanding accountability from the returning veteran, indicating that some Vietnamese did not offer unconditional forgiveness. For Larry and Burstall, genuine remorse and honest discourse was their avenue for acceptance, while Murphy's aggression ended the dialogue with his former enemy. However, the sparseness of these kinds of reports, particularly among more recent returnees, combined with the near-uniform acceptance in other veterans' memories, suggests that Vietnamese animosity toward returning veterans was suppressed. In the mid-2000s, US veteran Wayne Karlin returned to Việt Nam to facilitate a meeting between another US veteran and the family of the man he killed. He remembered:

... something [his friend] Due had told me about an American veteran who had participated in the My Lai massacre. Wracked – stretched on a mental rack for years with guilt over what he had done, he wanted to meet the survivors of a family

[64] Murphy, *Quiet Australians*, 195.   [65] Interview with Larry.   [66] Ibid.
[67] Burstall, *A Soldier Returns*, 89.   [68] Murphy, *Quiet Australians*, 195.

whose other members he had slaughtered, in order to confront his past, heal. What a terrible thing to do, I'd said to Due. He had met one of the family members, who had agreed – "with teeth clenched in hatred," Due said – to smile and meet the man; it was national policy now to be friendly to the Americans, and he would obey.[69]

Việt Nam's "national policy" of forgiveness permitted, and perhaps even encouraged, veterans to push further than they otherwise might in seeking atonement. As Karlin notes, the repenting veteran "find[s] his healing by opening wounds in [the Vietnamese], as if they existed only to heal or define him."[70] A continuous cycle of remorse, penance, and absolution was offered to veterans, who could continue revisiting trauma at the expense of the Vietnamese, their forgivers. This tension was suggested in some interviews. Suel, a former Marine turned anti-war activist, described challenging the forgiveness offered to him by a group of Vietnamese veterans because "they always say, 'the war is over, we forgive you, yadayadayada.'" Suel reminded them that "we bombed your country. We killed millions of your people. We raped your daughters, we made whores out of them. We poured poison all over it." The response he received – "I choose to live in the future. If you want to live in the pain, and you want to live in the past, don't bring it to me" – he interpreted as a lesson about forgiveness: "I said: Thank you. Thank you so much."[71] Yet the words of the man who responded could equally be interpreted as a rebuke: stop asking me for absolution, you are only reminding me of my pain.

The impact of this forgiveness-redemption dynamic on the Vietnamese was explained by Phạm Thành Công, a survivor of the My Lai massacre and the director of the Sơn Mỹ Museum and Memorial. Công was interviewed in 2015 by My Lai reporter Seymour Hersh. Công told him that in 2008, Charlie Company veteran Kenneth Schiel returned to Việt Nam and visited Sơn Mỹ, the site of the massacre. Unlike normalization interviewee Ron, who witnessed the massacre but "just shot with a camera," Schiel carried a weapon.[72] Also, unlike Ron, who handed his photographs to Hersh to expose the massacre, Schiel was accused of participating in the massacre and complying with the cover-up. A meeting at Sơn Mỹ between Schiel and Công was orchestrated by a documentary maker: Công did not know that Schiel had participated in the massacre, and Schiel did not know that Công was a survivor. These facts emerged during their meeting. Unlike other veterans who returned

---

[69] Karlin, *Wandering Souls*, 235. [70] Ibid.
[71] Interview with Suel. This encounter is described in detail in Chapter 2.
[72] Interview with Ron.

to My Lai to atone, Schiel was "less forthcoming."[73] He apologized, but would not discuss the massacre. This agitated Công: "'how did you feel when you shot into civilians and killed? Was it hard for you?' ... 'Maybe you came to my house and killed my relatives.'"[74] Công was infuriated by Schiel's reluctance to repent, and denied his request to join a community commemoration of the massacre because "he had no interest in easing the pain of a My Lai veteran who refused to own up fully to what he had done."[75] Công further demonstrated his need for genuine redemption when William Calley, the commanding officer and the only soldier to be prosecuted for My Lai, finally apologized publicly in 2009. Công responded by inviting Calley to Việt Nam: "I want him to come here to feel the forgiveness of the people and to see the rebuilding of lives from the debris of the destruction he caused in the past."[76] Calley has not gone back.

Công's stories show how the narrative of Vietnamese forgiveness has come to dominate American conceptions about attitudes toward veterans in Việt Nam. It is reasonable to conclude that Schiel would not have returned to My Lai and apologized had he anticipated anything less than a magnanimous response from the Vietnamese. Australian and US veterans rationalized this forgiveness in different ways. US veterans largely accepted the official Vietnamese narrative in which the repentant veteran is a victim in solidarity with Vietnamese war victims. Ralph, for example, explained how "the Vietnamese people recognize the humanity of the American people versus the American government ... they view the war as impressed, as most of us were drafted, impressed upon the American people by government, and impressed upon them."[77] This explanation could have been taken directly from one of Việt Nam's war museums, and despite its inaccuracy (most soldiers enlisted), variations on this line were repeated by almost every American I interviewed.

Australian veterans, however, rarely touched on these justifications for forgiveness. Instead, an entirely different rationale emerged. Australian veterans unanimously reported that the Vietnamese welcomed them back to Việt Nam because they loved and respected Australian soldiers during the war. This narrative highlighted the humanitarianism, skill, and honor of Australian soldiers in contrast with the American forces. According to

---

[73] Seymour Hersh, "The Scene of the Crime: A Reporter's Journey to My Lai and the Secrets of the Past." *New Yorker*, March 30, 2015.
[74] Phạm Thành Công, quoted in Hersh, "The Scene of the Crime."
[75] Hersh, "The Scene of the Crime."
[76] Phạm Thành Công, quoted in "Director Hopes Cinematic My Lai Tale 'Awakens Something.'" *Thanh Niên*, May 14, 2010.
[77] Interview with Ralph.

Australian veterans, RVN civilians remember the Australians as liberators. John W. remembered how fellow veteran Graham E. persuaded him to return to Việt Nam:

> ... he said, "they love us. They really truly love us." And they do, they genuinely do. These are kids, babies, they know because of their grandparents and their parents have told them what the Australians did, you know? And how the Australians helped them, and what they did, not just as a soldier, but in other ways, how they helped them. And we, to them, are their heroes.[78]

At the same time, Australians reported that the PAVN and NLF "have a huge respect for the Australian veteran" because "we were certainly a force to contend with."[79] Many Australian veterans also reported that the Vietnamese remembered their honorable conduct in war. Bill A. explained that "the Vietnamese people, they love the Australians. They've got a lot of respect for the Australians.... We captured a Viet Cong cache... one of the documents was at a very high level in the Viet Cong, and it did say that 'we respect the Australians because they respected our dead.' And it's still the same, you know?"[80] Their memories of Vietnamese acceptance were often coupled with statements such as Ken's: "I know they still detest the American with a vengeance, in many places."[81]

Australian returnees offered scant evidence for this narrative. Most made broad generalizations, like John W., implying that their stories of Vietnamese gratitude were not memories of personal thanks. Those who made specific claims about Vietnamese respect did not corroborate them – Bill A. did not elaborate on how his battalion received information about the content of the seized documents, for example, which were presumably passed on to intelligence for translation.[82] The largely positive American experiences in Việt Nam suggest that Australian perceptions of Vietnamese attitudes toward Americans were grounded in confirmation bias, reinforced by the narratives about American soldiers presented at sites such as the War Remnants Museum. Furthermore, Burstall's remark that "there are many Vietnamese, as there are many Australians, who will never forgive or forget" indicates that the Vietnamese feelings toward returning Australians were as varied, complex, and personal as their response toward returning Americans – and masked by the same "national policy" of friendliness.[83]

Rather than reflecting experiences of "meeting the enemy," the Australian narrative appeared to originate in the Australian veteran community. Stories of Vietnamese love and respect for Australians bore no

---

[78] Interview with John W. [79] Interview with Brian. [80] Interview with Bill A.
[81] Interview with Ken. [82] Interview with Bill A. [83] Burstall, *A Soldier Returns*, 69.

5 Meeting the Enemy   145

correlation to the timing of return or to exposure to Việt Nam at peace but were more prominent among those who returned on tours or who were tour guides. Dave, for instance, said that "they love us. The average Australian veteran does not know that."[84] Dave indicated that he encouraged veterans who returned on his tours to feel proud of their service. From the mid-2000s, there was also significant Australian media coverage of normalization returnee Derrill's "Operation Wandering Souls" project, as well as project outreach to the Australian veteran community, so more Australian veterans became informed of the importance of body recovery and burial rites in Việt Nam.[85] Peter, for instance, said that because "we buried their dead, and left markers ... when we did our trip back to Việt Nam that showed up, they knew what we'd done, and they knew that they could go to a certain spot and they would find their dead."[86] Thus returnees' interpretation that Vietnamese friendliness was a mark of respect for the Australian Task Force (ATF) drew more from Australian voices than Vietnamese ones.

The Australian narrative of Vietnamese love and respect illustrates the effect of "particular publics." In this case, the close-knit community of Australian veteran expatriates and returnees is the particular public – a small section of the broader Australian veteran community that centers its memories around the values of Anzac. As Chapter 2 discussed, the "Anzac Revival" played a role in shaping the form of the Australian return to Việt Nam in the pattern of Gallipoli pilgrimage. It also reshaped the way in which veterans remembered the war. Alistair Thomson observed that veteran memories of Vietnam after the Anzac Revival portrayed the Australian experience in Vietnam "as 'The Legend of Anzac Upheld,'" and evidently the Anzac filter has been applied to the return to Việt Nam as well.[87] The traits that veterans claim the Vietnamese remember and respect of the ATF are all qualities of the "digger," the "model of Anzac manhood," as historian Craig Stockings describes it, "fight[ing] hard but play[ing] by the rules ... [with] an innate sense of fair play and deep democratic urges."[88] The Anzac myth centers on the superiority of the Australians to their allies, not their enemies, hence the veterans' projection of their own anti-Americanism in their speculation about the hatred

---

[84] Interview with Dave.
[85] See for example: Tom Hyland, "Diggers Offer Peace at Last for 'Wandering Souls.'" *Sydney Morning Herald*, April 24, 2011.
[86] Interview with Peter.
[87] Alistair Thomson, *Anzac Memories: Living with the Legend* (Clayton, NC: Monash University Press, 2013), 252–53.
[88] Craig Stockings, "Let's Have a Truce in the Battle of the Anzac Myth." *The Australian*, April 25, 2012.

the Vietnamese must hold for Americans – in contrast to the Australian digger.

The Australian interpretation of Vietnamese friendliness demonstrates how dominant narratives and popular memories that emerged after the war affected the return to Việt Nam and shaped veterans' interactions with the Vietnamese. Another widespread perception among Australian veterans was of a clear difference between northern and southern Vietnamese. Australian Army veteran David W. said that he "can pick northerners, if one walked down the street now, I could tell you, they're from the north."[89] Australian veterans agreed that this difference was an effect of the war. Brian said that "there is a distinct difference between the southerners and the northerners. The southerners, you can walk down the street and just in passing say 'hello' to a person and they will respond. In the north, they are much [more], sort of, militarized."[90] These descriptions suggest that Australians continue to view Việt Nam through a wartime lens, dividing the people by the 17th parallel established by the 1954 Geneva Accords. Northerners were the enemy – communist, martial, cold, repressed – and southerners the ally – democratic, free, warm, open. Even Australians who had not travelled to northern provinces promoted this binary, demonstrating again the power of particular publics among veteran returnees. Through this division, these veterans perpetuated their wartime allegiances. "Hà Nội's a waste of time," said Les, "you can't even buy a smile there, and they were the winners, so they're pretty sad people."[91]

These divisions of people by region demonstrate how the wartime lens filtered returnees' interpretations of the Vietnamese, often reiterating colonial and essentialist ideas. However, a small handful of veterans reported that returning to Việt Nam at peace challenged the racist ideas that they had formed before or during the war. Most returnees avoided describing this experience in detail. Anti-war veterans, for example, focused on the experience of discovering the humanity of the Vietnamese, but elided the pre-discovery dehumanization that was implied. US Army veteran Bobby Muller described how he had "felt animosity towards the Vietnamese even though I felt the war was wrong. It wasn't until I went back to Việt Nam after the war that I came to look upon the Vietnamese people differently ... everyone – and I mean people on the street – were gracious and welcoming."[92] Suel also alluded to dehumanizing thoughts but concentrated on his self-reflection and transformation upon discovering Vietnamese humanity:

---

[89] Interview with David W. [90] Interview with Brian. [91] Interview with Les.
[92] American RadioWorks, "25 Years from Vietnam."

5   Meeting the Enemy   147

They said, "Welcome to Việt Nam," it just blew me away, I wasn't expecting it. It changed my mind about the Vietnamese. 'Cause I was taught, and I believed, that they were evil people. I mean if you're going to kill somebody, you can't kill good people. So, you got to come up with some way to .... And then I meet them, and I realize, you know. And this has been a hard question that I had to deal with. And I really had to deal hard with this. Am I an evil person?[93]

The aversion to discussing wartime racism explicitly was surprising. So much of the anti-war trajectory in the return to Việt Nam concerned self-enlightenment, and recognition of wartime racism and hatred would seem to fit with the redemption-forgiveness narrative. Several returnees implied that they were consciously involved in such a process, but they skated over their prejudices. This deflection contrasted with detailed explorations of other subjects that anti-war veterans felt enlightened about since returning to Việt Nam: they dwelled on their blind belief in God and country, their hatred for the anti-war movement, and their fears of masculine inadequacy. Yet acknowledgments that wartime ideologies, upbringing in American culture, basic training, combat coping mechanisms, or some combination of these factors had bred racism were only suggested, never unpacked and psychoanalyzed in the same way. Nor did they discuss how they felt when they first met their enemy: whether they felt resentment and fear toward these "evil people," or how stereotypes subsided as they built relationships.

A very small number of veterans were explicit about wartime racism and how this affected their return experience. These admissions occurred with more frequency in memoirs than in interviews, suggesting that it was easier for veterans to explore their feelings toward the Vietnamese in writing. Australian Army veteran Tony "Bomber" Bower-Miles wrote that in basic training, "it was instilled in you to hate them ... they drilled into us to hate and kill ... [the instructors] were there to teach the recruits to hate the slope-headed bastards. The loathing was hammered in."[94] Returnees who admitted in their interviews that they returned with any prejudice were more cagey. Graham E., for instance, explained,

... it just seemed to be they had a lack of courage, a lack of commitment. And you know, you look at the bars, and all they were interested in was making money. The women seemed to be, you know, very sort of loose morals, working in bars, you know, by the thousands. Corruption seemed to be rife, and trust was just not something you would attach to a Vietnamese person.

---

[93] Interview with Suel.
[94] Tony "Bomber" Bower-Miles and Mark Whittaker, *Bomber: From Vietnam to Hell and Back* (Sydney: Macmillan, 2009), 58, 85.

His prejudice "was one of the things I changed my mind about entirely... that [return] trip, it showed me a different side to the Vietnamese."[95] US Army veteran Mark was less detailed, but more forthcoming: "[in the war] we thought of them as animals. The people, as animals. Isn't that crazy? And now, guess what? We met them."[96]

Most returnees insisted that they had never felt hatred toward the Vietnamese on account of race. "I loved them when I was up there in 1970 – not the ones shooting at us, of course, but the civilian population," John W. said.[97] Occasionally, veterans acknowledged, regretted, and rationalized their prejudices toward the Vietnamese who were their enemy, all at the same time. Andy mused that

> ... they were a bit demeaned. But I don't think I had any real animosity towards the people, again, it's probably just taking this view that we're all probably part of the big game, but individuals in it are not necessarily bad people.... You certainly had a dim view of the North Vietnamese, thought that they were horrible people, trying to take over this lovely country and all that. But that was a pretty naïve view at the time.

He both acknowledged the "naiveté" of his biases and justified the wartime binary view of the Vietnamese. "I'm sure I didn't have any great feelings of animosity toward them, particularly the South Vietnamese, because I mean in our day we thought we were going over there to help them fight off these hordes that were trying to take over their country. So, they were pretty friendly towards us."[98]

These memories suggest a deep discomfort with the subjects of race and racism. Returnees' tendency to avoid or reject these subjects contrasted starkly with their widespread use of orientalist language and ideas in their representations of the Vietnamese. The prominence of racial essentialism in their narratives reflects wartime ideologies as well as the legacy of colonial thought in Australia and the United States that endures to this day. However, certain trends in their language demonstrate that their memories of "meeting the enemy" also reflect the experience of returning to Việt Nam. Most returnees described conversations where their Vietnamese tour guides and friends explained their national history and identity in ways that relied on essentialist notions of race, ethnicity, and nationhood. Many of these accounts indicated that the veterans were quoting their friends and associates. These conversations hinged both on political narratives that underlay Vietnamese discourses about

---

[95] Interview with Graham E. [96] Interview with Mark. [97] Interview with John W.
[98] Interview with Andy.

5   Meeting the Enemy   149

identity and national character, and on the language through which those narratives were communicated.

Vietnamese public discourse emphasizes an inherent "Vietnameseness." Anthropologist Terry Rambo argues that this focus on national character reflects the "constant preoccupation" of the SRV with enhancing national integration.[99] This preoccupation is an attempt in part to eradicate RVN memory of the war, but it is also a method of addressing ethnic tensions by quashing ethnic identities. Ongoing tensions between the dominant Việt Kinh and ethnic minorities pose a threat to SRV legitimacy, which rests on the narrative that all Vietnamese within current territories fought together against a succession of invading forces.[100] These tensions are fueled by the dominance of Kinh in Vietnamese political structures and by SRV policies that categorize and segregate Vietnamese by ethnicity, perpetuating an already pervasive essentialist construction of ethnicity. The SRV government attempts to smooth over these tensions by promoting a national character of "Vietnamese-ness" that subordinates ethnic divisions and promotes unity.[101] Returnees seemed to have absorbed this message of national unity and shared characteristics.

Equally important to these political undertones was the language in which returnees communicated. Most veterans spoke little to no Vietnamese, and none were fluent. Almost all their conversations with Vietnamese people were in English. Vietnamese speakers of English usually gain their speaking practice through classes with native English-speaking teachers. Cultural linguist Alistair Pennycook notes that "some of the central ideologies of current English Language Teaching have their origins in the cultural constructions of colonialism."[102] One ideology that Pennycook identifies as "endemic" to English Language Teaching theory and practice is the notion of "cultural fixity" in which students "are seen as belonging to a 'traditional' and static culture which defines their thoughts and behaviours ... when students are considered to have cultures, these tend to be fixed and static and deterministic."[103] This notion

---

[99] Terry Rambo, "Vietnam." In *Ethnicity in Asia*. Edited by Colin Mackerr as (London: Routledge, 2003), 114.
[100] Ibid., 112–13.
[101] Although representation of ethnic minorities in the National Assembly has increased in recent years, ethnic minorities are not represented in the Politburo or Central Committee of the Communist Party. For policies that classify Vietnamese by ethnicity, see for example the mandatory categorization of ethnicity on identity cards. "Each citizen must belong to one of the fifty-four recognized groups ... no ambiguity in classification is permitted." Rambo, "Vietnam," 115.
[102] Alistair Pennycook, *English and the Discourses of Colonialism* (London: Routledge, 1998), 48.
[103] Pennycook, *English and the Discourses of Colonialism*, 320.

permeates English discourse in Việt Nam, by native and Vietnamese speakers alike: comparisons about countries of origin are a common "icebreaker" topic between tourists, expatriates, teachers, and local Vietnamese, leading to reductive and generalizing statements about nations and races. The key point is: none of the veterans experienced how the Vietnamese self-perceive and conceptualize of their culture within their own linguistic framework. Their understanding of Vietnamese identity hinged on the colonial framework of English linguistic practices through which Vietnamese thoughts and memories were always filtered.

These factors were evident in veterans' descriptions of the Vietnamese. As this chapter has shown, many veterans commented on a particular Vietnamese character – a "spirit" or "essence" – and frequently ascribed the trait of resilience to this national identity. They admired how the Vietnamese coped with the struggles of war legacies and reconstruction, praising not only their survival but the ways in which they survived. US Army veteran Mike Boehm wrote that he "developed a profound respect for the Vietnamese, for their tenacity, industriousness, and most of all, their spirit."[104] Robert described how when he returned he "began to admire the tenacity of the Vietnamese struggling on a handful of rice."[105] The language veterans used to express their admiration for the Vietnamese directly mirrored descriptions of resilience, adaptability, and industriousness found in Vietnamese war museums and historical narratives. Thus, as Chapter 6 will show, by "meeting the enemy" veterans also engaged with new ways of remembering "their" war: the American War in Việt Nam.

---

[104] Mike Boehm, "VVRP Team IV." *Veterans Viet Nam Restoration Group.* www.vvrp.org/?page_id=152
[105] Interview with Robert.

6 Remembering the American War in Việt Nam

Việt Thanh Nguyễn writes that "all wars are fought twice: the first time on the battlefield, the second time in memory."[1] While many veterans returned to Việt Nam to reengage with memories of "their" war, they were often confronted with memories that belonged to their enemies. While some returnees embraced Vietnamese war memory, others rejected or challenged it, and many struggled with the tensions and contradictions between different versions of the war. Their reactions to memories of the American War highlighted the role of confirmation bias in memories of return, because while veterans' wartime biases continued to permeate their stories of return, they had a highly selective approach to Vietnamese war memory. Returnees drew out elements of Vietnamese memory that supported their personal war narratives and discarded those aspects that contradicted their point of view. This selectivity is somewhat ironic because, as this chapter discusses, many veterans felt that Vietnamese war memory was one-sided "propaganda."[2] The experiences discussed in this chapter were largely in response to open-ended questions I asked about returnees' emotional responses to how the war was remembered in Việt Nam, focusing on four spaces of memory: the War Remnants Museum in Hồ Chí Minh City; Hỏa Lò Prison Museum in Hà Nội; Sơn Mỹ Memorial and Museum in Quảng Ngãi; and Long Tân in Bà Rịa-Vũng Tàu.

The War Remnants Museum in Hồ Chí Minh City documents atrocities committed against the Vietnamese in the colonial period and in the Indochina wars, proposing that by showing evidence of "the crime and

---

[1] Nguyễn, *Nothing Ever Dies*, 4.
[2] My interviews strongly suggest that veterans used "propaganda" in the colloquial Western vernacular, meaning fabricated or very exaggerated material, rather than to describe information disseminated for political reasons. Statements such as "it doesn't bother us, it's just propaganda" make sense in the former context, not in the latter. To limit confusion between these meanings, I avoid using the term propaganda in my analysis.

consequences of war that the invasion force has caused to Vietnam," more people will understand the "mental struggle for independence and freedom of the country, the anti-war sense of invasion, to protect peace and solidarity friendship between the peoples of the world."[3] It is the most popular museum in Việt Nam, among visitors and locals, and almost every veteran I interviewed had visited it. The museum opened in 1975 as the "Exhibition House for US and Puppet Crimes," with a mandate to preserve "the heroic remnants of the Vietnamese people in the struggle against the invading forces, and to denounce the crimes and highlighted [sic] the devastating consequences of the war of aggression."[4] The evolution of the museum's name – changed to "Exhibition House for Crimes of War and Aggression" in 1990, and again to "War Remnants Museum" in 1995 – corresponded with shifts in the Socialist Republic of Việt Nam's (SRV's) diplomatic relationships, presenting a more conciliatory war memory to former enemy nations.[5]

Eight museum exhibits evolved alongside the name, so veterans saw different representations of Vietnamese memories at this site depending on when they returned. However, three exhibits were described by most veterans, and their descriptions indicate that the exhibits were maintained fairly consistently over the past three decades. The first included two rooms depicting atrocities committed against Vietnamese by American and "puppet" forces.[6] The main medium in this exhibit is photographs of acts of violence. The narrative produced by these photographs and the captions that accompany them describe the foreign forces as brutal invaders who used unwarranted aggression against defenseless Vietnamese victims. The second was an exhibit detailing the effects of Agent Orange, which includes a display of deformed fetuses in glass jars. The third exhibit celebrates the international anti-war movement. The selective attention veterans paid to these three exhibits – relative to the occasional references to exhibits depicting French and "puppet" torture

---

[3] "General Introduction," War Remnants Museum. http://warremnantsmuseum.com/posts/introduction-general

[4] Ibid.   [5] Schwenkel, *The American War in Contemporary Vietnam*, 164.

[6] Vietnamese museums name the Republic of Việt Nam (RVN) and Republic of Việt Nam Armed Forces (RVNAF) as a "puppet" (*ngụy*) regime with "puppet soldiers" (*lính ngụy*), and present them without agency, depicting them as brainwashed and stripping them of their Vietnamese identity. However, the most recent addition to the national history curriculum (implemented 2018–19) no longer refers to the southern regime and soldiers as "puppets," in order to present a more "objective" (*khách quan*) reading of history. This change in policy may soon be reflected at national museums. Phạm Thịnh, "GS Nguyễn Minh Thuyết: Không Chờ SGK Mới, Nên Bổ Sung Để Dạy Ngay Về Cuộc Chiến Chống Quân TQ Xâm Lược." *SOHA.VN*, August 22, 2017. http://soha.vn/gs-nguyen-minh-thuyet-khong-cho-sgk-moi-nen-bo-sung-de-day-ngay-ve-cuoc-chien-chong-quan-tq-xam-luoc-20170822094526365.html

methods, Japanese occupation practices, and the large collection of military hardware in the courtyard – indicates that (perhaps inevitably) veterans were preoccupied with how "their" war was presented in Vietnamese memory spaces.

Australian Army veteran John W. visited the War Remnants Museum in 2000, and remembered that "the first thing I saw was a bloke at My Lai. The photographs. Which I had seen in 1969. It's just gut-wrenching, it's just off. I saw that photograph, it took up half a wall, and I couldn't believe they could do that. It's like going to Dachau, Auschwitz. And I saw that and I thought, 'geez, that's in bad taste.'"[7] These museums are, for (some) Vietnamese, parallel sites to Dachau and Auschwitz: spaces for bearing witness to enormous pain and of reckoning with the past. The graphic representations of violence were intentional, as Schwenkel notes, because the "public documentation and visual displays of atrocities ... mobilize[d] memory, sentiment and action."[8] John W.'s statement that the exhibit was "just off" and "in bad taste" suggests that depicting the war as atrocity made him feel defensive, conflicting with his memory of the war. He went on:

I felt like I wanted to throw up. And I just looked at Graham and I said, "thank fuck, thank fuck there is not a photo of an Australian in here" ... I'm crying, like I am now ... I said, "Don't go in there. Do not go in there. That is not the war I fought in. That's not the war I fought in." I had to walk away. That turned my stomach, that's just ... the Vietnamese have every right, they have every right to be horrified as to what was done at My Lai, and Agent Orange, everything else like that. But I said to Graham, "thank god there were no Australians in there." It was like we didn't exist.[9]

Michael Roper argues that despite being composed through cultural frameworks and re-remembered according to social context, every memory has an "underlay," a core emotion at the heart of its expression, and that "re-remembering" that emotion is "a process motivated by the psychic needs of the past and present."[10] John W.'s reaction indicates a core tension in his experience visiting the War Remnants Museum. His memories of the museum oscillated between horror, defensiveness,

---

[7] Interview with John W. Based on my visits to the War Remnants Museum, I believe the photograph John W. referred to is the most famous image captured by Haeberle at My Lai. The photograph in question shows a dozen villagers massacred on a pathway. It appeared in *LIFE* magazine and was on the cover of the *Plain Dealer* when the My Lai story broke in 1969, and at the Museum it is a focal point of the American War exhibit. Author's notes from visit to War Remnants Museum, Hồ Chí Minh City, March 24, 2016.
[8] Schwenkel, *American War in Contemporary Vietnam*, 163.   [9] Interview with John W.
[10] Roper, "Re-Remembering the Soldier-Hero," 183.

disgust, and sympathy as he attempted to reconcile Vietnamese representations of the American War with the Australian experience in Vietnam.

Many Australian returnees were deeply offended by representations of Vietnamese war memories. John B. said of the War Remnants Museum, "we can't go there. We've gone in there, we can't spend any time in there. It's all propaganda. A lot of the people, they're ignorant. And you know the way to control the population is to keep them ignorant … you can control them, they don't know anything."[11] John B.'s use of the collection pronoun "we" to describe his aversion to the museum suggests that this is an agreed opinion among the Australian veteran community. His attitude demonstrated the Australians' tendency, described in Chapter 5, of categorizing the Vietnamese by region and politics according to wartime allegiances. The War Remnants Museum was considered a mouthpiece for the Communist Party: one veteran even misremembered the location of the museum as being in Hà Nội because it reflected the militaristic culture he associated with northern Việt Nam. "It's a little bit different up there, where they have the American War Museum."[12] The consensus that the museum exhibits were heavily manipulated or fabricated permitted veterans to deny any aspect of the Vietnamese experience that framed them as perpetrators of violence. "Their interpretation is absolute nonsense," said Kevin, an Australian Army veteran, "Absolute nonsense. The tour guide was a mouthpiece for Hồ Chí Minh, virtually."[13]

The Australian returnees' response to the War Remnants Museum reflected Scott Laderman's characterization of American responses to Vietnamese memory. Laderman argues that the "greater attention in Vietnam to Vietnamese suffering, such as the War Remnants Museum, has been angrily and repeatedly denounced because … it serves as an inherent affront to American collective memory and many Americans' sense of national identity."[14] While Laderman's description accurately describes Australian responses, it was not apparent among the US veterans I interviewed. Only the few who indicated feelings of patriotism and pride in their war service agreed with the Australian consensus that Vietnamese representations of the war were unfairly biased, mostly fabricated, and an attempt to exert political control. US Army veteran Robert J. Reilly, for example, wrote that the War Remnants Museum promoted "very heavy propaganda, capitalizing on the My Lai tragedy and some displaying blatantly contrived instances of 'atrocities' comprised the bulk of the museum's offerings. Unfortunately, there are few left in Vietnam or

---

[11] Interview with John B.   [12] Interview with Andy.   [13] Interview with Kevin.
[14] Scott Laderman, "From the Vietnam War to the 'War on Terror.'" In *Tourism and War*. Edited by Richard Butler and Scott Laderman (London: Routledge, 2013), 34.

among the tourists present today who are old enough to know the truth.... The Vietnamese have done a [sic] effective job of demonizing us!"[15]

The majority of US veterans, in contrast, supported Vietnamese memories. Michael remembered seeing the deformed fetuses and said "that was a crime. That was a crime, and that should be punished." When asked how he felt about the War Remnants exhibits, he explained: "so it makes me uncomfortable. It should. You know? It should. I am more of an advocate for the Vietnamese right now than I am the American government."[16] Because most American returnees were also strongly anti-war, they found that Vietnamese war narratives reinforced their views on American culture and the US military-industrial complex. Larry Rottmann, for instance, wrote that the "life-size (death size?) images" of My Lai at the War Remnants Museum "breaks my heart": "I'm ashamed to have been in the same army as these men ... such a wanton waste of life, such a terrible example of US xenophobia."[17] John Z. found the military hardware at the War Remnants Museum educational because he "wasn't really at the pointy end," so the courtyard collection of tanks, bombers, and unexploded ordnance "opened [his] eyes, the technowar we fought ... things like the Daisy Cutters, you know, one bomb clears acres ... I didn't realize any of that existed until I saw it at the museum."[18]

These accounts show two forceful reactions to Vietnamese memory, clearly divided along national and ideological lines. Across both nationalities, however, one of the most prevalent responses to Vietnamese memory was the conviction that "victor's history" always prevails. When I asked former Marine Bill E., for example, about the War Remnants Museum, he laughed and said, "it's better than it used to be! I mean, it's still biased, just like any museum is. Especially military museums .... They try to tell their side, their story. And none of what's up there is false." He paused. "Well, some of it." Over two decades, Bill E. guided countless veterans through the War Remnants Museum, so he witnessed shifts in language and representation over time. Repeated visits to the space, his attention to softening narratives, and his expatriate exposure to Vietnamese memories of the war left Bill E. with a relaxed if slightly cynical attitude toward official Vietnamese commemoration: "it's just that they show their side of the story. And I've been to the Marine Corps museum in the US, and same thing. I mean we tell our side of the story, and not the bad side of the story."[19] Other veterans took a consciously selective approach to museum exhibits, noting what they

---

[15] Robert J. Reilly, *Return of the Warrior*, 68.   [16] Interview with Michael.
[17] Rottmann, "A Hundred Happy Sparrows," 135.   [18] Interview with John Z.
[19] Interview with Bill E.

approved of and disregarding what they did not. Australian Army veteran Ric thought that "their Army museum in Hà Nội is quite good ... they've got bits and pieces there that are quite good. Lots of stuff about Uncle Ho, but it's very biased, obviously. It's a bit like that one where my picture is." Ric was referring to the Agent Orange exhibit in the War Remnants Museum, where his advocacy for victims of dioxin poisoning is implicitly framed as support for the SRV. "That's quite biased, but who cares?" He was unfazed by this political exploitation of his personal mission, and even enjoyed getting regular emails from veterans who have visited the museum, "they ask me what happened, I say, 'Oh, I'm Hanoi Ric!'"[20]

Ric's relaxed attitude can be explained by a broader trend in Australian reactions to Vietnamese memory, where returnees emphasized that it is the American War, and not the Australian War, in Việt Nam. They suggested that this name implicitly exonerated Australian participation. Les said that "their version of history is different to ours, and I suppose because they're in charge they can tell their people anything they want. I mean, there's a very strong resentment of what they call the American War, but they probably don't know we were in it. So, we probably fly under the radar a bit."[21] Australians also suggested that the American War memory spared returning Australians from facing fabricated claims and manipulated anger. Australian Army veteran Graham S. concurred:

... the propaganda from the Việt Nam perspective was all directed pretty much toward the Americans anyway. And the museums are full of what they term American atrocity. But it's propaganda in the main ... I'm not saying that everything the Americans did was right and honorable, but generally speaking it wasn't as bad as the North Vietnamese portrayed it at the time and how they've portrayed it since. And as far as the Australian involvement was concerned, I think that we were honorable.[22]

The dual response of dismissing Vietnamese memory as mostly exaggerated and highlighting the Vietnamese focus on American conduct is a twofold exculpation: the Vietnamese wrote myth rather than history, and the villain of the myth is American and not Australian.

US veterans had more difficulty separating "their" war from Vietnamese memory, which complicated their "victors' history prevails" approach. US Army veteran Francis, for example, thought that the War Remnants Museum showed how

---

[20] Interview with Ric. [21] Interview with Les.
[22] Interview with Graham S., Telephone, June 23, 2017.

... the advantage of being a writer of history is good because you can portray it –
I'm not saying we didn't do a bunch of terrible things. Not a bunch, we did some
terrible things. But it's certainly a one-sided perspective.... But it's their country,
it's their museum, it's their war and, in a sense, they won. Not in a sense. They
won. So, they can write about it however they want. But, they don't talk about
some of the things that they did either.[23]

He struggled to reconcile his respect for Vietnamese war memories with a lopsided portrayal of violence and victimhood. Other veterans were determined to accept Vietnamese war memory to demonstrate their solidarity with the Vietnamese, but this determination conflicted with their political views on the purpose of commemoration. Some, like Suel, resolved this internal conflict by disengaging from contentious spaces in Việt Nam. He campaigned against American war commemorations – which he described as "recruiting posters" – but when it came to Vietnamese commemorations, he explained, "I don't go to them. To me, they're just propaganda. Everybody's got their story to tell, their propaganda, and that's OK. They won their war, they can say what they want to."[24]

Some veterans discovered that their personal experiences were retold in Vietnamese victory narratives. In 1967, John McCain parachuted into Trúc Bạch Lake in Hà Nội after his plane was shot down and was dragged out unconscious, by city residents. The Vietnamese erected a statue of McCain by the lake, depicting him in surrender: on his knees, hands raised. McCain visited Trúc Bạch Lake in 1985 on his first return trip with Walter Cronkite and was amused to see the statue dedicated to "John Sney McKay."[25] In an interview following this first trip back, he said "I still have no idea why they built this monument.... A very large crowd of Vietnamese gathered, all pointing to me and repeating my name – 'Mahcain, Mahcain.' It was perhaps the first time that someone was more recognized than Walter Cronkite."[26] McCain's humor likely derived from exasperation with his political battles in the United States. He reveled in the irony that this statue, "often pointed to ... as proof of my collaboration with the enemy" by American activists, so obviously misrepresented him. McCain's response indicates that he was content to live with the truth between two fabricated narratives: neither a "Manchurian candidate" nor a pleading "American air pirate." This last mistake, identifying him as Air Force rather than Navy, was "an insult

---

[23] Interview with Francis.   [24] Interview with Suel.
[25] McCain and Salter, *Worth the Fighting For*, 262.
[26] John McCain, quoted in "Inside Vietnam: What a Former POW Found." *US News and World Report*, March 11, 1985.

that only partly dilutes the pleasure I take from the only statue in the world that bears my name, or a close approximation of it, anyway."[27]

McCain and fellow ex-prisoner of war (POW) Pete reacted differently to Hỏa Lò Prison museum. This museum tells the story of Vietnamese resistance through the history of the colonial prison. Many Western visitors are only aware of the prison's tenure as the "Hanoi Hilton," and are surprised to find just two small rooms depicting the experiences of American POWs. These exhibits emphasize the comfort and kindness extended toward the US prisoners by Vietnamese guards: there are photographs of prisoners playing basketball, decorating a Christmas tree, attending chapel, enjoying meals. The introductory caption outside the first "US" room states:

... the United States government carried out sabotage warfare by using their air and naval forces.... Thousands of planes were shot down and hundreds of United States pilots were arrested by the North Army and people. Some of them were imprisoned here. During the war, the national economy was having difficulties, but the Vietnamese government created the best living conditions that they could for the US pilots. They had a stable life during their temporary detention periods.[28]

These representations contrast starkly with the exhibits documenting French colonial torture practices. The overarching narrative of the museum is one of the righteousness, unity, and resilience of the Vietnamese people.

McCain and Pete first revisited Hỏa Lò together in 1992, on an official delegation regarding the POW/missing in action (MIA) issue. At the time, Hỏa Lò was still operating as a prison. In 1998, the jail was mostly demolished (a small part of the original walls remains) and turned into the museum. Neither veteran was impressed with the narrative at their "old lodgings."[29] Pete described it as "a complete fraud."[30] McCain sarcastically described photographs, orchestrated to galvanize the international anti-war movement, of prisoners "enjoying Hanoi's gracious hospitality."[31] Pete was at Hỏa Lò when these photographs were taken. He remembered how prisoners were brought over to Hỏa Lò from "The Plantation," another Hà Nội prison, and given luxuries for the photo shoot. "They had been locked up for a long time and 'oh wow! Ping pong table!' Of course, it was all being filmed. And brought out a bunch of neat food, 'wow, haven't eaten like this in a long time, or ever!' And so, of

---

[27] McCain and Salter, *Worth the Fighting For*, 262.
[28] Author's notes from visit to Hỏa Lò Prison, Hà Nội, April 2016.
[29] McCain and Salter, *Worth the Fighting For*, 262.   [30] Interview with Pete.
[31] McCain and Salter, *Worth the Fighting For*, 262.

course it was just all for propaganda, but staged."³² Before visiting, neither veteran had expected that the museum would accurately represent their incarceration. In 1985, before the museum opened, an interviewer asked McCain if the Vietnamese expressed regret for his suffering as a prisoner. "They still stick to this myth that the prisoners were treated well," he responded.³³ Still, the audacity of the Vietnamese perpetuating myths about the treatment of POWs in the very same space that they were tortured outraged them. Pete, invited in official capacity as Ambassador when the museum first opened, remembered his reaction to the exhibit: "Are you shitting me? That never happened!"³⁴

Pete's experience with and relationship to the exhibit was unusually direct, and the material obviously contrived. Yet many returnees were upset by exhibits that were more historically accurate. For example, the Sơn Mỹ Memorial and Museum remembers the victims of the My Lai massacre. The museum was built on the former hamlet of Tư Cung, one of the five hamlets attacked in the massacre, in the village of Tịnh Khê. Remnants of the hamlet remain in a garden, circled by a concrete pathway impressed with children's footprints and soldiers' bootprints. A statue in the center of the garden depicts survivors of the massacre cradling dying victims. Inside the small museum, a plaque covers the wall opposite the entrance. This "List of the Victims Killed by the GIs" has the names of the 504 civilians killed in the massacre etched into reflective black stone.³⁵ The museum is extremely graphic. Photographs of the massacre are spread across the single floor. There are several dioramas, and a replica well stands in one corner with bloody handprints on the lip: inside is a mannequin of a dying man in a pool of blood. There are displays of recovered items from burnt houses, with captions detailing who their owners were and explaining in detail how they were killed. Toward the end of the museum, there are photographs of atoning veterans, rebuilding projects, and diplomatic and commemorative events.³⁶ This turn in the story toward the recovery and reconciliation demonstrates again Schwenkel's observation of the role of the US veteran in Vietnamese postwar memory, in which the supplicating veteran elevates Vietnamese moral authority by revealing the Vietnamese capacity for forgiveness.³⁷ The reconciliation turn is particularly effective at Sơn Mỹ because the My Lai massacre was such an absolute demonstration of

---

³² Interview with Pete.   ³³ McCain, in "Inside Vietnam."   ³⁴ Interview with Pete.
³⁵ Veterans and other Western visitors sometimes note that plaques like this remind them of "The Wall" in DC, but there is no evidence suggesting that either memorial was based on the other.
³⁶ Author's notes from visit to Sơn Mỹ Memorial and Museum, Tịnh Khê, April 4, 2016.
³⁷ Schwenkel, *American War in Contemporary Vietnam*, 26–27.

American brutality and Vietnamese victimization. Thus, the narrative at Sơn Mỹ echoes the story of the War Remnants and Hỏa Lò museums: Vietnamese suffering, resistance, and endurance.

Classics scholar James Tatum argued that "for most Americans, [My Lai] . . . will have more resonance than any other memorial of the America [sic] War in Vietnam."[38] However, very few veterans visited Sơn Mỹ. Most did not indicate that they had considered visiting, which may simply reflect lack of opportunity: Tịnh Khê is three hours by train or car from the nearest cities with any major tourism infrastructure. Others explained that they found it too painful to visit. Suel reacted forcefully when I asked if he had visited the site: "I won't go there. I absolutely refuse to go there. I don't want to deal with it. No, I've never been there, and I'll never go there."[39] The few veterans I interviewed who chose to visit Sơn Mỹ were all sympathetic to Vietnamese war victims. Because Sơn Mỹ is much more difficult to visit than the War Remnants and Hỏa Lò museums, and because the museum remembers such a traumatic, controversial, and well-known event, their decision to make the journey to the site of the massacre indicated a recognition of Vietnamese pain. Perhaps more than any other space in Việt Nam, Sơn Mỹ is a place to make pilgrimage and grieve.

Despite their sympathy toward Vietnamese war victims, several of the veterans who visited Sơn Mỹ contested the way the events of My Lai were memorialized there. Ron, the US Army photographer of the My Lai massacre, testified in 1976 that he had first sold his photographs of the My Lai massacre because he "wanted to get it off my chest, let the people know exactly what had happened."[40] Ron was glad that his images were on display in the War Remnants Museum, because "American museums are trying to hide . . . what happened in Vietnam and that. And I think in Việt Nam they're trying to show more of a reality of what happened there." However, when I asked him about the captions on his photographs at Sơn Mỹ, Ron said, "some I can agree with, some I cannot agree with."[41] Captions were the common complaint among Sơn Mỹ visitors. James, a proudly anti-war American veteran, remembered "some propaganda there" at Sơn Mỹ, with "one photograph in particular, of GIs, American GIs [soldiers] standing around smoking cigarettes and [the

---

[38] James Tatum, "Memorials of the America War in Vietnam." *Critical Inquiry* 22:4 (Summer, 1996): 645.
[39] Interview with Suel.
[40] Testimony of Ronald Haeberle, April 23, 1970. In House Committee on Armed Services, *Investigation of the My Lai Incident*, Ninety-First Cong., Second Session, 1976, 268.
[41] Interview with Ron.

6   Remembering the American War in Việt Nam   161

caption] said 'GIs relaxing after the massacre.'"⁴² This caption is not inaccurate: Seymour Hersh collected accounts from survivors and participants in the massacre who remembered soldiers "taking a break, or loafing" while other soldiers continued the killing.⁴³ Yet James felt so strongly about this caption that he "talked to the young woman guide there .... I said, 'that's inappropriate, and you should revise that.' And I gave her some suggestions."⁴⁴

Ron and James both held the view that American violence against civilians was endemic during the war. However, when they were confronted with exhibits that remembered American violence in this way – as a casual, indifferent practice, rather than an aberrant, reactionary "snap" triggered by stress – they reacted defensively.⁴⁵ In the aftermath of war, both had questioned how and why their fellow soldiers could commit such acts of violence. The answers they found – military culture, ingrained racism and misogyny, psychological pressures of combat, and coping mechanisms for trauma – did not excuse but at least explained how people could learn to hurt others.⁴⁶ These factors of the American experience were rarely discussed in Vietnamese spaces for memory, and when they were, they were clinical and accusatory: flat dissections of enemy ideology and action. One caption reads: "America's secret documents about operation plan to kill civilians in Sơn Mỹ on March 16th, 1968." Another describes a 1969 bombing run through Quảng Ngãi: "the US bombing the area to rub out their crimes traces, one year later."⁴⁷ The focus of the Sơn Mỹ Museum is the Vietnamese experience as victim of atrocity, not the American experience as perpetrator. Consequently, these veterans found their feelings of solidarity tested by what they felt were exaggerated or one-sided representations.

For Ron, Sơn Mỹ also tested his personal war memory. He disapproved of "some of the objects they have there [at Sơn Mỹ], like you've probably seen the setup of the soldier and that, and all that? This one soldier holding the woman by the hair, that's a little ... kind of hard to comprehend. It could have happened there, I do not know, but the photographs

---

⁴² Interview with James. As of 2016, this caption reads "the US soldiers with a 'cold look' after Sơn Mỹ massacre."
⁴³ Seymour Hersh, *My Lai 4* (New York: Random House, 1970), 66.
⁴⁴ Interview with James.
⁴⁵ Exploring a similar response of American tourists to the War Remnants Museum, Laderman argues that for American visitors, "the war was an American tragedy, and if the museum failed to acknowledge American suffering ... then it was revealing its ideological bias." Laderman, "From the Vietnam War to the 'War on Terror,'" 33.
⁴⁶ Both veterans recommended Nick Turse's *Kill Anything That Moves* to explain their view on atrocities in Vietnam. Nick Turse, *Kill Anything That Moves: The Real American War in Vietnam* (New York: Metropolitan Books, 2013).
⁴⁷ Sơn Mỹ Memorial and Museum, April 4, 2016.

tell the whole story there."⁴⁸ Ron was describing a nearly life-size clay statue of a soldier forcing a woman onto the ground by her hair. His descriptions of inauthenticity at Sơn Mỹ were weighted by his sense of authority over My Lai memory: he was a witness to the massacre and so considered his memory, represented in his photographs, as the closest to "the whole story," or the historical truth. In his 1976 testimony, he described conduct very similar to that depicted by the diorama: American soldiers were "more or less tormenting these people, especially that woman [indicating a photograph] at the front. They were grabbing her and kicking her around."⁴⁹ Perhaps if the diorama presented this specific event in the way that he remembered it, he would not have disapproved. However, his critique avoids "the basic difficulty" of portraying atrocity: how to represent an event when cover-ups and ongoing warfare eradicated nearly all the evidence and only the trauma of survivors remains.⁵⁰ Furthermore, his sense of authority over memory of My Lai undermines how the Vietnamese tell their own story. Ron's images captured the event from one place, and from the point of view of one US Army photographer, but the massacre spanned four hamlets. Surviving the hundreds of murdered Vietnamese were the villagers who witnessed their deaths. The diorama of the woman Ron describes is likely based on the memory of a survivor.⁵¹

Thus, Vietnamese war memories that directly challenged veteran experiences elicited strong responses. Aspects of Vietnamese war narratives that implicitly contested veteran memories, on the other hand, were often overlooked or even readily accepted. The dominant official narrative in Việt Nam frames the American War as part of a long tradition of resistance to foreign invasion. Historian Patricia Pelley notes that this narrative emerged in the aftermath of Independence, when Communist Party historians "were urged to put greater emphasis on the 'fighting spirit' of the Vietnamese ... new narratives were centered on the idea of a totalizing unity inside the borders and an aggressive heterogeneity beyond."⁵² This nation-building narrative is prominent in general history museums, temples and other religious spaces, and in public discourse. I anticipated that many returnees would reject this narrative because it

---

⁴⁸ Interview with Ron.
⁴⁹ Haeberle, testimony on *Investigation of the My Lai Incident*, 502.
⁵⁰ Paul Williams, *Memorial Museums: The Global Rush to Commemorate Atrocities* (Oxford: Berg, 2007), 25. Charlie Company soldiers razed the hamlets after the massacre, and Quảng Ngãi province was heavily bombed from 1969 until 1972 by RVNAF and American aircraft to cripple National Liberation Front (NLF) resistance in the area.
⁵¹ The museum is directed by a survivor, Phạm Thành Công, and other survivors worked as guides at the memorial.
⁵² Pelley, *Postcolonial Vietnam*, 93.

presents the United States and Australia as two of many oppressive forces. Yet most veterans accepted this narrative and reproduced it in their memories of return.

For example, US Army veteran Harold Moore visited the Vietnam Historical Museum where he saw

> ... a timeline and a map of Vietnam's unhappy history dating back well over a thousand years .... Few Westerners seemingly had ever considered before marching their soldiers off into the jungles of a nation full of ardent nationalists who had demonstrated that they were fully prepared to fight for generations until the foreign occupier got tired of war, or choked on his own blood.[53]

Moore took this narrative as an answer to the question of why America lost the war in Vietnam. He did not see the implications of this narrative: that the United States invaded (and was not asked by the RVN), that they did so for imperial purposes (not for their allies), and that right was on the side of Democratic Republic of Việt Nam (DRV) and, by extension, the contemporary SRV. Many veterans like Moore – proud of their service, proud of their country, and ambiguous if not in agreement with the war – responded in similar fashion when they learned about Việt Nam's "thousand years" of resistance. They accepted it as an answer to "why we lost," but did not reflect on the ideological challenge this narrative posed to their worldview. Alistair Thomson's theory of "composure" suggests that for these returnees, reframing Vietnam as the "American War" somehow absolved returnees of the legacy of American violence in Việt Nam. Thomson notes that we draw on public references to compose a life story that is psychically comfortable.[54] While Vietnam in America means "tragedy ... the bad war, a syndrome, a quagmire, a stinging loss in need of healing and recuperation," in Việt Nam the American War is just one of many foreign invasions.[55] By remembering the war through Vietnamese memory – placed in a context of cyclic Vietnamese resistance – the American invasion is diminished relative to the "thousand years" of war against China, and American moral responsibility over Vietnam is reduced.

Anti-war veterans escaped the ideological challenge posed by public Vietnamese war memory. Most had concluded long ago that the DRV was on the "right" side of war, so the narrative of united resistance merely validated their view. Instead, they faced another contradiction. Anti-war

---

[53] Moore and Galloway, *We Are Soldiers Still*, 25.
[54] Alistair Thomson, "A Past You Can Live With: Digger Memories and the Anzac Legend." *Oral History Association of Australia Journal* 13 (1991): 13.
[55] Nguyễn, *Nothing Ever Dies*, 5.

returnees were strongly opposed to war commemoration in their own countries – not only Vietnam commemorations, but all venerations of the US military. Writer W.D. said that "if I had my way, I'd dynamite every war memorial in the United States of America."[56] Former Marine Larry argued that war commemoration whitewashed history and "immortalizes war, and makes it into something good."[57] Only memorials that were perceived to challenge war were exempt from critique: "The Wall," for example, was excused as a "stroke of genius" that "speaks only of loss."[58] However, this condemnation of war commemoration did not extend to Việt Nam.

For example, US Army veteran Deryle described Vietnamese war cemeteries as "holy places," focusing on a revolutionary cemetery in Kon Tom that he visited with local veterans who had built a memorial there. He used similar language to describe Angel Fire Memorial Chapel, built by the father of a soldier killed in Vietnam, in his home state of New Mexico: it was an "incredible temple ... a holy thing, a sacred thing." Over the years, the ownership of Angel Fire shifted from the father, Victor Westphall, to Disabled American Veterans, to the David Westphall Veterans Foundation, and finally to the state of New Mexico. The memorial was increasingly traditionalized as it changed hands, with the addition of a Visitors Center, an amphitheater, a Huey helicopter, and from 2018, a military cemetery. Deryle lamented the changes at Angel Fire: "it ended up being taken over by patriotic American veterans' groups, and that old man, Mia, he didn't start it to do that. You know? He didn't mean it to be a hagiography of war."[59]

The evolution of Angel Fire from a private memorial into a state memorial paralleled the expansion of Vietnamese memorials, including the one at Kon Tum. Both gradually grew to represent the memories and grief of a broader community of survivors, and were eventually recognized as national historic sites.[60] Both promoted whitewashed versions of "their" war and condemned the "other side." The Angel Fire Visitor Center depicts US soldiers playing with children and providing medical care, while the few representations of Vietnamese perpetuate wartime

---

[56] Interview with W.D. [57] Interview with Larry.
[58] Ibid.; Maya Lin, in Jon Wiener, "Chris Burdden and 'The Other Vietnam Memorial.'" *The Nation*, May 11, 2015. www.thenation.com/article/chris-burden-and-other-vietnam-memorial/
[59] Interview with Deryle.
[60] Angel Fire Memorial Chapel was recognized by Congress as a memorial of national significance in 1987; Khu Di Tích Chiến Thắng Đắk Tô – Tân Cảnh (Victory Monument Dak To – Tan Canh) was recognized as a historic monument with national importance in 1992.

stereotypes.⁶¹ As Deryle noted, Kon Tum's Victory Memorial includes a large plaque that remembers the revolutionary victory at Dak To: "there was the date when the commies ran the running dog capitalists out of the country … 'Vietnamese army forces blah blah blah took over the town of Kon Tum, ran Americans out.'"⁶² Despite (or perhaps because of) the political agendas apparent at both sites, many survivors still find meaning in these spaces. Like the Vietnamese veterans who return to the Kon Tum memorial every March, New Mexico veterans visit the site during a ritual motorcycle rally at Red River, and US veterans from around the country make pilgrimage to Angel Fire in the annual "Run For The Wall."⁶³

The parallel development of these two sites suggests that Deryle's initial preference for Angel Fire and his enduring attachment to Kon Tum was political. Patrick Hagopian notes that Victor Westphall stated that the chapel "honored all the dead of the Vietnam conflict, including North Vietnamese and Viet Cong."⁶⁴ This reconciliatory note of Angel Fire likely appealed to Deryle, but it became a cause of contention. Hagopian found that funding from the broader veteran community was conditional on a narrower memorial practice: "now that the [Disabled American Veterans] DAV is involved, [Vietnam Veterans Memorial] Fund officials are satisfied that there is no longer any thought that the Chapel will honor enemy veterans."⁶⁵ Through the participation of large veterans' organizations, Angel Fire came to perpetuate the ideology that recruited Deryle into the war in the first place: "I volunteered … pro-war, pro-America, yay go team, you know?" Deryle rejected the significance that traditional elements of Angel Fire held for more conservative veterans, because those elements represented the pro-war ideology that he had come to despise. But because Kon Tum was the site of his battle, and because he commemorated his battle there with former enemies, he could separate the politicized elements of the Kon Tum memorial from its spiritual significance. Deryle remembered his first return to Kon Tum in 1995. He asked his guide to translate the entire poster. "He sighed real

---

⁶¹ One of the few photographs in the Center in which Vietnamese are the subject is an image of three women in *áo dài*, traditional dress. The caption describes "Three fashionably dressed Vietnamese women stroll past a public execution site in downtown Saigon." Author's notes from visit to Vietnam Veterans Memorial Chapel, Angel Fire, New Mexico, May 19, 2017.
⁶² Interview with Deryle.
⁶³ "Run For The Wall" is an annual motorcycle ride from Los Angeles to Washington, DC in the week prior to Memorial Day. Vietnam veterans and supporters visit memorials and meaningful sites along the way.
⁶⁴ Hagopian, *Vietnam War in American Memory*, 180.
⁶⁵ Ibid. Disabled American Veterans is a politically conservative veterans' organization.

big, he looks up at me and he said, 'Deryle, it say: war is over.' And I looked at him and I said: 'And so it is.'"[66]

Other anti-war returnees exempted Vietnamese sites of memory because of their feelings of solidarity and guilt toward Vietnamese victims of the war. For example, Marine Larry, a former Marine, was interested in the My Lai massacre. He had interviewed survivors and read transcripts of Calley's court martial, and in his interview recounted many of the violent details he had learned to illustrate the horror of the massacre. He described the statue at Sơn Mỹ as "just awesome."[67] The statue at Sơn Mỹ depicts two men, two women, and two children. One man is slumped over the body of a child; another is collapsed in the arms of the seated woman. The other woman is standing, with fury and pain etched on her face, holding a child limp in one arm with her other fist raised in defiance. The standing woman is the central figure, a "Heroic Mother" or "Mother of Vietnam" icon that is prominent throughout Việt Nam.[68] Historian Heonik Kwon observes that Heroic Mothers play an important role in mobilizing support for and commemorating the revolutionary cause: they are honored for "sacrific[ing]" their children and are depicted "overcom-[ing] the grief of losing their children to the enemy's violence to stand defiantly against the machinery of violence."[69] Thus at Sơn Mỹ, the (civilian) victims and survivors of the My Lai massacre legitimize the revolutionary cause. Larry's admiration of the Sơn Mỹ statue reflects both his solidarity with victims of the massacre and his agreement with the narrative of a revolutionary war against American aggression.

Larry's admiration also speaks to his preoccupation with women war victims. He traced the trajectory of his return to Việt Nam to witnessing the death of a pregnant Vietnamese woman on My Khe beach during the war, which led him to write a novel about a woman who fought for the NLF. After returning to Việt Nam to live he focused on telling the stories of NLF women who survived political prisons. When he talked about his regret, grief, and anger about the war, he fixated on sexual violence and torture of women: "the only thing you hear about, you read about in America is the Hanoi Hilton. You don't read about Côn Đảo or Côn Sơn prison island, you don't read about women being strung up and raped to death with a poker."[70] He, along with many other veterans, perceived women as inherently calmer, more peaceful, and loving than men. The "maternal instinct" was central to their understanding of womanhood.

---

[66] Interview with Deryle.   [67] Interview with Larry.
[68] Heonik Kwon, "North Korea's Culture of Commemoration." In *Atheism and Its Discontents: A Comparative Study of Religion and Communism in Eurasia.* Edited by Tam T.T. Ngo and Justine B. Quijada (London: Palgrave, 2014), 127.
[69] Ibid.   [70] Interview with Larry.

Women fought only when necessary, and never for ego: therefore, women soldiers were more virtuous both in their femininity and in their sacrifice. This view corresponds to Vietnamese constructions of women in combat. Historian Hue-Tam Ho Tai notes that the "popular saying 'when war comes, even women must fight' ... suggests that women are recruits of last resort into the fight to defend the homeland."[71] These gendered combat values are reflected in the Sơn Mỹ statue, where the women figures are positioned with agency: they cradle the dying man and killed child, and with a raised fist suggest that they will avenge the deaths. They are both carers and fighters, with each role intrinsically linked to the other. Vietnamese memorials to women legitimized anti-war returnees' views on gender and on war: subverting Western martial masculinity while upholding anti-war variations of traditional gendered values. It is ironic, then, that Heroic Mother memorials do not challenge Vietnamese patriarchal norms, but exploit the "gendered national imaginaries" of Việt Nam.[72] Tai argues that mother figures in Vietnamese commemoration make "use of images of the country as victim of oppression and as family whose home is being invaded."[73] The Heroic Mother concentrates the identity of the war victim around Việt Nam's most sacred figure, and doing so, immortalizes those that were sacrificed.

Perhaps the most striking bias in veteran appreciation of Vietnamese commemoration was the lack of recognition of the erasure of the RVN. Suel, who loathed most memorials, reminisced:

I'll tell you where I do like to go. And we do it every year, we go up to the National Memorial here in Việt Nam, for the veterans that died. And I go up there, and I light incense. I go up there every year, to give honor to these men. Bill and I do every year. There's a place we go to, and we always give a toast to the brothers. The ones who made it, and the ones who didn't, on all sides. There's no ... I mean it's everybody. North, south, east, west, I don't care. You're a brother. And we go every year.[74]

Trường Sơn National Cemetery, where he toasted to "the brothers ... on all sides," only remembers revolutionary soldiers. RVNAF are not remembered and cannot be buried in Martyrs' cemeteries, and many of their own cemeteries were destroyed after the war. Yến Lê Espiritu describes this "organized forgetting" of RVNAF in Việt Nam as "a form of forced disappearance ... literally razing the dead [Army of the Republic of Việt Nam] ARVN soldiers from the landscape."[75] Ruins of RVNAF

---

[71] Hue-Tam Ho Tai, "Faces of Remembering and Forgetting." In *Country of Memory: Remaking the Past in Late Socialist Vietnam*. Edited by Hue-Tam Ho Tai (Berkeley, CA: University of California Press, 2001), 174.
[72] Till, "Places of Memory," 293.   [73] Ibid., 173.   [74] Interview with Suel.
[75] Espiritu, *Body Counts*, 108.

cemeteries dot the landscape of southern provinces, their tombstones crumbling and overgrown with weeds. Near some of the larger memorials and cemeteries, such as the one in Kon Tum, locals maintain small shrines to RVNAF soldiers. These alternative sites of memory contrast starkly with the impressive state-sponsored cemeteries and memorials, drawing attention to the limits of national reconciliation. Yet returnees seemed to respond to Martyrs' ceremonies as if they were memorials for all soldiers. Many felt honored to join in official commemorations at these cemeteries. This response was not limited to anti-war veterans or those sympathetic to the SRV. Australian veteran Rod felt that these moments of shared mourning in sacred spaces were the foundation stone of Australian-Vietnamese veteran relationships. It was "the way we began our friendship with the Vietnamese ... we've been back there for the memorial to their dead from the Binh Ba battle .... They do their own way, but it's the same as us. We mourn our dead."[76]

Few returnees spoke about the lack of representation of their former allies. American veteran Mike P. observed in 1989: "only the graves of the winners were allowed to be cared for and memorialized as the Honored Dead." Mike P. felt very deeply about the erasure of RVNAF soldiers. He remembered a former RVNAF cemetery where "the gravestones of the losers had been uprooted and the place re-landscaped."[77] Veterans who observed erasure were acutely aware of the importance of ancestor worship in Việt Nam. When Reilly observed in 2010 that RVNAF military cemeteries had "disappeared," which he understood to mean "desecrated, bulldozed out of existence," he noted that "for a culture that venerates their ancestors, this is horrible blasphemy."[78] These few returnees also indicated that the repression of RVN memory was common knowledge among returning veterans. US Army veteran Mark described visiting a cemetery with the Veterans Viet Nam Restoration Project (VVRP) – the same organization that Mike P. returned with in 1989 – and some Vietnamese hosts:

We went out and lit these punks [of incense] and set them [on] each one of the graves. And then I find out that those are all Viet Cong. They gave them good graves. The South Vietnam Army guys, they just bulldozed them. I didn't feel good about that. And a lot of guys from the VVRP: "we got to put up with this, we got to honor that." Well, I didn't like that, so I didn't go back there and do it anymore. I'm not putting a prayer out for a communist that killed ... you know, didn't seem right to me.[79]

---

[76] Interview with Rod. [77] Mike P., "1989 VVRP Journal w Intro."
[78] Reilly, *Return of the Warriors*, 52. [79] Interview with Mark.

Early observers of this erasure interpreted it in different ways. Mike P. thought that the erasure of memory indicated that "the Vietnamese have not yet worked through the war, the old regime, and perhaps even their various regional identities; have repressed or avoided the problem."[80] William Broyles Jr. had a less generous interpretation. He viewed Vietnamese remembrance practice as *damnatio memoriae*, a deliberate erasure with explicit political purposes. "The Communists stand in the flood of history and pluck from the water only what serves the State. If reality is inconvenient, it can simply be hanged. If history falls short of the ideal, it can be transformed into myth."[81] Where Mike P. saw an inability to acknowledge, reconcile and heal from conflict, Broyles saw "a moral certainty so strong as to make the suffering of the individuals invisible."[82] By the time Mark and Reilly returned in 2009 and 2010 respectively, there was little doubt that the erasure of RVNAF graves and memories was a deliberate act of repression, and not merely a sign of deep wounds that would eventually scar over.

Only these four Americans – Reilly, Mark, Mike P., and Broyles – commented on the deliberate erasure of their former allies from the memory landscape of Việt Nam. Some other interviewees acknowledged that both countries "hang," as Broyles put it, their "inconvenient" histories, but implied that Việt Nam's purpose was purer. Chuck, for instance, saw Vietnamese commemoration as promoting "peace, and stability, and a unified nation. So, I don't quibble too much with that."[83] Others took a relativist approach: after advocating the destruction of American war memorials, W.D. proposed new memorials to suffragettes, unionists, civil rights leaders, and Native American resistance fighters. He viewed SRV memorials as commemorating a comparable righteous cause: "the Vietnamese have good reason to memorialize their war dead. Those men and women died fighting for their country's freedom."[84] Aside from indicating that Americans do not have a good reason to memorialize their war dead, his statement erases the RVNAF who died fighting for their freedom. These responses suggest that many Americans may have preferred not to engage with the contentious aspects of Vietnamese commemoration that undermined the SRV – and anti-war – perspective on the war.

Australian veterans, in contrast, focused on the desecration of RVNAF memory in their discussions of Vietnamese commemoration. Army veteran David W. explained, "it's all one-sided. All the memorials are for the winners. There are none for the people we fought with. Not a thing . . .

---

[80] Mike P., "1989 VVRP Journal w Intro." [81] Broyles Jr., *Brothers in Arms*, 167–68.
[82] Ibid., 267. [83] Interview with Chuck. [84] Interview with W.D.

they bulldozed and put blocks of units on [the graves of the RVNAF]."[85] Many Australians continued to promote the domino theory justification for Australia's involvement upon their return, and so interpreted Vietnamese remembrance practices within this framework. Kevin explained: "any myth propagated by the Vietnamese government that it was a war of liberation, an anti-American War, and united the South, that's propaganda. It was a war of conquest, they colonized the South, they plundered the hell out of the place."[86] Most Australians were suspicious of the SRV and its political agenda. Some found conflict and disrespect wherever they looked. Army veteran Brian, for instance, noted that the graves of NLF soldiers that Australians fought against had disappeared when he returned. He interpreted this as malicious desecration: "at war's end, the North Vietnamese destroyed all those graves. Why? Boy, that's just opening up all wounds. The only thing I can think is that they were South Vietnamese people. Irrespective of their views, of supporting the North, they were South Vietnamese, so they were treated as all of South Vietnamese. Very little respect." The bodies of these NLF soldiers were likely removed from their hasty war graves to a final resting place close to their families, in keeping with Vietnamese ancestor worship. Brian was aware of this ritual: "I understood the Asian mind, the Asian way of respect and treatment of family dead ... unless they have a body that they can give a rightful burial to, the body's spirit remains wandering."[87] Yet because of his negative views of the SRV, he interpreted the absence of these NLF graves as a reminder of the vindictive regional hierarchies in socialist Việt Nam.

The focus on wartime purpose and the distrust of the Vietnamese government link to a broader reason why Australians reacted so strongly against SRV memory narratives. As Part I shows, where Americans found healing and friendship largely through reconciliation projects, Australians tended to work through their trauma by invoking and recreating the Anzac tradition of commemorative pilgrimage. Memories of the war that conflicted with the Australian narrative were met with hostility and anger. This tension between Australian and Vietnamese memory was particularly evident at the site of the Battle of Long Tan.

On August 18, 1966, D Company of 6th Battalion, Royal Australian Regiment (6RAR) clashed with an NLF battalion in a rubber plantation near the village of Long Tân. Seventeen Australians and one New Zealander were killed, and 24 soldiers were wounded, marking the highest single-day loss of life for the ATF in Vietnam, along with what Australian forces estimated at 245 NLF. Both sides claimed victory.

[85] Interview with David W.   [86] Interview with Kevin.   [87] Interview with Brian.

Three years later, 6RAR erected a cross on the site "in memory of those ... who gave their lives near this spot during the Battle of Long Tan."⁸⁸ After the war, the cross was removed and in 1984 relocated to Đồng Nai Museum in Biên Hòa. In Australia, the anniversary of the battle was increasingly associated with Vietnam veteran identity and in 1987 was designated "Vietnam Veterans Day." The Long Đất People's Committee erected a replica cross on the site of the battle between 1986 and 1989, likely in response to increasing interest from the small number of Australians who had returned.

Veteran attitudes toward Long Tân shifted significantly over the years. Terry Burstall, a veteran of the battle, returned in 1986 and found the site "foreboding and stagnant .... Part of me wanted to walk around the plantation and part of me wanted to get out of the accursed place." Burstall was shown the original cross by his guide in 1987 and was unsure if it would be meaningful to other veterans because it "really did not mean a thing to me."⁸⁹ In 1990, Australian Army veteran Graham E. received permission from the People's Committee to hold an Anzac Day ceremony at the site. Graham E. remembered how an NLF veteran and member of the Local People's Committee named Mr. Huy argued passionately for Graham E.'s right to hold the service. Huy and several other NLF veterans attended Graham E.'s service, and Huy then helped Graham E. find the nearby location where he had trod on a mine. "It was a very emotional moment for me. But I never forgot the sort of courage and the kindness of that bloke."⁹⁰ Both Burstall and Graham E. felt somber at Long Tân, and both demonstrated respect for Vietnamese sovereignty. Their experiences indicate a negotiation of personal trauma through reconciliation.

Graham E.'s official Anzac Day ceremony at Long Tân in 1990 established a precedent for other Australians and coincided with the "Anzac Revival" in Australia. As increasing numbers of Australians began to return for commemorations at Long Tân in the 1990s, the local government put visitation rules in place to protect the private property on which the cross stands. Prescheduled visits and small-scale, unofficial commemorations were permitted. While these rules were obeyed, Australian veterans also began to exert influence over the site. Graham S. created an organization to fund the upkeep of the replica cross and site because "we knew how important it was to veterans going back, they needed a focal point, and the Long Tan Cross [replica] had become that focal point."⁹¹

---

[88] Photograph of the original Long Tan Cross. Accession number P09951.002. Australian War Memorial Collection. www.awm.gov.au/collection/C1271355
[89] Burstall, *A Soldier Returns*, 88–89, 136.   [90] Interview with Graham E.
[91] Interview with Graham S.

The growing symbolic significance of Long Tân to Australian war memory demonstrates the process of "inventing tradition."[92] As Boym notes, "invented tradition does not mean a creation ex nihilo or a pure act of social constructivism; rather, it builds on the sense of loss of community and cohesion and offers a comforting collective script for individual longing."[93] Graham S.'s group liaised with the Vietnamese government through an Australian veteran charity group, and the replica cross was formally recognized as a war memorial in 2002. The original cross, still in the Biên Hòa museum, was rarely visited. "The original cross is a symbol really," Graham S. explained, while the replica has "become iconic."[94]

Returning veterans gradually began to push the boundaries of Vietnamese conditions. The fortieth anniversary in 2006 saw increasing tension between veterans' feeling of entitlement to Long Tân and Vietnamese authority. Australian veteran and local liaison Paul Murphy gave a radio interview complaining about "the amount of work that was required was just mind-blowing ... it went on and on, police permits ... [songs] had to be submitted to the cultural department in Hà Nội for approval ... it has been a very sensitive issue."[95] Expatriate groups began to run tours to Long Tân without permits, and veteran guides contested Vietnamese history on their tours. Australian boundary-pushing in Việt Nam mirrors anxieties about (lack of) sovereignty at Gallipoli, the site of the first Anzacs, where historian Bart Ziino observes a continued "basic insecurity about the apparent contradiction between [Australia's] own 'Valhalla' and its status as alien soil."[96] The shift in attitude toward Long Tân also reflected a pronounced shift toward the heroic in Australian Vietnam war memories. The *60 Minutes* program that followed commemoration returnee Dave and fellow Long Tan veteran Bob Buick on their first trip back to the battlefield for the fortieth anniversary promoted an Anzac narrative of the battle of Long Tan. Strategic stakes were exaggerated, NLF advantages overstated, Australian support minimized, and the Vietnamese version of history was dismissed as "stubbornly claim[ing] victory."[97] The climactic moment of the program was two NLF Long Tan veterans stating that "you won this battle, but we won the war."[98] Dave emphasized this concession: "they recognized that we won our war. And that is what they respect and admire."[99]

---

[92] Eric Hobsbawm and Terence Ranger, *The Invention of Tradition* (Cambridge: Cambridge University Press, 1983).
[93] Boym, *Future of Nostalgia*, 42.   [94] Interview with Graham S.
[95] Paul Murphy, "40 Years On – Long Tan." *ABC Radio National*, August 18, 2006.
[96] Ziino, "Who Owns Gallipoli?" 3.
[97] "The Forgotten Heroes." *60 Minutes*, produced by Hamish Thomson (Sydney: Nine News, August 13, 2006). http://battleoflongtan.com/60-minutes-the-battle-of-long-tan/
[98] DD45 veteran, interview in ibid.   [99] Dave, interview in ibid.

Australian veterans – both those who fought in the battle and those who did not – demonstrated that they had absorbed this narrative, invoking Gallipoli in their stories of Long Tan. Graham S. explained that Long Tan "typified the spirit of the Australian soldier, and that was forged at Gallipoli ... it's taken on the same sort of significance as Gallipoli."[100] Army veteran Ray argued that had the NLF won Long Tan, the revolutionary forces would have "take[n] out all the Australians ... the South Vietnamese government would have fallen."[101] John W. described how "the Aussies took on 2000, a bloody platoon kicked the arse of 2000!"[102] Some returnees claimed that after Long Tan the Vietnamese were afraid to face the Australians in battle, effectively pacifying the province of Phước Tuy for the remainder of the war.[103] This war memory fed into the Australian consensus that the Vietnamese welcomed them back to Việt Nam because of their wartime conduct, working to validate the growing numbers of Australian returnees. Long Tân was often cited as evidence for this Australian consensus, with returnees pointing out the rarity of memorials to foreign soldiers on Vietnamese land. In his 2006 radio interview, Murphy explained that "Dien Bien Phu was a huge victory for the Vietnamese, whereas in this particular case, the situation was reversed. So, to actually have a monument when the situation didn't work out for them is pretty special. And that comes about by the respect that they have for Australians, the respect that they have for Australian soldiers."[104]

Vietnamese tolerance of foreign commemoration indicates that is inaccurate. Aside from the French memorial to the tens of thousands killed or captured at Điện Biên Phủ, there is also a plaque in Hồ Chí Minh City commemorating US servicemen who were killed defending the US Embassy from an attack in the 1968 Tet Offensive.[105] The Tet Offensive and Điện Biên Phủ were epic battles that demonstrated the power of Vietnamese resistance. Both memorials were erected to remember foreign soldiers who were killed, not battles that were won. These sites promote the memory of Vietnamese resistance while extending a benevolent gesture of reconciliation toward former enemies which, as Chapter 5 discussed, is an established Vietnamese framework for maintaining political legitimacy while developing diplomatic relations. Long Tân serves a similar function: the battle was memorialized in 1969 by Australians because so many soldiers died, not because it was a great victory. It was the Vietnamese who took the initiative of erecting the

---

[100] Interview with Graham S.   [101] Interview with Ray.   [102] Interview with John W.
[103] Interview with Dave.   [104] Murphy, "40 Years On – Long Tan."
[105] Justin Corfield, "United States Embassy," *Historical Dictionary of Ho Chi Minh City* (London: Anthem Press, 2013), 314–15.

replica cross and plaque, promoting their national image of compromise and reconciliation by encouraging commemorations that remembered the soldiers killed on both sides of the battle. Taken in context of the memorials at Điện Biên Phủ and the US Consulate and the dominant attitude of friendship toward returning veterans, Vietnamese actions suggest that permissions for Australian commemorations at Long Tân are part of the national narrative of forgiveness and reconciliation.

Australian reactions to Long Tân illustrate how returning veterans easily accepted those aspects of Vietnamese memories of the American War that validated their personal memories of war, often misinterpreting the meaning behind Vietnamese memories to blend them into their own. Aspects of Vietnamese memory that were harder to contend with were dismissed, condemned, disputed, or ignored. As Part II has shown, veteran memories and feelings of attachment to Vietnamese spaces were in constant tension with Vietnamese memories and gestures of reconciliation. Returnees navigated this tension by threading selected parts of Vietnamese memory through their existing understandings of the war. In Part III, I consider how this tension affected veterans' reflections on legacies of the Vietnam War.

Part III

Legacies

7   Revisiting Vietnam

After the war, Vietnam veterans grappled with complex and politically charged narratives about the war that shaped how they viewed their individual experiences. Those that returned to Việt Nam faced new stories and memories about the war that often undermined or contradicted these narratives. Yet the experience of returning to Việt Nam tended to verify and validate veterans' views on war legacies rather than challenge or change them. This is not surprising: neurological research shows that challenges to political beliefs and personal memories are processed emotionally and are experienced as attacks on the self.[1] People are inclined to rationalize evidence that contradicts their views and threatens their identity rather than reassess their ideology, and accept misinformation when it supports their views and affirms their identity.[2] This chapter explores veterans' views on four war legacy issues, in light of returning to Việt Nam: perceptions of defeat (or victory) in Vietnam; the anti-war movement; the association between "their" war and war crimes; and the justness of the war. While I did not pose direct questions about loss, justness, or crimes, the majority of veterans raised these issues in their interviews without prompting, suggesting that these are key legacies that continue to cause contention about the meaning of "their" war.

American veteran William Broyles Jr. returned to Việt Nam in 1986 to search "for the clues to the character of Vietnam, for the sources of its tenacious resistance, for the reasons why we lost."[3] One of the lasting questions about Vietnam is why, how, and even whether the Western

---

[1] Jonas T. Kaplan et al., "Neural Correlates of Maintaining One's Political Beliefs in the Face of Counterevidence." *Scientific Reports* 6: 39589 (2016). N.p. http://dx.doi.org/10.1038/srep39589
[2] Ibid.; Dan Kahan, "Misconceptions, Misinformation, and the Logic of Identity-protective Cognition." Working Paper No. 164, *The Cultural Cognition Project*, Yale Law School. https://papers.ssrn.com/sol3/papers.cfm?abstract_id=2973067
[3] Broyles Jr., *Brothers in Arms*, 101.

allies lost the war. Historian Robert J. McMahon outlines four broad perspectives within the United States: the orthodox position that the war was "morally ambiguous" and a "tragic mistake; the radical leftist position that the war was an imperialist invasion; the revisionist position that it was a "noble cause," fought well and failed by the home front or weak allies; and the vindicationist position that America in fact won the war.[4] Australian perspectives largely mirror these positions.[5] These broad categories of Vietnam retrospectives have endured for fifty years. While proponents of the orthodox position remain dominant in academia, alongside adherents of the radical critique, both revisionists and vindicationists were increasingly common in the political sphere and among veterans' groups.

Among returnees, one of the dominant reflections on "the reasons why we lost" was that communist victory was inevitable because Vietnamese willpower was such as to outlast any invading force. "It was never going to be a winnable show," Australian Army veteran Ric explained, "even if America had the opportunity to attack North Vietnam [with ground troops], I don't think they'd have beaten the will of the people who just wanted a united country."[6] This reasoning reproduced a prominent narrative at official Vietnamese sites of memory, such as state-directed museums. Sites like the Củ Chi tunnels link victory in the American War to innate national characteristics of tenacity and fortitude and present those characteristics as having evolved over years of resistance to foreign invasions.[7] Veterans absorbed this message in their interpretations of the loss of the war. Ric explained that "we went to their history museums, and we come away with the conclusion ... if we were going to win, if the Americans were going to win that, if they were serious about winning it, they would have had to do things a whole lot different, and shot and killed every one of them, because they weren't giving up. They weren't going to give up at all. They'd just go down fighting, basically."[8]

These state narratives were bolstered by interactions with Vietnamese veterans and survivors. John K. described Vietnamese pride in their history of resistance:

I talked to one of the guys in the army when I was there, and he said, "you know, we were willing to fight as long as you guys wanted to fight. If you wanted the war

---

[4] McMahon, "Contested Memory"; Robert J. McMahon, "Changing Interpretations of the Vietnam War." In *The Oxford Companion to Military History*. Edited by John Whiteclay Chambers II (Oxford: Oxford University Press, 1999), 767.
[5] Jeff Doyle, "Dismembering the Anzac Legend: Australian Popular Culture and the Vietnam War." *Vietnam Generation* 3:2, Special Issue: Australia R&R – Representations and Reinterpretations of Australia's War in Vietnam (1991): 110.
[6] Interview with Ric. [7] Schwenkel, *American War in Contemporary Vietnam*, 91.
[8] Interview with Ric.

to last five more years, ten more years, if you wanted it to last to 1999, we were perfectly willing to sacrifice all our kids. 'Cause when they came over the border, the DMZ, we never thought we'd see them again. So, we would have done that. Regardless of what you folks did." And I believe them. That's dedication.[9]

Returnees from across the political spectrum repeated this narrative of inevitable revolutionary victory. For anti-war veterans, the narrative validated their political views. For others, inevitable victory offered an exculpatory story that absolved veterans' governments of the responsibility of military failure. Making willpower the key to victory – over superior knowledge of terrain, intelligent strategy, military cohesion, and effective propaganda – erases American and Australian ignorance of Vietnamese history, culture, and local politics; ignores the cruel fallacy of "destroy[ing] the town in order to save it" tactics and the absurd "body count" measurement for victory; disregards the low morale and friction among allied troops; and neglects the powerful dissent of the international anti-war movement.[10] This willpower narrative was the answer that Broyles settled on. He reflected on the revisionist position in the United States, writing that

... many American advocates of air power now believe we failed because we did not bomb enough. But the argument had one basic flaw: whatever the price of winning the war ... the North Vietnamese were willing to pay it ... that was the fallacy at the core of our strategy of a graduated response; gradually increasing the pain does not necessarily affect an opponent who is willing to lose everything.[11]

The notion of dedication and willpower was also present in returnees' discussions of their Vietnamese allies. Many veterans suggested that the Western allies lost because the Republic of Việt Nam (RVN) was corrupt, its military was weak and cowardly, and its civilians were disloyal. "There was no unity in the South Vietnamese government. In the populace it was every man, woman and child for themselves," US Army veteran Robert J. Reilly wrote.[12] "Basically, they didn't want to fight," Australian Army veteran Rod said, "I won't say they were cowards or anything like that, [but] they didn't really want to be in a fight."[13] Veterans thus reflected the broader Western narrative of "dependency and tragic victimhood" in the RVN, which Long T. Bui argues is a scapegoating device: "if the South Vietnamese nation could not muster enough strength to stand on its

---

[9] Interview with John K.
[10] An unnamed Major to journalist Peter Arnett in the aftermath of a battle in Bến Tre, in which 456 civilians were killed. Peter Arnett, "Ruined Ben Tre, after 45 Days, Still Awaits Saigon's Aid: Regime Has Offered Nothing in Effort to Rebuild Town." *New York Times*, March 15, 1968, 3.
[11] Broyles Jr., *Brothers in Arms*, 45. [12] Reilly, *Return of the Warriors*, 111.
[13] Interview with Rod.

own ... the debacle that followed was the fault of *those* people for not loving freedom enough to fight and die for it."[14] This narrative of RVN weakness was closely entwined with the perception of revolutionary willpower. After he praised the "dedication" of a People's Army Việt Nam veteran, John K. added, "I don't think South Việt Nam had the will to fight. And without that, there's no way that we could send more arms, and more money, and we just would not have made it."[15]

Historian Carie Uyen Nguyen notes that while Republic of Việt Nam Armed Forces (RVNAF) soldiers were scapegoated in American popular culture as "incompetent cowards who often shirked their duties," her oral history research shows that veterans had much more complex perspectives: "some Americans ... believed the [Army of the Republic of Việt Nam] ARVN soldiers were good soldiers, fighting as hard as they could to defend their country ... others resented what they saw as an unequal burden."[16] It is very likely that many veterans held both beliefs simultaneously. The emphasis on RVNAF weakness in return narratives suggests that engaging with the contemporary Socialist Republic of Việt Nam (SRV) undermined the already-ambiguous RVN in memory. As Karen Till notes, different social groups can contest "official representations of the past" and offer "alternatives to claim a political 'voice' in the public realm."[17] However, if the political voice of social groups is silenced – such as it is for RVNAF veterans – their memory of the past is erased and the official representation is sustained. When veterans revisited the wartime space, symbolic meanings invested in two political entities were physically affirmed: Sài Gòn fell, but Hà Nội stands. Where revolutionary willpower and resilience were heavily emphasized, the story of RVN weakness and corruption was reinforced. The RVNAF were reduced to *ngụy*, "puppets," reiterating notions of dependency. Finally, as this book has shown, many veterans returned to Việt Nam with an agenda to meet and understand their enemy, and found healing in the connections they made. Perhaps for these connections to be sustained as veterans explored their shared experiences with revolutionary veterans, another figure – a new Other – was required to bear responsibility for the war. Scapegoating the RVN and its forces may have allowed Australian and American returnees to reflect with revolutionary veterans on their war experiences.

Veterans' views of Vietnamese willpower reflected the orthodox perspective that Western intervention in Vietnam was wrongheaded, and the war "a lost, pointless, morally ambiguous conflict."[18] Former prisoner of

---

[14] Bui, *Returns of War*, 11–12. [15] Interview with John K.
[16] Nguyen, "Whose War Was It Anyway?" [17] Till, "Places of Memory," 293.
[18] McMahon, "Contested Memory," 178.

war (POW) and US Air Force veteran Pete said that in hindsight, "we totally misread who the South Vietnamese were, and we totally, totally misread who the North Vietnamese were."[19] McMahon observes that this point of view was dominant in popular culture and reflected in public opinion polls, with a majority of Americans viewing US intervention as "a tragic mistake."[20] This narrative gained prominence in reconciliation discourses in the aftermath of US-Việt Nam normalization. In 2001, General Võ Nguyên Giáp was interviewed for a *CNN* special on the Cold War. "The Americans fought the Vietnamese, but they did not know much about Vietnam or anything at all about the Vietnamese people," Giáp explained, "Vietnam is an old nation founded in a long history before the birth of Christ ... the Americans knew nothing about our nation and her people."[21]

Veterans who promoted this conclusion often presented themselves as students of history. They emphasized the hypocrisy of democratic rhetoric without democratic principles: "if you just read the history of the conflict you'll see," US Army veteran John C. said, "they set up a government, they put their man in power and then fought a war defending the status quo, so to speak, but they never had the support of the majority of the people."[22] The return experience likely reaffirmed such positions, as returnees learned more of Vietnamese history and culture. Pete explained the follies of US support for the South and opposition of the North: "there was no way in hell we were ever going to get the Vietnamese to follow a leader who didn't agree with them from a religious standpoint ... Hồ Chí Minh was actually never a communist. He was a socialist nationalist ... we didn't understand the big picture."[23]

The entwined themes of Western hubris and Vietnamese resilience dominated veterans' discussions of strategy failure. Former Marine Mike P. remembered that he "felt that we were fighting the war in the wrong way."[24] In this, returning US veterans reflected common themes in veterans' narratives: historian John A. Wood writes that in memoirs, "almost never is the impression given that the actions of the authors and their comrades, including killing scores of ['Viet Cong'] 'VC' and [North Vietnamese Army] NVA, somehow contributed to an ultimate victory."[25] Just as returning affirmed veterans' convictions about the ignorance of

---

[19] Interview with Pete.   [20] McMahon, "Contested Memory," 176.
[21] Võ Nguyên Giáp, interview in "Episode 11: Vietnam." CNN: Cold War. Produced by Pat Mitchell and Jeremy Isaacs (New York: CNN, June 10, 2001). http://web.archive.org/web/20010610022952/http://www.cnn.com/SPECIALS/cold.war/episodes/11/interviews/giap/
[22] Interview with John C.   [23] Interview with Pete.   [24] Interview with Mike P.
[25] Wood, *Veteran Narratives and the Collective Memory of the Vietnam War*, 29.

Vietnam intervention, returning also confirmed what many veterans had suspected when in the field. US Army veteran Ralph described how on search-and-destroy missions, "we're going around, we're clearing land, and we just travelled through. You never stay and secure anything. So, you realize, this can't last, because we're not holding land ... you could see that we weren't going to win anything, so we were just kind of there. Just hope you get through it, try to help your friend." Like many returnees, Ralph "used to think we could have won, but when you get back [to Việt Nam] and see the ineffectiveness of the bombing, I mean the Hồ Chí Minh trail, you can hardly think you'll control that by bombing."[26]

The revisionist position emerged in the late 1970s from historians such as Guenter Lewy, who argued that the United States won its battles in Vietnam and that lack of will from American political leaders lost the war.[27] This position became popular among traditional veterans' organizations in the 1980s and was embraced by the Reagan administration.[28] Among the predominantly anti-war Americans who returned to Việt Nam, however, this was not a popular position. Only John McCain, who lamented the "terribly misguided political interference in the war's conduct," and US Army veteran Mark, who argued that "[if we had] kept bombing for two more weeks, we would have won," held the revisionist position.[29] The revisionist position suggests that America won most if not all of its battles in Vietnam – a measure that, as Ralph shows, seemed irrelevant to many of those in combat. However, as Ralph also indicates, many liberals believed that the full might of American techno-power could have (not necessarily that it should have) won the war. It was returning, and understanding how the Vietnamese survived the devastating bombing campaigns, that led Ralph to conclude that the war was unwinnable.

The revisionist position was, however, very popular among Australian veterans. The Australian revisionist position narrowed the Australian Task Force's (ATF's) purpose in Vietnam: "our charter was to cease the fighting in South Việt Nam, that's what we went over there for. When the Paris Peace Accords were signed in 1971 [sic], North signed a peace treaty with South. Our political masters then seen an avenue to get us out, 'cause it was unpopular. So, we did what we had to do, we did

---

[26] Interview with Ralph.
[27] Guenter Lewy, *America in Vietnam* (Oxford: Oxford University Press, 1978), 160, 251.
[28] See for example, "who can doubt that the cause for which our men fought was just?" Ronald Reagan, "Remarks at the Veterans' Day Ceremony at the Vietnam Veterans Memorial." November 11, 1988. Online by Gerhard Peters and John Woolley, *The American Presidency Project*. www.presidency.ucsb.edu/ws/?pid=35155
[29] McCain and Salter, *Worth the Fighting For*, 15; Interview with Mark.

achieve our goals."³⁰ Australian returnees pointed to differences between their strategies and the American conduct to make this point. "I've got a thing about Americans anyway," said Special Air Service Regiment (SASR) veteran Ken, "it's because of the war, it's the way the Americans went about it. That's why they lost ... [we] learned how to conduct counter-insurgency warfare ... whereas the Americans were all firepower. They would bomb the shit out the place."³¹ Fellow SASR veteran Robin argued that "we basically over the years had pacified the province, so that the opposition from D445 in particular was very limited by the time our last squadron pulled out. I think Australia's mission, as far as it operated, yes, in the province, yes, I thought it was [successful]."³²

The Australian revisionist narrative thus promoted the idea that "we won *our* war." Historian Jeffrey Grey notes that this idea is "tied to a persistent belief in American tactical incompetence and South Vietnamese cowardice," contrasted with the notion of superior tactical understanding by the Australians. This narrative emerged during the war itself, when the "archetypal phlegmatic character of the Anzacs was frequently commented on, serving to position Australian soldiers as ready, willing, and more than able to deal with the difficulties of this new conflict."³³ The Australian revisionist narrative is thus an echo of the Anzac tradition of comparing the digger favorably with the ally, rather than the enemy. While Grey notes that "it is possible to deduce" from decreasing Australian contacts with enemy forces in the late 1960s and early 1970s, as well as decreasing Australian casualties, that Australian operations were successful and that the National Liberation Front (NLF) had been defeated in Phước Tuy, he argues that it is equally plausible, "even likely," that the NLF was merely waiting out the Australian withdrawal.³⁴ Military historian Albert Palazzo concurs, noting that "despite six years of effort 1ATF had not severed the insurgents' grip on the population."³⁵ Further, as Grey argues, "the whole idea of 'winning our war' divorced from consideration of the wider fortunes of the Saigon Government is fatuous, and based on a very curious notion of winning."³⁶

The last position McMahon identifies is the vindicationist belief that the Western powers won by limiting the spread of communism in neighboring countries.³⁷ None of the Americans discussed in this book held this point of view. However, several Australians presented their national

---

[30] Interview with Ray. [31] Interview with Ken. [32] Interview with Robin.
[33] Garton, "War and Masculinity in Twentieth Century Australia," 88.
[34] Grey, "In Every War but One?" 194, 195–96.
[35] Albert Palazzo, *Australian Military Operations in Vietnam* (Canberra: Army History United, 2011), 182.
[36] Grey, "In Every War but One?" 196. [37] McMahon, "Contested Memory," 173.

strain of vindicationist theory in the wake of the Cold War. "For them it was a civil war," explained Robin, "for the Western world it was a line in the sand against communism. And strategically that worked."[38] The vindicationist argument drew on counterfactual scenarios explored by prominent historians of the war in Australia. Peter Edwards, Official Historian at the Australian War Memorial, notes that "in the longer view one form of the domino theory gained a degree of credibility. This was the argument that that intervention ... had served a useful purpose by delaying the fall of the RVN by ten years ... [during which] numerous changes in Southeast Asia affected the regional impact of Hanoi's victory." Edwards suggests a "plausible" vindication of domino theory in the emergence of pro-Western governments in Indonesia and Thailand during the Vietnam War.[39] This line of argument was taken up by the Australian veteran community. Veterans Bruce Davies and Gary McKay argue that the war provided "improved strategic security" for Australia and that "the war provided a bulwark that allowed the peoples of the nearby Southeast Asia dominoes to prosper and to develop into mini economic powerhouses."[40] Veterans clung to this narrative that offered meaning to "their" war: "the Vietnam War did slow the communism war down, moving into other countries," Army veteran Rodney said, "I know they went into Laos and Cambodia, but that was going to happen anyway, really. Might have stopped them going into Thailand, Malaya, you don't know."[41]

The popularity of the Cold War narrative among recent Australian returnees suggests that the vindicationist position is linked to the intertwining of social valuation of wars, social recognition of veterans, and the emphasis on deprivation in Vietnam veteran identity. Australia's Anzac legend hinges on themes of betrayal and martyrdom, and the Vietnam Anzac identity interweaves these themes with memories of exclusion.[42] In mapping his theory of the "underlay" of memory, Michael Roper suggests that in memory narratives, "emotional processes connected to the war

---

[38] Interview with Robin.   [39] Edwards, *Australia and the Vietnam War*, 272.
[40] Bruce Davies and Gary McKay, *Vietnam: The Complete Story of the Australian War* (Crows Nest: Allen & Unwin, 2012), 591.
[41] Interview with Rodney.
[42] As historians Uilleam Blacker and Julie Fedor note, "martyrdom is a key node within a cluster of semantically rich and interlinked concepts – victimhood, sacrifice, and persecution – all of which can be used to mount compelling claims to legitimacy and authority." Uilleam Blacker and Julie Fedor, "Soviet and Post-Soviet Varieties of Martyrdom and Memory." *Journal of Soviet and Post-Soviet Politics and Society* 1:2 (2015): 198. On the use of martyrdom in Australian military identity, see Frank Bongiorno, "A Century of Bipartisan Commemoration: Is Anzac Politically Inevitable?" In *The Honest History Book*. Edited by David Stephens and Alison Broinowski (Sydney: NewSouth, 2017), 118.

experience and to present life-dilemmas coalesce in the narrative, revealing the psychic as well as the social structuring of memory."[43] In the Australian vindicationist narrative, this social-psychic structuring is evident. The explicit linking between the ATF mandate and a Cold War victory suggests strong emotions of rejection over a lack of recognition that has become central to the identity of the Australian Vietnam veteran. Robert – who did not even support the domino theory – lamented: "the First World War blokes were recognized, the Second World War blokes were recognized, but I mean from '67 to '87, twenty years before they said, 'oh youse have done a good job, you did stop the domino effect that they were saying.' Not that it was ever going to happen, but they did acknowledge it."[44]

Soldier recognition, or lack thereof, was entwined with the memories of the anti-war movement. War memory in both the United States and Australia is dominated by the notion that Vietnam veterans were ostracized and abused by anti-war protesters. In the United States, stories of the "spat-upon" Vietnam veteran have circulated widely since the 1980s. American Vietnam veteran Jerry Lembcke explored this story and found no reports of anti-war protesters spitting on veterans prior to the 1980s. He concluded that a confluence of visual and emotional memories from the Vietnam era led to a gradual process of social amnesia, pointing to metaphor-laden speeches by President Nixon, altercations between anti-war protesters and law enforcement, and hostility from the pro-war lobby toward anti-war veterans. Lembcke argues that the "spitting" story "displace[s] the anxiety of defeated male warriors into scapegoats."[45] Elements of the spitting myth manifest in Australian narratives of Vietnam, which historian Ann Curthoys investigated and found no evidence of.[46] Historian Chris Dixon explored a parallel Australian myth of red paint or blood being thrown over returning soldiers. He locates the origin of the myth in a one-woman protest at a Welcome Home parade in 1966, but finds no evidence that paint or blood were used regularly by anti-war protesters to shame Vietnam veterans.[47] My own research explores the epithet "baby killer" in memories of a hostile homecoming, tracing imagery in veterans' memories to a blurring of anti-war, women's liberation, and anti-abortion protests throughout the late 1970s before the epithet was explicitly linked to Vietnam veterans in *Rambo: First Blood*.[48] Like Lembcke, Curthoys, and Dixon, my research suggests veterans felt

---

[43] Roper, "Re-Remembering the Soldier-Hero," 201. [44] Interview with Robert.
[45] Lembcke, *Spitting Image*, 7–9. [46] Curthoys, "Vietnam," 113–30.
[47] Dixon, "Redeeming the Warriors."
[48] Parts of the above discussion on apocryphal memories of anti-war abuse originally appeared in Martin Hobbs, "We Went and Did an Anzac Job."

emasculated and displaced by a new young male authority: the anti-war protester.

I asked veterans how they felt about the anti-war movement during the war, and if their views had changed over time. Many veterans viewed the anti-war movement with contempt. They felt they had been targeted by the anti-war movement, even if they themselves had come to agree with anti-war views. "I resent people condemning troops because of the job they were doing. I mean, we weren't baby killers, we weren't any of those sorts of things," Australian Army veteran Derek explained, "when you had people that were supporting the enemy that we were fighting, that was a very bad thing. So, from that perspective, I was very much opposed to them using the Army as scapegoats. On the bigger picture . . . ." He went on to describe his reading on Hồ Chí Minh and US interference in the war of independence against the French. "Had they given it to the Vietnamese I don't think we'd have seen a Điện Biên Phủ and I don't think we'd have seen a Vietnam War."[49] Many veterans held views that were informed primarily by media coverage of sensationalist pro-NLF student protests by students. "They just went about it the wrong way," Mike P. explained, "'NLF is gonna win! Ho Ho Ho Chi Minh!' You know, that rubbed it in."[50] Other veterans saw anti-war activists as ignorant opportunists rather than people with different world views. Australian Army veteran Kevin explained:

. . . they're still a bunch of useless arseholes in my view. The pseudo-intelligentsia that couldn't even find Vietnam on the map and raced to the high ground to claim the moral position were totally exposed in '75, '78, '79, when Vietnam fell, when the South fell to the North, and huge bloody atrocities were committed against the South Vietnamese: not a peep out of them.[51]

This disdain for protesters indicated a resentment that was ultimately more about protecting or elevating veteran identity than it was about the war itself: "[the protesters] gave me a wider view as to how ignorant people can be. How short sighted they can be. I thought that people were more intelligent than that," Australian Army veteran Dave said. "It just gave me a sense that I was a lot more intelligent for having gone there [to Vietnam], I was a lot wiser for having been there."[52] US veterans, who were generally less critical of the protesters, also compared themselves favorably with the anti-war movement. US Air Force veteran Ted remembered thinking, "I don't give a damn about them because I've already been to Vietnam, I know what it's about. And they have no idea what they're talking about." He didn't see "any connection between what

[49] Interview with Derek.   [50] Interview with Mike P.   [51] Interview with Kevin.
[52] Interview with Dave.

they were saying and how I felt."[53] Ted later became involved in anti-war projects, so his wartime defensiveness toward protesters suggests that postwar readjustment made it very difficult for veterans, even those with anti-war views, to listen to the views of students who had never been to war. Former Marine veteran Greg, who returned from war to his hometown of Oakland, explained, "they were too radical for me. They were way too … anti-American. They didn't just want to end the war, they wanted to lose it. And I wasn't ready to make that jump yet, I couldn't give up that we were right. That we were honorable in what we were doing."[54]

The enduring hostility toward the anti-war movement indicates that veterans viewed the anti-war movement as undermining their status as soldiers. Some veterans who later became anti-war inverted these values, describing their past selves as ignorant or brainwashed and the anti-war protesters as intelligent and enlightened. John K. explained:

… [now] I think [protest] was the right thing to do, yeah, absolutely. At the time I was defending my country against the Vietnamese coming to California and invading us. I mean I was so completely and totally brainwashed, as most of us were. But I feel now they were instrumental in saving lives and they should have been listened to them a long time ago. They were on the right side of it.[55]

Mirroring the Australian accounts, American reflections on the anti-war movement hinged on intelligence, ignorance, and authority to speak about the war. Former Marine David E. explained, "I thought they just didn't know about the guys dying over here, you know? And I just didn't know. I just didn't know."[56]

Most US veterans had changed their minds about the anti-war movement. Pete had first heard of the anti-war movement in a Hà Nội prison cell and assumed it was propaganda: "are you kidding me? Not going to happen in my America." When asked how he reacted when he was released from prison, returned to the United States, and realized the stories were true, he explained that he "had bigger problems" to think about, and focused on rebuilding his life. Through his professional life, particularly his friendship with Vietnam veteran, anti-war activist, and fellow politician John Kerry, he came to appreciate the anti-war movement. He realized, "that's their [civilians] only out. And, so, if they don't [protest], they're doing a disservice. Because that's their voice, and in a democracy that's the only thing you got, you better protect it. And by getting out on the streets and protesting is certainly an effective way to do it." Pete suggested that returning to Việt Nam had reaffirmed this value, explaining: "one of the biggest arguments we have with Việt Nam right

[53] Interview with Ted.   [54] Interview with Greg.   [55] Interview with John K.
[56] Interview with David E.

now ... they are reluctant to allow people, to, quote, 'assemble.' Well, assemble means protest. And we're having a real contest with Việt Nam on their really sitting down on people who get out on the streets and demonstrate ... [it's] a very clear democratic issue that one has to protect."[57]

Many US veterans regretted not joining the anti-war movement. Some had undergone radical changes in belief systems in the war and felt that joining the protests would break their last anchor to their former self. When Suel was discharged from the Marines, he "was totally against the war, but I still wanted to please my parents. Cause I knew I'd be isolated if I went against the war ... [and] I had all of the damn war in Vietnam I ever wanted. And that's a disappointment, I wish I had."[58] As Suel suggests, another reason for not joining the protest was a desire to escape conflict. Former Marine John A. remembered how during the war he was resolved to "tell it like it is" to the media after his tour, but when he returned home, "I didn't want to be in a setting where there would be a confrontation. 'Cause if some policeman gave me a shove with a stick I'd attack him, I would, without even thinking. I was still pretty amped up."[59] Other veterans did join and described it as a "stepping-stone" in their path back to Việt Nam. The few veterans that joined the anti-war movement during the war itself found that protest allowed them to begin to heal. US Army veteran Chuck left Vietnam with anti-war sentiments, "both angry and questioning, you know, what I'd done here and what we'd done as Americans." He "knew that I needed to do something, desperately, when I got back, but I didn't know what that was ... [it] worked out a lot of the anger and bitterness that I felt I probably would have kept inside."[60] Contrary to popular memory, anti-war veterans remembered that "the demonstrators actually treated us a lot better, I thought, than a lot of other people did. They were happy to have a Vietnam veteran standing out on the street with them. And I always felt welcome."[61] For these veterans, acceptance from the movement validated their wartime doubts and gave them a sense of community. US Army draftee James described feeling part of something in the anti-war movement, more so than he did in the war, not as a veteran protester but just as "one person protesting against an unjust war."[62]

Veterans' views on the anti-war movement were closely linked with their views on the conduct of their military in Vietnam. Veterans who joined the anti-war movement did so out of anger at what they had seen in Việt Nam. On the other hand, veterans who still felt anger toward the

---

[57] Interview with Pete. [58] Interview with Suel. [59] Interview with John A.
[60] Interview with Chuck. [61] Interview with John Z. [62] Interview with James.

anti-war movement felt they had been vilified for war crimes that they had not committed. "We had blood thrown over us, we were called baby killers and rapists and murderers," said John W., "It was just horrendous, you know? And we didn't do any of that."[63] Acknowledging carnage in war – or refusing to acknowledge it – is a way of measuring, justifying, or regretting war, and Vietnam, more so than other wars, drew attention to the politics of the "production of dead human bodies" in war.[64] Veterans' views on war crimes in Vietnam demonstrates the difficulty of what Việt Thanh Nguyễn terms a "just memory" of warfare: "of seeing and remembering how the inhuman inhabits the human ... not just by ghostly others, but by the horrors we have done, seen, and condoned."[65]

Because my fieldwork concerned the return to Việt Nam, and out of ethical concern for research with subjects who may have trauma issues, none of my questions were about combat or war crimes. However, many veterans volunteered combat narratives, and the ways in which they described combat provided insight into their perspectives on methods of war. Additionally, because of the lasting association between Vietnam and war crimes in the collective war memories of Australia and the United States, atrocities such as My Lai were frequently discussed. How veterans made sense of their conduct in service, in light of the lingering association between Vietnam and war crimes, revealed an ongoing struggle to come to grips with profoundly unsettling information and find culturally and morally comfortable ways of remembering violence.

The only actions that were uniformly described by veterans as crimes were acts of interpersonal violence that indicated malevolence: rape, mutilating corpses for trophy collection, torture in non-interrogation circumstances, deliberate mass killings of unarmed civilians. These crimes were clearly distinguished from military actions. In contrast, actions such as torture in interrogations, corpse mutilation for efficient burial or psychological warfare, bombing cities, strafing villages, individual and small-group civilian killings in free-fire zones, and the forced dislocation of civilians were generally described using military terminology: SOPs (Standard Operating Procedures), Task Force policy, psy-ops, mop-up. Such actions were only described as crimes by those whose wartime responsibilities or postwar careers provided them with specific knowledge regarding the laws of warfare. This suggests that veterans sometimes learned criminal actions as strategies or tactics and were unaware of the legal ambiguity or criminality of such actions. It also

---

[63] Interview with John W.
[64] Mary Dudziak, "'You Didn't See Him Lying ... Beside the Gravel Road in France': Death, Distance, and American War Politics." *Diplomatic History* 42:1 (2018): 8.
[65] Nguyễn, *Nothing Ever Dies*, 19.

suggests that a military framework and language provided a level of psychic comfort for veterans when remembering such actions, implicitly justifying violence under an acceptable moral code.

For example, Australian Army veteran Tony "Bomber" Bower-Miles reflected in his memoir:

> I blew up bodies.... It saved time digging a hole. They used to call it an engineer's burial. I was well aware of the psych ops angle of it because they'd always try and take their dead away with them. If you understand the Asian mind, you know they all want to go to the happy hunting ground in one piece and have a proper burial. So, by blowing the body to shithouse, it will piss off the ones that are still alive.[66]

Bomber's use of "they used to call it" indicates this was not an isolated incident. Australian Army veteran Terry Burstall also suggested that corpse mutilation and display was an established ATF method in Vietnam: a "policy of dumping VC bodies in town market squares or dragging them behind Armoured Personnel Carriers (APCs), in sight of the village children, both methods supposedly meant to draw out further VC sympathisers."[67] However, Derrill, an Australian Army veteran, said that engineer's burials "would be an anomaly. I only knew of one occasion that that did happen by Australian soldiers, that was an ambush at a place called Thừa Tích." Derrill explained that eleven NLF were killed by Australian forces at Thừa Tích. Some of the bodies were destroyed on the spot with an "engineer's burial" before a request came through from the Vietnamese district chief asking for the bodies to be returned to the village. The remaining bodies were strapped to APCs rather than secured inside the vehicles, and transported to the village of Xuyên Mộc. As the Australians approached Xuyên Mộc, "these bodies supposedly fell off, according to [the Australians], and they dragged them into the village behind the ACPs. And they all happened to be tied by the leg."[68]

The differences between these descriptions of "engineer's burials" – as a regular practice versus an anomaly, with casual descriptions versus graphic detail – indicates that military frameworks clouded the ability of soldiers in combat to distinguish acceptable violence or proportional responses to threats from war crimes. Roper suggests that "the 'underlay'

---

[66] Bower-Miles and Whittacker, *Bomber*, 104.
[67] Terry Burstall, "Policy Contradictions of the Australian Task Force Vietnam, 1966." *Vietnam Generation* 3:2, Special Issue – Australia R&R: Representations and Reinterpretations of Australia's War in Vietnam (1991): 44.
[68] Interview with Derrill. This specific incident has been reported in the Australian media and discussed in another veteran's memoir. Matthew Benns, "Australian Federal Police May Investigate Claims Diggers Committed Atrocities During the Vietnam War." *News.com.au*, December 29, 2013; Don Tate, *The War Within* (Sydney: Murdoch Books, 2008), 263–64.

of memory ... is structured through the nature of the war experience itself ... [and] motivated as much by the need to address feelings which date from the event itself as from the imagined expectations of his audience."[69] Bomber and Burstall served in the field and witnessed a great amount of violence and death. The strategic language used by Burstall and the rough army slang used by Bomber suggests a practiced distance, indicating that the military framework provided a way of processing abject violence in a way that they could live with day to day. Consequently, this framework appeared to limit veterans' considerations of the effects of their actions. In contrast, Derrill worked in psy-ops: both distanced from the field and attuned to the psychic violence and moral violation of an engineer's burial. He described the "absolute horror" on the faces of villagers when they saw the ACPs dragging bodies into Xuyên Mộc. Finally, both Bomber and Burstall reported engineer's burials in books, which provided distance from their audience. Derrill spoke directly to me, and thus may have felt the social pressure to clarify his awareness of the illegal action. "It's actually a war crime," he said, "it, to me, was a war crime. The bodies were blown up, that was the first thing, and the second thing is, dragging the bodies. I mean, they claimed it was accidental, but bullshit."[70]

The moral framework Derrill used to explain corpse mutilation drew out the impact of combat methods, indicating that certain legally or morally ambiguous behaviors had ripple effects that were conducive to a climate that permitted atrocities and consequently detrimental to the war effort. For example, the pacification strategies of the RVN, US, and Australian militaries in Việt Nam focused on isolating rural civilians in the RVN from the NLF by resettling civilians in high-risk areas into refugee camps.[71] In order to secure the ATF base at Nui Dat, for example, the nearby villages of Long Tân and Long Phước were destroyed and the villagers resettled. Robert described the process of "clearing patrols" on Operation Ainslie in 1967:

... we'd put up huts and then we'd go into a village and say, "right, we are going to shift you into this lovely beaut place you're going to live in." And you'd take them out of there, take everybody out. Then you'd burn them [the villagers' huts]. And

---

[69] Roper, "Re-Remembering the Soldier-Hero," 184.   [70] Interview with Derrill.
[71] Military displacement of civilians in warfare was legally ambiguous in contemporary international law: "Individual or mass forcible transfers ... are prohibited, regardless of motive. Nevertheless, the Occupying Power may undertake total or partial evacuation of a given area if the security of the population or imperative military reasons so demand." "Deportations, Transfers, Evacuations," Article 49, Convention IV, Geneva Conventions, August 12, 1949. https://ihl-databases.icrc.org/applic/ihl/ihl.nsf/Article.xsp?action=openDocument&documentId=77068F12B8857C4DC12563CD0051BDB0

then you start to hear screaming. And then they'd all come out, because some of them were Viet Cong.⁷²

Army veteran Paul Murphy also took part in Operation Ainslie and remembered how "crying, weeping, protesting, struggling peasants were moved to Sui Nghi [sic] as the bulldozer and Zippo were put to good use to eradicate the villages." Murphy wrote that "Sui Nghi is discussed at length today by those who participated back in '67 in what was an 'unforgettable civilian relocation experiment gone wrong,'" suggesting that veterans remember the action with sadness and regret.⁷³ However, there was no indication from Murphy or Robert that the aims and methods of Operation Ainslie had broader repercussions.

Heonik Kwon argues that these policies of displacement directly facilitated atrocities against civilians. American and Australian forces conducted "search-and-destroys" in free-fire zones with the understanding that civilians from these areas had been resettled and warned that their ancestral homes were now off-limits. Civilians, on the other hand, endured years of occupation and total war. Kwon outlines how resettled civilians monitored the situation in their homes carefully, with elders staying behind to tend to family plots and children and grandchildren moving "back and forth between the village and the refugee camp, whenever the situation allowed, to help on the family farm."⁷⁴ Villagers often petitioned local authorities to establish more permanent visitation rights.⁷⁵ Their returns home corresponded with the requirement of Article 49 of Geneva Convention IV, which only allows for displacement under "imperative" circumstances, that "persons thus evacuated shall be transferred back to their homes as soon as hostilities in the area in question have ceased."⁷⁶ Underlying the movements of civilians was an ongoing war of disinformation. Villages perceived to be safe attracted returning inhabitants and temporary settlers, but as Kwon notes, "the 'safe village' and the 'return village' could turn into a site of mass death when the identity of the village suddenly shifted and it became a 'VC' village circled in red on the battle map. This shift in identity was abrupt, unknown to the village inhabitants."⁷⁷ In the case of My Lai, for example, the villagers "considered the US soldiers in My Khe to be friends."⁷⁸

Returnees' memories of small-scale civilian killing during search-and-destroys show that soldiers were trained to think about free-fire zones as their territory. Australian Army veteran Ben Morris explains in his master's

---

⁷² Interview with Robert.   ⁷³ Murphy, *Quiet Australians*, 196, 198.
⁷⁴ Kwon, *After the Massacre*, 30.   ⁷⁵ Ibid., 31.
⁷⁶ "Deportations, Transfers, Evacuations," Article 49, Convention IV.
⁷⁷ Kwon, *After the Massacre*, 32.   ⁷⁸ Ibid., 31.

thesis that a "restricted" or free-fire zone was established around the ATF base in Nui Dat "to improve the security of the base by allowing Australians to fire without fear of wounding or killing civilians." The presence of civilians was thus an intrusion: Morris described how his platoon was "involved in an ambush that resulted in the death of civilians who had wandered into a restricted zone."[79] Anthropologist Kenneth Maddock argues that the distinction between military actions and atrocities occur when "our cultural consciousness draws a line, and says that it is atrocious to overstep."[80] Some veterans indicated an awareness of this line. Bomber described a search-and-destroy: "we turned that village upside down … I remember thinking to myself this could end up another My Lai in a millisecond."[81] Yet most veterans who described actions in free-fire zones indicated an enduring mental distinction between civilian and enemy territory. "I flew infantry on helicopters," Mark explained, "and we did search-and-destroy missions. We would fly into a village, enemy village, and we would kill everything and every pig and chicken and water buffalo and burn down every hooch in the place, just because it's enemy territory."[82]

The kinds of actions described here relate to debates over why the war was lost. Philosopher Michael Waltzer reflected on Vietnam in *Just and Unjust Wars*, his influential 1977 text on just war theory. Waltzer argues that in guerrilla warfare, "if the killing of civilians were sufficient to win civilian support, the guerrillas would always be at a disadvantage, for their enemies possess far more firepower than they do. But killing will work against the killer."[83] The revolutionary war rested on the ability of revolutionary forces to recruit southerners into the NLF and to win and sustain the allegiance of southern civilians. Those who aligned themselves with the Democratic Republic of Việt Nam (DRV) did so for personal as well as ideological reasons. Activist author Arlene Eisen wrote *Women and Revolution in Việt Nam* (1984) after a 1981 trip to Việt Nam, listing the reasons why women joined the revolutionary movement: "to reunify the country"; because they were "enraged by the rape of their sisters"; "to avenge the death of people they loved"; "to defend their villages rather than be herded into concentration camps"; "to increase their chances of survival by joining the liberation struggle."[84] All but one of these reasons were responses to RVNAF, US, and Australian policies. Veterans who

---

[79] Ben Morris, "Remembering Vietnam: Official History, Soldiers' Memories and the Participant Interviewer." Master's thesis, University of Wollongong, 2014, 51, 49.
[80] Kenneth Maddock, "Atrocities and Culture: Revisiting the Vietnam War." *Journal of Polynesian Society* 48: Memoirs, Man and a Half (1991): 297.
[81] Bower-Miles and Whittacker, *Bomber*, 124. [82] Interview with Mark.
[83] Michael Waltzer, *Just and Unjust War* (New York: Basic Books, 1977), 185.
[84] Arlene Eisen, *Women and Revolution in Viet Nam* (London: Zed Books, 1984), 95.

enquired about the effects of their policies when they returned to Việt Nam had their concerns verified by Vietnamese experiences. After meeting with survivors in Phước Tuy, Burstall concluded:

> ... war itself is an atrocity, but there was no need for the mindless brutality toward the civilian population. Our war was to fight the VC, not the people. If we say the VC were the people, we are then admitting that we were fighting against our own beliefs, as our rationale was to help the people. In fact, the war could never be won without the support of the people.[85]

As Bomber summarized: "it didn't exactly win the hearts and minds of the people as you're driving this great steel rod down through grandma's chest."[86]

Returnees' discussions of atrocity sometimes broadened to the meanings behind violence: what level of violence veterans felt they could be driven to, what factors could drive them there, how they would react in a massacre. In these instances the "composure" of memory – the references and scaffolding veterans used to find "psychic comfort" with their war experiences – was quite clear.[87] John A., for instance, was convinced he had killed civilians during a search-and-destroy but had repressed the memory because he could not process the violence.[88] He carefully delineated the difference between a "snap," which he defined as "a break with reality," and My Lai: "it's not ... you know where they have this elaborate deal and then they go on and kill some people and they go back and try to get other people to go with them and get some more ... a snap is a snap. It's not that long."[89] In his memoir, he reflected on My Lai: "rage and hatred toward non-combatants are not qualities found in true warriors," and remembered that when his patrol team heard of the massacre, "we all wished we could have been there to help [Hugh] Thompson quell that atrocity."[90] He repeated this hope for a chance to perform righteous violence each time we spoke, "[his patrol team] 116 was six klicks [kilometers] from My Lai ... we wished we had been there to take down some of these murderers."[91] John A.'s own recognition of having participated in violence against civilians drove him to draw a moral distinction between himself and Charlie Company: he was not hateful, he was not racist, he would have done the right thing. Others contemplated whether they would have been capable of standing against orders. Bill E. wondered:

---

[85] Burstall, *A Soldier Returns*, 187.   [86] Bower-Miles and Whittacker, *Bomber*, 103.
[87] Dawson, *Soldier Heroes*, 23.   [88] Discussed in Chapter 2.   [89] Interview with John A.
[90] Akins, *Drowning Out the Drums*, 167–68. US Army officer Hugh Thompson Jr. led a small crew of soldiers who tried to stop the My Lai massacre as it occurred.
[91] Interview with John A.

... what I would have done if I had been there. You know, if you're told by your commanding officer to do something, and there's shots being fired all around you, what do you do? .... I give these guys that did stand up against it all the respect in the world, because that had to be a tough thing to do .... A lot of guys just stepped back and didn't participate, that's probably where I would have been. I'd like to think I would have stood up there and say stop it, stop it, but I don't think I would have had the guts to.[92]

Anti-war returnees agreed that My Lai signified a broader problem in Việt Nam. They explained how the actions of troops in Vietnam turned the Vietnamese into an enemy and created what psychologist Robert J. Lifton describes as an "atrocity-producing situation"; a military culture that was "inevitably genocidal."[93] US veteran and My Lai witness Ron said that "there were things that happened I think that were worse than My Lai over there and the only thing is, I happened to be there that day, with the camera, and recorded some of the events [at My Lai]."[94] Many described a policy of shooting near civilians to "test" them. US veteran Don explained that he refused to participate in destruction and killing on search-and-destroy missions, and so was put on security, watching the villagers. He remembered asking, "'What happens if they run?' 'Well, that means they're a VC.' 'Well then what do you do?' They just look at you, like: you dumb shit. 'You shoot them.' They're pronounced guilty, when they run."[95] James described how this "test" turned into a game among soldiers outside of missions:

guys taking out their rifles and shooting farmers from the truck, from the moving truck ... that kind of thing was done all the time. You know, when we showed up, people were scared and they ran, and so the American soldiers and the officers assumed that they were running because they were guilty. Well, they were running to save their lives. And, so, they were killed for being frightened. And, of course, they were frightened, because they knew they might be killed.[96]

This game, itself derived from a "test," then turned into a "policy ... to shoot near them. If they ran, jumped for cover, they were the enemy ... how many are gonna stand there? The instinct is going to be to jump."[97] For many veterans, therefore, My Lai came to signify something larger than the violence and death of one massacre: it was a single moment that embodied the Vietnam War.

Others approached the question of war crimes in Việt Nam with more ambiguity. "Calley was wrong, but My Lai, [there were] a lot of VC

---

[92] Interview with Bill E. [93] Lifton, *Home from the War*, 41 [94] Interview with Ron.
[95] Interview with Don. [96] Interview with James. [97] Interview with Larry.

there," Mark said.[98] Some were uneasy about the singular focus on American crimes. US Air Force veteran Mike M. said, "a lot of people wanted to lambast the United States for their dealings over there, but the communist regime was pretty brutal too."[99] US Air Force veteran Jim felt that the United States had been "fairly upfront" about My Lai and thought it was time for the SRV to acknowledge their crimes. "I mean, it took a while ... and yeah, we had a lot of soldiers that had a lot of stuff they really shouldn't've been doing. But that was a lot more out in the open than the Vietnamese government, which – now, there had been massacres too, on their side, of their own people, but you don't hear anything about that."[100] Veterans alluded to mass summary executions after the Battle for Hué in 1968 for evidence of revolutionary crimes. Yet as Laderman notes, "there is no credible evidentiary basis for this version of events" of the "Hue Massacre."[101] The methodical execution of between 2,000 and 14,000 of civilians by revolutionary forces over 3 weeks was an apocryphal story that vindicated Cold Warrior justifications for US involvement in the war.[102] The "Hue Massacre" became embedded in Western popular memory as part of a broader re-remembering of the war as one of "mutual destruction."[103] Returnees' focus on war crimes at Hué suggests that for some, the linking of war crimes and the US military in memories of Vietnam was an unfair distortion, and returning to Việt Nam may have exacerbated feelings of resentment because of the singular focus there on American atrocity. "Our moral sense is exquisitely tuned to My Lai and the effects of our bombing," Broyles wrote, "but we are deaf to the brutalities of our enemies. Before Vietnam we could do no wrong – then we could do no right. History is seldom so simple."[104]

These ambiguous responses to American war crimes infuriated antiwar veterans. "I see so many people not being able to admit that it was wrong, it was criminal, and sinful, and they just can't admit it," Larry said. In response, he had embarked upon a relentless pursuit of uncovering and exposing the "horror of it all." "I want them to know," Larry said,

---

[98] Interview with Mark.   [99] Interview with Mike M.   [100] Interview with Jim.
[101] Laderman, *Tours of Vietnam*, 89.
[102] The evidence suggests that NLF soldiers killed between 300 and 710 non-combatant police and RVN officials during the Tet Offensive in Hué. US Information Agency official Douglas Pike, who initially promoted the "bloodbath theory," acknowledged in 1988 that the numbers of those killed by the NLF were drastically inflated. Of the mass graves uncovered in Hué after the eight-week siege, many of the thousands of civilian fatalities were a result of American airpower, as well as an estimated one thousand assassinated by RVN forces. Laderman, *Tours of Vietnam*, 89, 91–94, 116–17.
[103] For discussion on the reconfiguration of the United States as the principal war victim through the narrative of "mutual destruction," see: Martini, *Invisible Enemies*, 41–76.
[104] Broyles Jr., *Brothers in Arms*, 168.

7 Revisiting Vietnam

"know more about what happened in this country." He repeatedly described, unprompted, the kinds of violence experienced by women in various RVN political prisons: "the most horrible things that you think might be happening ... women abused, all kinds of different, having snakes put in their pants, beat the snakes, make them bite. The eels, putting those up their vaginas ... they were digging up skeletons, and they had nails this long [he held up his finger and thumb an inch apart] driven through the tibia." Larry's fixation on torture practices may indicate vicarious trauma. Constant minimizations and denials of Vietnamese suffering in broader US political culture led him to relentlessly reach for more evidence to prove the violence. In doing so, he reduced Vietnamese lives to tortured bodies. Larry became transfixed by the abject cruelty of the war, leading him to revere victims of suffering. "When I saw those nails through those bones, you know, I could – all I saw was like [he held his arms out in a crucifixion pose], on the cross, with the nails being driven through the feet." Caught in a loop of bearing witness, under the logic that doing so was both virtuous and enlightening, he consumed memories of war crimes. "My god ... I've got so much on it, I feel like I've been there," Larry said, "I am still learning, still growing."[105]

Because of the notoriety of My Lai, US veterans were forced to grapple with the conduct of their military in Vietnam. Australians, however, were not. Their narrative on war crimes was that Australians "did the job they were there to do, and they did it with honor."[106] "We didn't have a My Lai," Dave explained; "we shot the odd woman we saw in the bush under circumstances which were wartime circumstances."[107] Many Australian veterans were anxious to exonerate not only themselves but the entire ATF in Vietnam: "I don't know any Australian troop that ever raped a woman. And I don't know any Australian troop that ever killed a baby. You know? It went on, it most certainly happened, but no Australian troops were ever guilty of that. Certainly not the battalion that I served with."[108] They felt the anti-war movement "tarred us with the American brush."[109] "Why didn't they find out the Australians were doing things honorably? I mean we were just baby killers, none of our guys killed fucking babies, we helped them for fuck's sake! I was a patrol medic in SAS! That was saving them, that wasn't killing them."[110] In an extension of the "we won our war" narrative, many Australians made a point of comparing their honorable conduct to that of the Americans. "Most observers of the Vietnam War, including myself have nothing but contempt for the way in which the war was conducted by the US," Murphy

---

[105] Interview with Larry.   [106] Interview with Peter.   [107] Interview with Dave.
[108] Interview with John W.   [109] Ibid.   [110] Interview with Ric.

wrote, "Thank god we were in the Australian armed services and can hold our heads high in what we achieved."[111]

This chapter has explored questions of how, why, or if the Western allies lost, what to make of the anti-war movement, and how to comprehend and remember violence and crimes in Vietnam. Returnees' thoughts and reflections on these subjects, in light of their return to Việt Nam, are connected to a broader set of questions: was the war just? Was it the right course of action? What is the legacy of the Vietnam War? Their answers emerged from their memories, anecdotes, and perspectives on the war and return to Việt Nam.

Australian returnees could be grouped according to two distinct positions that correlated strongly with the time of return. The first, correlated with early returns, was that Australian involvement was a mistake, arising out of politicians' efforts to maintain the US alliance. "Most people now realize the folly of our involvement in the Vietnam War," army veteran Graham E. explained. "I think most people now see it as having been a political war."[112] Burstall wrote that Australian involvement amounted to "boot-licking to an American insurance policy."[113] The prevalence of this view among early returnees overlaps with an anti-American sentiment that was widespread in 1980's Australian writing on the war.[114] Adherents viewed the commitment to Vietnam as a continuation of Australian subservience to fighting "'other people's wars' ... at the behest of our 'great and powerful friend,' the United States," with no benefit and at considerable cost to Australian citizens, soldiers, and national interest. The "other people's wars" argument had broad appeal, because it touched, as Doyle describes, "upon the too easy appropriation of the well-known betrayal myth underlying Gallipoli's adduction as the founding myth of the nation."[115] This conclusion therefore allowed veterans to judge the war from a distance while maintaining the virtue of Australian soldiers: "Australia was committed long term to backing the US," Murphy wrote, "this commitment arrived at a point in history where an Australian Prime Minister declared publicly ... that Australia was 'all the way with LBJ.' From then on it was downhill for all parties concerned in the conflict. Not that this was Australia's doing, hell we never lost a battle!"[116]

However, as Grey notes, "the notion that Australians have always fought 'other people's wars' rests on the assumption that the wars we have fought in

---

[111] Murphy, *Quiet Australians*, 529.   [112] Interview with Graham E.
[113] Burstall, *A Soldier Returns*, 9–10.
[114] Doyle, "Dismembering the Anzac Legend," 118.
[115] Grey, "In Every War but One?" 192–93, 119.   [116] Murphy, *Quiet Australians*, 18.

were not in our national interest."[117] The second major Australian reflection on Vietnam incorporates the war into Australia's national interest, arguing that Australian involvement was justified by the threat of communism. These returnees emphasized that Vietnam was not a "people's war," at least not on the side of the NLF: "the North Vietnamese would never beat the Americans, it was China and Russia," Rodney insisted.[118] "It was called the Yellow Peril, you know?" David W. explained, "China was on the march, down into Indonesia ... I always wonder, if we hadn't – we might have won it."[119] This viewpoint was more common among veterans who returned in the 2000s and later and overlapped with veterans who argued that the Cold War ended in Vietnam. Dave explained how the dominoes would fall: "After Sài Gòn, went into Cambodia. Then they go into Burma, and they probably go back to Malaya, they were already – Indonesia under Sukarno was already communist. So, if you can't see the progression: North Korea, North Việt Nam, Cambodia, Malaya, Indonesia, if you can't see a progression there, then you're not thinking."[120]

Some veterans of both nationalities suggested that the war was just, but fought badly. "I could understand why we did it," Mike M. said, "because we were involved in the SEATO [Southeast Asia Treaty Organization]. We were a member of that, so we had a reason to be there.... I'm not sure the way we fought the war was credible, but the domino theory has some credibility to it."[121] These veterans avoided any indictment of the troops themselves, focusing on broad strategy. Others suggested that Western intervention was misplaced, but that the war was fought well or had positive effects. Mark said that although "I don't think communism has expanded since Vietnam ... communism doesn't work very well," he also thought "we did a lot of good here [during the war] ... this was a third world nation when we got here. Women didn't wear bras, most of them didn't wear tops when we got here in 1950-something. And then they taught them how to do that."[122] Mark's belief that the military presence educated the Vietnamese is classic orientalist paternalism and reflects an idea that critical refugee studies scholar Mimi Nguyen describes as "liberal war," which "perpetuates violence that it claims is incidental to its exercise of power to free others."[123] "We've taught them what freedom is like. We taught North Vietnam what freedom is like."[124] Mark's perspective reflects the increasingly common interpretation of Vietnam as a "noble cause."

---

[117] Grey, "In Every War but One?" 193.   [118] Interview with Rodney.
[119] Interview with David W.   [120] Interview with Dave.   [121] Interview with Mike M.
[122] Interview with Mark.
[123] Mimi Nguyen, *The Gift of Freedom: War, Debt, and Other Refugee Passages* (Durham, NC: Duke University Press, 2012), 20.
[124] Ibid.

Indeed, several veterans argued that the cause was just, and their warfare was moral, but the war itself was a lost cause. "I think we could have stayed there. We were doing a lot," said Australian veteran Ray. He added: "It was unwinnable; we never could have won it. We could never have got rid of communism in the short term."[125] These contradictory reflections on the legacy of the war suggest that many veterans struggled with the dominant academic and pop culture perspective that the war was a "quagmire": they wanted to find meaning in their service by locating value in "their" war.

For veterans who felt that the war was just or noble – even if it was unwinnable – the end of the war was extremely painful. John W. said that the Australian withdrawal "was part of my guilt. We didn't do what we said we were going to do . . . . It has reduced me to tears to see little kids that have lost arms and legs, innocent victims of war, and they're terrified, absolutely terrified. Here's this bloody great big Aussie with a pair of big army boots on. . .," John W. became increasingly emotional as he described, "he reaches down and gives that kid something out of his ration pack, and the appreciation and the love that they have for these people who come there and given them hope, and then we turn our back on them?" Returning to Việt Nam only "reinforced" his shame:

We should never bloody have been involved in this war, we should never have gotten in there, but when we did get in there, we should have fought to the last man, to the very last man, not to let these people down. Because what we did is, we went in there and we promised all these bloody people that we were going to be there and be their allies and take away this horrendous invasion of the North that was communist, everything else. And then when it got too hot politically, come on boys, you've got to get out of there. And we left them high and dry. We left those people high and dry. And that's wrong. That, to me, is wrong.[126]

Many returnees concluded that the war was simply "a horrible waste. Of time, effort, money, people. I think in the back of my mind I thought it was inevitable anyway."[127] This conclusion was very difficult for some, and facing the reality of wasted effort in peacetime Việt Nam was challenging. When US Air Force veteran Heiko returned to Việt Nam,

. . . I didn't really feel comfortable that the communists now owned this place, you know. I mean we busted our horns for so long, doing what we did. And know looking back at it, it wasn't really our war, but it just seemed a waste of people, and time, and bodies, and all of that kind of stuff, you know. That's what really came to mind, was all the people we lost. You know, it was sad.[128]

---

[125] Interview with Ray. [126] Interview with John W. [127] Interview with Ken.
[128] Interview with Heiko.

Yet for others, returning provided some comfort. Francis explained that "when the war was officially ended, we thought if we left ... we thought it was going to be a blood bath, and it was going to be terrible, and communism would take over, there'd be mass murder, all these terrible scenarios. It didn't really happen that way." Francis found that returning to Việt Nam "gave me the sense that all of our fears of what was going to happen [didn't], I mean on a small scale it did, but for the majority."[129] Many of these veterans considered Western intervention in Vietnam to be an honest mistake. They recognized the blinkers of identity and ideology, of trusting the known and fearing the unknown, on American policymakers. "[It] was a terrible mistake," Pete explained, "because we should have told the French to sit down and shut up and get their act together on the European continent, and let Việt Nam go its way. We failed to do that."[130]

Finally, many anti-war returnees viewed the Western involvement in Việt Nam as fundamentally immoral. They argued that the United States intervened for personal profit and power, rather than through a misguided notion of rescuing the Vietnamese from communism. These veterans were angry. "The Johnsons owned stock in Bell helicopters!" David A. said, "have you ever seen a video or newsreel of Vietnam where you didn't see helicopters everywhere? .... What was their motivation to end the war?... the Gulf of Tonkin incident! They attacked our ship? No, they didn't! That was a lie that our government and the media told to justify our coming here."[131] Anti-war veterans often expressed the radical critique that emerged among the New Left in the 1970s, which conceptualized the United States as a "rapacious superpower" conducting an imperialist agenda through military intervention.[132] Historians such as Gabriel Kolko argued that the Vietnam War revealed an American goal of "imposing its hegemony" on "states and social systems opposed to the international order Washington sought to establish."[133] Such analysis reflected anti-war returnees' experiences in Vietnam. It also provided veterans with a target for their rage. "Henry Kissinger is a war criminal, Nixon's a war criminal, a lot of them that were in the State Department," John A. said. "I would have danced on Lyndon Bain Johnson's grave, for escalating that war."[134] The radical critique was hardened by the return to Việt Nam. "The longer I stay here, the more anti-war I get," Suel explained, "when I look at the devastation, what we did to these people for absolutely no reason. I mean there was not even

---

[129] Interview with Francis. [130] Interview with Pete. [131] Interview with David A.
[132] McMahon, "Changing Interpretations of the Vietnam War," 767.
[133] Gabriel Kolko, *Anatomy of a War* (Allen & Unwin: London, 1986), 547.
[134] Interview with John A.

a plausible reason for what we did. It just really hardened me, my thoughts. I am totally and completely anti-war now."[135]

Veterans' conclusions on the legacies of the war demonstrate that rather than challenging their views, the experience of returning to Việt Nam often reinforced their existing values and beliefs. This trend of reinforcement was apparent across both nationalities, various political positions, and all return periods. Veterans' discussions of loss (or victory) in Việt Nam, the anti-war movement, war crimes, and the justness or morality of the war also demonstrate that these debates are far from settled. On the contrary, the force and passion with which veterans discussed these topics demonstrated how polarizing and contentious the Vietnam War continues to be. Nguyễn notes that "the tendency is to remember any given war, to the extent that it is remembered at all, for a detail or two."[136] For those who lived through it, reducing the war down to a "detail or two" was a reduction of their entire experience. Consequently, many responded to discussions about the return experience by launching into debates around the morality of "their" war, revealing how much their sense of identity was connected to the war. In the following final chapter(Chapter 8), I explore how veterans negotiated the space of contemporary Việt Nam with these entrenched wartime views and identities.

[135] Interview with Suel.   [136] Nguyễn, *Nothing Ever Dies*, 4.

8 Veteran Legacies in Việt Nam

"Yeah, hell yeah I got a right to be here. I spilt blood on this ground."[1] Many veterans returned to Việt Nam with strong feelings of diasporic connection to the physical space of the country, feelings that were often challenged and tested by local practices, national memories, and the effects of the passage of time. This final chapter explores how veterans responded to that challenge, working to reassert their sense of connection through their individual engagements with Vietnamese society and through the growing enclaves of the veteran-expatriate community. I first introduce several nostalgic social practices I observed among veterans in Việt Nam before turning to explore how veterans justified their presence in Việt Nam, showing how they harnessed Australian and American wartime culture, values, and knowledge in order to establish their authority. Finally, I analyze how Australian and US returnees made sense of their return to Việt Nam as living legacies of war.

Throughout my research, conversations I had about my work with Australian, American, and Vietnamese civilians indicated a widespread, cross-cultural perception that veterans return to Việt Nam to engage in sex tourism and find young Vietnamese wives. While Thailand was and remains the most notorious destination for "intercourse and inebriation," the country's history as a Rest and Relaxation (R&R) site and the role of Vietnam veterans as Thailand's first sex tourists linked veterans to the concept of sex tourism and located the practice in a war-related Asian setting.[2] In Australia, media coverage of the trafficking of Filipino brides – itself a wartime legacy – also contributed to the widespread idea that

---

[1] Interview with Deryle.
[2] See for example: Keith B. Richburg, "In Thailand, Some Vietnam Vets Are Still Missing by Choice." *Washington Post*, June 5, 1988, 1; Stevenson, *Hard Men Humble*, 12–15.

Vietnam veterans returned to Việt Nam for sex.[3] Western popular culture representations of Southeast Asia entrenched this association between sex tourism in Asia and veterans. One colleague suggested that veterans were returning to Việt Nam "like in 'Khe Sanh,'" a Vietnam veteran anthem containing the lyrics: "Been back to Southeast Asia ... the answer sure ain't there / But I'm drifting north, to check things out again ... nothing like the kisses / from a jaded Chinese princess / I'm gonna hit some Hong Kong mattress all night long."[4] These ambiguous connections between the war, veterans, the sex industry, and Asia thus created the idea that veterans returned to Việt Nam primarily to meet Vietnamese women.

War histories and returnee narratives implicitly support this stereotype. Historian Heather Stur argues that the US military depicted Vietnamese women in traditional dress, *áo dài*, as the "national symbol" of the Republic of Việt Nam (RVN), while folklore among soldiers represented Vietnamese women as "sexual playthings."[5] Laderman concurs, observing that Vietnamese women were presented in wartime guidebooks as "touristic sights (or sites) ... both sexualized objects and emblems of Asian tradition." Laderman further notes that soldiers received military-issue pocket guidebooks that used "colorful imagery ... typical of the idyllic visions of Vietnam appearing in the broader tourism literature."[6] Soldier memoirs show the impact of this gendered marketing. Many justify the development of an Asian fetish through the "Dear John" letter. The term "Dear John" to describe a letter announcing a break up was popularized in World War II, but in Vietnam the term narrowed to suggest that the woman ended the relationship because she supported the anti-war movement, often through a relationship with an anti-war man.[7] "Dear John" letters in Vietnam narratives are thus shorthand for personal and political betrayal. In memoirs, receiving a "Dear John" letter often led soldiers to turn away from "round-eyes" toward client relationships with Asian sex workers.[8] Scurfield described how his "own Dear John experience was a catalyst that seemed to turn me further away from American women and towards Asian women. I, and perhaps other American soldiers, found *The Guess Who's* song 'American Woman (Get Away From Me)' to become a very meaningful personal

---

[3] Nikki Barrowclough, "The Shameful Story of Australia's Serial Husbands." *Good Weekend*, May 6, 1995. www.smh.com.au/good-weekend/gw-classics/the-shameful-story-of-australias-serial-husbands-20140827-109b5i

[4] Cold Chisel, "Khe Sanh." *Cold Chisel* (Sydney: Trafalgar Studios, 1978).

[5] Stur, *Beyond Combat*, 38–40. [6] Laderman, *Tours of Vietnam*, 33, 34, 51.

[7] Emanual Tay, "The Dear John Syndrome During the Vietnam War." *Diseases of the Nervous System* 37:1 (1976): 165–67.

[8] Wood, *Veterans Narratives and the Collective Memory of the Vietnam War*, 72.

anthem."[9] In return narratives, many veterans lauded Vietnamese women as graceful, elegant, and "the most beautiful women in the world," with emphasis on the "sensual" and "traditional" (submissive) elements of their femininity.[10]

The extent to which individual veterans' sexual preferences were shaped by the wartime sex industry, and how far desire for companionship factored in to their returns to Việt Nam, is unclear. Most returnees did not introduce the subject of sex in their interviews, in discussing either war or return. A handful of veterans offered unprompted declarations that they did not return to Việt Nam seeking relationships. David E. explained that when he returned,

> ... the last thing I want[ed] to do is get hooked up with a Vietnamese woman. I see these guys, these old men, running around with these little twenty-two-year-olds, and I just think they're wacked out. And then they're having kids! What the hell! Excuse me, sixty-six, sixty-seven, years old, they got a two-year-old daughter? So anyway, it was not in my game plan.

As it happened, however, David E. did go on to marry a Vietnamese woman, Ushi, after returning. His descriptions of marriage centered on the intellectual, emotional, and spiritual equality he valued in his relationship. His declaration established a distinction between himself and the "alcoholic sex addicts" that "sadden" him, creating an alternative narrative of love in Việt Nam.[11] Other veterans, like Mike C. and Bill E., offered a subtler distinction. They discussed their marriages to Vietnamese women in ways that emphasized equality and respect. They worked together, grew to love each other, suggesting that their relationships developed away from the "bar culture" of Nha Trang and Đà Nẵng. Each of these veterans discussed the agency of their wives throughout their interview, with the implicit message that they did not view Asian women as submissive. Their awareness suggests that the stereotype of returning to Việt Nam to engage in sex tourism is apparent within the expatriate veteran community.

Several of my Australian interviewees talked frankly with other (male) researchers and journalists about their participation in the sex industry in Vũng Tàu.[12] My age and gender likely influenced dialogue on the subject in my interviews, as many veterans responded to me with an avuncular attitude. Other returnees directed me to memoirs or biographical media

---

[9] Scurfield, *A Vietnam Trilogy*, 52.
[10] Interview with David A; Reilly, *Return of the Warriors*, 47. [11] Interview with David E.
[12] For example: Lindsay Murdoch, "Swearing They'd Never Go Back, Many Veterans Now Call Vietnam's Vung Tau Home." *Canberra Times*, December 10, 2016. www.canberratimes.com.au/good-weekend/swearing-theyd-never-go-back-many-veterans-now-call-vietnams-vung-tau-home-20161207-gt5ww6.html

pieces in which their wartime and postwar sex lives were openly discussed, but did not broach the subject with me.[13] The juxtaposition between silence in my fieldwork data and explicit content in memoirs suggests that social norms may have constrained veterans during interviews. Oral historian Noah Riseman explores the "reticence" of Australian veterans to discuss "misbehavior" on R&R in his oral history interviews. Riseman suggests that this reticence is in part to protect the veteran group and avoid "reinforcing negative stereotypes," and in part to protect the individual from embarrassment with stories that "fell outside the bounds of acceptable social behavior."[14] In the case of veterans who shared explicit memoirs but were reticent in interviews, the latter almost certainly is the case. For example, John A. explained in a memoir how sex and combat became inextricably linked for him during the war: "a fire fight is sexual. Killing became seductive." In the "gentle world" he found with a Vietnamese sex worker, he was reassured of his morality even as he transgressed his own boundaries: "this was war and there was no taboo... she whispered in my ear: 'you good man. You good man, John.'" In the early 2000s, he had a relationship with a young Vietnamese woman named Tuyet. John A. psychoanalyzed his attraction: "Tuyet takes me back to a mind-set where I flaunted death.... [She] has no idea that she is another connection to the war for me, a conduit back to the dark night. She can't comprehend that I want to save her. I realize that I associate her with the attractive, young Viet Cong woman I killed.... Thirty years later, I'm making love to her corpse."[15]

Other memoirs were less introspective. Australian Army veteran Paul Murphy provided a scathing critique of return relationships, describing how "gullible veterans" were "duped" by unfaithful Vietnamese women who make the same empty promises to "one or two oilmen... to ensure her future." He pitied veterans "who had done the lot on the whiff of a sweet smelling, beautiful courtesan."[16] As Murphy's perception that veterans were "duped" by sex workers suggests, foreign clientele in the sex tourism industry demand emotional as well as physical labor. Women in this market develop long-term, intimate relationships (even marriages) with repeat customers by framing remuneration explicitly as a power that clients bestow, tapping into Western notions of "Third World poverty."[17]

---

[13] For example, Mike C. in Martin Naperstek, *War Song* (Bloomington, IN: iUniverse, 2000).

[14] Noah Riseman, "'Describing Misbehaviour in Vung Tau as "Mischief" is Ridiculously Coy': Ethnographic Refusal, Reticence, and the Oral Historian's Dilemma." *Oral History Review* 45:1 (2018): 88, 90.

[15] Akins, *Nam Au Go Go*, 133, 143, 91.   [16] Murphy, *Quiet Australians*, 173.

[17] Hoang, *Dealing in Desire*, 150.

Workers ask clients to support specific needs – rent, children's school fees, English or business classes, family emergencies – in order to make the client "feel empowered and needed in their financial ability to care for a poor third-world woman."[18] From the worker's point of view, this role-play is what the client is paying for: "wife nurturing, men providing."[19] Despite this blurring of economy and emotion, both parties are aware of the transactional nature of these relationships. Workers and clients set prices together. An anecdote I heard numerous times among Australian and US veteran communities was that local women referred to expatriates as "ATMs" (automated teller machines), indicating veterans' awareness of the ongoing financial aspect of these long-term relationships.[20] Conflict emerges when the clients began to feel entitled to physical and emotional labor without payment. Just as client-worker relationships reenact Western wartime values – liberating the Vietnamese woman – Murphy's description of veterans being "duped," or denied free labor, was tinged with sexism and racism that echoed Western wartime perceptions of Asian women. Tourism scholar Damien Garrick notes that sex tourists draw on wartime slang: Asian women are described as "'LBFM's' or 'Little Brown Fucking Machines Powered by Rice.'"[21] Garrick argues that wartime justifications for sex tourism "reinforce the power dynamics of race that exist between Western men and Third World women and allow Westerners to rationalize their participation in sex tourism as justifiable."[22] Murphy's dual feelings of entitlement to and contempt for "young, very attractive Vietnamese bar girl[s]" underlie his resentment that "hapless 'old warrior[s]'" were "beguiled" by sex workers. This scorn for Vietnamese women turned out to be an explanation for his own marriage, where "I too fell into the honey pot ... but hell, why should I be any different? I am only human."[23]

Murphy's discussion of Vietnamese-expatriate relationships suggest that the space of Việt Nam provided the veteran-expatriate community with a permissive context for reproducing wartime values. Tourism scholars Bob McKercher and Thomas G. Bauer argue that tourism "offers a liminal environment away from the constraints of home, which reduces inhibitions .... Western tourists in particular are allowed to escape the normal gender, social, and even racial constraints when they travel."[24]

[18] Hoang, "Economies of Emotion, Familiarity, Fantasy, and Desire," 263–66, 270.
[19] Hoang, "Flirting with Capital," 517.
[20] Hoang, "Economies of Emotion, Familiarity, Fantasy, and Desire," 264.
[21] Damien Garrick, "Excuses, Excuses: Rationalisations of Western Sex Tourists in Thailand." *Current Issues in Tourism* 8:6 (2005): 498.
[22] Ibid., 499. [23] Murphy, *Quiet Australians*, n.p. (author's forward), 174.
[24] Bob McKercher and Thomas G. Bauer, "Conceptual Framework of the Nexus between Tourism, Romance, and Sex." In *Sex and Tourism: Journeys of Romance, Love, and Lust.*

For veterans, these constraints were also ones of time. Australian and American societies had rapidly progressed since the war around issues of race and gender. The liminal space offered by a non-Western context was heightened by the connection of the place to war, offering a kind of memory template for "more radical behavior."[25] Furthermore, "industrial prostitution" is disguised in Việt Nam through the hospitality industry, replicating the wartime "bar culture" in which bars operate as brothels.[26]

This bar culture is an integral part of a deliberate nostalgic war memory promoted by the Vietnamese tourism industry since Đổi Mới. Communications scholars Laurel B. Kennedy and Mary Rose Williams argue that the Vietnamese tourism industry isolates and reproduces war memory as niche tourism experiences, promoting an image of "Asian exoticism and its mystique, as well as a muted and angerless history."[27] I have already discussed some elements of this nostalgic war memory, such as the kitsch reproductions of war artifacts, that veterans consumed.[28] Bar culture, however, was an aspect of nostalgic war memory that veterans actively participated in: the portrayal of war as a social activity.[29] Historians and anthropologists have written at length about this production of nostalgic war memory in Vietnamese tourism: with "bars like the 'Apocalypse Now' and the 'B4-75' opened in the early 1990s, inviting patrons to step into a peculiar re-created past, of the war as experienced by a partying GI."[30] As the return to Việt Nam became normalized and the return demographic aged, such explicit war nostalgia became unfashionable.[31] Veteran-expatriate bars began blending war memories into their culture instead of (or as well as) their aesthetic, developing a mixture of nostalgia, sex tourism, and war tourism that was pronounced and encoded among the veteran community in Việt Nam.

The liminality of travel, memory of wartime space, and replication of wartime culture thus collapsed time through space, permitting veterans to express wartime (both of the war and of the time of the war) views in a peacetime environment. Many of the conversations in expat bars revolved around "what's wrong with Australia/America," with migration and multiculturalism, identity politics, the "nanny-state," coddled youth,

---

Edited by Thomas G. Bauer and Bob McKercher (New York: Haworth Press, 2003), 10, 11.
[25] Ibid., 10.
[26] Bruce Prideaux et al., "Exotic or Erotic – Contrasting Images for Defining Destinations." *Asia Pacific Journal of Tourism Research* 9:1 (2004): 9.
[27] Kennedy and Williams, "The Past Without Pain," 126.   [28] Discussed in Chapter 4.
[29] Kennedy and Williams, "The Past Without Pain," 151.   [30] Ibid., 146.
[31] One reconciliation veteran told me that "No one goes to Apocalypse Now anymore. It used to be crazy, though."

and shifts in gender roles as the main complaints. Richard, a former Marine and expatriate in Đà Nẵng, explained that he liked living in Việt Nam because "living's easy. The United States is fucked up, [but] here, one race, all little people, you don't have to deal."[32] Australian veterans in particular suggested that they felt relieved from Western cultural and social norms in Việt Nam. At an official gala dinner in 2016 commemorating the 50th anniversary of the Battle of Long Tan, several veterans on my table rejoiced that they "didn't have to be politically correct over here."[33] Cultural historian Robin Gerster argues that the coinciding of the Vietnam War with counterculture movements in Australia and the United States led Vietnam veterans to feel emasculated by the new "anti-war warriors."[34] Many Australian veterans felt that dominant "PC" (politically correct) culture in Australia was arbitrating individual morality and restricting individual freedom, and implied that these repressions were produced by the social dominance of the "anti-war warriors": the same people who had emasculated them during the war. These veterans exhibited what scholars Megan Mackenzie and Alan Foster describe as "masculinity nostalgia": "a yearning for a set of gender norms and relations linked to fantasies of a secure, 'traditional', and ordered past."[35] They remembered Việt Nam at war as a time and space – the last time and space – where veterans' traditional masculinity was not repressed by an increasingly progressive culture. Expatriate areas of peacetime Việt Nam were carved out as safe spaces for the performance of 1960's values of race, sex, and power as their traditional masculinity was protected by a barrier of wealth and whiteness. Thus where many diasporic communities "strive to create a comforting and invigorating home away from home," veteran-returnees attempted to recreate the lost homeland in Việt Nam.[36]

In this recreation, veteran-returnees mark an ironic deviation from diasporic patterns. Political scientist William Safran argues that while diasporic consciousness fixates on the homeland, this consciousness "does not – and is not intended to – lead its members to prepare for the actual departure to the homeland." Some members of diasporas can and

---

[32] Interview with Richard.
[33] Author's notes from attendance at the Vietnam Australia Friendship Dinner, Vũng Tàu, August 18, 2016.
[34] Robin Gerster, "A Bit of the Other: Touring Vietnam." In *Gender and War: Australians at War in the Twentieth Century*. Edited by Joy Damousi and Marilyn Lake (Melbourne: Cambridge University Press Archive, 1995), 225.
[35] Megan Mackenzie and Alan Foster, "Masculinity Nostalgia: How War and Occupation Inspire a Yearning for a Gender Order." *Security Dialogue* 48:7 (2017): 206.
[36] Martin Baumann, "Diaspora: Genealogies of Semantics and Transcultural Comparison." *Numen* 47:3 (2000): 329.

do return to their homeland, but the core purpose of diasporic imaginings of homeland is a "defense mechanism against slights committed by the host country."[37] Yet veteran-returnees harnessed this defensiveness to the United States and Australia *in* Việt Nam, as part of a diasporic claim. This deviation raises another difference between veteran-returnees and other diasporas: unlike diasporic groups united by common awareness of a lost homeland, the warzone homeland is a feature of returnee memories, not Vietnam veteran memories more broadly. While my interviewees felt that "there was something about this place that was always with us," there are many veterans who do not feel that sense of connection or belonging to Việt Nam, and most veterans never returned.[38] Importantly, I only interviewed veterans after they returned, once they had encountered Việt Nam at peace. The diasporic consciousness among my interviewees may itself reflect the displacement they faced upon return, leading them to emphasize their wartime connections to the physical space of Việt Nam.

This tendency to emphasize wartime connections to space was reflected in returnees' preoccupation with the legitimacy of their war experience. Within veteran communities, war and combat were understood as fundamentally masculine experiences that imparted esoteric knowledge which could not be communicated to or comprehended by civilians.[39] This "war knowledge," or wisdom gained through the experience of warfare, gained particular significance for Vietnam veterans. Continuing debates over the purpose, meaning, and result of the Vietnam War in Australia and the United States imparted exclusivity to the Vietnam war experience. Unlike many of the politicians, academics, and journalists who debated the war, they (veterans) were there.[40] At the same time, and in large part in reaction to the Vietnam War, parallel social and cultural forces in the United States and Australia increasingly conferred authority and legitimacy through military service.[41] The importance of war knowledge among the returnee community became apparent as I initiated fieldwork. While I made it clear repeatedly that I was interested in a variety of postwar experiences and memories, prospective

---

[37] Safran, "Diasporas in Modern Societies," 94. [38] Interview with Mike C.
[39] Despite their commitment to truth-telling, anti-war veterans sometimes become agitated when non-veterans promote anti-war arguments without centering veteran knowledge. See for example, Michael Uhl, "An Enfant Terrible Stumbles Upon the Vietnam War." *Counterpunch*, April 9, 2013.
[40] Veterans occasionally conceded that embedded war correspondents had experiential war knowledge, usually with qualifiers.
[41] Bacevich, *New American Militarism*, 1–7; Fitzgerald, "Support the Troops," 1–22; Reynolds and Lake, "Epilogue: Moving On?" In *What's Wrong with ANZAC? The Militarisation of Australian History*. Edited by Marilyn Lake et al. (Sydney: University of New South Wales Press, 2010), 161–73.

interviewees focused intently on whether their personal war experience was sufficient for my research project, even apologizing in a few instances for "only" being in a support position. Like other diasporic groups, veterans "carry their social hierarchies with them," including, for returnees, back to Việt Nam.[42] War knowledge thus became the key to claiming a place in the former warzone home upon return to Việt Nam.

Initially, it was knowledge of Vietnamese war experiences that granted access to the warzone home. Reconciliation returnees described how meeting their former enemies and discovering their point of view gave them a sense of belonging: "we did share those common circumstances," US Army veteran Ralph explained. "Even though you're on opposite sides, you're still kind of brothers in that war."[43] In their memoirs, articles, and interviews, reconciliation veterans referred to Vietnamese stories they had heard and suggested I speak to specific locals about their lives, reflecting on the sheer scale of warfare experienced by the Vietnamese. However, as increasing numbers of veterans returned and veteran-expatriates established enclaves, Australian and American experiences began to dominate as the legitimizing diasporic knowledge. During my fieldwork in 2016, recent returnees in expatriate bars in Đà Nẵng and Vũng Tàu – the respective enclaves of American and Australian veterans – recommended I interview specific veterans who were "really at the pointy end," who were embedded in the local expatriate community, and/or who were tour guides. These veterans were essentially unofficial spokespeople for their diasporic community, and others deferred to their war experiences: "You should talk to him, he's got some good ones!" At the same time, Vietnamese experiences were diminished as veteran communities created hierarchies for Vietnamese truth. In the Australian community, for instance, Vietnamese who countered veteran narratives were dismissed as "dinky-di [deeply] north Vietnamese," whereas those who verified veteran knowledge were assumed to be associated with the RVN.[44]

In their interviews, some returnees expressed their diasporic claim – their sense of belonging to the space of Việt Nam as a result of their war experience – through nostalgic practices. In Part I, I explored how longing for resolution or peace manifested in nostalgia for the warzone home, drawing veterans back to Việt Nam. Yet "nostalgic love can only survive in a long-distance relationship."[45] The Việt Nam that veterans longed for was in part manufactured by tourism representations of Việt Nam as an idyllic paradise – what Kennedy and Rose describe as the isolated

---

[42] Sigona et al., "Introduction: The Self as Plural," xix.   [43] Interview with Ralph.
[44] Interview with John B.   [45] Boym, *Future of Nostalgia*, xiv.

"depiction of war as a localized and provincial event."[46] By situating war memory in a pastoral landscape, the tourism industry promotes an idea of "real Việt Nam" as a land that time forgot: a pastiche that collapses the colonial, feudal, and dynastic histories of Việt Nam into the image of peasant villages. Films such as *The Deer Hunter* and *Apocalypse Now* also depict Việt Nam as untouched jungle and bucolic rice paddies.[47] In these films, the "real Việt Nam" is represented in fragments before being obliterated with napalm strikes and bombing runs. The wartime destruction of this "real Việt Nam" in film puts a high value on the authentic pastoral, fueling foreign demand for the romantic idyll of prewar Việt Nam in the tourism sector. This cultural memory of Việt Nam at war is also embedded in veteran memories of combat, which center on guerrilla warfare in the jungles. Urban areas were generally remembered as the site of large bases and R&R centers, while battles that took place in warzone towns, such as the house-to-house fighting in Sài Gòn and Huế during the Tet Offensive, were understandably remembered on a terrain of ruins rather than in cosmopolitan cities.[48] These memories erase the prewar history of urban populations in the "Pearl of the Far East" and the Imperial Capital. When veterans returned – particularly since the early 2000s – they found bustling cities, industrial areas, and modern technology that jarred with these romanticized war memories.

Many veterans responded to challenges to war memory by framing peacetime Việt Nam as a corrupted paradise. Australian Army veteran Ray said: "I think it's changed for the worse. It's lost its innocence, I guess. Lost its innocence ... I think that's the worst part of what I see of it. And that's looking at it from a person who was there when it was really raw Asia." This dismayed response to postwar Việt Nam occurred across all veteran demographics, irrespective of time of return, frequency of return, nationality, or political affiliation. The nostalgia for a wartime idyll and the disapproval of peacetime Việt Nam indicates the cultural power of film and marketing on veteran war memory: Ray had also described war as a "dirty, horrible thing."[49] This nostalgic discontent can be seen as a way of reiterating the diasporic claim to place. Veterans remember Việt Nam before it "changed"; they were there when it was authentic. Reactions of nostalgic discontent thus locate a sense of belonging that supersedes the contemporary reality of peacetime Việt Nam.

---

[46] Kennedy and Williams, "The Past Without Pain," 154.
[47] *The Deer Hunter, Apocalypse Now*. The major exception to this cinematic trope is *Full Metal Jacket*, which depicts the fighting in Huế during the Tet Offensive. *Full Metal Jacket*, directed by Stanley Kubrick (Burbank, CA: Warner Bros., 1987).
[48] Eighty percent of Huế was destroyed in the siege during the Tet Offensive.
[49] Interview with Ray.

Veterans supported their memories of an idyllic wartime past by implying that (most of) peacetime Việt Nam was inauthentic. Ray went on a Mekong Delta tour on his return trip in 2008. He determined that "along the [Mekong] river, they're still really peasants, and that's the only way you see the real village life."[50] His conclusion was based partly on the marketing of Việt Nam as a bucolic paradise, as these Delta tours draw on nostalgia by offering tourists a "last chance" insight into "authentic rural lifestyles."[51] His sense of authority over what was "real" Việt Nam suggested confirmation bias for his wartime perception of "raw Asia."[52] Veterans who projected authority over what was authentic may have found that the chaotic, urban reality of contemporary Việt Nam threatened their psychic comfort. To accept bustling cities, industrial growth, and luxury resorts as "real" Việt Nam would undermine the legitimacy of their memories, knowledge, and claim to space in Việt Nam.

Representations of peacetime Việt Nam as a corrupted paradise were most common among the most recent returnees to Việt Nam. This attitude was also more prevalent among Australians, who tended to be more politically conservative. Among US veterans, particularly those who returned early and visited frequently, war memory was displaced with a different nostalgic image. These veterans pinpointed the time of their first return as Việt Nam's idyllic moment, and expressed nostalgic discontent at Việt Nam's evolution since their return. John A. suggested that since he first returned in 2000, Vietnamese culture had changed for the worse. He tied this to urbanization and aspirational consumerism: "the ones in the city are becoming like Americans. You know, just stressed out, you see them grimacing in the morning, early in the morning and late in the evening they come back with grimaces on their faces, 'cause they're trying to work and get a bigger motorbike and a bigger screen and the latest new cellphone."[53]

This perception that Việt Nam was "purer" before it was affected by globalization is not unique to veterans. Many civilian tourists are similarly nostalgic for foreign spaces that are or were "untouched" by capitalism. But veterans also returned with a memory of war that they wanted to replace. "Half my life I have longed to witness peace in this land I have never been able to see in my mind's eye except in the midst of war," W. D. wrote, and in 1985 he began "to feel a strangely satisfying sense of déjà vu …. This is the Vietnam I remember: rural, simple, almost eternal.

[50] Interview with Ray.
[51] "Floating Market Tour," *Mekong Tours*. http://mekongtours.info/; "Mekong Delta Tours," *Buffalo Tours*. www.buffalotours.com/Popular-Destinations/Mekong-Delta-Tours.html
[52] Interview with Ray.   [53] Interview with John A.

What's different is the absence of war."[54] These first, longed-for experiences in peacetime Việt Nam were precious. Many veterans formed close attachments with the time as well as the space of their first return, and resented subsequent changes to these spaces. Ralph reminisced that Hà Nội in 1989 "had a real beauty to it, even though it was run down and what not."[55] His brother agreed: "whoosh, whoosh, whoosh ... this almost silent bicycle city."[56] US veterans returned in greater numbers than Australians in the reconciliation and normalization period, and American returnees were often broadly anti-capitalist. Reflecting on the pace of change in Việt Nam, Suel lamented: "I knew the WTO [World Trade Organization] was having a greater effect on Vietnam than Uncle Ho."[57] As Boym notes, nostalgia can be "a defense mechanism against the accelerated rhythm of change and the economic shock therapy."[58] It was unclear to what extent this nostalgia for Việt Nam in the early stages of reconstruction was a critique of globalization or an expression of personal longing. Given that anti-war veterans were unlikely to frame wartime culture in positive terms, this romanticization of predevelopment poverty may have acted as a placeholder for the wartime fantasy that they recognized as problematic.

Each of these social practices – performing wartime values, participating in diasporic communities, and expressing nostalgic discontent – worked to reiterate veterans' sense of belonging in Vietnamese space by bringing the past into the present, constantly linking "their" Việt Nam with the contemporary country. Veterans also claimed connections to Vietnamese space through philanthropy. The prominent "healing-through-helping" narrative that many veterans drew on to explain the effects of their return journeys implied a mutual benefit to local Vietnamese. Even those who did not promote the healing-through-helping narrative were involved (albeit inadvertently) in philanthropy through the veteran-expatriate bars, tours, and community events that patronized local nongovernmental organizations (NGOs). Because of this implicit benefactor role in veterans' returns, I asked interviewees whether they felt their presence was beneficial to Việt Nam.

Early American returnees considered normalized relations to be a beneficial result of their presence in Việt Nam. Pete, the former Ambassador, explained:

... when I went to Việt Nam in '91, pathetic, you know. It's only a couple years before that [that] people were dying from hunger on the streets. When I went back

---

[54] Ehrhart, *Going Back*, 21. [55] Ralph, interview in *Going Back: Echoes of War*.
[56] John C., interview in ibid. [57] Jones, *Meeting the Enemy*, 234.
[58] Boym, *Future of Nostalgia*, 64.

in '97, it wasn't a hell of a lot better, but it was better. And now, look at the quality of life. And I'm not going to pat myself on the back a lot, but the fact is, a lot of the stuff I did contributed to the improvement of the quality of life for 93 million people. That's a pretty good accomplishment.[59]

Veterans who returned on humanitarian missions emphasized their person-to-person diplomacy, sometimes viewing their contribution to normalization as superior to that of political veterans. "Our group," Don said of the Veterans for Peace (VFP):

... actually helped pave the way for improved relations between Việt Nam and America. More so than our Embassy has, to tell you the truth, because the Embassy is just a mouthpiece for government policy .... They know that there are American veterans who are very interested in helping the country to make up for the scars of war, and that has helped pave the way, and I feel good about that, very good about that.[60]

Because of the enduring hostility toward Việt Nam from within their own countries, US veterans also felt it was important that they showed the Vietnamese – former enemies, allies, the civilians caught in between, and their descendants – that not all soldiers bore a grudge. Reconciliation returnee John Z. explained, "we were still, technically, enemies. And so, they saw people that came through and said, hey, we're here to be friends. And I think that, you know, hopefully, that changed some of their opinions as well."[61] Some thought this demonstration of care was important because it gave the Vietnamese the opportunity to forgive. Normalization returnee Deryle thought,

... in some way maybe it'll help them, 'cause they still got their war wounds, you know? ... I mean, that's really neat, really to be able to pass over someone who's done something to you. You know forgiveness is powerful, forgiveness and thankfulness. And we're thankful ... most of us appear to be kind of thankful to be able to go there and not have the Vietnamese spit on us, you know?[62]

This perspective conforms to the dominant redemption-forgiveness narrative in Việt Nam. However, former Marine Suel disputed this: "they don't even want to hear us say: 'I'm sorry.' That's not part of the deal. They just want us to understand kind of what they want through. So, yeah, I think that's important for them. And me." Suel said that initially, he did not recognize how valuable the act of returning was: "the Vietnamese are so grateful that some of us come back and care about them. I didn't realize that at first, but I realize it now. I think it's very important that we show that. 'We care about you, we like you.'"[63]

---

[59] Interview with Pete. [60] Interview with Don. [61] Interview with John Z.
[62] Interview with Deryle. [63] Interview with Suel.

This demonstration of care was connected to prereturn expectations. Most veterans returned with some degree of suspicion or fear of the Vietnamese. These negative views were confounded by their return experience. Veterans' emphasis on the importance of showing care, or even love, for the Vietnamese was in part a remediation of these prereturn views and an expression of gratitude for the kindness they received. David E. explained:

When I was here in 1968, as a Marine ... I carried that M16, and I tried to look like the baddest, meanest, motherfucker in the whole damn valley. And I stuck that M16 in every Vietnamese man, woman, and child's face I could. 'Cause I wanted them to fear me as much as they possible could. 'Cause I felt if they feared me, my chances of survival were greater, they would leave me alone. Today, when I go around here ... I make a little extra effort to learn some phrases in Vietnamese. When you go and you speak a little Vietnamese to these people, they are just so grateful that you have taken the time to know their language. It just puts a smile on their face. That's sort of my way to make amends to these people.[64]

David E.'s suggestion that learning Vietnamese was an apology for wartime actions may seem insufficient as "amends," particularly given that he lived in a Vietnamese-speaking country, was married to a Vietnamese woman, and had Vietnamese step-children and step-grandchildren. However, his "little extra effort" to learn the language also relates to wartime conduct. Most US and Australian troops who served in Vietnam learned no Vietnamese aside from the wartime slang that bastardized the local language, blended it with slang developed in wars with other Asian countries (e.g. "mamasan"), and turned it into a tool of aggression and dominance: boo coo dinky dow (from the French "*beaucoup*" – many, and *điên cái đầu* – crazy); didi mow (from "*đi đi*" – go away, and "*mau*" – fast, confusingly used by troops to mean "hurry up"); *noojin* (Nguyễn, a common Vietnamese name – used to refer to any Vietnamese).

Where Americans highlighted emotional connections, Australian returnees tended to frame their gestures of goodwill in terms of diplomacy. Derrill listed the benefits of his project, Operation Wandering Souls: "we have had a number of things that we've either returned to the museum in Vũng Tàu or the museum in the old Biên Hòa, which is now Đồng Nai. And we've returned things to the Vietnamese government, and when we've gone back, we've also had meetings with their equivalent of a[n] [Royal Services League] RSL on a national scale in Hà Nội." He then explained the benefit: "it's a positive thing reflecting on Australia .... It's helped on a government-to-government level, it's

---

[64] Interview with David E.

certainly on a personal level, and certainly with positive feelings from Vietnamese toward Australia."[65] This focus on state-level relationships was surprising given that Australia recognized the Democratic Republic of Việt Nam (DRV) in 1973, without the aid of Vietnam veterans. Perhaps the emphasis on "foster[ing] good relationships between the two countries" was simply a way of discussing emotional connections in terms that the returnees were comfortable with.[66]

Some veterans used personal anecdotes to explain the benefit of their presence. This was most common among veterans on humanitarian missions, who returned repeatedly to the same village or town. On these return visits, they saw the progress of their projects and got to know the people they were supporting. US Army veteran Mike Boehm, who set up a loan funds program with a group of Quakers from Madison, demonstrated his benefit through the story of Phạm Thị Hương. Two of Hương's children were killed in a massacre by American troops in Trường Khánh in April 1969. When Boehm first met Hương, she told him that she "cannot forget the smell of the decomposing bodies of my children." Boehm remembered, "from what I could see, she had died that day. She was walking and talking, but dead inside." Boehm returned two years later and "the change in Mrs. Hương was amazing – almost unbelievable. She was smiling, laughing, and talking, just vibrant with new life." Her neighbors told Boehm and Do that with the loan, Hương started farming cows. "The crushing burden of poverty she had been living under finally lifted enough for her to begin to heal." Boehm's use of personal anecdote to measure his contribution reflects the medium he chose to discuss his humanitarian work. The story about Hương was published in *The Veteran*, the biannual newsletter for Vietnam Veterans Against the War. It was a call for other veterans to atone: "we cannot walk away from the people there ... our obligations do not end with the ending of the war."[67]

Other veterans drew on personal anecdotes because they were emotionally attached to their beneficiaries. US Army veteran Larry was introduced to Hoa and her family on his first journey back to Việt Nam in 2008. The family included Hoa; her mother; two teenage sons; four daughters, one still in high school; and three grandchildren. The teenage boys, Nghĩa and Toàn, were quadriplegic because of illness linked to Agent Orange exposure. Hoa's family was living in deep poverty, with Hoa as the sole provider.

---

[65] Interview with Derrill. [66] Interview with Andy.
[67] Mike Boehm, "Hope Rises from the Ashes of My Lai." *The Veteran*, 35:2 (2005): 22.

I put three hundred dollars in [her bank account] then, and I said, "you need a different motorbike, this is going to crater on you any time." They couldn't speak English. She had tears in her eyes; she didn't know what to say.... The last trip back I made, she proudly showed me the different motorbike she had, and then when I went inside I got tears in my eyes. For the first time in this woman's life... she had a small refrigerator. She didn't have to worry about salting the fish, that sort of thing..... And I just kept it up, just kept going back from the States, made sure they had an extra fifty dollars a month.[68]

Larry eventually moved to Đà Nẵng, bought a house, and Hoa and her family moved in. He began paying the children's school fees and Nghĩa and Toàn's medical fees, as well as campaigning for assistance for victims of Agent Orange. Given his closeness to Hoa and her children, whom Larry described as "my family," it is understandable that he, like Boehm, focused on personal relationships and Vietnamese gratitude. Toàn entered the intensive care unit in 2015, and Nghĩa died in September 2017. Larry's information campaign, "Child of War Viet Nam," is dedicated to them.[69]

Personal anecdotes of healing-through-helping implicitly validate veterans' presence in Việt Nam. Australian Army veteran Ric explained that "it makes you feel good, and as I say, the Vietnamese people, they really welcome me in, because they say, 'we know you help Vietnamese people.'"[70] This dynamic puts pressure on the Vietnamese to perform gratitude. Murphy wrote of the local response to a school built by the Australian Vietnam Veterans Reconstruction Group in Vũng Tàu in 1994: "the Vietnamese could not have been more appreciative and many speeches assured us that our efforts were not wasted, that this near brand new facility was badly needed and the kids had a dry safe school to study in."[71] This response spurred him to commit to humanitarian work in Việt Nam. By the mid-2000s, Việt Nam was recovering economically and previously poverty-stricken areas were increasingly self-sufficient. Veteran agencies were no longer major centers of community development, and their donations no longer prized. In the late 2000s or early 2010s, Murphy asked his Vietnamese liaison with the Women's Union where a donation of computers, intended to support a microfinance initiative, had gone.[72] They were in storage. This rankled Murphy: "the Women's Union has selective memory loss and does not

---

[68] Interview with Larry.   [69] Child of War Viet Nam. http://childofwarvietnam.com/
[70] Interview with Ric.
[71] Murphy, *Quiet Australians*, 237. The Reconstruction Group was renamed the "Australian Vietnam Volunteers Resource Group" in 2009, after Murphy had left the organization.
[72] Murphy mentions at several points in his memoir that he was writing in 2011.

mention nor show any gratitude for the computers we purchased for them in 2006."[73] Murphy later walked away from the Reconstruction Group and from Việt Nam.

Murphy's response speaks to what writer Teju Cole describes as the "White Savior Industrial Complex." Cole observes a trend of self-validating attention to global injustice among wealthy, white communities in which "the world is nothing but a problem to be solved by enthusiasm" and where humanitarian support "is about having a big emotional experience that validates privilege."[74] Beneficiaries are conceptualized as victims without agency and are expected to be unconditionally grateful for white philanthropy. If these expectations are not met, donors feel deprived of their entitled emotional reward. Cole argues that a common thread in the White Savior Industrial Complex is the privileging of good intentions on behalf of the donor over the effect for the beneficiary, and notes that "there is much more to doing good work than 'making a difference.' There is the principle of first do no harm, and the idea that those who are being helped ought to be consulted over matters that concern them."[75] Murphy's angry responses to Vietnamese "ingratitude" overlooked the need and capability of the communities he was trying to help. In 1997, the Reconstruction Group built a public toilet in Bến Súc, a very poor fishing village. The facilities were pay-per-use to cover water and electricity costs, and so they went unused. The power was switched off and the facilities fell into disrepair. Murphy blamed the "putrid" state of the facilities on "recipients [who] are not prepared to help themselves," detailing the repeated efforts of the Group to maintain the facilities until they were totally rebuilt in 2005. "It is a shame that the Vietnamese have a problem in appreciating aid that is provided for their welfare and see no need to keep clean or maintain a gift horse," Murphy concluded.[76]

Some veterans measured their benefit to Việt Nam through the longevity of their involvement and the credibility of their "Nobel-winning" campaigns and organizations.[77] Australian Army veteran Graham E., for instance, reflected that "I've managed to assist in a number of areas, regarding to improvements in Việt Nam. I was patron of an organization for many years that work[ed] on rehabilitation programs. I campaigned for the end to the use of landmines and for more support for victims or

---

[73] Murphy, *Quiet Australians*, 271.
[74] Teju Cole, "The White Savior Industrial Complex." *Known and Strange Things: Essays*, reproduced in *The Atlantic*, March 21, 2012. www.theatlantic.com/international/archive/2012/03/the-white-savior-industrial-complex/254843/
[75] Ibid.   [76] Murphy, *Quiet Australians*, 266.
[77] American RadioWorks, "25 Years from Vietnam."

survivors of, civilian survivors of landmines."[78] Other veterans were more understated. When I asked former Marine Greg, who taught for two decades in Hồ Chí Minh City, whether he felt his presence in Việt Nam was beneficial, he shrugged and said, "sure, to some."[79] These veterans balanced the benefit they brought to Việt Nam with the benefit afforded to them. US Army veteran Mike C., for example:

> ... wanted to move away from dealing only with the war, and I wanted to get into education, and I wanted to build something ... my first love, my first career was in education, so I thought, finish it! So that's what I'm doing .... I've seen many wonderful improvements, and been a good service to many, many people, in universities and language centers. So that gives me a sense of contribution.[80]

Expatriates who were integrated into their local community through humanitarian work were similarly modest. US Army veteran Chuck cofounded Project Renew, which remediates unexploded ordnances (UXOs) in Quảng Trị, and liaised with NGOs to support various war legacy issues, including prosthetics for victims of UXOs and support for people affected by Agent Orange. He was hailed by other veterans and was well known by many Vietnamese for the impact of his work over the decades. His response to my question regarding his benefit to Việt Nam was: "in very small ways, I think so, yeah. I hope so."[81]

These returnees indicated an awareness of the White Savior critique. All had worked directly or indirectly with the Western nonprofit sector, and several had first-hand experience in the fields of politics and development. I was advised by one returnee that some of the more prominent expatriate-veterans had been hurt by charges of paternalism and self-indulgence from academics and journalists. Their responses to my question could be read as a buttress against such charges. However, the inverse correlation between measurable contributions and modesty regarding the significance of their contribution also suggests that those who had long-term exposure to the complexity and depth of Vietnamese society became more aware of the limits of individual contributions.

International relations scholar Michael Barnett observes a transformation of humanitarianism in the 1990s. The traditional NGO sector shifted away from notions of neutrality and independence and began to see themselves as potentially major actors in world politics, leading to accusations of corruption and paternalistic imperialism.[82] Disastrous interventions in Somalia, the former Yugoslavia, and

---

[78] Interview with Graham E.   [79] Interview with Greg.   [80] Interview with Mike C.
[81] Interview with Chuck.
[82] Michael Burnett, "Humanitarianism Transformed." *Perspectives on Politics* 3:4 (2005): 724–25.

Rwanda illustrated the fallibility of humanitarian organizations and left the aid sector in crisis. At the same time, global suffering appeared to be on the rise. Traumatic television coverage of war and atrocity created what became known as "the CNN effect," in which constant media coverage of crises engendered a "surge of concern for distant strangers."[83] Compassionate watchers turned away from established organizations to a do-it-yourself model of aid: the MONGO (My Own NGO).

There are costs and benefits to MONGOs. The costs epitomize Cole's White Savior critique: amateurs often tackle problems with a great deal of enthusiasm, but without much contextual understanding. MONGOs can be ineffective or counterproductive, lack transparency and accountability, and more performative of virtue than responsive to need. On the other hand, MONGOs who consult with intended beneficiaries can target a specific need more efficiently than larger NGOs, particularly in countries like Việt Nam where governmental permissions and negotiations are notoriously slow. In 2015, six years after he first returned with the Veterans Viet Nam Restoration Project (VVRP), US Army veteran Mark set up a "Bikes for Vietnam Kids" GoFundMe campaign to target education access in A Lưới.[84] He explained his process: "we contact the schools, and they contact the kids that aren't coming to school, that live maybe ten kilometers away, they can't walk to school ... every bike that we give them changes a whole family up there. And they can bring two or three kids to school on one bike, if they want to." After donating several hundred bikes, he decided to address another problem. Children in rural areas had to cycle in the dark to make it to school on time, putting them at risk of road accidents. Mark started raising funds to bulk-buy reflective tape.[85]

The appeal of MONGOs to veterans in Việt Nam is understandable. They provide the veteran with a direct relationship to their recipient, ensuring an emotional reward. They allow the veteran to justify their participation or leadership in remediation as a moral imperative: "we were the ones on the ground here," Larry said, "so let's get back on the ground here and help."[86] Because returnees tended to establish aid services in their former wartime locations, MONGOs further provide a tangible authority for the veteran in Việt Nam: tying him to the space in the present as well as the past. US Air Force veteran Francis returned to Nhơn Đức, a small hamlet near Hồ Chí Minh City, where he was

---

[83] Michael Burnett, *Empire of Humanity: A History of Humanitarianism* (Ithaca, NY: Cornell University Press, 2011), 116.
[84] "Bikes for Vietnam Kids." GoFundMe, 2015. www.gofundme.com/vietnambikes
[85] Interview with Mark.   [86] Interview with Larry.

stationed for six months during the war. While wartime relationships sometimes gave veterans an inflated sense of their own understanding of local problems, repeated return visits and lasting relationships also provided them with genuine insight. "When I go back to Việt Nam I always go back to the village and see some of the families, some of the kids that I've known," Francis explained. Through these relationships, he consulted with the local community about specific needs. "We spent a couple weeks building a sidewalk in this little village, so that the kids could get to school in the muddy season. Motorcycles, they could get to their local shop to get whatever they wanted easier. Could they survive without that? Sure, they're survivors. But it was a little thing that makes their lives easier."[87]

The tendency of veterans to return and work within communities where they had been stationed highlighted key differences between Australian and US veterans. American soldiers were stationed throughout the southern and central provinces of Việt Nam, and their return projects dotted provinces throughout the country. The individual focus and management of different MONGOs reflected the disjointed American experience of war. Australian charity work was mostly centralized in Bà Rịa-Vũng Tàu, formerly Phước Tuy province, where the Australian Task Force (ATF) had been based. Australian veterans worked with and donated to a handful of small but established NGOs, indicating that the more cohesive Australian war experience shaped the returnee community and its relationship to Việt Nam. One veteran explained the rationale for veteran NGOs: "there were a lot of Vietnamese civilians that worked for the Australian army who were treated pretty poorly after the war, so they look after them and their kids."[88] This assistance was further framed as a continuation of wartime allegiance, blurring peacetime philanthropy with military conduct. "We left a lot of goodwill, Australia, I reckon," answered commemoration returnee Peter, "which I've talked about, the respect the Vietnamese have got for the Australians. We built orphanages, schools, wells, bridges, the engineers did a magnificent job. So, there's a legacy there. After the war, when Australia could get back in there, they continued to do that type of situation. And that's ongoing."[89] Australian veterans thus interpreted the question of benefit as within a national frame or within the veteran community, rather than their own personal contribution: "there's a lot of good coming out of Australia for Việt Nam."[90]

Finally, there were some who answered by pointing to negative effects of the veteran presence in Việt Nam. John A. said that "there are some

[87] Interview with Francis.   [88] Interview with Andy.   [89] Interview with Peter.
[90] Interview with Rod.

veterans that, I've seen them in Sài Gòn, that are ugly Americans. That are drinking at ten a.m. and treat Vietnamese like ugly Americans."[91] Part of this complaint stemmed from a perception that increasing numbers of disinterested, holidaying veterans were ruining the image of the conscientious minority. Australian Army returnee Graham S. described how "they sit in bars, on their big fat wallets, full of Vietnamese currency, taking their pensions from Australia. They have young Vietnamese wives, and in some cases children, and they might find it easy to live in Việt Nam, money certainly does go a lot further there, but does their presence do us any good? No, I don't think so."[92] These critiques indicate that growing numbers of veterans in Việt Nam threatened the legitimacy of individual feelings of belonging. "I don't really know how to describe them," Larry said, "[but] I don't see ... a burning desire to help those here in Việt Nam. To a certain degree, but not necessarily the way I feel it. I'm not judging, I'm just saying, I notice that."[93] In the face of this challenge, returnees developed hierarchies for assessing each other's values in order to justify their own presence. "If Vietnam veterans go back and write their story," Australian Army veteran Rob said, "that will have impact. But if you go back and you go drinking in the bars and you go to Vũng Tàu and you do this tourist trip and you stand around with your mates at Nui Dat and remember this bloke or that gun, you come back and you've had a great experience, but you haven't changed the legacy of the war."[94]

Rob's comment about changing "the legacy of the war" introduces the final part of this chapter. I view veterans as living legacies of war. Their lives shape how war is remembered and understood. To understand how they made sense of their personal experiences in Việt Nam in the context of the war, the last question I asked every veteran was: "how do your actions in Việt Nam affect the legacy of the war here?" Some veterans concluded that their actions in Việt Nam had no effect at all. "I don't think I individually affect the legacy of the war," Ralph said, "I'm just a dot, and the legacy is huge. I think I'm much too small to affect the legacy."[95] However, the majority responded to questions by linking their individual actions to broader political, social, cultural, and even spiritual shifts, in Việt Nam and in their home countries.

The earliest American returnees saw themselves as channels for normalization. Bobby Muller suggested that the return his Vietnam Veterans of America (VVA) group in 1981 broke through a barrier with Việt Nam and allowed for the later politician-veteran advocacy:

---

[91] Interview with John A.   [92] Interview with Graham S.   [93] Interview with Larry.
[94] Interview with Rob. Skype. March 28, 2017.   [95] Interview with Ralph.

... everybody was afraid to get involved with anything to do with Việt Nam ... we told them how much [the prisoner of war/missing in action (POW/MIA) issue] meant to the American people. And when we finished telling our story, they told us their story. How much the missing from the war meant to them.... [Shortly afterwards] the US government did go to Hà Nội, and the Vietnamese did give them remains of US servicemen. And that really provided an opening... a bridge, to get things going, which led fairly quickly to a renewal of government-to-government relations.[96]

Political returnees also focused on the POW/MIA issue, although they did so without mention of the "opening bridge" of Bobby Muller's controversial tour. Scholarship on early reconciliation efforts between Việt Nam and the United States concurs with veterans' assessments, concentrating on the figurehead role of returnees and former POW politicians as legitimizing the normalization and POW/MIA recovery project to the American public.[97] Returnees suggested that their common experience of grief and loss helped to establish relationships with the Vietnamese. Pete remembered that "the MIA/POW issue was a common denominator between the US and Việt Nam that gave us a platform to develop trust and confidence between the two sides. And it was really from that activity that we were able to graduate from specific search efforts to more political and diplomatic efforts. And that, then essentially was the stepping stone into normalization."[98]

Other veterans, the redeemers, saw their defining legacy as taking responsibility for their participation in the war. Chuck reflected that his work in Việt Nam "has allowed me to live with myself with some level of hope that I've been able to correct, in small ways, some of the damage that we did here, during the war."[99] Australian Army veteran Robert explained:

> The big picture, OK, I came over to your country, I was part of the atrocity. I thought, prior to my arrival, it was the right thing to do. I know now in my frame of mind that it wasn't the right thing to do. And you people, you're the innocent ones. You're born after all that, and you're still paying the costs of what we created. So, for me those return visits are in essence to say well, yeah, I know what we did was wrong. This is my apology. In my terms. I got to be responsible for myself.[100]

---

[96] Bobby Muller, interview in *Going Back: Echoes of War.*
[97] See for example: Myra MacPherson, *Long Time Passing, New Edition: Vietnam and the Haunted Generation* (Bloomington, IN: Indiana University Press, 2009), xxxii; H. Bruce Franklin, "Missing in Action in the Twenty-First Century." In *Four Decades On: Vietnam, the United States, and the Legacies of the Second Indochina War.* Edited by Scott Laderman and Edwin A. Martini (Durham, NC: Duke University Press, 2013), 287; Allen, *Until the Last Man Comes Home,* 271.
[98] Pete, interview in *Going Back: Echoes of War.*   [99] Interview with Chuck.
[100] Interview with Robert.

This sense of responsibility corresponds with the broader trend of "politics of regret" on the global stage. Sociologist Jeffrey K. Olick coined this phrase to describe the emergence of apology and redress in the 1990s as "a new principle of political legitimation" among states. Olick argues that the "morally shattering experiences of total war and genocide," the emerging notion of universal human rights, post-Cold War questions of "how to marry justice and reconciliation," and increasingly fractured postmodern societies undermined the coherence of grand narratives. Rather than promote a "heroic golden age," states turned inward and performed redemption. The governments of the United States and Australia have each apologized for a variety of incidences, actions, inactions, and atrocities. Neither has apologized to Việt Nam. Olick suggests that the trauma of Vietnam to the American psyche created "an unassimilable breach in the collective narrative."[101] This breach is also evident in Australia, where a popular heroic narrative of Vietnam is perpetually threatened by an antiwar counter-narrative. Under the new politics of regret, this static collective trauma became a driving force for redeeming veterans. The absent atonement by the nation-state created a moral imperative for them to take personal responsibility. David E. drew on a military analogy to explain this action: "there was always a saying in the Marine Corps, after we'd been on the firing range. They'd say, 'clean up the brass' [pick up the bullet shells] ... the last two years I've been pretty dedicated to that ... cleaning up the brass, Project Renew, that's what we're doing, cleaning up our brass."[102]

Some American redeemers used New Age mantras to explain their legacy. "We're on this earth for a reason," Larry said, "after the war I did have some spiritual experiences ... I don't know if you'd want to call it the vibrations of the heart, or whatever, there is something real, spiritual ... things can perceptibly change from that imperceptible spiritual beginning."[103] Anthropologist Susan Love Brown suggests that New Age philosophies are particularly attractive to Baby Boomers: a generation that came of age at time of cultural crisis and "rebelled against the exclusivity and hypocrisy inherent" in the values of their parents' generation.[104] For veterans, this crisis was compounded by a war experience that was incomprehensible within the moral framework of their society. Suel explained that after Vietnam, "I didn't trust my

---

[101] Jeffrey K. Olick, *The Politics of Regret: On Collective Memory and Historical Responsibility* (New York: Routledge, 2007), 14, 122, 129, 122, 32.
[102] Interview with David E. [103] Interview with Larry.
[104] Susan Love Brown, "Baby Boomers, American Character, and the New Age: A Synthesis." In *Perspectives on the New Age*. Edited by James R. Lewis and J. Gordon Melton (Albany, NY: SUNY Press, 1992), 92.

religion, they fucking lied to me. I didn't trust my school, I didn't trust my parents, I didn't trust my politicians, I didn't trust anything I read, heard, I had no trust of anything. And it took me years to rebuild my foundation as a human being."[105] New Age philosophies provided an alternative structure in which the spiritual development of the self was the core ethical tenet, rendering the untrustworthy institutions obsolete. This offered veterans a way to make sense of the war experience, compartmentalizing trauma through individual acts of good and magnifying the legacy of their redemption with spiritual significance. "The wheel of life on this planet is huge," Larry told me, "and we're all one little cog in it. We can remember that, we keep our little place going strong, and then we can inspire others."[106]

Very occasionally, these veterans would break from spiritual justifications and acknowledge that the New Age narrative was a tool for them to make sense of war and trauma. These candid admissions tended to follow lengthy philosophizing discussions on the possibility and virtue of true altruism. Deryle, for example, meditated:

> ... all my adult life I've been intrigued by the idea of alchemy. How do you turn something base into something finer? How do you turn, well, lead into gold? Alchemy is not about a base material kind of thing, the whole philosophy around it is: How do you turn a rock into a light stream. How do you make something – here's what we we've got, here's what we exist in the world with, how do we make it something finer? So, I'm determined ....

He trailed off. "Ah, shit. I say that, but then I fart around like a regular human being. I don't want this Vietnam crap on me the rest of my life."[107]

Bich Ngoc Do argues that participation in reconciliation, normalization, and redemption processes allowed veterans to "not only play an altruistic role and serve their country but also to reassert their manly morality" by justifying "American tutelage in Vietnam during the war, naturaliz[ing] American paternalism today, and defin[ing] American neoliberal capitalism as benevolent and necessary."[108] Schwenkel agrees, arguing that return "healing journeys" were "concurrently moral journeys imbued with paternalistic meaning, convictions, and desires to rescue Vietnam from the privations of communism with capitalist models of development, progress and aid as their tools."[109] Pete's descriptions of his legacy as the first US Ambassador reflected this critique:

> ... we normalized a whole host of aspects of our relationship, but the really big one was to get the bilateral trade agreement passed .... That document shaped Việt

---

[105] Interview with Suel.   [106] Interview with Larry.   [107] Interview with Deryle.
[108] Do, "Normalizing Vietnam," 24.
[109] Schwenkel, *American War in Contemporary Vietnam*, 28.

8 Veteran Legacies in Việt Nam   227

Nam's economic future. Because it educated the Vietnamese to what their potential was economically, and they started to seriously pursue it. Prior to that they were, "we don't know, we don't know, shall we do this, shall we not, we're a socialist country, you're talking free market, how's this going to work."[110]

Veterans in the private sector mirrored this tutelage framework. Former Marine Joe Bangert returned in 1985, obtained an exception to the Trading with the Enemy Act, and became the first American businessman in Việt Nam with Sea Air Vietnam, an aviation service:

> Everyone else is told, don't do business in Việt Nam, they're fucking lousy commies and they beat our fucking ass, and we'll punish them for fucking twenty years. Oh, but by the way, if I got a license to do business and I have an exception to the trade embargo, all of a sudden, I got capital.... I started bringing American aircraft into Hà Nội. I got them permission to land. I got them permission to fly over Việt Nam ... I showed the Vietnamese how to tell the Americans that were avoiding their territory because of the trade embargo that you could make money on the trade embargo. By fucking letting them land and get gas and fly over your fucking territory. Two hundred dollars a plane. And the Vietnamese said "Oh, Mr. Joe, Mr. Joe, we had no idea!" See not only that, you're training Americans to come into Việt Nam again.[111]

Bangert's memories illustrate Schwenkel's characterization of "moral masculinity," and particularly Do's observation of veteran attraction to the role of instructor. He "showed the Vietnamese how" to negotiate, just as Pete "educated" them in their own potential.

The paternalism that Do and Schwenkel identify among US veterans was also performed by Australian veterans. However, where Americans focused on education for the future, Australians framed their role as history teachers and truth tellers. Kevin, for instance, explained that he hoped the legacy of his and other veterans' return journeys to Long Tân would lead

> ... young Vietnamese, the under 25s, [to] start to ask questions about why. Why do so many foreigners come back, what was so significant about a place they haven't even heard of in their own country, for this particular group of foreigners? And if they do that, and they ask why, then that leads to further questions, and then they start to challenge their own government's version of events.[112]

Returnees' perception that their legacy in Việt Nam was disrupting communist control by de-indoctrinating civilians directly mirrors, as Do suggests, the wartime perception of Western "tutelage."

A significant number of veterans indicated that broadening Australian and American understandings was their core legacy. Although my

[110] Pete, interview in *Going Back: Echoes of War*.   [111] Joe Bangert, interview in ibid.
[112] Interview with Kevin.

question was focused on war legacies in Việt Nam, many veterans pointed out that they had more influence in their home countries. Pete explained that "as an Ambassador ... one of your biggest responsibilities is to educate your own country." Pete became so frustrated with the war-centered media coverage of Việt Nam that he barred his Embassy from talking to the press and developed a documentary about his ambassadorship that was made by "essentially following me around. And talking to the Vietnamese people, talking to Vietnamese officials, talking to American businesspeople, talking to the Vietnamese educators, talking to the Viet Khieu [Vietnamese refugees] ... and on and on and on .... It was incredibly effective."[113] Storytelling was widely recognized as a powerful mode of turning a personal history into a political legacy. "It's my anti-war effort, to tell it like it is," said John A.[114] They had an important truth to share, one that could only be relayed by veterans who had returned. Francis explained: "there's value of me talking to people about my experiences in Việt Nam. Mine is a very unique experience .... The more exposure you have to different points of view, different perspectives, the better able you are to understand what happened."[115] The focus on truth-telling to American and Australian civilians suggests that the "moral masculinity" performed by these veteran-educators came from the perception that as veterans, they had more knowledge, more authority, and more capacity for understanding than other actors – Vietnamese, American, or Australian. Pete's "essential" negotiation tactic between the "90 percent [of America that was] against the idea of reconciliation" and the Vietnamese, who "were very narrow-minded as well," was his history: "I've suffered about as much as any American during the war. Just short of dying. And if I can have reconciliation, why can't you?"[116]

---

[113] Interview with Pete. [114] Interview with John A. [115] Interview with Francis.
[116] Interview with Pete.

Conclusion

In 2016, Vietnam veteran and former US Senator Bob Kerrey was appointed Chair of Fulbright University Việt Nam (FUV). Kerrey served as in the US Navy Sea, Air, and Land (SEAL) Teams in Vietnam from 1966 to 1969. In 1969, Kerrey led his unit in a raid of Thạnh Phong, a village in Bến Tre province. The raid was part of the Phoenix Program: Kerrey's unit were sent in on a "takeout" of National Liberation Front (NLF) leaders who were controlling the area.[1] Twenty civilians were killed, but because the raid was in a free-fire zone, the civilians were counted as enemy dead. Kerrey was awarded a Bronze Star. In 2001, following pressure of a media exposé on Thạnh Phong, Kerrey took responsibility for ordering retaliatory fire as per "standard operating procedure ... to dispose of the people we made contact with" under the "unwritten rules of Vietnam."[2] He maintained that he personally had not killed anyone. Former SEAL team member Gerhard Klann remembered the raid differently: he recalled Kerrey instructing the unit to cut the throats of five unarmed civilians, including children, whom they discovered in a hooch on the edge of the hamlet.[3] He and another SEAL team member remembered Kerrey helping Klann kill an elderly man.[4] Klann further remembered no enemy fire as they searched the hamlet, lined up unarmed civilians, and shot them.[5] His account was independently supported by a Vietnamese woman who survived the massacre, Phạm Thị Lành. The Thạnh Phong raid is remembered in the War Remnants Museum as an atrocity, representing the memories of Lành and Klann, and a monument at Thạnh Phong remembers the "brutal

---

[1] Gregory L. Vistica, "One Awful Night in Thanh Phong." *New York Times*, April 25, 2001. www.nytimes.com/2001/04/25/magazine/one-awful-night-in-thanh-phong.html
[2] Bob Kerrey, quoted in Vistica, "One Awful Night in Thanh Phong."
[3] David Kohn, "Memories of a Massacre, Part II: Klann Tells His Version of the Story." 60 Minutes, *CBS News*, May 1, 2001.
[4] Kohn, "Memories of a Massacre." [5] Ibid.

murder of civilians" who were "massacred barbarously" by Kerrey's SEALs.⁶

Kerrey's appointment to the chair of the FUV board resulted in a furious debate in Việt Nam that centered on healing, reconciliation, forgiveness, and who is permitted to forgive. Politburo member Đinh La Thăng "urged Vietnamese to recognize Kerrey's moral courage and forgive his crime, honoring the tradition of 'faith in the future.'"⁷ Many agreed with this position, arguing that Vietnamese veterans and war victims "did not want to live with hatred."⁸ Political commentator Xuân Lộc Duẩn argued that opposition to Kerrey's appointment "means the country is still reluctant to rise above the past."⁹ The healing narrative surrounding returning veterans was seized as an effective method of silencing critique and expressions of trauma from war victims who opposed Việt Nam's embrace of US capital and business in Việt Nam. Others disagreed with the implication that the Vietnamese were hindering reconciliation by refusing to "rise above" and forgive. Lawyer Thái Bảo Anh said that forgiveness was "the rights of the dead victims and their still living family members."¹⁰ Bảo Anh questioned whether Kerrey had considered how his appointment was "opening an old wound in Vietnamese people's minds."¹¹ War Remnants Director Huỳnh Ngọc Vân was concerned that if Kerrey worked in Vietnamese education, students would have to defer to him with "the respected term 'teacher.'"¹² Some suggested that the appointment and defenses such as Thăng's demonstrated the government's priorities: putting business with the United States ahead of Vietnamese trauma and using forgiveness as a way to erase the past. Former Socialist Republic of Việt Nam (SRV) diplomat Tôn Nữ Thị Ninh stated that "we cannot obliterate such facts by invoking the need to look for the future."¹³ Thị Ninh argued that the

---

⁶ Calvin Godfrey, "Forgetting Thanh Phong." *VnExpress International*, January 5, 2017. https://e.vnexpress.net/news/travel-life/forgetting-thanh-phong-3523710.html

⁷ Chau Hoang, "In Debate Over Bob Kerrey's Wartime Role, Vietnam Confronts Its Past Demons." CogitASIA, *Center for Strategic & International Studies*, July 7, 2016. www.cogitasia.com/in-debate-over-bob-kerreys-wartime-role-vietnam-confronts-its-past-demons/

⁸ Ben Bland, "Ex-US Senator's Role in Vietnam University Opens Wartime Wounds." *Financial Times*, May 31, 2016. www.ft.com/content/5f7054a2-26f3-11e6-8b18-91555f2f4fde?mhq5j=e5

⁹ Xuân Lộc Duẩn, "Vietnam's Kerrey Dilemma: Fulbright University Appointment Is Lightening Rod for US Ties." *Asia Times*, June 21, 2016. www.atimes.com/vietnams-kerrey-dilemma-fulbright-u-appointment-is-lightning-rod-for-us-ties/

¹⁰ Thái Bảo Anh, quoted in Bland, "Ex-US Senator's Role in Vietnam University Opens Wartime Wounds."

¹¹ Ibid.   ¹² Huỳnh Ngọc Vân, quoted in Godfrey, "Forgetting Thanh Phong."

¹³ Tôn Nữ Thị Ninh, "Bob Kerrey in Vietnam." *New York Times*, June 7, 2016. www.nytimes.com/2016/06/08/opinion/bob-kerrey-in-vietnam.html

appointment was inappropriate, disregarded Vietnamese "self-respect and dignity" and should not be masked "as an opportunity to atone for past wrongdoings."[14]

American returnees joined the debate. Several of the veterans interviewed for this book signed an open letter calling for Kerrey to resign. In the letter, they note the "many US veterans who have returned to do penance" and who find the return "therapeutic and cathartic," indicating that they saw themselves, unlike Kerrey, as authentic redeemers.[15] Kerrey, for his part, responded: "honestly and with the pain of memories forever haunted, I apologize to the people whom I have harmed."[16] He acknowledged that apologizing was "inadequate," suggesting that his involvement in normalization and reconciliation processes and the Fulbright education initiative were acts of atonement: "I try to help the Vietnamese wherever possible."[17] As Việt Thanh Nguyễn argued, with Kerrey's appointment and the ensuing debate, "we are returning to the familiar story about an American soldier's redemption ... at the expense of remembering Vietnamese suffering."[18]

Also in 2016, over a thousand Australian veterans returned to Việt Nam for the 50th anniversary of the Battle of Long Tan, overwhelming the small city of Vũng Tàu. They planned to visit the site of the Long Tan Cross en masse to commemorate the battle. The day before the anniversary of the battle, the Vietnamese government cancelled access to the site and prohibited speeches at the commemorative events, citing "deep sensitivities."[19] They relented at the last minute to allow small numbers at the cross in staggered visits. On Long Tan Day, busloads of veterans lined up on a main road nearby the rubber plantation where the battle was fought. Between heavy falls of August monsoon rains, hundreds of veterans climbed out of their coaches and glared at the local police guarding the entry to Long Tân, retreating into the buses when the rain began

---

[14] Thị Ninh, "Bob Kerrey in Vietnam."
[15] Mark A. Ashwill et al., "47 Signatories Urge Bob Kerrey to Resign from Fulbright University Viet Nam Position." markaswhill.com, September 7, 2016. https://markashwill.com/2016/09/08/23-signatories-urge-bob-kerrey-to-resign-from-fulbright-university-viet-nam-position/
[16] Bob Kerrey, quoted in Nguyễn Thanh Tuấn, "Lãnh Đạo ĐH Fulbright Xin Lỗi Việc Gây Ra Trong Chiến Tranh," Zing.VN, May 30, 2016. https://news.zing.vn/lanh-dao-dh-fulbright-xin-loi-viec-gay-ra-trong-chien-tranh-post653446.html
[17] Kerrey, quoted in Tuấn, "Lãnh Đạo ĐH Fulbright Xin Lỗi Việc Gây Ra Trong Chiến Tranh."
[18] Việt Thanh Nguyễn, "Bob Kerrey and the 'American Tragedy' of Vietnam." *New York Times*, June 20, 2016. www.nytimes.com/2016/06/20/opinion/bob-kerrey-and-the-american-tragedy-of-vietnam.html
[19] Liam Cochrane, "Long Tan: Vietnamese Authorities Cancel 50th Anniversary Commemoration Event." *ABC News*, August 18, 2016. www.abc.net.au/news/2016-08-17/vietnam-police-block-access-to-long-tan-site/7756984

again. This cycle of postured enmity went on for hours as one busload at a time was let through to hold a small ceremony. Most veterans eventually turned back without attending the cross.[20]

Veterans interpreted the cancellation as evidence of government repression – not only of the Australians, but of local Vietnamese whom the veterans believed supported them. "When old foes meet," Kevin explained to me, "the truth comes out. It comes out from the wrong side. It comes out from their side. Which is what the government does not want the people of Việt Nam to know. That's pretty common from any communist regime."[21] Others suggested that the Vietnamese cancelled at the last minute deliberately, to "show them who was boss."[22] Even the few Australians who sympathized with Việt Nam's cancellation implied that the Vietnamese reaction was a repression of historical truth. Long Tan veteran Graham S., who established the fund to care for the cross, explained:

> A Việt Nam based group of people decided that they were going to have this great big celebration of Long Tan . . . . And, of course, the Việt Nam government had never recognized that they suffered a defeat at Long Tan, so this flew in the face of all their propaganda, and they really didn't have any alternative other than to shut it all down, which is exactly what they did . . . everything was fine until this mob over there decided that they were going to have this great big celebration of a great victory. Now it was a victory, there's no doubt about that, but not in the eyes of the Vietnamese.[23]

Australian Vietnam veterans therefore viewed themselves as subverting communist propaganda and disseminating historical truth to local Vietnamese through their commemorative activities.

This interpretation of the anniversary cancellation omitted some key facts. The local government permitted access to Long Tân only on certain conditions, including low-key ceremonies and crowd control, as the cross stands on private farmland. Political speeches, regalia, and fanfare were not allowed. For the 50th anniversary, however, the local veteran-expatriate community had planned extravagant events, including a concert and a gala dinner, each with hundreds of veterans attending. Long Tan veteran Dave gave a presentation about the battle in which he

---

[20] Author's note, Long Tân and Vũng Tàu, August 18, 2016. I travelled with veterans to Long Tân on one of the buses and waited with them for several hours. That evening at an official dinner in Vũng Tàu, almost everyone I spoke to said they had eventually turned back.
[21] Interview with Kevin.
[22] This was the consensus among veterans at the Little Pattie concert, who spoke to me on background.
[23] Interview with Graham S.

claimed that the Australians had killed over a thousand Vietnamese, leading other veterans to repeat this "fact."[24] Bill A., another veteran of the battle, confided in me on the morning of the anniversary his hopes that the Vietnamese government would finally concede defeat at Long Tan as a mark of respect to the visiting Australians.[25] Not only were veterans testing Vietnamese conditions for access to Long Tân, they were violating Vietnamese laws. Graham S. explained that the veteran-expatriate community had been "taking illegal tours to Long Tân for years," bypassing the Vietnamese permit system because "they say it's all a rip off."[26] These veterans – including fellow Long Tan veterans – had organized tours to Long Tan for the 50th anniversary, selling tickets to visiting veterans and pilgrims.[27] These efforts to exert social, physical, historical, and financial control over the site of Long Tân demonstrate a profound sense of entitlement to Vietnamese space.

This book has shown that veterans returned to Việt Nam to find resolution, or peace, in their personal relationship to the war. Returnees conceptualized Vietnam as the place where their identity was forged, the locus of their trauma, the root of their connection with other veterans, and the source of ongoing debates around the legacy of "their" war. Veteran-returnees thus acted as a diasporic community, imagining Vietnam as a lost, warzone home. Their desire for resolution manifested in nostalgia for this home: reacting to the "needs of the present" by turning back toward the past, veterans were reawakened to Vietnam.[28]

By tracing their returns through economic, cultural, and political shifts in Việt Nam, Australia, and the United States, three distinct periods of return emerged. Reconciliation veterans returned in response to a groundswell of reflective activity in Australia and the United States, as well as signs of change in Việt Nam. These returnees had been unable to move on from war, preoccupied with memories, doubts, and in some cases, physical reminders Vietnam, and many returned as soon as it seemed possible for them to do so.[29] Their journeys gradually normalized the idea of returning, culminating in the normalization of diplomatic relations between Việt Nam and the United States. Many normalization veterans returned to Việt Nam in response to traumatic shifts in their personal lives. In the context of a rising therapy culture in Australia and

[24] Interview with Bill A. The Australian Task Force (ATF) body count after the battle was 250 casualties; Vietnamese estimates were 150.
[25] Ibid.   [26] Interview with Graham S.
[27] Ibid. Supported by author's observations in Vũng Tàu, August 15–21, 2016.
[28] Boym, *Future of Nostalgia*, xvi.
[29] It is notable that the only two returnees in this group who were disabled through war injury – Bobby Muller and Graham E. – were among the very first to return, when Việt Nam was most difficult to navigate.

the United States, they turned to a new story about the war – one shared by the reconciliation returnees – of healing in Việt Nam. Through this healing story the concept of returning to Việt Nam was fully normalized, leading to the commemoration stage of veterans' returns. During this period, discourse in Australia, the United States, and Việt Nam centered on national commemorative events. Veterans' returns in this period mirrored the commemorative shift, as their journeys were characterized by ritual and memorial practice. This period of return was marked by later stages of life: commemoration veterans returned after their children had left home or moved away, in their retirement, or with the financial support of belated compensation for their war service.

Australian and American returnees approached the return in different ways. The first Americans returned when the United States considered Việt Nam an enemy state. Many had been called "traitors" or "commies" for returning to Việt Nam in the 1980s and early 1990s.[30] Even after diplomatic relations were normalized, Americans reported that in the United States, Việt Nam was still treated with suspicion, with recent returnees describing hostility from friends, family, and their local veteran community for deciding to return. So, for Americans, the return to Việt Nam was a radical act. For Australians, however, diplomatic relations had been established in 1973, and the first Australian returns coincided instead with the beginnings of a huge resurgence of national commemorative activity known as the "Anzac Revival." Australian returns thus occurred in context of a growing national tradition of battlefield pilgrimage. Two dominant national narratives about the war in Australia and the United States shaped veterans' desire to return: anti-war and Anzac. The Anzac narrative was part of a broader re-remembering of Australia's contribution to wars that focused on the virtues of soldiers, while the anti-war narrative focused on atoning for American participation in a war that many American returnees saw as a moral crime. While not every Australian returnee subscribed to the Anzac mythology, and not every American felt the war was entirely unjust, the majority in both groups conformed to these positions.[31] Consequently, these war narratives came to define the national stories of veterans' returns in Australia and the United States.

When veterans arrived in Việt Nam, they found that their warzone home was unrecognizable, replaced with unfamiliar places, politics, and people. Returnees were faced with conflicting challenges and rewards.

---

[30] Interview with Greg.
[31] Thirty-five of the forty-three Americans demonstrated a radical anti-war worldview; twenty of the twenty-six Australians indicated agreement with revisionist and vindicationist perspectives on the war through the Anzac lens.

Many returnees reported that their memories of war were diluted by visiting Việt Nam at peace and found friendship and solidarity with their former foes. Most described a sense of relief. These rewards were framed through discourse from the veteran's return period: reconciliation returnees focused on connecting with former enemies; normalization returnees on healing; and commemoration returnees on the remembrance of service on all sides. Most veterans thus achieved their goal for returning: finding a degree of resolution and a measure of peace.

Yet this peacetime reality also disrupted their diasporic connection to Vietnamese spaces. Returnees navigated this challenge by drawing from the same wartime narratives that had informed their return. Anti-war and Anzac memories shaped how returnees interpreted and interacted with peacetime Việt Nam, as they recaptured their sense of belonging by relying on familiar stories about a suddenly unfamiliar place. Thus, while the return experiences challenged returnees' wartime memories, the return did not change their views so much as reinforce their existing perspectives. Furthermore, while returning to Việt Nam helped many veterans to put Vietnam behind them, there was not total separation between war and country. As the numbers of returnees rose and expatriate-veteran enclaves emerged, the wartime narratives and nostalgic practices through which veterans navigated the return took on greater impact, collapsing time through space to relocate the warzone home. Veterans' return journeys then reveal the impossibility of fully resolving "their" war in Việt Nam.

It is unlikely that returning veterans will continue to exert influence over Việt Nam in the future. The numbers of returnees will decrease as significant anniversaries pass and the veterans themselves age and pass away; already many veteran-expatriates are returning to Australia and the United States for health, family, or security reasons. And Việt Nam is moving on, with or without its former enemy soldiers.

After insisting that he would not resign the Fulbright chairmanship, Kerrey conceded that he would step down if his presence put the Fulbright initiative at risk.[32] Although his appointment caused only a brief flurry of attention in the United States, in Việt Nam, his chairmanship was an ongoing public relations issue. In early 2017, Minister for Information and Communications Trương Minh Tuấn published an article in several Vietnamese newspapers decrying the state of the Vietnamese press. One of his charges against the press was the excessive

---

[32] Richard C. Paddock, "Bob Kerrey's War Record Fuels Debate in Vietnam on His Role at New University." *New York Times*, June 2, 2016. www.nytimes.com/2016/06/03/world/asia/vietnam-fulbright-university-%20kerrey.html?_r=0

and "sensationalist" debate in op-eds over Kerrey's appointment which, he argued, unnecessarily revived painful memories of war.[33] Tuấn suggested the media was "complicit" in justifying Kerrey's actions in Thạnh Phong, "wounding the souls" of those who died.[34] Tuấn's critique was the final blow to FUV's credibility with Kerrey at the helm. In May of 2017, he resigned his position at FUV.

Six months later, the Vietnamese government quietly gave the Long Tan Cross to the Australian War Memorial. Just as Kerrey's FUV appointment caused a brief stir in American headlines, the Long Tan anniversary scandalized Australia for a week or so before fading away, with Australian media generally sympathetic to the veterans.[35] In Việt Nam, however, frustrations between the expatriates and local government persisted, and the government maintained their ban on official ceremonies at Long Tân for Anzac Day in 2017. The following November, Vietnamese officials approached the Australian embassy in Hà Nội and offered to hand over the Long Tan Cross to Australia – on the condition that the handover be quick and quiet.[36] Again mirroring the FUV fallout, it appears that tensions around Long Tân were potentially threatening to an Australian-Vietnamese strategic partnership.

In 1995, the newly appointed Vietnamese Ambassador to the United States Lê Văn Bàng made a public appeal to Americans to put the war behind them and reconcile with Việt Nam. Bàng pointed to the handful of early returnees that had bridged the hostility with their former enemies and achieved reconciliation, encouraging Americans to look to these veterans as a model. In spite of veterans' nostalgic longing, and despite their best efforts to recreate their warzone home, Việt Nam's responses to these latest veteran-scandals show an unrelenting march away from war-oriented relationships. More than twenty years later, Bàng's words take on new meaning: "veterans returning to Vietnam are discovering that it is a country, not a war."[37]

---

[33] Trương Minh Tuấn, "Vui Buồn Với Báo Chí Việt Nam Năm 2016" (Sad Vietnamese Press in 2016). *Nhân Dân*, January 3, 2017. www.nhandan.com.vn/chinhtri/item/31732502-vui-buon-voi-bao-chi-viet-nam-nam-2016.html

[34] Ibid.

[35] Liam Cochrane, "Long Tan Veterans 'Sitting on Tenterhooks' After Being Refused Entry to Battlefield." *ABC News*, August 17, 2016. www.abc.net.au/news/2016-08-17/long-tan-veterans-refused-entry-to-battlefield/7760398

[36] Simon Bensen, "Secret Return from Vietnam for Long Tan Cross." *The Australian*, December 6, 2017. www.theaustralian.com.au/national-affairs/defence/secret-return-from-vietnam-for-long-tan-cross/news-story/176478d7f4c998c57dad1d4306ca6d8e

[37] Lê Văn Bàng, "How the US and Vietnam Can Manage Peace." *Chicago Tribune*, April 27, 1995. http://articles.chicagotribune.com/1995-04-27/news/9504270100_1_vietnamese-veteran-vietnam-war-family-altar

Appendix 1 Veteran Subjects

Andy
    Lance-Corporal, Infantry, Australian Army. Conscripted.
    Vietnam tour: 1968–69.
    Returned to Việt Nam in 2008.

Bangert, Joe
    Sergeant, Marine Corps. Enlisted.
    Vietnam tour: 1968–69.
    Returned to Việt Nam in 1985, lived in Hà Nội 1992–97.

Bill A.
    Lance-Corporal, 6RAR, Infantry, Australian Army. Enlisted.
    Vietnam tour: 1966–67; 1969–70.
    Returned to Việt Nam in 2006; 2016.

Bill E.
    Gunner, US Marines. Enlisted.
    Vietnam tour: 1969.
    Returned to Việt Nam in 1994. Multiple subsequent visits.
    Relocated to Đà Nẵng in 2008.

Bobby Muller
    Lieutenant, US Marines. Enlisted.
    Vietnam tour: 1968–69.
    Returned to Việt Nam in 1981. Multiple subsequent visits.

Boehm, Roy Mike
    US Army. Enlisted.
    Vietnam tour: 1968–69.
    Returned to Việt Nam in 1992. Multiple subsequent visits.

Bowen, Kevin
    1st Air Cavalry, US Army. Drafted.
    Vietnam tour: 1968–69.
    Returned to Việt Nam in 1987.

Bower-Miles, Neil Antony (Bomber)
    Sapper, 21EST; 1FS, Engineers, Australian Army. Enlisted.

Vietnam tour: 1969–70.
Returned to Việt Nam in 2001. Multiple subsequent visits.

Brian
Private, 1ARU; 3RAR, Infantry, Australian Army. Conscripted.
Vietnam tour: 1968.
Returned to Việt Nam in 2002. Multiple subsequent visits.

Broyles Jr., William
First Lieutenant, US Marines. Enlisted.
Vietnam tour: 1969–71.
Returned to Việt Nam in 1984.

Burstall, Robert Terence (Terry)
Lance-Corporal, 1RAR; 6RAR, Infantry, Australian Army. Enlisted.
Vietnam tour: 1966–67.
Returned to Việt Nam in 1986; 1987.

Champagne, Fredy
Infantry Sergeant, US Army. Enlisted.
Vietnam tour: 1965–66.
Returned to Việt Nam in 1989. Multiple subsequent visits.

Chuck
Intelligence Specialist, US Army. Enlisted.
Vietnam tour: 1967–68.
Returned to Việt Nam in 1992. Multiple subsequent visits.
Relocated to Hà Nội in 1995.

Dave
Second Lieutenant, 6RAR, Infantry, Australian Army. Conscripted.
Vietnam tour: 1966–67.
Returned to Việt Nam in 2006. Multiple subsequent visits.

David A.
Officer, US Army. Drafted.
Vietnam tour: 1968–69.
Returned to Việt Nam in 2016.

David E.
US Marines. Enlisted.
Vietnam tour: 1969.
Returned to Việt Nam in 2007.
Relocated to Đà Nẵng in 2011.

David W.
Gunner, 1FS, Artillery, Australian Army. Enlisted.
Vietnam tour: 1966–67.
Returned to Việt Nam in 2004. Multiple subsequent visits.

Derek
Sergeant, 32SSS; 21EST; 1FS; HQAFV, Engineers, Australian Army.

Enlisted.
Vietnam tour: 1966–71.
Returned to Việt Nam 1999.
Multiple subsequent visits since 2007.

Derrill
Sergeant, 8RAR; 1PSYOP; 4RAR, Infantry, Australian Army. Enlisted.
Vietnam tour: 1969–70; 1971.
Returned to Việt Nam in 2003. Multiple subsequent visits.

Deryle
Infantry, US Army. Enlisted.
Vietnam tour: 1967.
Returned to Việt Nam in 1995. Multiple subsequent visits.

Don
Private, US Army. Enlisted.
Vietnam tour: 1967.
Returned to Việt Nam in 2004.
Relocated to Nha Trang in 2005.

Francis
US Army. Enlisted.
Vietnam tour: 1966–67.
Returned to Việt Nam in 1998. Multiple subsequent visits.

Graham E.
Private, 7RAR, Infantry, Australian Army. Enlisted.
Vietnam tour: 1970.
Returned to Việt Nam in 1990.
Multiple subsequent visits.

Graham S.
Lance-Corporal, 6RAR, Infantry, Australian Army. Enlisted.
Vietnam tour: 1966–67.
Returned to Việt Nam in 2010; 2014.

Greg
US Marines. Enlisted.
Vietnam tour: 1966–67.
Returned to Việt Nam in 1988.
Relocated to Hồ Chí Minh City in 1992.

Heiko
US Air Force. Enlisted.
Vietnam tour: 1962–63.
Returned to Việt Nam in 2011.

Heselton, Ted
Engineer, US Army. Enlisted.

240   Appendix 1

Vietnam tour: Unknown
Returned to Việt Nam in 1990.

James
Specialist, US Army. Drafted.
Vietnam tour: 1966.
Returned to Việt Nam in 1993.
Relocated to Hà Nội in 2008.

Jim
US Air Force. Enlisted for the draft.
Vietnam tour: 1970.
Returned to Việt Nam 2012. Multiple subsequent visits.

John A.
Private, US Marines. Enlisted for the draft.
Vietnam tour: 1967–69.
Returned to Việt Nam in 2000. Multiple subsequent visits. Lived half of each year in Nha Trang.

John B.
Private, 3RAR, Infantry, Australian Army. Conscripted.
Vietnam tour: 1967–68.
Returned to Việt Nam in 2007; 2008.

John C.
Private, US Army. Enlisted for the draft.
Vietnam tour: 1966–67.
Returned to Việt Nam in 1989. Multiple subsequent visits.

John K.
US Marines. Enlisted.
Vietnam tour: 1969–72.
Returned to Việt Nam in 2016.

John W.
Corporal, 7RAR, Infantry, Australian Army. Enlisted for conscription.
Vietnam tour: 1970.
Returned to Việt Nam in 2000.

John Z.
Private, US Army. Enlisted for the draft.
Vietnam tour: 1970.
Returned to Việt Nam in 1989.

Ken
Corporal, 2SASR, Infantry, Australian Army. Enlisted.
Vietnam tour: 1968–69; 1971.
Returned to Việt Nam in 2010.

Kevin
Lance-Corporal, 3SASR; 1SASR; 2SASR, Infantry, Australian Army.

Veteran Subjects

Enlisted.
Vietnam tour: 1969–71.
Returned to Việt Nam in 1993; 2009; 2016.

Larry
US Marines. Enlisted.
Vietnam tour: 1965–66; 1968–69.
Returned to Việt Nam in 2008.
Relocated to Đà Nẵng in 2012.

Les
Private, 2AOD, Ordnance, Australian Army. Conscripted.
Vietnam tour: 1968–69.
Returned to Việt Nam in 2010.

Mark
US Army. Enlisted.
Vietnam tour: 1970–71.
Returned to Việt Nam in 2009. Multiple subsequent visits.

Maurice
Specialist, US Army. Enlisted.
Vietnam tour: Unknown.
Returned to Việt Nam in 1974; 1983.

Michael
US Navy. Enlisted.
Vietnam tour: 1967.
Returned to Việt Nam in 2014. Multiple subsequent visits.

Mike C.
US Army. Enlisted.
Vietnam tour: 1966–67.
Returned to Việt Nam in 1998.
Relocated to Nha Trang in 2008.

Mike M.
US Air Force. Enlisted.
Vietnam tour: 1969–70.
Returned to Việt Nam in 2013.

Mike P.
CAP, US Marines. Enlisted.
Vietnam Tour: 1968–70.
Returned to Việt Nam in 1989; 2013.

McCain, John
Captain, US Navy. Enlisted.
Vietnam tour 1967–73.

Prisoner of War 1967–73.
Returned to Việt Nam in 1985. Multiple subsequent visits.
Moore, Harold
Lieutenant General, US Army. Enlisted.
Vietnam tour: 1965–66.
Returned to Việt Nam in 1991; 1993.
Murphy, Paul
Private, 2RAR, Infantry, Australian Army. Enlisted.
Vietnam tour: 1967.
Returned to Việt Nam 1990. Multiple subsequent visits.
Paul R.
US Army. Enlisted.
Vietnam tour: 1966–67.
Returned to Việt Nam in 2016.
Paul S.
Staff Sergeant, US Marines. Enlisted.
Vietnam tour: 1964–65; 1968–69.
Returned to Việt Nam in 1995; 1999; 2002.
Pete
Colonel, US Air Force. Enlisted.
Vietnam tour: 1966–73. Prisoner of War 1966–73.
Returned to Việt Nam in 1991; 1993. Relocated to Hồ Chí Minh City as US Ambassador, 1997–2001.
Peter
Lance-Bombardier, 131 DLB, Artillery, Australian Army. Enlisted.
Vietnam tour: 1968–69.
Returned to Việt Nam in 2013.
Ralph
Sergeant, US Army.
Drafted. Vietnam tour: 1968.
Returned to Việt Nam in 1989.
Ray
Private, 1ARU; 5RAR, Infantry, Australian Army. Conscripted
Vietnam tour: 1969; 1969–70.
Returned to Việt Nam in 2008. Multiple subsequent visits.
Reilly, Robert J.
Major, US Army. Enlisted.
Vietnam tour: 1966–Unknown.
Returned to Việt Nam in 1998.
Ric
Trooper, 1SASR, Infantry, Australian Army. Enlisted.

Vietnam tour: 1970.
Returned to Việt Nam in 2006. Multiple subsequent visits.
Richard
    US Marines. Enlisted.
    Vietnam tour: 1968–69.
    Returned to Việt Nam in 2002.
    Relocated to Đà Nẵng in 2004.
Rob
    Private, 4RAR, Infantry, Australian Army. Conscripted.
    Vietnam tour: 1971.
    Returned to Việt Nam in 2009.
Robert
    Private, 7RAR, Infantry, Australian Army. Conscripted.
    Vietnam tour: 1967.
    Returned to Việt Nam in 2013. Multiple subsequent visits.
Robin
    Second Lieutenant, 1SASR, Infantry, Australian Army. Enlisted.
    Vietnam tour: 1970–71.
    Returned to Việt Nam in 2016.
Rod
    Private, 1ARU; 4RAR; 9RAR; Infantry, Australian Army. Conscripted.
    Vietnam tour: 1969.
    Returned to Việt Nam in 2012.
    Relocated to Vũng Tàu in 2014.
Rodney
    Private, 1ARU; 6RAR; 2RAR, Infantry, Australian Army. Conscripted.
    Vietnam tour: 1967.
    Returned to Việt Nam in 2016.
Ron
    Sergeant, US Army. Drafted.
    Vietnam tour: 1968.
    Returned to Việt Nam in 2000; 2011; 2013.
Rottmann, Lawrence
    First Lieutenant, US Army. Enlisted.
    Vietnam tour: 1967–68.
    Returned to Việt Nam in 1987. Multiple subsequent visits.
Scurfield, Raymond
    Captain, US Army. Enlisted.
    Vietnam tour: 1968–69.
    Returned to Việt Nam in 1989; 2000.
Suel
    US Marines. Enlisted.

Vietnam tour: 1968–69.
Returned to Việt Nam in 1998.
Multiple subsequent visits. Lived in Hà Nội 2000–10 (approximately).

Ted
Sergeant, US Air Force. Enlisted.
Vietnam tour: 1968–69.
Returned to Việt Nam in 1989.

W. D.
Infantry Sergeant, US Marines. Enlisted.
Vietnam tour: 1967–68.
Returned to Việt Nam 1985; 1990; 2011.

Wal
Private, 1 ARU; 5RAR; 7RAR; Infantry, Australian Army. Enlisted.
Vietnam tour: 1969–70.
Returned to Việt Nam in 2015.

Appendix 2 Interview Questions

Interviews were semi-structured, so these questions were threaded through ongoing conversation with veterans. Some veterans were not asked many of these questions because they offered narratives that covered most of the preliminary questions.

1. Why did you decide to return to Việt Nam?
2. When did you return to Việt Nam?
3. Why did you return when you did?
4. Do you or have you ever felt isolated from your country? If so, could you describe how?
5. How did you feel about the anti-war movement when you returned from the war? How do you feel about it now?
6. Did your experience in the Vietnam War change your political views? If so, when and how did they change?
7. Did your experience in Việt Nam after the war change your political views? If so, when and how did they change?
8. Do you think that your experiences in Việt Nam, either during the war or when you returned, changed your attitude to or opinion of your home country?
9. In your experience, how is the Vietnam War discussed in your country?
10. How do you feel about the ways in which the Vietnam War is discussed in your country?
11. How do you feel about the ways in which the Vietnam War is remembered in your country?
12. Have there been changes in how you feel about war commemoration?
13. Have your memories of wartime experience changed since you have returned to Việt Nam?
14. What do you feel being in Việt Nam has accomplished?
15. Do you feel your presence is beneficial to the country?
16. How do you think Việt Nam has changed since the war?

17. What do you think the war did to Việt Nam?
    – I began following up this question with "how do you think the war affected the Vietnamese?" or "how do you think the war impacted on their way of life?" to raise the human dimension of war legacies (see Chapter 4).
18. How do your actions in Việt Nam affect the legacy of the war here/there?

Bibliography

Interviews

Interview with Andy. Melbourne. June 13, 2016.
Interview with Bill A. Vũng Tàu. August 18, 2016.
Interview with Bill E. Đà Nẵng. April 19, 2016.
Interview with Brian. Skype. June 23, 2016.
Interview with Chuck. Hà Nội. April 21, 2016.
Interview with Dave. Melbourne. June 27, 2016.
Interview with David A. Hồ Chí Minh City. March 29, 2016.
Interview with David E. Đà Nẵng. April 8, 2016.
Interview with David W. Vũng Tàu. August 17, 2016.
Interview with Derek. Skype. May 16, 2016.
Interview with Derrill. Skype. June 27, 2016.
Interview with Deryle. Skype. August 29, 2016.
Interview with Don. Nha Trang. March 31, 2016
Interview with Francis. Skype. May 11, 2016.
Interview with Graham E. Perth, December 18, 2015.
Interview with Graham S. Telephone. June 23, 2017.
Interview with Greg. Hồ Chí Minh City. March 25, 2016.
Interview with Heiko. Skype. May 10, 2016.
Interview with James. Hà Nội. April 23, 2016.
Interview with Jim. Hồ Chí Minh City. March 23, 2016.
Interview with John A. Facetime. August 12, 2016.
Interview with John B. Skype. May 16, 2016.
Interview with John C. Skype. June 23, 2016.
Interview with John K. Skype. August 2, 2016.
Interview with John W. Skype. May 23, 2016.
Interview with John Z. Skype. November 15, 2016.
Interview with Ken. Melbourne. May 25, 2016.
Interview with Kevin. Long Tân. August 18, 2016.
Interview with Larry. Đà Nẵng. April 18, 2016.
Interview with Les. Skype. July 1, 2016.
Interview with Mark. Đà Nẵng. April 14, 2016.
Interview with Maurice. Skype. July 26, 2016.
Interview with Michael. Đà Nẵng. April 15, 2016.
Interview with Mike C. Nha Trang. March 31, 2016.

Interview with Mike M. Skype. May 20, 2017.
Interview with Mike P. Skype. May 11, 2016.
Interview with Paul R. Hồ Chí Minh City. March 28, 2016.
Interview with Paul S. Skype. January 19, 2016.
Interview with Pete. Melbourne. May 12, 2016.
Interview with Peter. Melbourne. February 8, 2016.
Interview with Ralph. Skype. June 27, 2016.
Interview with Ray. Melbourne. May 19, 2016.
Interview with Ric. Telephone. August 5, 2016.
Interview with Richard. Đà Nẵng. April 16, 2016.
Interview with Rob. Skype. March 28, 2017.
Interview with Robert. Melbourne. July 1, 2016.
Interview with Robin. Melbourne. July 26, 2016.
Interview with Rod. Vũng Tàu. August 19, 2016.
Interview with Rodney. Vũng Tàu. August 17, 2016.
Interview with Ron. Skype. April 5, 2016.
Interview with Suel. Đà Nẵng. April 14, 2016.
Interview with Ted. Skype. February 19, 2016.
Interview with W.D. Email. January 12, 2016.
Interview with Wal. Skype Interview. May 18, 2016.

Private Correspondence and Manuscripts

James. "Hoi An Epiphany." Private journal entry shared with the author. 1993.
John A. "More High Weirdness." Personal essay shared with the author. 2020.
Mike P. "1989 VVRP Journal w Intro." Private journal shared with the author. 1989.

Museum Sources

"General Introduction." War Remnants Museum. http://warremnantsmuseum.com/posts/introduction-general
"The Australian Vietnam Forces National Memorial." *Vietnam Veterans of Australia Association.* www.vvaa.org.au/memorial.htm
"Photograph of the Original Long Tan Cross." *Australian War Memorial Collection.* www.awm.gov.au/collection/C1271355

News Media

"25 Years from Vietnam: An Online Chat with Bobby Muller." Revisiting Vietnam.
American RadioWorks. April 28, 2000. http://americanradioworks.publicradio.org/features/vietnam/muller_chat.html
"A Place Called Long Tan with Meaning for All." *The Age.* August 18, 2002.
"Câu Chuyện Của Cựu Chiến Binh Mỹ, Larry Vetter Tại Việt Nam." *VTV4.* July 24, 2015. http://vtv.vn/video/gap-go-khan-gia-vtv4-24-7-2015-85646.html

"Cựu Binh Mỹ Và Hành Trình Trở Lại Việt Nam Giúp Đỡ Nạn Nhân Chiến Tranh." *Thanh Niên*. April 30, 2016. https://thanhnien.vn/the-gioi/cuu-binh-my-va-hanh-trinh-tro-lai-viet-nam-giup-do-nan-nhan-chien-tranh-697567.html

"Director Hopes Cinematic My Lai Tale 'Awakens Something.'" *Thanh Niên News*. May 14, 2010.

"Inside Vietnam: What a Former POW Found." *US News and World Report*. March 11, 1985.

"Vietnam as a Tourist Spot for Veterans." *Canberra Times*. September 30, 1992.

"Vietnam: Bill and Hillary Clinton Visit Hanoi." *AP Archive*. www.aparchive.com/metadata/youtube/92023f9b409a456f39e610084b653a23

"Welcome to Viet Nam." *Tuổi Trẻ News*. September 23, 2015. http://tuoitrenews.vn/news/national/20150923/watch-viral-tourism-promotion-clip-elcome-to-vietnam/38531.html

Albrecht, Brian. "Vietnam Surprises Vets Returning to Battleground." *Plain Dealer*. November 11, 2016. www.cleveland.com/metro/index.ssf/2016/11/vietnam_vets_return_to_old_bat.html

Andelman, David A. "49 US Citizens and Dependents Fly from Saigon." *New York Times*. August 2, 1976, 1.

Arnett, Peter. "Ruined Ben Tre, after 45 Days, Still Awaits Saigon's Aid: Regime Has Offered Nothing in Effort to Rebuild Town." *New York Times*. March 15, 1968, 3.

Ashwill, Mark A., et al. "47 Signatories Urge Bob Kerrey to Resign from Fulbright University Viet Nam Position." September 7, 2016. https://markashwill.com/2016/09/08/23-signatories-urge-bob-kerrey-to-resign-from-fulbright-university-viet-nam-position/

Baker, Mark. "Going Back." *Good Weekend*. November 10, 2001, 21.

Ball, Martin. "What the Anzac Revival Means." *The Age*. April 24, 2004.

Bàng, Lê Văn. "How the US and Vietnam Can Manage Peace." *Chicago Tribune*. April 27, 1995. http://articles.chicagotribune.com/1995-04-27/news/9504270100_1_vietnamese-veteran-vietnam-war-family-altar

Barrowclough, Nikki. "The Shameful Story of Australia's Serial Husbands." *Good Weekend*. May 6, 1995. www.smh.com.au/good-weekend/gw-classics/the-shameful-story-of-australias-serial-husbands-20140827-109b5i

Benns, Matthew. "Australian Federal Police May Investigate Claims Diggers Committed Atrocities During the Vietnam War." *News.com.au*. December 29, 2013.

Bensen, Simon. "Secret Return from Vietnam for Long Tan Cross." *The Australian*. December 6, 2017. www.theaustralian.com.au/national-affairs/defence/secret-return-from-vietnam-for-long-tan-cross/news-story/176478d7f4c998c57dad1d4306ca6d8e

Bland, Ben. "Ex-US Senator's Role in Vietnam University Opens Wartime Wounds." *Financial Times*. May 31, 2016. www.ft.com/content/5f7054a2-26f3-11e6-8b18-91555f2f4fde?mhq5j=e5

Boehm, Mike. "Hope Rises from the Ashes of My Lai." *The Veteran* 35:2 (2005).

Bowen, Kevin. "Seeking Reconciliation in Vietnam." *Christian Science Monitor*. November 10, 1988.

Broyles Jr., William. "The Road to Hill 10: A Veteran's Return to Vietnam." *The Atlantic* 225: April 1, 1985.
Callick, Rowan. "Battles Put to Rest." *The Australian.* August 18, 2006.
Cochrane, Liam. "Mass Fish Kill in Vietnam Solved as Taiwan Steelmaker Accepts Responsibility for Pollution." *ABC News*. July 1, 2016. www.abc.net.au/news/2016-07-01/mass-fish-kill-in-vietnam-solved-as-steelmaker-admits-pollution/7559906
  "Long Tan Veterans 'Sitting on Tenterhooks' After Being Refused Entry to Battlefield." *ABC News.* August 17, 2016. www.abc.net.au/news/2016-08-17/long-tan-veterans-refused-entry-to-battlefield/7760398
  "Long Tan: Vietnamese Authorities Cancel 50th Anniversary Commemoration Event." *ABC News.* August 18, 2016. www.abc.net.au/news/2016-08-17/vietnam-police-block-access-to-long-tan-site/7756984
Crossette, Barbara. "Vietnam Set for Tourists." *New York Times.* November 5, 1985.
Dao, James. "Vietnam Legacy: Finding GI Fathers, and Children Left Behind." *New York Times.* September 15, 2013.
Dapin, Mark. "At the Vung Tau RSL." *The Monthly.* April 2013.
Davidson, Linda. "Legacies of War: Forty Years After the Fall of Saigon, Soldiers' Children are Still Left behind." *Washington Post.* April 17, 2015.
Duẩn, Xuân Lộc. "Vietnam's Kerrey Dilemma: Fulbright University Appointment Is Lightening Rod for US Ties." *Asia Times.* June 21, 2016.
Ervin, Bill. "US Marine: This Is Why I Returned to Vietnam to Stay." *PRI.org.* May 6, 2015. www.pri.org/stories/2015-05-06/us-marine-why-i-returned-vietnam-stay
Fallows, James. "Shut Out." *The Atlantic Monthly* 267:3 (March 1991): 42–43.
Godfrey, Calvin. "Forgetting Thanh Phong." *VnExpress International.* January 5, 2017. https://e.vnexpress.net/news/travel-life/forgetting-thanh-phong-3523710.html
Hawley, Samantha. "US Veterans Who Fathered Children in Vietnam Gather on 50th Anniversary." *AM: The Full Story. ABC News.* May 15, 2015.
Herman, Elizabeth. "The Women Who Fought for Hanoi." *New York Times.* June 6, 2017.
Hersh, Seymour. "The Scene of the Crime: A Reporter's Journey to My Lai and the Secrets of the Past." *New Yorker.* March 30, 2015.
Hoang, Chau. "In Debate Over Bob Kerrey's Wartime Role, Vietnam Confronts Its Past Demons." CogitASIA, *Center for Strategic & International Studies.* July 7, 2016.
Hood, Lucy. "Maine Native to Help Build Clinic in Vietnam." *Bangor Daily News.* September 3, 1990.
Hyland, Tom. "Diggers Offer Peace at Last For 'Wandering Souls.'" *Sydney Morning Herald.* April 24, 2011. www-smh-com-au/national/diggers-offer-peace-at-last-for-wandering-souls-20110423-1ds2x.html
Kaufman, Dan. "Reconciliation at My Lai." *New Yorker.* March 24, 2013.
Kilian, Michael. "The War Hero Is a Senator Now." *Chicago Tribune.* July 19, 1987.

Kohn, David. "Memories of a Massacre, Part II: Klann Tells His Version of the Story." 60 Minutes, *CBS News*. May 1, 2001.
Kranish, Michael. "No Retreat, No Surrender." *Boston Globe*. March 9, 2003. www.boston.com/ae/music/articles/2003/09/03/no_retreat_no_surrender/
Lauras, Didier. "A Pilgrimage to the Battlefields." *Sydney Morning Herald*. January 2, 2005.
Lloyd-Roberts, Sue. "A US Soldier Searches for His Vietnamese Son." *BBC News*. April 27, 2014.
Malan, Andre. "Return to Vietnam." *Canberra Times*. May 13, 1990.
Mastony, Collen and Tet Gregory. "Real or Fake, Vietnam Dog Tags Stir Up Emotions." *Chicago Tribune*. October 30, 2002.
McCain, John. "A Former POW on Vietnam, Four Decades Later." *Wall Street Journal*. March 13, 2013.
McGrory, Mary. "For a Moment at Christmas, Vietnam Evokes the Old Emotions." *Washington Post*. December 29, 1981.
Miller, Alan C. "Veterans Find Peace in Vietnam." *Los Angeles Times*. July 5, 1990. http://articles.latimes.com/1990-07-05/news/mn-136_1_vietnam-veterans
Mullen, William. "At Peace, At Last: After 11 Years and an Emotional Parade, Vietnam Vets Finally Feel Welcome." *Chicago Tribune*. August 17, 1986. www.chicagotribune.com/news/tribnation/chi-1986-chicago-tribune-magazine-vietnam-parade-article-20110610-story.html
Murdoch, Lindsay. "Why Vietnam Objected to the Long Tan Commemoration." *Sydney Morning Herald*. August 18, 2016. www.smh.com.au/world/why-vietnam-objected-to-the-long-tan-commemoration-20160817-gqv9aw.html
"Swearing They'd Never Go Back, Many Veterans Now Call Vietnam's Vung Tau Home." *Canberra Times*. December 10, 2016. www.canberratimes.com.au/good-weekend/swearing-theyd-never-go-back-many-veterans-now-call-vietnams-vung-tau-home-20161207-gt5ww6.html
Murphy, Paul. "40 Years On – Long Tan." *ABC Radio National*. August 18, 2006.
Nguyễn, Việt Thanh. "Bob Kerrey and the 'American Tragedy' of Vietnam." *New York Times*. June 20, 2016. www.nytimes.com/2016/06/20/opinion/bob-kerrey-and-the-american-tragedy-of-vietnam.html
Nicholson, Brendan. "Vietnam's Long Tan Reunion Ban Fuels Outrage." *The Australian*. August 18, 2016. www.theaustralian.com.au/national-affairs/defence/vietnams-long-tan-reunion-ban-fuels-outrage/news-story/602e1dd87f7e1701f4ddd9ee860335e1
Ornstein, Charles and Terry Parris Jr. "40 Years After Vietnam, Blue Water Navy Vets Still Fighting for Agent Orange Compensation." *ProPublica*. September 11, 2015. www.propublica.org/article/after-vietnam-blue-water-navy-vets-fighting-agent-orange-compensation
Paddock, Richard C. "Bob Kerrey's War Record Fuels Debate in Vietnam on His Role at New University." *New York Times*. June 2, 2016. www.nytimes.com/2016/06/03/world/asia/vietnam-fulbright-university-kerrey.html?_r=0

Palmer, Laura. "A City of Forgotten Children." *Deseret News*. September 1, 1989.
Piccininni, Ann. "Author Details How He Helps Veterans Heal." *Daily Herald (Arlington Heights)*. November 10, 2005.
Richburg, Keith B. "In Thailand, Some Vietnam Vets Are Still Missing by Choice." *Washington Post*. June 5, 1988, 1.
"Returning to Vietnam for Comfort – or Cash." *Washington Post*. April 27, 1995.
Rottmann, Larry. "A Hundred Happy Sparrows: An American Veteran Returns to Vietnam." *Vietnam Generation*. January 1, 1989, 118.
Shatan, Chaim. "Post-Vietnam Syndrome." *New York Times*. May 6, 1972, 35.
Stockings, Craig. "Let's Have a Truce in the Battle of the Anzac Myth." *The Australian*. April 25, 2012.
Thị Ninh, Tôn Nữ. "Bob Kerrey in Vietnam." *New York Times*. June 7, 2016. www.nytimes.com/2016/06/08/opinion/bob-kerrey-in-vietnam.html
Tick, Edward. "Apocalypse Continued." New York Times. January 13, 1985, 60.
Thịnh, Phạm. "GS Nguyễn Minh Thuyết: Không Chờ SGK Mới, Nên Bổ Sung Để Dạy Ngay Về Cuộc Chiến Chống Quân TQ Xâm Lược." *SOHA.VN*. August 22, 2017. http://soha.vn/gs-nguyen-minh-thuyet-khong-cho-sgk-moi-nen-bo-sung-de-day-ngay-ve-cuoc-chien-chong-quan-tq-xam-luoc-20170822094526365.html
Tuấn, Nguyễn Thanh. "Lãnh Đạo ĐH Fulbright Xin Lỗi Việc Gây Ra Trong Chiến Tranh." *Zing.VN*. May 30, 2016. https://news.zing.vn/lanh-dao-dh-fulbright-xin-loi-viec-gay-ra-trong-chien-tranh-post653446.html
Tuấn, Trương Minh. "Vui Buồn Với Báo Chí Việt Nam Năm 2016." *Nhân Dân*. January 3, 2017. www.nhandan.com.vn/chinhtri/item/31732502-vui-buon-voi-bao-chi-viet-nam-nam-2016.html
Uhl, Michael. "An Enfant Terrible Stumbles Upon the Vietnam War." *Counterpunch*. April 9, 2013.
Vistica, Gregory L. "One Awful Night in Thanh Phong." New York Times. April 25, 2001. www.nytimes.com/2001/04/25/magazine/one-awful-night-in-thanh-phong.html
Weiner, Jon. "Chris Burdden and 'The Other Vietnam Memorial.'" *The Nation*. May 11, 2015. www.thenation.com/article/chris-burden-and-other-vietnam-memorial/
Weinraub, Bernard. "Vietnam Invites 4 US Veterans to Visit Hanoi." *New York Times*. December 13, 1981.
"Vietnam Veterans Take Emotional Journey to Hanoi." *New York Times*. December 19, 1981.
"American Veterans Treated Warmly in a Threadbare Hanoi." *New York Times*. December 22, 1981.
"Hanoi, in Economic Straits, Seeks to Move Toward Ties with US." *New York Times*. December 28, 1981.
"Hanoi Asks US Veterans for Talks." *New York Times*. April 22, 1984.
Wilson, George C. "Back to the Land of Nightmares: Vietnam Vets Come Full Circle with Therapy." *San Francisco Chronicle*. March 18, 1990, 8.

Blogs, Campaigns, Websites, and Video Footage from Veterans Returns

"About VFP Chapter 160." *Veterans Chapter for Peace 160: Hòa Bình Việt Nam.* https://vfp160.org/about-vfp-chapter-160/

"Bikes for Vietnam Kids." *GoFundMe.* 2015. www.gofundme.com/vietnambikes

"Cheap Charlie (ANZAC Day 2013 Tommy's Sports Bar Vung Tau Viet Nam)." YouTube. www.youtube.com/watch?v=3CjH2dMpl0M

"Child of War Viet Nam." http://childofwarvietnam.com/

Akins, John. "Vietnam War Books & Writing." www.johnakins.com

Boehm, Mike. "A Union of Like Hearts – A Unique Collaboration." *Project Leaders, MQI Vietnam.* www.mqivietnam.org/project-leaders

"VVRP Team IV." *Veterans Viet Nam Restoration Group.* http://www.vvrp.org/?page_id=152

Champagne, Fredy. "The Founding of the VVRP." *Veterans Viet Nam Restoration Project.* www.vvrp.org/?page_id=133

Heselton, Ted. "Ted Heselton's Yen Vien Journal: Team III." *Veterans Viet Nam Restoration Project.* http://033a4c3.netsolhost.com/?page_id=1123

"Veterans for Peace Annual Spring Tour to Việt Nam 2017." *Veterans for Peace.* October 21, 2016. www.veteransforpeace.org/who-we-are/member-highlights/2016/10/21/veterans-peace-annual-spring-tour-viet-nam-2017

Wilson, Brian. "History of the Idea of the Veterans Peace Action Teams." *Brianwilson.com.* February 1, 1987, republished online by the author in 2017. www.brianwillson.com/history-of-the-idea-of-the-veterans-peace-action-teams-vpat/

Memoirs and Books

Self-published memoirs listed here were given or sold to me personally by the author

Akins, John. *Nam Au Go Go: Falling for the Vietnamese Goddess of War.* Port Jefferson, NY: Vineyard Press, 2005.
    Drowning Out the Drums: A Marine Comes Homes. Hà Nội: Thế Giới Publishing, 2014.

Blackburn, Don. *Into the Heart.* N.p.: CreateSpace, 2013.

Bower-Miles, Tony and Mark Whittaker. *Bomber: From Vietnam to Hell and Back.* Sydney: Macmillan, 2009.

Broyles Jr., William. *Brothers in Arms: A Journey from War to Peace.* New York: Alfred A. Knopf, 1986.

Burstall, Terry. *A Soldier Returns: A Long Tan Veteran Discovers the Other Side of Vietnam.* Brisbane: University of Queensland Press, 1990.
    "Policy Contradictions of the Australian Task Force Vietnam, 1966." *Vietnam Generation* 3:2, Special Issue – Australia R&R: Representations and Reinterpretations of Australia's War in Vietnam (1991): 35–49.

Ehrhart, W.D. *Going Back: A Poet Who Was Once a Marine Returns to Vietnam.* Wallingford, CT: Pendle Hill Pamphlet, 1987.
 In the Shadow of Vietnam: Essays, 1977–1991. Jefferson, NC: McFarland, 1991.
Hersh, Seymour. *My Lai 4.* New York: Random House, 1970.
Jones, Suel D. *Meeting the Enemy: A Marine Goes Home.* N.p.: Booksurge.com, 2008.
Karlin, Wayne. *Wandering Souls: Journeys with the Dead and the Living in Viet Nam.* New York: Nation Books, 2009.
McCain, John and Mark Salter, *Worth the Fighting For: A Memoir.* New York: Random House, 2002.
Moore, Lt. Gen. Harold G. and Joseph L. Galloway. *We Are Soldiers Still: A Journey Back to the Battlefields of Vietnam.* New York: HarperCollins, 2008.
Murphy, Paul. *The Quiet Australians: Saints and Sinners.* N.p.: Book Pal, 2011.
Napersteck, Martin. *War Song.* Bloomington, IN: iUniverse, 2000.
Reilly, Major Robert J. *Return of the Warriors: Vietnam War Veterans Face the Ghosts of Their Past on Their Personal Battleground.* Victoria, BC: Trafford Publishing, 2010.
Scurfield, Ray. *A Vietnam Trilogy: Veterans and Posttraumatic Stress, 1968, 1989, 2000.* New York: Algora Publishing, 2004.
 Healing Journeys: Study Abroad with Vietnam Veterans. Vol. 2 New York: Algora Publishing, 2006.
Tate, Don. *The War Within.* Sydney: Murdoch Books, 2008.
Tick, Edward. *War and the Soul: Healing Our Nation's Veterans from Post-traumatic Stress Disorder.* Wheaton, IL: Quest Books, 2005.

Music, Television, and Film

Apocalypse Now. Directed by Francis Ford Coppola. Beverly Hills, CA: United Artists, 1979.
Cold Chisel. "Khe Sanh." *Cold Chisel.* Sydney: Trafalgar Studios, 1978.
Deathdream. Directed by Bob Clark. Toronto: Quadrant Films, 1974.
"Episode 11: Vietnam." *CNN: Cold War.* Produced by Pat Mitchel and Jeremy Isaacs. New York: CNN, June 10, 2001. http://web.archive.org/web/20010610022952/http://www.cnn.com/SPECIALS/cold.war/episodes/11/interviews/giap/
First Blood. Directed by Ted Kotcheff. Los Angeles, CA: Orion Pictures, 1982.
First Blood II. Directed by George P. Cosmatos. Los Angeles, CA: Anabasis Investments and Estudios Churubusco, 1985.
Full Metal Jacket. Directed by Stanley Kubrick. Burbank, CA: Warner Bros., 1987.
Going Back: Echoes of War. Directed by Kaley Clements. US version 2016. Unreleased documentary shared with the author.
Honor, Duty and a War Called Vietnam. Directed by Burton Benjamin. New York: CBS, 1985.
Missing in Action. Directed by Joseph Zito. Beverly Hills, CA: The Cannon Group, 1984.
Motorpsycho! Directed by Russ Meyer. Hollywood, CA: Eve Productions, 1965.

Nam's Angels. Directed by Jack Starrett. Hollywood, CA: Fanfare Films, 1970.
Platoon. Directed by Oliver Stone. Los Angeles, CA: Orion Pictures, 1986.
Redgum, "I Was Only Nineteen (A Walk in the Light Green)." *Caught in the Act*. Sydney: Epic Records, 1983.
Taxi Driver. Directed by Martin Scorsese. Los Angeles, CA: Columbia Pictures, 1976.
The Deer Hunter. Directed by Michael Cimino. Los Angeles, CA: Universal Pictures, 1978.
"The Forgotten Heroes." *60 Minutes*. Produced by Hamish Thomson. Sydney: Nine News, August 13, 2006. http://battleoflongtan.com/60-minutes-the-battle-of-long-tan/
Vietnam. Directed by Chris Noonan and John Duigan. Sydney: Roadshow, February 23–April 27, 1987.
Vietnam: Two Decades and a Wake-Up. PBS. Produced by Steven Smith. Arlington, VA: PBS, 1990.

Nongovernmental Organization Sources

"Father Founded." *Father Founded*. http://fatherfounded.org/
"Impact on Vietnam." Agent Orange Record. www.agentorangerecord.com/impact_on_vietnam/health/
"Veterans' and Veterans' Family Counselling Service – Summary of Background and Current Events." Vietnam Veterans Association of Australia. www.vvaa.org.au/vvcs2.htm

Official Government and Intergovernmental Reports

"Vietnam-Era Unaccounted for Statistical Report." Vietnam-Era Prisoner of War/Missing-in-Action Database, POW/MIA Databases & Documents, Library of Congress. http://lcweb2.loc.gov/frd/pow/Nov0701.html
MARIN. "The Information Center for Martyrs." Nhan Tim Donh Doi. www.nhantimdongdoi.org/?mod=gioithieu
Viet Nam National Administration of Tourism. "International Visitors to Vietnam from 1995 to 2003." *Ministry of Culture, Sports, and Tourism*. December 1, 2003. http://vietnamtourism.gov.vn/english/index.php/items/489
"International Visitors to Viet Nam in December and 12 Months of 2016." *Ministry of Culture, Sports and Tourism*. December 27, 2016. http://vietnamtourism.gov.vn/english/index.php/items/11311

Speeches, Parliamentary Debates, Official Testimonies, Statutes

Clinton, William J. "Announcement of Normalization of Relations with Vietnam." American Presidency Project. Online by John Wooley and Gerhard Peters. July 11, 1995. www.presidency.ucsb.edu/ws/?pid=51605

Fischer, Tim. "Visit to Brunei Darussalam and Vietnam by Deputy Prime Minister and Trade Minister, the Hon. Tim Fischer MP." Department of Foreign Affairs and Trade, Australia. August 9, 1996. http://trademinister.gov.au/releases/1996/tr53.html

Convention IV, Geneva Conventions. August 12, 1949. https://ihl-databases.icrc.org/applic/ihl/ihl.nsf/Article.xsp?action=openDocument&documentId=77068F12B8857C4DC12563CD0051BDB0

Hawke, Bob. "Speech by the Prime Minister: Dawn Service Gallipoli." April 25, 1990. http://pmtranscripts.pmc.gov.au/release/transcript-8013

House Committee on Armed Services. *Investigation of the My Lai Incident*. Ninety-First Congress, Second Session, 1976.

Keating, Paul. "Anzac Day: 25 April 1992." Ela Beach, Port Moresby. April 25, 1992. www.keating.org.au/shop/item/anzac-day-25-april-1992

Reagan, Ronald. "Peace: Restoring the Margin of Safety." Veterans of Foreign Wars Convention. Chicago. August 18, 1980. www.reagan.utexas.edu/archives/reference/8.18.80.html

"Inaugural Address." *The American Presidency Project*. Online by John Woolley and Gerhard Peters. January 20, 1981. www.presidency.ucsb.edu/ws/?pid=43130

"Remarks at the Veterans' Day Ceremony at the Vietnam Veterans Memorial." American Presidency Project. Online by John Woolley and Gerhard Peters. November 11, 1988. www.presidency.ucsb.edu/ws/?pid=35155

Scott, Bruce. "Vietnam Veterans' Delegation to Vietnam." Ministerial Statements, Australian Senate, 38th Parliament, 1st Session, 1st Period, Canberra. September 11, 1996, 3283–85.

Tourism Sources

"Floating Market Tour." *Mekong Tours*. http://mekongtours.info/

"Mekong Delta Tours." *Buffalo Tours*. www.buffalotours.com/Popular-Destinations/Mekong-Delta-Tours.html

Secondary Sources

Abrams, Lynn. "Memory as Both Source and Subject of Study: The Transformations of Oral History." In *Writing the History of Memory*. Edited by Stefan Berger and Bill Niven. London: Bloomsbury, 2014, 89–109.

Agrusa, Jerome, John Tanner, and Judy Dupris. "Determining the Potential of American Vietnam Veterans Returning to Vietnam as Tourists." *International Journal for Tourism Research* 3 (2006): 222–34.

Allen, Michael J. *Until the Last Man Comes Home: POWs, MIAs, and the Unending Vietnam War*. Chapel Hill, NC: University of North Carolina Press, 2009.

Alneng, Victor. "'What the Fuck Is a Vietnam?' Tourist Phantasms and the Popcolonization of (the) Vietnam (War)." *Critique of Anthropology* 22 (2002): 461–91.

Appy, Christian. *American Reckoning: The Vietnam War and Our National Identity.* New York: Penguin, 2015.
Athukorala, Prema-chandra and Tran Quang Tien. "Foreign Direct Investment in Industrial Transition: The Experience of Vietnam." *Journal of the Asia Pacific Economy* 17:3 (2012): 446–63.
Bacevich, Andrew. *The New American Militarism: How Americans Are Seduced by War.* New York: Oxford University Press, 2005.
Barrett-Meyering, Isobelle. "Pilgrimage to Vietnam: Australian Veterans as 'Ambassadors of Peace.'" *Venour V. Nathan Prize (Undergraduate).* Sydney: University of Sydney, 2007.
Bass, Thomas A. *Vietnamerica: The War Comes Home.* New York: Soho, 1996.
Baumann, Martin. "Diaspora: Genealogies of Semantics and Transcultural Comparison." *Numen* 47:3 (2000): 313–37.
Beamish, Thomas D, Harvey Molotch, and Richard Flacks. "Who Supports the Troops? Vietnam, the Gulf War, and the Making of Collective Memory." *Social Problems* 42:3 (1995): 344–60.
Bean, Charles. *The Official History of Australia in the War of 1914–1918, Vol. 11, The Story of Anzac from 4 May, 1915, to the Evacuation of the Gallipoli Peninsula.* 11th ed. Canberra: Australian War Memorial, 1941.
Beavers, Herman. "Contemporary Afro-American Studies and the Study of the Vietnam War." *Vietnam Generation* 1:2 A White Man's War: Race Issues and Vietnam (1989): 6–13.
Ben-Moshe, Danny, Joanna Pyje, and Liudmila Kirpitchenko. "The Vietnamese Diaspora in Australia: Identity and Transnational Behaviour." *Diaspora Studies* 9:2 (2016): 112–27.
Berdahl, Daphne. "Voices at the Wall: Discourses of History and National Identity at the Vietnam Veterans Memorial." *History and Memory* 6:2 (1994): 88–124.
Blacker, Uilleam and Julie Fedor. "Soviet and Post-Soviet Varieties of Martyrdom and Memory." *Journal of Soviet and Post-Soviet Politics and Society* 1:2 (2015): 197–216.
Bleakney, Julia. *Revisiting Vietnam: Memoirs, Memorials, Museums.* New York: Routledge, 2006.
Blight, David. W. *Race and Reunion: The Civil War in American Memory.* Cambridge: Harvard University Press, 2001.
Bongiorno, Frank. "A Century of Bipartisan Commemoration: Is Anzac Politically Inevitable?" In *The Honest History Book.* Edited by David Stephens and Alison Broinowski. Sydney: NewSouth, 2017, 106–19.
Boym, Svetlana. *The Future of Nostalgia.* New York: Basic Books, 2001.
Bozcar, Amanda. "Economics, Empathy and Expectation: History and Representation of Rape and Prostitution in Late 1980s Vietnam War Films." In *Selling Sex on Screen: From Weimar Cinema to Zombie Porn.* Edited by Karne Ritzenhoff and Catriona McAvoy. Lanham, MA: Rowman & Littlefield, 2015, 69–94.
Brown, Susan Love. "Baby Boomers, American Character, and the New Age: A Synthesis." In *Perspectives on the New Age.* Edited by James R. Lewis and J. Gordon Melton. Albany, NY: SUNY Press, 1992, 87–96.

Brubaker, Rogers. "The 'Diaspora' Diaspora." *Ethnic and Racial Studies* 28:1 (2005): 1–19.
Bui, Long T. *Returns of War: South Vietnam and the Price of Refugee Memory.* New York: New York University Press, 2018.
Burnett, Michael. "Humanitarianism Transformed." *Perspectives on Politics* 3:4 (2005): 723–40.
 Empire of Humanity: A History of Humanitarianism. Ithaca, NY: Cornell, 2011.
Camacho, Paul. "From War Hero to Criminal." In *Strangers at Home: Vietnam Veterans Since the War.* Edited by Charles R. Figley and Seyour Leventman. New York: Praeger Publishers, 1980, 267–72.
Carruthers, Ashley. "Vietnamese Language and Media Policy in the Service of Deterritorialized Nation-Building." In *Language, Nation and Development in Southeast Asia.* Edited by Lee Hock Guan and Leo Suryadinata. Singapore: Southeast Asian Studies, 2007, 195–216.
Chambers, Thomas A. *Memories of War: Visiting Battlegrounds and Bonefields in the Early American Republic.* Ithaca, NY: Cornell University Press, 2012.
Cole, Teju. "The White Savior Industrial Complex." *Known and Strange Things: Essays.* Reproduced in *The Atlantic.* March 21, 2012. www.theatlantic.com/international/archive/2012/03/the-white-savior-industrial-complex/254843/
Corbin, Juliet and Janice M. Morse. "The Unstructured Interactive Interview: Issues of Reciprocity and Risks When Dealing with Sensitive Topics." *Qualitative Inquiry* 9:3 (2003): 335–54.
Corfield, Justin. "United States Embassy." *Historical Dictionary of Ho Chi Minh City.* London: Anthem Press, 2013.
Creswell, Tim. *Place: A Short Introduction.* Oxford: Blackwell Publishing, 2004.
Crocq, Marc-Antoine and Louis Crocq. "From Shell Shock and War Neurosis to Posttraumatic Stress Disorder: A History of Psychotraumatology." *Dialogues in Clinical Neuroscience* 2:1 (2000): 47–55.
Curthoys, Ann. "'Vietnam': Public Memory of an Anti-War Movement." In *Memory in Twentieth Century Australia.* Edited by Kate Darian-Smith and Paula Hamilton. Melbourne: Oxford University Press, 1994, 113–35.
Curtis, Paulette. "Locating History: Vietnam Veterans and Their Returns to the Battlefield, 1998–1999." PhD Diss., Harvard University, 2003.
Damousi, Joy. "Why Do We Get So Emotional About Anzac?" In *What's Wrong with ANZAC? The Militarisation of Australian History.* Edited by Marilyn Lake, Henry Reynolds, and Mark McKenna. Sydney: University of New South Wales Press, 2010, 84–102.
Dapin, Mark. "'We Too Were Anzacs': Were Vietnam Veterans Ever Truly Excluded from the Anzac Tradition?" In *The Honest History Book.* Edited by David Stephens and Alison Broinowski. Sydney: NewSouth, 2017, 77–91.
Davies, Bruce and Gary McKay. *Vietnam: The Complete Story of the Australian War.* Crows Nest: Allen & Unwin, 2014.
Dawson, Graham. *Soldier Heroes: British Adventures, Empire, and the Imagining of Masculinities.* New York: Routledge, 1994.
Dean Jr., Eric T. "The Myth of the Troubled and Scorned Vietnam Veteran." *Journal of American Studies* 26:1 (1992): 59–74.

DeMonaco, Marykim. "Disorderly Departure: An Analysis of the United States Policy Toward Amerasian Immigration." In *Asian Indians, Filipinos, and other Asian Communities, and the Law*. Edited by Charles McClain. New York: Garland Publishing, 1994, 217–86.

Dixon, Chris. "Redeeming the Warriors: Myth-Making and Australia's Vietnam Veterans." *Australian Journal of Politics & History* 60:2 (2014): 214–28.

Do, Bich Ngoc. "Normalizing Vietnam: Vietnam Veterans and the Reconstruction of Postwar US-Vietnam Relations, 1985–2010." PhD Diss., University of Hawai'i, 2011.

Donaldson, Carina and Marilyn Lake, "Whatever Happened to the Anti-War Movement?" In *What's Wrong with ANZAC? The Militarisation of Australian History*. Edited by Marilyn Lake, Henry Reynolds, Mark McKenna. Sydney: University of New South Wales Press, 2010. 57–83.

Doyle, Jeff. "Dismembering the Anzac Legend: Australian Popular Culture and the Vietnam War." *Vietnam Generation* 3:2, Special Issue: Australia R&R – Representations and Reinterpretations of Australia's War in Vietnam (1991): 109–66.

Dudziak, Mary. *War Time: An Idea, Its History, Its Consequences*. Cary, NC: Oxford University Press, 2012.

———. "'You Didn't See Him Lying … Beside the Gravel Road in France': Death, Distance, and American War Politics." *Diplomatic History* 42:1 (2018): 1–16.

Ebron, Paulla A., "Tourists as Pilgrims: Commercial Fashioning of Transatlantic Politics." *American Ethnologist* 26:4 (November 1999): 910–32.

Edwards, Peter. *Australia and the Vietnam War*. Kensington: NewSouth, 2014.

———. "Fifty Years On: Half-Century Reflections on the Australian Commitment to the Vietnam War." In *New Perceptions of the Vietnam War: Essays on the War, the South Vietnamese, the Diaspora and the Continuing Impact*. Edited by Nathalie Huynh and Chau Nguyen. Jefferson, NC: McFarland, 2015.

Eisen, Arlene. *Women and Revolution in Viet Nam*. London: Zed Books, 1984.

Ekins, Ashley. "Australian MIAs of the Vietnam War – 'Missing in Action' or 'No Known Grave?'" *Wartime* 23 (2003). www.awm.gov.au/wartime/23/no-known-grave/

Espiritu, Yến Lê. "About Ghost Stories: the Vietnam War and 'Rememoration.'" *PLMA* 123:5 (2008): 1702.

———. *Body Counts: The Vietnam War and Militarized Refugees*. Berkeley, CA: University of California Press, 2014.

Field, Sean. "Beyond 'Healing': Trauma, Oral History and Regeneration." *Oral History* 34:1 (Spring 2006): 31–42.

Figley, Charles R. and Seymour Leventman. "Introduction: Estrangement and Victimization." In *Strangers at Home: Vietnam Veterans Since the War*. Edited by Charles R. Figley and Seyour Leventman. New York: Praeger Publishers, 1980, xxi–xxxi.

Fitzgerald, David. "Support the Troops: Gulf War Homecomings and a New Politics of Military Celebration." *Modern American History* 2 (2019): 1–22.

Franklin, Bruce H. *MIA, or, Mythmaking in America*. New Brunswick, NJ: Rutgers University Press, 1993.

"Missing in Action in the Twenty-First Century." In *Four Decades On: Vietnam, the United States and the Legacy of the Second Indochina War*. Edited by Scott Laderman and Edwin A. Martini. Durham, NC: Duke University Press, 2013, 259–96.

Garrick, Damien. "Excuses, Excuses: Rationalisations of Western Sex Tourists in Thailand." *Current Issues in Tourism* 8:6 (2005): 497–509.

Garton, Stephen. *The Cost of War: Australians Return*. Melbourne: Oxford University Press, 1996.

"War and Masculinity in Twentieth Century Australia." *Journal of Australian Studies* 22:56 (1998): 86–95.

Gatewood, John B. and Catherine M. Cameron. "Battlefield Pilgrims at Gettysburg National Military Park." *Ethnology* 43:3 (Summer, 2004): 193–216.

Gerster, Robin. "A Bit of the Other: Touring Vietnam." In *Gender and War: Australians at War in the Twentieth Century*. Edited by Joy Damousi and Marilyn Lake. Melbourne: Cambridge University Press Archive, 1995, 223–38.

Giang, Le Minh, et al. "Substance Use Disorder and HIV in Vietnam since Doi Moi (Renovation): An Overview." *Journal of Food and Drug Analysis* 21:4 (2013): S42–S45.

Glassman, Jim. "Counter-Insurgency, Ecocide and the Production of Refugees: Warfare as a Tool of Modernization." *Refuge* 12:1 (June 1992): 27–30.

Gottschang Turner, Karen with Phan Than Hao. *Even the Women Must Fight: Memories of War from North Vietnam*. New York: Wiley, 1998.

Grey, Jeffrey. "In Every War but One? Myth, History and Vietnam." In *Zombie Myths of Australian Military History*. Edited by Craig Stockings. Sydney: NewSouth, 2010. 190–212.

Gustafsson, Mai Lan. *War and Shadows: The Haunting of Vietnam*. Ithaca, NY: Cornell University Press, 2009.

Hagopian, Patrick. *The Vietnam War in American Memory: Veterans, Memorials and the Politics of Healing*. Boston, MA: University of Massachusetts Press, 2009.

Hanh, Phung Thi. *South Vietnam's Women in Uniform*. Sài Gòn: Vietnam Council on Foreign Relations, est., 1970.

Hart, Gavin. "Sexual Behavior in a War Environment." *Journal of Sex Research* 11:3 (August 1975): 218–26.

Hellman, John. *American Myth and the Legacy of Vietnam*. New York: Columbia University Press, 1986.

Herman, Judith. *Trauma and Recovery*. New York: Basic Books, 1992.

Hoang, Kimberley Kay. "Economies of Emotion, Familiarity, Fantasy, and Desire: Emotional Labor in Ho Chi Minh City's Sex Industry." *Sexualities* 13:2 (2010): 255–72.

"Flirting with Capital: Negotiating Perceptions of Pan-Asian Ascendency and Western Decline in Global Sex Work." *Social Problems* 61:4 (2014): 507–29.

Dealing in Desire: Asian Ascendency, Western Decline, and the Hidden Currencies of Global Sex Work. Berkeley, CA: University of California Press, 2015.

Hobsbawm, Eric and Terence Ranger. *The Invention of Tradition*. Cambridge: Cambridge University Press, 1983.
Hunt, Steven. *The Carter Administration and Vietnam*. London: Macmillan, 1996.
Hutchinson, Garrie. *Pilgrimage: A Traveller's Guide to Australia's Battlefields*. Collingwood: Black Inc., 2006.
Inglis, Ken and Jan Brazier. *Sacred Spaces: War Memorials in the Australian Landscape*. Melbourne: The Miegunyah Press, 2008.
Isaacs, Arnold R. *Vietnam Shadows: The War, Its Ghosts, and Its Legacy*. Baltimore, MA: JHU Press, 2000.
Jeffords, Susan. *The Remasculinization of America*. Indianapolis, IN: Indiana University Press, 1989.
Jones, Sidney, Joseph Saunders, and Malcolm Saunders. *Repression of the Montagnards: Conflicts Over Land and Religion in Vietnam's Central Highlands*. New York: Human Rights Watch, 2002.
Junger, Sebastian. "The Bonds of War." *Psychotherapy Networker Magazine* 42:46 (September 1, 2016): 42–48.
Kahan, Dan. "Misconceptions, Misinformation, and the Logic of Identity-Protective Cognition." Working Paper No. 164. *The Cultural Cognition Project*. Yale Law School (2017). N.p. https://papers.ssrn.com/sol3/papers.cfm?abstract_id=2973067
Kaplan, Jonas T., Sarah Gimbel, and Sam Harris. "Neural Correlates of Maintaining One's Political Beliefs in the Face of Counterevidence." *Scientific Reports* 6:39589 (2016). http://dx.doi.org/10.1038/srep39589
Karageorgos, Effie. *Australian Soldiers in South Africa and Vietnam: Words from the Battlefield*. London: Bloomsbury Publishing, 2016.
Karageozian, Nanor. "Diasporic 'Return' Migrations." In *Diasporas Reimagined: Spaces, Practices and Belonging*. Edited by Nando Sigona et al. Oxford: Oxford University Press, 2015.
Kennedy, Laurel B. and Mary Rose Williams. "The Past Without Pain: The Manufacture of Nostalgia in Vietnam's Tourism Industry." In *Country of Memory: Remaking the Past in Late Socialist Vietnam*. Edited by Hue-Tam Ho Tai. Berkeley, CA: University of California, 2001, 135–64.
Keys, Barbara. *Reclaiming American Virtue: The Human Rights Revolution of the 1970s*. Cambridge: Harvard University Press, 2014.
King, Claire Sisco. *Washed in Blood: Male Sacrifice, Trauma and the Cinema*. New Brunswick, NJ: Rutgers University Press, 2011.
Kizer, Kenneth W. "The 'New VA': A National Laboratory for Health Care Quality Management." *American Journal of Medical Quality* 14:1 (January, 1999): 3–20.
Kolko, Gabriel. *Anatomy of a War*. London: Allen & Unwin, 1986.
Vietnam: Anatomy of a Peace. London: Routledge, 1997.
Korinek, Kim and Bussawaran Teerawichitchainan . "Military Service, Exposure to Trauma, and Health in Older Adulthood: An Analysis of Northern Vietnamese Survivors of the Vietnam War." *American Journal of Public Health* 104:8 (2014): 1478–87.
Kwon, Heonik. *After the Massacre: Commemoration and Consolation at Ha My and My Lai*. Berkeley, CA: University of California Press, 2006.

"North Korea's Culture of Commemoration." In *Atheism and Its Discontents: A Comparative Study of Religion and Communism in Eurasia*. Edited by Tam T. T. Ngo and Justine B. Quijada. London: Palgrave, 2014, 112–33.

Laderman, Scott. *Tours of Vietnam: War, Travel Guides, and Memory*. Durham, NC: Duke University Press, 2009.

"From the Vietnam War to the 'War on Terror': Tourism and the Martial Fascination." In *Tourism and War*. Edited by Richard Butler and Scott Laderman. London: Routledge, 2013, 26–35.

Lake, Marilyn. "How Do Schoolchildren Learn About the Spirit of Anzac?" In *What's Wrong with ANZAC? The Militarisation of Australian History*. Edited by Marilyn Lake, Henry Reynolds, and Mark McKenna. Sydney: University of New South Wales Press, 2010, 113–60.

Lê, Phan Huy, et al. *Lịch Sử Việt Nam-Tập 1*. Hà Nội: Ministry of Education and Training, 1983.

Lema, Joseph and Jerome Agrusa. "Revisiting the War Landscape of Vietnam and Tourism." In *Tourism and War*. Edited by Richard Butler. New York: Taylor and Francis, 2013, 245–53.

Lembcke, Jerry. *The Spitting Image: Myth, Memory and the Legacy of Vietnam*. New York: New York University Press, 1998.

Lewy, Guenter. *America in Vietnam*. New York: Oxford University Press, 1978.

Leys, Ruth. *Trauma: A Genealogy*. Chicago, IL: University of Chicago Press, 2000.

Lifton, Robert J. *Home from the War: Vietnam Veterans, Neither Victims nor Executioners*. New York: Simon & Schuster, 1973.

Limerick, Brigid, Tracey Burgess-Limerick, and Margaret Grace. "The Politics of Interviewing: Power Relations and Accepting the Gift." *International Journal of Qualitative Studies in Education* 9:4 (2006): 449–60.

Linenthal, Edward Tabor. *Sacred Ground: Americans and Their Battlefields*. Chicago, IL: University of Illinois Press, 1993.

Lipman, Jana K. "'The Face is the Roadmap': Vietnamese Amerasians in the US Political and Popular Culture, 1980–1988." *Journal of Asian American Studies* 14:1 (2011): 33–68.

Loftus, Elizabeth. "The Reality of Repressed Memory." *American Psychologist* 48:5 (May 1993): 518–37.

Long, Lynellyn, D. "Viet Kieu on a Fast Track Back?" In *Coming Home? Refugees, Migrants, and Those Who Stayed Behind*. Edited by Lynellyn D. Long and Ellen Oxford (Philadelphia, PA: University of Pennsylvania Press, 2004), 67–68.

Mackenzie, Megan and Alan Foster. "Masculinity Nostalgia: How War and Occupation Inspire a Yearning for a Gender Order." *Security Dialogue* 48:7 (2017): 206–23.

MacPherson, Myra. *Long Time Passing, New Edition: Vietnam and the Haunted Generation*. Bloomington, IN: Indiana University Press, 2009.

Maddock, Kenneth. "Atrocities and Culture: Revisiting the Vietnam War." *Journal of Polynesian Society* 48: Memoirs, Man and a Half (1991): 293–98.

Martin Hobbs, Mia. "'We Went and Did an Anzac Job': Memory, Myth, and the Anzac Digger in Vietnam." *Australian Journal of Politics and History* 64:3 (2018): 480–97.

Martini, Edwin A. *Invisible Enemies: The American War on Vietnam, 1975–2000*. Amherst, MA: University of Massachusetts Press, 2007.

Agent Orange: History, Science, and the Politics of Uncertainty. Amherst, MA: University of Massachusetts, 2012.

McAlister, Elizabeth. "Listening for Geographies: Music as Sonic Compass Pointing Towards African and Christian Diasporic Horizons in the Caribbean." In *Geographies of the Haitian Diaspora*. Edited by Regine O. Jackson. New York: Routledge, 2011.

McKay, Gary. *Going Back: Australian Veterans Return to Vietnam*. Crows Nest: Allen & Unwin, 2007.

McKenna, Mark. "Anzac Day: How Did It Become Australia's National Day?" In *What's Wrong with ANZAC? The Militarisation of Australian History*. Edited by Marilyn Lake, Henry Reynolds, and Mark McKenna. Sydney: University of New South Wales Press, 2010, 103–32.

McKercher, Bob and Thomas G. Bauer. "Conceptual Framework of the Nexus between Tourism, Romance, and Sex." In *Sex and Tourism: Journeys of Romance, Love, and Lust*. Edited by Thomas G. Bauer and Bob McKercher. New York: Haworth Press, 2003, 3–16.

McMahon, Robert J. "Changing Interpretations of the Vietnam War." In *The Oxford Companion to Military History*. Edited by John Whiteclay Chambers II. Oxford: Oxford University Press, 1999, 767.

"Contested Memory: The Vietnam War and American Society, 1975–2001." *Diplomatic History* 26: 2 (2002): 159–84.

Morris, Ben. "Remembering Vietnam: Official History, Soldiers" Memories and the Participant Interviewer." Master's Thesis, University of Wollongong, 2014.

Nguyen, Carie Uyen. "Whose War Was It Anyway?" *New York Times*. August 18, 2017.

Nguyen, Mimi. *The Gift of Freedom: War, Debt, and Other Refugee Passages*. Durham, NC: Duke University Press, 2012.

Nguyen, Nathalie Huynh Chau. *Memory Is Another Country: Women of the Vietnamese Diaspora*. Santa Barbara, CA: Praeger, 2009.

South Vietnamese Soldiers: Memories of the Vietnam War and After. Santa Barbara, CA: Praeger, 2016.

Nguyen, Phuong Tran. *Becoming Refugee American: The Politics of Rescue in Little Saigon*. Chicago, IL: University of Illinois Press, 2017.

Nguyễn, Việt Thanh. *Nothing Ever Dies: Vietnam and the Memory of the War*. Cambridge: Harvard University Press, 2016.

Nguyễn-Võ, Thu-Hương. "Forking Paths: How Shall We Mourn the Dead?" *Amerasia Journal* 31:2 (2005): 157–75.

The Ironies of Freedom: Sex, Culture and Neoliberal Governance in Vietnam. Seattle, WA: University of Washington Press, 2008.

Novaco, Raymond W. and Claude M. Chemtob. "Anger and Combat-Related Posttraumatic Stress Disorder." *Journal of Traumatic Stress* 15:2 (2002): 123–32.

Ognibene, Brig. Gen. Andre J. , Colonel O'Neill Barret Jr., John J. Deller, et al. *Internal Medicine in Vietnam, Volume II: General Medicine and Infectious Diseases*. Washington, DC: Surgeon General and Center of Military History United States Army, 1982, 233–36.

Olick, Jeffrey K. *The Politics of Regret: On Collective Memory and Historical Responsibility*. New York: Routledge, 2007.

Oulton, Jacinta M, Melanie K.T. Takarangi, and Deryn Strange. "Memory Amplification for Trauma: Investigating the Role of Analogue PTSD Symptoms in the Laboratory." *Journal of Anxiety Disorders* 42 (August, 2016): 60–70.

Palazzo, Albert. *Australian Military Operations in Vietnam*. Canberra: Army History United, 2011.

Pelley, Patricia M. *Postcolonial Vietnam: New Histories of the National Past*. Durham, NC: Duke University Press, 2002.

Pencak, William A. *Encyclopedia of the Veteran in America*. Santa Barbara, CA: ABC-Clio, 2009.

Pennycook, Alistair. *English and the Discourses of Colonialism*. London: Routledge, 1998.

Phan, Hai-Dang Doan. "Rumor of Redress: Literature, the Vietnam War, and the Politics of Reconciliation." PhD Diss., University of Wisconsin-Madison, 2012.

Pitt-Rivers, Julian. "The Law of Hospitality." *HAU: Journal of Ethnographic Theory* 2:1 (2012): 506–09.

Prideaux, Bruce, Jerome Agrusa, Jon G. Donlon, and Chris Curran. "Exotic or Erotic – Contrasting Images for Defining Destinations." *Asia Pacific Journal of Tourism Research* 9:1 (2004): 5–17.

Rambo, Terry. "Vietnam." In *Ethnicity in Asia*. Edited by Colin Mackerras. London: Routledge, 2003, 108–35.

Reynolds, Henry and Marilyn Lake. "Epilogue: Moving On?" In *What's Wrong with ANZAC? The Militarisation of Australian History*. Edited by Marilyn Lake, Henry Reynolds, and Mark McKenna. Sydney: University of New South Wales Press, 2010, 161–73.

Reynolds, Robert. "Trauma and the Relational Dynamics of Life-History Interviewing." *Australian Historical Studies* 43:1 (2012): 78–88.

Riseman, Noah. "'Describing Misbehaviour in Vung Tau as "Mischief" is Ridiculously Coy': Ethnographic Refusal, Reticence, and the Oral Historian's Dilemma." *Oral History Review* 45:1 (2018): 84–100.

Roemer, Lizabeth, Brett T. Litz, Susan M. Orsillo, and Amy Wagner. "A Preliminary Investigation of the Role of Strategic Withholding of Emotions in PTSD." *Journal of Traumatic Stress* 14:1 (2001): 149–56.

Roper, Michael. "Re-Remembering the Soldier-Hero: The Psychic and Social Construction of Memory in Personal Narratives of the Great War." *History Workshop Journal* 50 (Autumn 2000): 181–204.

———. *Secret Battle: Emotional Survival in the Great War*. Manchester: Manchester University Press, 2009.

Safran, William. "Diasporas in Modern Societies: Myths of Homeland and Return." *Diaspora* 1:1 (Spring 1991): 83–99.

Sagona, Antonio, Mithat Atabay, C.J. Mackie, Ian McGibbon, and Richard Reid. *Anzac Battlefield: A Gallipoli Landscape of War and Memory.* Melbourne: Cambridge University Press, 2016.
Said, Edward. *Orientalism.* London: Penguin, 1978.
Scates, Bruce. *Return to Gallipoli: Walking the Battlefields of the Great War.* Cambridge: Cambridge University Press, 2006.
Schwenkel, Christina. "Recombinant History: Transnational Practices of Memory and Knowledge Production in Contemporary Vietnam." *Cultural Anthropology* 21:1 (February 2006): 3–30.
  The American War in Contemporary Vietnam: Transnational Remembrance and Representation. Bloomington, IN: Indiana University Press, 2009.
  "Socialist Mobilities: Crossing New Terrains in Vietnamese Migration Histories." *Central and Eastern European Migration Review* 4:1 (2015): 13–25.
Sharpley, Richard and Philip R. Stone. "(Re)presenting the Macabre: Interpretation, Kitschification and Authenticity." In *The Darker Side of Travel: The Theory and Practice of Dark Tourism.* Edited by Richard Sharpley and Philip R. Stone. Bristol: Channel View, 2009, 109–28.
Shatan, Chaim. "The Grief of Soldiers: Vietnam Combat Veterans' Self-Help Movement." *American Journal of Orthopsychiatry* 43: 4 (July, 1973): 640–53.
Shay, Jonathan. *Achilles in Vietnam: Combat Trauma and the Undoing of Character.* New York: Atheneum, 1994.
  Odysseus in America: Combat Trauma and the Trials of Homecoming. New York: Scriber, 2002.
Sidel, Mark. *The Constitution of Vietnam: A Contextual Analysis.* London: Hart Publishing, 2009.
Sigona, Nando, et al. (eds.). "Introduction: The Self as Plural." In *Diasporas Reimagined: Spaces, Practices and Belonging.* Oxford: Oxford University Press, 2015, xvii–xxiii.
Siminski, Peter. "Employment Effects of Army Service and Veterans' Compensation: Evidence from the Australian Vietnam-Era Conscription Lotteries." *The Review of Economics and Statistics* 95:1 (2013): 87–97.
Siracusa, Joseph and Hang Nguyen. "Vietnam-US Relations: An Unparalleled History." *Orbis* 61:3 (2017): 404–22.
Sontag, Susan. *Trip to Hanoi.* New York: Farrar, Straus and Giroux, 1968.
Stellman, Jeanne Mager, Steven D. Stellman, Richard Christian, Tracy Weber, and Carrie Tomasello. "The Extent and Patterns of Usage of Agent Orange and Other Herbicides in Vietnam." *Nature* 422 (April 2003): 681–87.
Stevenson, Jonathan. *Hard Men Humble: Vietnam Veterans Who Wouldn't Come Home.* New York: The Free Press, 2002.
Stewart, Elizabeth. "Vietnam: The Long Journey Home." In *New Perceptions of the Vietnam War: Essays on the War, the South Vietnamese Experience, the Diaspora and the Continuing Impact.* Edited by Nathalie Huynh Chau Nguyen. Jefferson, NC: McFarland, 2015, 108–28.
Strange, Deryn and Melanie K. T. Takarangi. "False Memories for Missing Aspects of Traumatic Events." *Acta Psychologica* 141:3 (November 2012): 322–26.

Stur, Heather. *Beyond Combat: Women and Gender in the Vietnam War Era.* Cambridge: Cambridge University Press, 2011.

———. "'Hiding Behind the Humanitarian Label': Refugees, Repatriates, and the Rebuilding of America's Benevolent Image after the Vietnam War." *Diplomatic History* 39:2 (April 2015): 223–44.

Tai, Hue-Tam Ho. "Faces of Remembering and Forgetting." In *Country of Memory: Remaking the Past in Late Socialist Vietnam.* Edited by Hue-Tam Ho Tai. Berkeley, CA: University of California, 2001, 135–64.

Takaki, Ronald. *Strangers from a Different Shore: A History of Asian Americans.* New York: Penguin, 1989.

Tal, Kali. *Worlds of Hurt: Reading the Literatures of Trauma.* Cambridge: Cambridge University Press, 1994.

Tatum, James. "Memorials of the America War in Vietnam." *Critical Inquiry* 22:4 (Summer, 1996): 634–78.

Tay, Emanual. "The Dear John Syndrome During the Vietnam War." *Diseases of the Nervous System* 37:1 (1976): 165–67.

Taylor, Sandra C. "Long-Haired Women, Short-Haired Spies: Gender, Espionage, and America's War in Vietnam." *Intelligence and National Security* 13:2 (1998): 61–70.

———. *Vietnamese Women at War: Fighting for Ho Chi Minh and the Revolution.* Lawrence, KS: University Press of Kansas, 1999.

Taylor, T. S. "Sex Tourism and Inequalities." In *Tourism and Inequality: Problems and Prospects.* Edited by S. Cole and N. Morgan. Cambridge: CABI, 2010, 49–66.

Teerawichitchainan, Bussawaran and Kim Korinek. "The Long-Term Impact of War on Health and Wellbeing in Northern Vietnam: Some Glimpses from a Recent Survey." *Social Science & Medicine* (2012): 1995–2005.

Thomas, Sabrina. "Blood Politics: Reproducing the Children of 'Others' in the 1982 Amerasian Immigration Act." *Journal of American-East Asian Relations* 26 (2019): 51–84.

Thomson, Alistair. "A Past You Can Live With: Digger Memories and the Anzac Legend." *Oral History Association of Australia Journal* 13 (1991): 12–18.

———. "Anzac Stories: Using Personal Testimony in War History." *War & Society* 25:2 (2006): 1–21.

———. *Anzac Memories: Living with the Legend.* Clayton, NC: Monash University Press, 2013.

———. "Anzac Memories Revisited: Trauma, Memory and Oral History." *Oral History Review* 42:1 (2015): 1–29.

Till, Karen E. "Places of Memory." In *A Companion to Political Geography.* Edited by John Agnew, Katharyne Mitchell, and Gerard Toal. Oxford: Blackwell, 2003, 289–301.

Tran, Vu Mei Yen. "Vietnamese Expressions of Politeness." *Griffith Working Papers in Pragmatics and Intercultural Communication* 3:1 (2010): 12–21.

Turse, Nick. *Kill Anything That Moves: The Real American War in Vietnam.* New York: Metropolitan Books, 2013.

Twomey, Christina. "Trauma and the Reinvigoration of Anzac: An Argument." *History Australia* 10:3 (2013): 85–103.

Valverde, Caroline Kieu-Linh. "From Dust to Gold: The Vietnamese Amerasian Experience." In *Racially Mixed People in America*. Edited by Maria P. Root. London: Sage, 1992, 144–61.

Varzally, Allison. *Children of Reunion: Vietnamese Adoptions and the Politics of Family Migrations*. Chapel Hill, NC: University of North Carolina Press, 2017.

Villa, Valentine M. "Health and Functioning among Four War Eras of US Veterans: Examining the Impact of War Cohort Membership, Socioeconomic Status, Mental Health, and Disease Prevention." *Military Medicine* 167:9 (2002): 783–89.

Vo, Nghia M. *The Bamboo Gulag: Political Imprisonment in Communist Vietnam*. Jefferson, NC: McFarland, 2003.

Walker, Graham. "The Official History's Agent Orange Account: The Veterans' Perspective." In *War Wounds: Medicine and the Trauma of Conflict*. Edited by Elizabeth Stewart. Wollombi: Exisle Publishing, 2011, 148–61.

Waltzer, Michael. *Just and Unjust War*. New York: Basic Books, 1977.

Williams, Paul. *Memorial Museums: The Global Rush to Commemorate Atrocities*. Oxford: Berg, 2007.

Wilson, John P. and Jacob D. Lindy. *Trauma, Culture, and Metaphor: Pathways of Transformation and Integration*. New York: Routledge, 2013.

Wood, John A. *Veteran Narratives and the Collective Memory of the Vietnam War*. Athens, OH: Ohio University Press, 2016.

Wu, Ellen D. "It's Time to Center War in US Immigration History." *Modern American History* 2:2 (2019): 215–35.

Wu, Judy Tzu-Chun. *Radicals on the Road: Internationalism, Orientalism, and Feminism During the Vietnam Era*. Ithaca, NY: Cornell University Press, 2013.

Yarborough, Trin. *Surviving Twice: Amerasian Children of the Vietnam War*. Washington, DC: Potomac Books, 2005.

Yeomans, Peter and Evan M. Forman. "Cultural Factors in Traumatic Stress." In *Culture and Mental Health: Sociocultural Influences in Theory and Practice*. Edited by Sussie Eshun and Regan A.R. Gurung. Oxford: Blackwell, 2009, 221–44.

Yow, Valerie. "'Do I Like Them Too Much?': Effects of the Oral History Interview on the Interviewer and Vice-Versa." *The Oral History Review* 24:1 (Summer 1997): 55–79.

Yuh, Yi-Jeon. "Moved by War: Migration, Diaspora, and the Korean War." *Journal of Asian American Studies* 8:3 (October 2005): 277–91.

Yule, Peter. *The Long Shadow: Australia's Vietnam Veterans Since the War*. Sydney: NewSouth, 2020.

Ziino, Bart. "Who Owns Gallipoli? Australia's Gallipoli Anxieties 1915–2005." *Journal of Australian Studies* 88 (2006): 1–12.

Index

Agent Orange, 29, 46, 77, 113–16
  advocacy for victims, 52, 67, 82, 156, 218
  health issues associated with, 69, 82, 83, 113, 152
Amerasians, 109–13
American War
  SRV narrative, 122, 162, 178
  See also Hỏa Lò Prison Museum, Hà Nội; Long Tan, Battle of; Sơn Mỹ Memorial and Museum, Quảng Ngãi; Vietnam War; War Remnants Museum, Hồ Chí Minh City
Angel Fire Memorial Chapel, New Mexico, 164
animosity, 140–42
anti-war activism, 7, 55–57, 58, 59
anti-war movement, veteran's views on, 185–89, 202
Anzac tradition, 35, 74, 76, 145, 171, 173, 183, 184, 234
Apocalypse Now (movie), 30, 212
Appy, Christian, 16
atonement, 46, 69, 91
  See also forgiveness; reconciliation
atrocities
  See war crimes
Australia–Việt Nam diplomatic relations, 11, 49, 51
Australian narrative of Vietnamese love and respect, 143–46, 173
Australian Vietnam Forces National Memorial, 34, 36, 55
Australian Vietnam Veterans Reconstruction Group, 218

Balmoral, Battle of, 68, 79, 109
Bàng, Lê Văn, 236
Bangert, Joe, 38, 227
Barnett, Michael, 220
battlefield pilgrimage, 4–7, 11, 73–76, 79, 83, 91, 171–74
  See also tourism

battles
  See Balmoral, Battle of; Huế, Battle for; Ia Drang, Battle of; Long Tan, Battle of
Bauer, Thomas G., 203–09
Beamish, Thomas D., 55
Berdahl, Daphne, 34
Bird, Tom, 40
Bleakney, Julia, 13
Boehm, Mike, 19, 31, 42, 150, 217
Bowen, Kevin, 33, 39, 42, 44
Bower-Miles, Tony ("Bomber"), 147, 190, 191, 193, 194
Boym, Svetlana, 5, 31, 38, 39, 56, 63, 172
Bozcar, Amanda, 117
Brown, Susan Love, 225
Broyles, William, 34, 40, 111, 120, 169, 177, 179, 196
Brubaker, Rogers, 14
Bui, Long T., 14, 179
Burstall, Terry, 38, 40–41, 44, 46, 87, 140, 144, 171, 190, 191, 194, 198

Calley, William, 143, 166
Camacho, Paul, 134
Cameron, Catherine, 4
Carruthers, Ashley, 51
Chambers, Thomas, 4
Champagne, Fredy, 30, 32, 83
Cheap Charlie (song), 119
civilian killings, 189, 192, 229
  See also war crimes
civilian relocation, 191–92
Clinton, Bill, 51, 55
Cole, Teju, 219
combat memories
  See war memories and narratives
commemoration of war
  See war commemoration
commemoration returnees, 4, 20, 73–97, 233
composure of memories, 21, 58, 163, 194
Công, Phạm Thành, 142

268

conscripts, 19
Coral-Balmoral, Battle of, 68
corpse mutilation, 189–91
   See also war crimes
Cresswell, Tim, 8
Củ Chi tunnels, 108
Curthoys, Ann, 185

Da Nang Air Base, 86
Damousi, Joy, 4
Davies, Bruce, 184
Dawson, Graham, 21, 78
Deer Hunter, The (movie), 212
defeat/victory, perceptions of, 177–85, 202
Democratic Republic of Việt Nam (DRV, North Vietnam), 138, 163
demons metaphor, 88–90
diasporas, 14–16
   Vietnamese diaspora, 14, 15, 51, 92
diasporic community, Vietnam veterans as, 2–4, 14–16, 31, 209–14, 233
diasporic intimacy, 31, 39
diasporic longing, 8, 31, 209
Điện Biên Phủ, 173
dioxins, 82, 83, 114, 115, 156
   See also Agent Orange
Disabled American Veterans, 77, 164, 165
Dixon, Chris, 185
Do, Bich Ngoc, 226
domino theory, 169, 184, 199
draft volunteers, 19
draftees, 19
Dudziack, Mary, 16

Edwards, Peter, 184
Eisen, Arlene, 193
emotion and masculinity, 21, 66
environmental issues, 114–16
   See also Agent Orange
Espiritu, Yến Lê, 14, 167

familial grief, 124
Father Founded, 82
Field, Sean, 17
First Blood:
   Part II (movie), 30
Fischer, Tim, 51, 55, 75
fish kill, 115
forgiveness, 7, 69, 92–95, 139, 142–43, 230
   See also atonement; reconciliation
Foster, Alan, 209
Friendship Village, Hà Nội, 58, 67, 70
Fulbright University Việt Nam (FUV)
   chairmanship issue, 229–31, 235

Garrick, Damien, 207
Gatewood, John, 4
Gerster, Robin, 209
"ghosts" and "demons" metaphors, 88–90
Giáp, General Võ Nguyên, 132, 133, 181
Glassman, Jim, 116
Grey, Jeffrey, 183
Gustafsson, Mai Lan, 124

Hà Nội, 46, 51
Hagopian, Patrick, 13, 165
Hawke government, 36
Hawke, Bob, 74
healing journeys, 3, 11–14, 50–72, 77, 84, 122, 233
healing-through-helping
   See philanthropic and humanitarian initiatives
herbicidal warfare, 82, 114
   See also Agent Orange
Herman, Judith, 59
Heroic Mother memorials, 166, 167
Hersh, Seymour, 142
Heselton, Ted, 39, 40, 45, 47
Hjort, Brian, 82
Hồ Chí Minh City, 45, 88, 104
   sex workers, 117
   street children, 110, 111
   US Embassy memorial plaque, 173
   See also War Remnants Museum, Hồ Chí Minh City
Hỏa Lò Prison, 41
Hỏa Lò Prison Museum, Hà Nội, 158–59
Hoang, Kimberly Kay, 117
Huế, Battle for, 196
humanitarian initiatives See philanthropic and humanitarian initiatives

Ia Drang, Battle of, 47
identity politics, 134
interviews
   See Vietnam veteran returnee interviews
Iraq War, 76
Isaacs, Arnold R., 121

Junger, Sebastian, 122

Karlin, Wayne, 141
Kennedy, Laurel B., 208, 211
Kerrey, Bob, 229–31, 235
Khe Sanh, 107
kitsch memorabilia, 103
Klann, Gerhard, 229
Kolko, Gabriel, 117, 201

270 Index

Kon Tom Victory Memorial, 164, 165
Korinek, Kim, 123
Kurtz, Colonel (fictional character), 30
Kwon, Heonik, 166, 192

Laderman, Scott, 116, 154, 196
Lê, Phan Huy, 122
legacies of Vietnam War
   See Vietnam veteran returnee perceptions and attitudes
Lembcke, Jerry, 185
Lewy, Guenter, 182
Lifton, Robert J., 195
Long Tan, Battle of, 36, 40–41, 51, 73, 87, 133, 170–74
   anniversaries, 74, 75, 209, 231–33, 236
   memorial cross and replica, 91, 171, 172, 173, 231, 236

Mackenzie, Megan, 209
Maddock, Kenneth, 193
Martini, Edwin A., 16, 115
masculinity and emotion
   See emotion and masculinity
McCain, John, 29, 38, 41, 48, 157, 158, 182
McKay, Gary, 184
McKenna, Mark, 4
McKercher, Bob, 203–09
McMahon, Robert J., 178, 181, 183
meeting the enemy (concept), 127–50
memorabilia, 103
memory
   composure of, 21, 58, 163, 194
   instability and malleability, 62–65, 87
   politics of, 8
   recovery/verification, 84–86, 87
   repressed, 63, 194
   research, 21
   underlay, 21, 153, 184, 191
   within small social groups, 21, 78
   See also war memories and narratives
military sites and structures, 104–08
MONGOs (My Own NGO), 221
Moore, Harold, 47, 133, 140–42, 163
moral injury, 59, 121, 122, 124
   See also war crimes
Morris, Ben, 193
mother figures
   See Heroic Mother memorials
mourning, 41
   familial grief, 124
Muller, Bobby, 3, 28, 47, 133, 139, 146, 223

Murphy, Paul, 140, 172, 173, 192, 206, 218
My Lai massacre, 64, 141, 142, 153, 155, 159–63, 166, 194, 195
   photographs, 54, 159, 160, 161
   See also Sơn Mỹ Memorial and Museum, Quảng Ngãi

National Liberation Front (NLF)
   respect for Australians (alleged), 144
   veterans, 132, 137
New Age mantras, 225
New Zealanders in Vietnam, 6
NGOs, 92, 220, 222
   MONGOs (My Own NGO), 221
Nguyen, Carie Uyen, 180
Nguyen, Mimi, 199
Nguyễn, Việt Thanh, 109, 151, 189, 202, 232
Nguyễn-Võ, Thu-Hương, 14, 117
normalization returnees, 3, 20, 50–72, 223, 233
North Vietnam
   See Democratic Republic of Việt Nam (DRV, North Vietnam)
North Vietnamese Army (NVA)
   See People's Army Việt Nam (PAVN, North Vietnamese)
nostalgia, 6, 8, 53, 119
   forms of, 5, 63
   masculinity nostalgia, 208
   nostalgic discontent, 211–14
   reflective, 5, 31, 38, 64
   restorative, 5, 63, 70, 75, 86
Nui Dat, 91, 105, 191, 193

Olick, Jeffrey K., 224
Operation Ainslie, 191
Operation Ranch Hand
   See herbicidal warfare
Operation Wandering Souls, 68, 124, 145, 216
oral history approach
   See Vietnam veteran returnee interviews
Orderly Departure Program, 111

Palazzo, Albert, 183
particular publics (concept), 21, 78, 145
People's Army Việt Nam (PAVN, North Vietnamese)
   atrocities (alleged), 196
   respect for Australians (alleged), 144
   veterans, 132, 137
Peterson, Douglas ("Pete"), 29, 41, 48, 50, 115, 158, 180, 187, 214, 224, 226, 228

Index

Phạm, Văn Đồng, 27
Phan, Doan, 13
philanthropic and humanitarian initiatives, 30, 32, 67–69, 82, 83, 92, 214–23
Pitt-Rivers, Julian, 131
place, attachment to, 2–4, 91, 105–09, 120, 209–14
Platoon (movie), 30
politics of memory, 8
politics of regret, 224
post-traumatic stress disorder
  See PTSD
post-Vietnam syndrome
  See PTSD
Prisoners of War (POW)/Missing in Action (MIA) issue, 27–29, 48, 49, 223
Project Renew, 220
PTSD, 43, 50–72, 81, 88–90, 120, 125
puppet forces (narrative), 52, 127, 152

racism, 146–49
Rambo, *First Blood* (movie), 185
Rambo, John (fictional character), 30
Rambo, Terry, 149
Reagan, Ronald, 32
reconciliation, 47, 230, 236
  between former soldiers, 47, 132–37
  See also forgiveness
reconciliation returnees, 3, 20, 122, 139, 233
redemption
  See atonement; forgiveness
Redgum
  I Was Only Nineteen (A Walk in the Light Green), 36, 74
regret, politics of, 224
Reilly, Robert J., 52, 53, 57, 66, 71, 129, 154, 168, 179
Republic of Việt Nam (RVN, South Vietnam), 163, 179
Republic of Việt Nam Armed Forces (RVNAF, South Vietnamese)
  lack of recognition/memorials, 167–70
  perceptions of, 179
  puppet forces (SRV narrative), 52, 127, 152, 180
  veterans, 127
returnees
  See Vietnam veteran returnees
Riseman, Noah, 206
Roper, Michael, 19–22, 153, 184, 191
Rottmann, Larry, 39, 42, 44, 46, 155

Schiel, Kenneth, 142
Schwenkel, Christina, 103, 109, 134, 135, 153, 226

Scurfield, Raymond, 43, 56, 57, 60, 102, 106, 204
sex work and sex tourism, 116–19, 203–09
Shay, Jonathan, 56, 59, 121
Socialist Republic of Việt Nam (post-war united government), 163
  American War narrative, 122, 162, 178
  Australian diplomatic relations with, 11, 49, 51, 216
  economic reforms (Đổi Mới), 27, 36
  Orderly Departure Program, 111
  outreach to Vietnamese in exile, 51
  recognition of effects of herbicidal warfare, 82
  stance toward returnees, 133
  US diplomatic relations with, 50–53, 79
  US embargo, 36
  US POW/MIA issue, 27–29, 48, 49, 223
  view of American people vs. American government, 134, 143
  See also Việt Nam (country)
solidarity among soldiers, 47, 132–37
Sơn Mỹ Memorial and Museum, Quảng Ngãi, 42, 64, 142, 159–63, 166, 167
  See also My Lai massacre
South Vietnamese forces
  See Republic of Việt Nam Armed Forces (RVNAF, South Vietnamese)
Stockings, Craig, 145

Tai, Hue-Tam Ho, 167
Tatum, James, 160
Taylor, T. S., 116
Teerawichitchainan, Bussarawan, 123
Tet Offensive, 173, 212
Thạnh Phong, 229, 236
Thomson, Alistair, 21, 58, 145, 163
Tick, Edward, 56, 62
Till, Karen, 8, 180
tourism, 13, 27, 48, 53, 73, 80, 83, 136, 207
  hospitality, 131, 208
  sex work and sex tourism, 116–19, 203–09
  souvenirs, 102
  war sites, 107
  See also battlefield pilgrimage
tradition, invented, 172
trauma and effects of war in Vietnamese people, 67, 109–16, 120–26
  See also moral injury; PTSD
Tun, Trương Minh, 235
tunnel networks, 108

unexploded ordnances (UXOs), 113, 220
United States
　diplomatic relations with Việt Nam, 50–53, 79
　political and diplomatic embargo on Việt Nam, 36, 48, 49
　remilitarization, 76
urbanization, 116, 213

veterans
　See Vietnam veterans
Veterans for Peace (VFP), 18, 67, 68, 77, 82, 94, 118, 133, 215
Veterans of Foreign Wars (VFW), 76
Veterans Viet Nam Restoration Project (VVRP), 31, 32, 48, 83
Viet Cong (VC)
　See National Liberation Front (NLF)
Việt Nam (country)
　history, 163
　media interest and rhetoric, 38
　post-war reconstruction, 30, 45
　returnee settlement in, 70, 96
　scale of wartime loss, 124, 131
　urbanization, 116, 213
　veterans' attitudes in peacetime, 7, 9, 91, 119, 208–14, 234
　See also tourism; Vietnam War; Vietnamese people
Việt Nam (political entities)
　See Democratic Republic of Việt Nam (DRV, North Vietnam); Republic of Việt Nam (RVN, South Vietnam); Socialist Republic of Việt Nam (post-war united government)
Vietnam Historical Museum, 163
Vietnam Syndrome (fear of US decline), 32
Vietnam veteran returnee interviews
　interview process, 16–19
　interview questions, 245
　interviewees, 19–22, 237–44
Vietnam veteran returnee perceptions and attitudes, 177, 202
　on anti-war movement, 185–89, 202
　on defeat/victory, 177–85, 202
　on justness of the war, 180, 198–202
　on meeting the enemy, 127–50
　on peacetime Việt Nam, 7, 9, 91, 119, 208–14, 234
　on Vietnamese memory (American), 151–58, 159–69
　on Vietnamese memory (Australian), 151–58, 169–74
　on Vietnamese people, 46, 127–50
　on war crimes, 188–98, 202
Vietnam veteran returnees
　animosity to, 140–42, 234
　as living legacies, 22, 223–28
　attachment to place, 91, 105–9, 120
　Australian narrative of Vietnamese love and respect, 143–46
　Australian-American differences, 6, 49, 143, 222, 234
　commemoration returnees, 4, 20, 73–97, 233
　differences, 69, 75, 79, 81, 143
　effect of returning, 13, 22, 40–49, 62–64, 65–72, 88–97
　forgiveness in Việt Nam, 7, 69, 92–95, 139, 142–43
　language of communication, 149, 216
　motivations, 2–4, 15, 76, 77, 81–85, 96, 233
　motivations, civilian perceptions of, 203
　normalization returnees, 3, 20, 50–72, 223, 233
　race, 136
　reconciliation returnees, 3, 20, 122, 139, 233
　reluctance to return, 79
　scholarship on, 9–14
　settlement in Việt Nam, 70, 96
　solidarity among soldiers, 47, 132–37
　SRV stance, 133
　war knowledge, connection to space and warzone home, 2–4, 209–14
Vietnam veterans
　and anti-war movement, 185–89
　anti-war veterans, 13, 30, 58–59, 76, 77, 129, 163, 201
　as diasporic community, 2–4, 14–16, 31, 209–14, 233
　as living legacies, 22, 223–28
　as victims, 134
　Australian vs. American identity, 35
　depiction of, 29–31, 134
　mistreatment narrative, 55–57, 185
　pride in service, 47, 56, 76, 89, 119
　reintegration and social cohesion, 122
　scholarship on, 9–14
　See also PTSD
Vietnam Veterans Association, 18
Vietnam Veterans Day (Australia), 36, 171
Vietnam Veterans Memorial, Washington DC ("The Wall"), 32, 33, 39, 55
Vietnam Veterans of America (VVA), 3, 28, 31, 47, 52, 77, 133, 223

Index

Vietnam Veterans War Memorial, Canberra
See Australian Vietnam Forces National Memorial
Vietnam War
  anti-war protests, 55–57
  commemoration of, 32–36, 61, 73
  controversy, 2
  defeat/victory perceptions, 177–85, 202
  demographics, 19
  domino theory, 169, 184, 199
  justness of, 180, 198–202
  narratives, 8–9, 178, 224, 234
  narratives, SRV, 122, 162, 178
  POW treatment, 158–59
  POW/MIA political issue, 27–29, 48, 49, 223
  racism, 146–49
  scale of loss, 124, 131
  See also American War; war memories and narratives; war relics and remnants
Vietnamese diaspora, 14, 15, 51, 92
Vietnamese people
  Amerasians, 109–13
  and contrite foreigners, 69
  animosity to returnees, 140–42
  effects of war, 46, 67, 109–16, 120–26
  forgiveness by, 7, 69, 92–95, 139, 142–43
  national character in public discourse, 149–50, 178
  northern/southern differences (perceived), 146, 148
  returnee attitudes to and perceptions of, 46, 127–50
  women veterans, 137
  See also moral injury; Việt Nam (country)
volunteering
  See philanthropic and humanitarian initiatives
Vũng Tàu, 51, 74, 80, 117, 118, 120, 133, 205, 216, 218, 231

"Wall, The"
  See Vietnam Veterans Memorial, Washington DC ("The Wall")
Waltzer, Michael, 193
war commemoration, 4, 32–36, 47, 76, 234

memorials to foreign soldiers in Vietnam, 173
  of Vietnam War, 32–36, 61, 73
  opposition to, 157, 163
  See also Anzac tradition; battlefield pilgrimage
war commemoration, Vietnamese
  lack of recognition of RVNAF, 167–70
  See also Hỏa Lò Prison Museum, Hà Nội; Long Tan, Battle of; Sõn Mỹ Memorial and Museum, Quảng Ngãi; War Remnants Museum, Hồ Chí Minh City
war crimes, 188–98, 202
  Australian narrative, 197
  See also moral injury; My Lai massacre
war memories and narratives, 2, 8–9, 21, 38–47, 84–88
  contested, 86
  in tourism, 208
  instability and malleability, 62–65, 87
  See also American War; Vietnam veteran returnee perceptions and attitudes; Vietnam War
war relics and remnants, 101–08
  memorabilia, 103
  military sites and structures, 104–08
  tourist souvenirs, 102
War Remnants Museum, Hồ Chí Minh City, 151–58, 229
war, manifest in culture and peacetime, 16, 22
wartime friends, searches for, 71, 81, 95
wartime racism, 146–49
Westphall, Victor, 164, 165
White Savior Industrial Complex, 219, 220
Williams, Mary Rose, 208, 211
women
  See women veterans; Heroic Mother memorials; sex work and sex tourism
women veterans, 137, 166, 193
Wood, John A., 130, 181
Wu, Ellen, 16
Wu, Judy Tzu-Chun, 129

Yule, Peter, 16

Milton Keynes UK
Ingram Content Group UK Ltd.
UKHW021922010924
447408UK00025B/347